ESSENTIAL OPERATIONS MANAGEMENT

ALEX HILL & TERRY HILL

palgrave
macmillan

First published 2011 by
PALGRAVE MACMILLAN

Palgrave Macmillan in the UK is an imprint of Macmillan Publishers Limited, registered in England, company number 785998, of Houndmills, Basingstoke, Hampshire RG21 6XS.

Palgrave Macmillan in the US is a division of St Martin's Press LLC, 175 Fifth Avenue, New York, NY 10010.

Palgrave Macmillan is the global academic imprint of the above companies and has companies and representatives throughout the world.

Palgrave® and Macmillan® are registered trademarks in the United States, the United Kingdom, Europe and other countries.

ISBN-13: 9780230232594

This book is printed on paper suitable for recycling and made from fully managed and sustained forest sources. Logging, pulping and manufacturing processes are expected to conform to the environmental regulations of the country of origin.

A catalogue record for this book is available from the British Library.

A catalog record for this book is available from the Library of Congress.

10 9 8 7 6 5 4 3 2
20 19 18 17 16 15 14 13 12

Printed and bound in China

Contents in brief

Contents

Part one – Introduction   1

1   Managing Operations   1

2   Operations Strategy   31

List of figures

List of case studies

Preface

Why choose this book?

Essential Operations Management is a uniquely concise and accessible guide to operations management, ideally suited to an introductory module taken as part of an undergraduate degree in business studies or related disciplines. The book may also be suited to some MBA courses due to its concise nature and managerial approach. Here are just a few reasons why you should choose this book:

- **Written and championed by a highly respected author team** Both Alex and Terry Hill worked in operations management in the business sector for a decade or more before switching careers. They are now respected and leading academic figures in the field of operations management as researchers, teachers and authors.
- **Concise yet comprehensive** The book is far more concise and focused than many of the competitor texts, covering exactly what students need to know for their introductory course and being divided clearly into a manageable number of chapters, easily fitting into an average 12-week/one-semester course.
- Written in **an accessible, friendly manner** suitable for students with little experience of the working world.
- The material is supported by a **comprehensive pedagogy**, and a **modern and dynamic page design** to draw students in.
- Reflects the **mix of service and manufacturing sectors within most national economies** in terms of content, illustrations and examples.
- **Excellent coverage of strategy** This is one of the key areas that students often find difficult to grasp. *Essential Operations Management* covers strategy in a clear and focused way.
- **International slant** Case studies and illustrations from a range of countries match the international demographic of today's student population.
- **Fully up to date** by covering topics such as just-in-time, lean operations and enterprise resource planning, and taking into account current developments such as the adoption of e-commerce in retailing and financial services and advances in digital technology.

Context

The trend of increasing competition in the production and delivery of services and products that began during the 1980s and 90s has continued into the 21st century. Customer demand for more choice, faster deliveries, competitive prices, delivery on time and the right first-time provision of services and products continues to grow. Operations is the function that provides most or all of these competitive features and, as a result, how well operations is managed to bring these about is a key corporate issue for all businesses and organizations.

This book reflects these developments and the capabilities that go hand in hand with the task of providing services and products. It focuses on the role of operations management, which as readers will discover, is made up of a complex and varied series of tasks. At its core, operations management involves using the essential contributions of staff to meet the needs of customers so that they will return and buy again. *Essential Operations Management* highlights the fact that how well a service or product is provided results in:

- Establishing the reputation (or brand name) that leads to customers choosing the service or product and recommending it to others (the first sale)
- Customers returning to buy again (the second sale).

Structure and content

The text reflects the sets of tasks and challenges that make up operations management. By glancing at the chapter list, you will see the wide range of issues and responsibilities that make up this field of study. Each aspect of the overall task is substantial in its own right both in terms of:

- Its day-to-day management
- Meeting customer needs.

To help in understanding operations as a substantial part of any organization, the chapters have been arranged into four Parts.

Introduction to operations management

The first two chapters take an overview of the nature and tasks that fall within operations management. Chapter 1 explains where operations fits into an organization, outlines the role of operations management and how inputs (such as materials, people, information and energy) are transformed into the services and products (outputs) sold to customers. The second chapter deals with the key role of operations strategy and explains its nature and content, how it fits into the strategy of a business, how it is developed and the essential task of implementation.

Designing and delivering services and products

The next four chapters deal with the core tasks of design through to the delivery of services and products, as well as the associated issues of choosing appropriate locations and developing the layout that will best meet the chosen service delivery system or manufacturing process.

Managing operations

The five chapters that make up this part of the book look at several substantial tasks within an organization that fall within the remit of operations:

- Managing capacity (the people, systems, processes and equipment mix) to meet demand
- Scheduling and executing operations' activities in line with customer requirements
- Managing inventory (the materials within the service delivery system or manufacturing process)
- Managing quality (ensuring that the design specification of a service or product is met)
- Managing the supply chain in a way that enhances operations' ability to meet schedules and promises made to customers.

Improving operations

The final chapter deals with the ongoing task of measuring and improving operations performance, including an exploration of why companies need to improve their operations, how operations can be improved and the alternative approaches, tools and techniques for making improvements.

Learning features

The text is complemented by several features to help student learning. These include:

- **Learning objectives** at the start of a chapter to highlight the core takeaways
- **Key ideas** that highlight key themes from the text
- **Key terms** – an on-page glossary highlighting important terminology
- **Cases** throughout each chapter to illustrate current developments and practices in operations management and to support, by example, the concepts, developments and approaches explained in the accompanying text. These are taken from a variety of companies and other organizations to reflect the mix of sectors and the breadth of operations activities that the book addresses. Each case includes questions to encourage critical reflection on the issues discussed, as well as weblinks (if appropriate) to enable further investigation
- **Figures** providing data or concepts in a tabular or graphic format to provide a deeper illustration of the issues under discussion
- **Critical reflections** at the end of each chapter that discuss the issues addressed in a chapter and encourage readers to reflect and critically evaluate key topics
- **Longer cases** at the end of each chapter that provide the basis for a study group, tutorial or class discussion of the issues covered in the corresponding chapter.

Alex and Terry Hill
March 2011

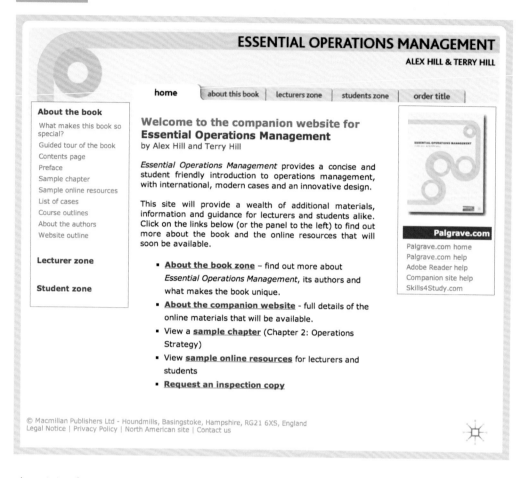

A variety of supporting materials are available for lecturers and students using *Essential Operations Management* via the companion website at www.palgrave.com/business/hillessential.

For **lecturers**, the website will include:

- PowerPoint lecture slides
- Case study teaching notes for the end-of-chapter case studies
- Answers to selected short cases to allow lecturers to set these as problems
- Guideline answers to discussion questions
- Guideline answers to assignments
- Sample examination questions
- Sample course outlines
- Guidelines on teaching operations management through film, including student worksheets and lecture notes.

For **students**, the website will include:

- Useful weblinks
- Chapter summaries
- A searchable online glossary of key terms
- Answers to selected short cases studies for self-learning
- Multiple choice questions for each chapter that can be used to revise and test knowledge and comprehension

About the authors

ALEX HILL is a Principal Lecturer at the Kingston University, UK, an Associate Fellow at the University of Oxford, UK, part of the Duke Corporate Education, US, learning resource network and Visiting Professor at the University of Pretoria, South Africa, the Academy of National Economy, Russia, and the BEM Management School, France. Prior to moving into university education, he worked extensively in industry and researches and consults in a wide range of service and manufacturing organizations.

TERRY HILL is an Emeritus Fellow at the University of Oxford, UK, an Affiliate Professor at the Milan Polytechnic, Italy and at the Ohio State University, USA, and a Visiting Professor at the University of Pretoria, South Africa. He is a leading international figure in the field of operations management and operations strategy. Terry spent several years in operations management and continues to work as a consultant. He has held previous professorial appointments at London Business School, UK, and the University of Bath, UK.

How to use each chapter

Learning objectives

- These show what you should have learned by the time you reach the end of the chapter
- Each objective is linked to a central topic or issue in operations management

Chapter outline

The chapter outline highlights the key topics to be covered in the chapter

Introduction

The introduction sets the scene and provides an overview of the chapter by explaining the key topics that will be covered.

Text within the chapter

The text explains the key concepts and ideas relating to the aspect of operations management being discussed.

Key terms – the key terms used within the chapter are explained in speech bubbles placed in the page margin

> KEY IDEAS

Key ideas contained within the chapter are highlighted and summarised within the text. These provide a useful overview of arguments being made within the chapter, which can also help students to revise for their exams.

CASES

A large number of case examples are scattered throughout each chapter to illustrate current developments and practices in operations management and show how the concepts, developments and approaches identified can be applied within organizations. These cases show a wide variety of companies reflecting the mix of sectors and the breadth of operations activities discussed within the book. Each case includes questions to encourage critical reflection on the issues discussed plus web links enabling further investigation.

Example answers to these questions can be found at www.palgrave.com/business/hillessential.

Figures

A large number of figures are also provided to show data or concepts in a tabular or graphic format. This provides a deeper illustration of the issues being discussed within the chapter.

Critical reflections

At the end of each chapter, critical reflections discuss the issues addresses in the chapter and encourage readers to reflect on and critically evaluate the key topics that have been discussed.

Summary

- The key points from the chapter are summarised as bullet points.
- As with the key ideas, these can help students revise for their exams.

Exploring further

Examples of journal articles, books and other sources are provided allowing you to further explore the ideas and concepts discussed within the chapter.

Study activities

Study activities containing discussion questions that will help students to debate and apply the key learnings from the chapter. There are also assignments that suggest more in-depth individual or group exercises.

END OF CHAPTER CASE

As well as cases being scattered throughout the chapter, there is a longer case at the end of each chapter. This can be used for a tutorial, study group or class discussion based on the concepts and ideas covered within the chapter.

Extensive teaching notes for each of these cases can be obtained from www.palgrave.com/business/hillessential.

Acknowledgements

Alex Hill would like to thank LK, DT and AV for their support. In addition, Terry Hill would like to thank PM, JB, SA, OJ, FJ and HH.

The authors are also grateful to Judith Wilding, the book's designer (www.deliciousindustries.com) and photographer Jonathan Harris (www.jonathanharrisphotography.com).

Publishers' Acknowledgements

The authors and publishers are grateful to the following for permission to reproduce copyright material:

The American Marketing Association for Figure 10.8, 'The gap model for understanding the difference between customer expectations and perceptions', adapted from Parasuraman, A. et al (1985) 'A conceptual model of service quality and implications for future research', *Journal of Marketing*, 49 (Fall 1985), pp. 41–50.

The Baldrige National Quality Programme for permission to reproduce Figure 10.13.

Barclays Bank PLC for permission to reproduce the image used in Case 4.4.

The Benetton Group for permission to reproduce the image of the Regent Street Benetton Store (Oxford Circus) in Case 2.4.

Canon (UK) Ltd. for permission to reproduce the image of a Canon camera used in Case 11.6.

The Central Intelligence Agency for Figure 1.6, 'Percentage of GDP by sector for selected countries, 2001 and 2008'.

The EFQM for Figure 10.10, 'EFQM Excellence Award categories and weights' © EFQM 2009.

Elsevier for permission to reprint Figures 11.4, 11.5 and 11.6 from R.H. Lowson, 'Offshore sourcing: and optimal operational strategy?', *Business Horizons* (Nov–Dec 2001), pp. 61–6.

Pearson Education Limited for Figure 10.8, 'The gap model for understanding the difference between customer expectations and perceptions', from Slack, N., Chambers, S. and Johnston, R. (2010) *Operations Management*, 6th edn), Essex. [Adapted from Parasuraman, A. et al. (1985) 'A conceptual model of service quality and implications for future research'. Reproduced by permission of the American Marketing Association.]

The authors and publishers are also very grateful to the following: Aldi, Asahi Breweries Inc., BMW Group, British Airways Plc., Dyson Ltd., Google, Inditex, Lloyds Banking Group, Nissan Motor Ltd., Pret A Manger Ltd., Porsche Cars Ltd., TED Conferences, LLC and Volvo Group.

Every effort has been made to trace all copyright holders, but if any have been inadvertently overlooked, the publishers would be pleased to make the necessary arrangements at the first opportunity.

Learning objectives

After completing this chapter, you should be able to:

- Explain the role of operations management in an organization

- Appreciate the dimensions that make up the operations management task

- Identify where the operations function fits within an organization

- Illustrate the crucial role of operations management in organizational success

- Set the scene for the rest of the book

Chapter outline

Introduction

What does operations management do?

- How operations management fits into an organization

- The role of operations management

- Inputs and outputs

- The mix of sectors in different economies

Variations in the operations management role

- Variations in complexity

- Variations in output: services versus products

Critical reflections

Summary

Operations function –
the function in an
organization that is
responsible for the
resources necessary
to deliver services
and/or make products

Operations
management –
the activities,
responsibilities
and decisions
that make up the
task of managing
of the process of
transforming inputs
such as materials,
people, energy and
information into
services and products

Introduction

Operations management is about the activities, responsibilities and decisions that transform inputs (such as materials, people, energy and information) into outputs (services and products), and is core to what an organization does. Whether it produces insurance, ice-cream, jeans, haircuts or hospital check-ups, an **operations function** has a critical role to play in how efficient and effective an organization is, the level of sales and profitability it achieves and how well it meets its long-term strategic plans: if managed well, **operations management** contributes hugely to business success – and if managed badly, it can lead to disaster.

But what is operations management? What do operations managers do? How do they do it? And why is it all so important? This book sets out to answer these questions, giving you an understanding of this interesting and varied area so that you will be ready to go into the business world fully equipped for the challenges you will face. This introductory chapter will give you a broad overview of the 'what' and the 'why' of operations management and set the scene for the rest of the book, which looks in more detail at different elements of the 'how' of operations management. In brief, however, the following key functions of operations should give you a sense of why it is so important:

- Typically, operations spends 60–70 per cent of costs, uses 60–70 per cent of investment funds and manages 60–70 per cent of staff. How well it manages its short- and long-term tasks will determine whether companies meet both their short-term and long-term targets.
- Operations handles a sale once it has been made. If this is done well, customers come back. If not, customers go elsewhere.

What does operations management do?

A good place to begin our investigation of the subject is to take a look at the role of, and tasks undertaken by, the operations function (also referred to as 'operations'). This will provide an overview of what is involved in managing this function, and what is covered by this book. Let's start by considering what organizations (both commercial and non-commercial) actually do. In essence, they provide **services** and/or **products** to customers. In a commercial organization (such as a shop, insurance company or steel plant), the services and products are likely to be exchanged for money; in a non-commercial organization (such as a state hospital, government agency or charity), there may be no financial exchange with customers, but they nevertheless receive services or products. The task of operations is to provide these services and products through a mix of the skills of the people employed by the organization, the equipment available and the **service delivery systems** or manufacturing processes used. In addition to this central task, operations is responsible for putting systems and procedures in place – for example, negotiating the purchase and supply of services and products from suppliers, scheduling customers or products through the operations process and distributing the completed items to customers (where this is required). The complexity of this 'processing' phase varies, as the examples shown in Case 1.1 illustrate.

Services – intangible
items (i.e. you cannot
touch them) that are
consumed at the
time of provision

Products (also
known as goods) –
tangible items
(i.e. you can touch
them), purchased
by individuals or
organizations for
subsequent use

Service delivery
systems – the
processes used
to deliver services
to customers

> **KEY IDEA**
> Operations' task is to provide the services or make the products sold to customers

CASE 1.1 OPERATIONS TASKS IN DIFFERING ORGANIZATIONS

- **Large retail organization** The operations task within a large retailer with several outlets would typically be handled partly centrally and partly in each store. Central operations would negotiate purchasing and supply contracts with suppliers, while operations in each store would be responsible for agreeing delivery schedules, staffing rotas and arrangements, managing commercial transactions with customers, organizing security and handling banking arrangements. Decisions on the range of products to sell would, however, fall outside operations' remit.

paring food in line with acceptable **customer lead-times**, serving drinks and contracting laundry services.

- **Garment manufacturer** A garment manufacturer buys in fabrics in a range of material types and colours, together with threads, trims, buttons, zips and other accessories. The materials are then cut in line with delivery schedules to meet different style and size requirements, and sewn together with relevant trim, buttons, zips and other accessories. After pressing and final inspection, the garments are packed and despatched to different customers. As with other businesses, operations would be responsible for material and accessory supply contracts, arranging deliveries from suppliers, fixing staffing requirements in line with customer demand, and scheduling, making and despatching garments to meet customer delivery agreements.

- **Restaurant** A restaurant buys in food and prepares it into a range of menus. In addition it purchases various types of soft drinks, bottled water, wines and other alcoholic drinks, stores and then serves them with relatively little additional processing. Operations activities here would be split between the kitchen (referred to as '**back office**' or 'back stage') and dining area (referred to as '**front office**' or 'front stage') and would involve arranging food and beverage supplies, agreeing staffing rotas, establishing and managing procedures for greeting and serving customers, pre-

Question

Select a service business other than those used above and complete a similar overview.

Students: www.palgrave.com/business/hillessential provides learning resources for this case

> **Customer lead-time** – the length of time a customer expects or is prepared to wait for a service or product from the point of making an order

> **Back office** – the area of a service delivery system in which there is normally no contact with customers

> **Front office** – the area of a service delivery system in which contact with customers normally takes place

As you can see from these examples, operations management is responsible for providing and delivering services and products to customers by managing the people, materials, resources and delivery systems involved, together with the other activities that support this core task.

How operations management fits into an organization

We have seen that organizations exist to provide services and products to customers, and that in order to achieve this, certain tasks must be completed. Now let's look more closely at what these tasks are. Essentially, organizations need to:

- Design the services or products
- Purchase materials and/or services from others
- Create the services or make the products to meet the needs of customers (for example, by adding to them in some way, providing diagnostic services, changing the shape of materials, assembling parts, giving advice and processing information or requests)
- Selling services and products to customers
- Accounting for the cash or credit transactions involved.

When an organization is small, several of these tasks are typically completed by one person. As the organization grows, the tasks it must perform remain the same (albeit being larger and more complex), but the organizational structure required to manage and provide them is altered. Sets of tasks are typically separated off into departments or functions and managed by different people. For example, the sales and marketing function would be responsible for selling services and products to customers, the operations function would be responsible for providing the services and products that had been sold, while the accounting and finance function would send out the invoices for the services and products sold and collect payment, categorize costs and revenues and prepare financial statements. In addition, these 'executive' or 'line' functions, as they are called, will be supported by specialist departments (for example, IT) that provide advice and expertise within a given field to help those responsible to better manage these 'executive' or 'line' functions and the organization overall (Figure 1.1).

Figure 1.1 **Some typical functions within a business**

Task	Function responsible		Type of function
· Generating new service and product ideas · Designing and developing new services and products	Services	Sales and marketing	Executive/line
	Products	Research and development	
· Promoting services and products · Selling services and products	Sales and marketing		
· Delivering the services and making the products sold to customers	Operations		
· Sending out invoices · Collecting payment · Preparing financial statements	Accounting and finance		
· Introducing new systems · Developing existing systems · Supporting the IT infrastructure	Information technology		Specialist support
· Recruiting staff · Employee relations	Human resources		

The role of operations management

As the function responsible for providing the services and products sold to customers, operations plays a key role in any organization, no matter what its size. But what does operations management actually involve? There are two distinct – but complementary – aspects to the role:

1 *Content* – what an operations manager *does*, that is, the tasks and responsibilities involved:
   - *The day-to-day or operational role* This involves managing the tasks and responsibilities within operations necessary to provide the required services or products – for example, managing **capacity** and controlling costs.
   - *The strategic role* This concerns meeting the **order-winners** and **qualifiers** within a company's markets for which operations is solely or jointly responsible – for example, providing a service right first time and delivering a service on time.

2 *Style* – *how* an operations manager manages people:
   - *The internal role* This concerns managing the people within the operations function itself and also the interaction of employees in operations with those in other functions within an organization, so as to meet the personal needs of employees within the operations function and overall business.
   - *The external role* This involves managing the people interface outside the organization at both the supplier's and customer's end of the supply chain.

> **KEY IDEA**

Day-to-day aspects of the operations role include managing within budgets, scheduling, serving customers, meeting output targets, and communicating and liaising with other functions in the organization

> **KEY IDEA**

Strategic aspects of the operations role involve providing those order-winners and qualifiers for which it is solely or jointly responsible in an effective manner in order to make the company competitive

The breadth of the tasks and range of skills involved make operations management a demanding and, at the same time, fascinating area. It links strategy to action, requires coordination across functions and involves managing the largest part of an organization. To accomplish this, operations manages most of the people, assets, costs and other resources necessary to produce and deliver the services and products sold to consumers or other organizations. In the area of strategy, the operations role is equally critical. For example, an organization's competitiveness may depend on delivering its services and products quickly (known as **delivery speed**), to the right requirements (known as **quality conformance**) and at the right price – and the achievement of each of these competitive factors depends crucially on successful operations management.

The operations role is best described as exciting, rich in issues, full of challenges, central to the process of a business and about managing through and with people. The day-to-day role is full of interest and variety, while its strategic contribution is central to maintaining and growing sales and profits.

We have looked so far at the operations role in broad terms. Now let's begin to examine in more detail the kinds of task that operations management might fulfill. As a taster, take a look at Case 1.2, which discusses Portioli's, a sandwich and coffee bar located in London's financial centre.

Capacity – comprises the staff, equipment and processes that make up the value-adding activities to meet a certain level of demand in a given time period

Order-winners – features of a service or product that contribute directly to its being chosen over that of other competitors (who also meet the minimum customer requirements)

Qualifiers – features of a service or product that mean a customer will shortlist it for purchase. They do not in themselves win orders but provide or create the opportunity to compete against other service/product providers

Delivery speed – the customer's lead-time (the length of time a customer expects or is prepared to wait) needs to be matched by the operations lead-time. Short customer lead-times create a delivery speed requirement

Quality conformance – providing a service or product to the design specification

CASE 1.2 OPERATIONS MANAGEMENT TASKS AT PORTIOLI'S SANDWICH AND COFFEE BAR

Opening at 7 am to catch the early breakfast and coffee demands of nearby office staff, Portioli's remains open throughout the day until 5.30 pm, when customer demand falls away. A customer visiting Portioli's will expect the full product range to be available, for these products to be of an appropriate quality (in terms of taste and freshness) and not to have to wait too long in a queue to be served. How does operations meet these expectations while ensuring that the business meets its profit targets?

Capacity management Customer numbers and ordering habits/quantities can be predicted using past experience of demand: operations will look at how demand fluctuates in terms of the hour of the day, the day of the week and the week of the year, and use these insights to determine staff levels and to ensure that queue lengths are in line with waiting time targets, while keeping staff costs to a minimum.

Supply chain and inventory management Operations also uses demand forecasts to manage the supply of beverages and food while taking existing stock into account. This role includes ensuring that product specifications (for example, taste, freshness and appearance) are met by Portioli's suppliers and maintained using appropriate storage and refrigeration provision. To this end, daily deliveries of a range of breads, pastries, food ingredients and salads are scheduled before 7 am, while other food and beverages (such as butter, coffee, tea and some sandwich fillings) are held in stock, with deliveries arranged once, twice or sometimes three times a week. Working with suppliers to guarantee that ingredients meet agreed specifications and that deliveries are on time is a key task for this outlet.

Scheduling, delivery systems and managing quality Other aspects that directly affect the smooth running of the business include layout, procedures and the movement of staff between different sets of tasks. As food preparation starts at 6 am and staff typically work an eight-hour day, scheduling appropriate levels of staff in terms of the mix of skills needed at different times is a key operations task, especially given the need for occasional overtime working to cover for holidays and absence. Scheduling staff to ensure that the necessary skills are available is an integral part of managing food quality and service levels at all times.

The market Demand has increased year on year over the last decade. The competitive criteria that are considered a key features in Portioli's sales growth include the quality and freshness of the food and beverages sold, the range of products on sale, short waiting times, prices that are in line with nearby competitors and a no-quibble refund should customers feel dissatisfied. The outlet itself is well located in relation to underground and bus services and, while some seating is available, most customers prefer the takeaway service on offer.

Questions

Review Portioli's sandwich and coffee bar and identify, using the contents list at the beginning of this chapter:

1 How the operations function works.

2 Which chapter topics in the book are reflected in the details provided.

© Alex Hill and Terry Hill 2011

As the Portioli case shows, operations is usually responsible for a whole range of tasks within an organization. These tasks will, of course, differ depending upon the type of organization and the nature of its services and products. Figure 1.2 illustrates this diversity by showing three different organizations and outlining the core operations tasks, support functions involved, and range of specialist functions on hand.

Organization	Some typical jobs in operations		Typical specialist functions that report elsewhere in the organization
	Core tasks	Support functions	
Hospital	Hospital director Medical staff – Doctors – Ward sisters – Nurses	Reception Maintenance Cleaning Porters	Microbiology Pathology Pharmacy Physiotherapy Accounting
Print company	V-P operations[a] Print manager Finishing manager Supervisors Team leaders Operators	Ink manager Plate production Scheduling	Design Pay office Accounts Quality assurance
Transport company	V-P operations[a] Depot managers Drivers	Vehicle maintenance Scheduling	Building and equipment maintenance Pay office Accounting

Figure 1.2 **Operations jobs and specialist functions in three organizations**

Note: [a] Vice-president of operations; also termed operations director.

As you would expect, the role of the operations manager reflects the aspects of the operations function we have already identified above – so some tasks relate to managing the day-to-day tasks and some to the strategic tasks, while others highlight the key role of managing people. The features of the operations tasks and their size and importance create a demanding and absorbing management role. It is concerned with detail yet must address corporate issues of significant size and importance. The key aspects of the job are now outlined below.

Managing a large cost centre

Operations accounts for a large part of the **asset investment** (typically 60–70 per cent) and usually has the largest budget within an organization (again, typically 60–70 per cent). One consequence is that operations managers are responsible for a large **cost centre**. If operations meets its budget and output targets, the cost structure of a business will be in place.

- *Assets* With regard to fixed assets (assets held long term for business use and not to be converted into products or services to be sold), operations is usually accountable for land, buildings and equipment. With regard to current assets (assets that are held short term and are intended to be sold or transformed into products and/or services), operations is responsible for managing and controlling **inventory**.
- *Costs* The operations function accounts for the major portion of an organization's expenditure. The majority of the direct costs, such as staff and materials, are incurred here, together with much of the **overhead costs** involved (for example, managers' and supervisors' salaries, power and utilities expenditure and maintenance of buildings and equipment).

Asset investment – the investment in a range of valuable or useful items, including land, buildings, equipment and inventory

Cost centre – a group of costs controlled by a part of the business (such as a function)

Inventory – also known as stock, comprises the inputs (materials) into the delivery system or manufacturing process, part-finished items (services or products) within the service delivery system or manufacturing process and outputs (finished items) to be sold or supplied to customers

Overhead costs – those costs (for example, management salaries, building and equipment maintenance and interest on loans) incurred in the general running of a business or organization

Managing people

As most employees are usually involved in providing services and/or making products, the task of managing people – in terms of the needs of customers and of the organization itself, as well as the personal development needs of the individuals involved – falls within the operations manager's remit and emphasizes this key element of the operations management job. Added to this, operations managers and their staff are likely to interact with other people, both within and outside the organization – and must do so professionally and effectively. So the 'people management' aspect of the operations manager's role is both sizeable and critical to the well-being of an organization. Creating a working environment that taps into the innate capability of individuals and groups is essential if real, lasting changes and improvements are to be made and maintained.

Managing the short and long term

Operations managers need to think in terms of both short- and long-term timescales. Obviously, it is important that operations is managed efficiently in the short term, so let's begin by investigating this aspect. A key short-term goal is to provide services or products efficiently and effectively: a day's lost output will never be recovered without additional costs being incurred, and customers who go elsewhere are lost business, sometimes for ever. That is the nature of the short-term operations task. It is thus essential that operations activities are well controlled and coordinated, and meet budgeted outputs. Achieving monthly targets requires that each day's target is met. Other departments may work on different timescales: for example, in sales and marketing, no one would expect the period sales target to be met pro rata each day. As a consequence, substantial pressure is, and has to be, exerted to meet short-term operations targets. At no time can the pressure to meet short-term goals be lifted, as costs and schedules are set in line with available capacity and meeting these ensures that customers' expectations, output schedules and profit targets are met.

> **KEY IDEA**
> Operations managers need to think and work in terms of both short- and long-term timescales

---

So what are some of the consequences of needing to meet these short-term goals, in terms of the operations manager's role?:

- The job is problem-oriented and solution-driven. Operations managers need to react quickly to resolve problems at source. Handling the symptoms as they appear will only bring temporary respite: the causes need to be identified and handled.
- It is a job that requires practical outcomes.
- 'Pressure is also a distinctive feature'[1] of the job due to the tasks involved, the time constraints imposed and the dependency upon a whole range of activities, some of which are outside the direct control of the operations function, either because of the organization's reporting system or because they are externally sourced.

The time pressures on operations managers often result in them having to make as good a decision as possible in any given situation. Thinking of a better decision at a later date is of little value – the consequences of the delay usually outweigh the gains involved. It is essential, therefore, that operations managers use their experience to good effect.

Sitting alongside these short-term considerations is the equally important long-term dimension of the job. Given the size of the day-to-day element of operations, managers need to be careful that the short term does not dominate the role and that adequate time and attention are given to the effective management of long-term objectives, which can lead to sizeable benefits. For example, improving the ways in which tasks are completed will typically reduce the time taken and the staff costs involved, while redesigning a service or product to reduce material costs will result in sizeable gains over time.

'**Operations transforms materials** into products and **services** to meet customer needs'

Similarly, improving the layout, for example of a restaurant, will increase the available space, allowing more customers to be served from existing facilities.

Managing the strategic contribution

Whereas operations' day-to-day task concerns essential activities such as managing within budgets, scheduling and communicating with other functions, its strategic task concerns providing those order-winners and qualifiers for which it is wholly or jointly responsible. For example, operations has a sizeable strategic role in retaining and growing market share – we will explore this in more detail in the next chapter. In brief, however, it is essential to the short- and long-term success of an organization that operations moves from being good in itself to being a front runner in meeting the needs of customers by creating competitive advantage. For example, in some markets, such as a fast-food chain, delivering products extremely fast (known as delivery speed) could lead to a competitive advantage over neighbouring outlets; in others, price might be the key factor in the market, and operations would be responsible for delivering products and services at a level of cost that allows them to be competitively priced. As Figure 1.3 illustrates, operations has a role both in gaining the first sale and securing the second. Whether or not customers return depends largely on how well their needs were met on their previous visit or how well their order was fulfilled, and this falls within the remit of operations. As you can see from this, it is the development and implementation of both the day-to-day and strategic activities that characterize the key role of the operations manager.

Figure 1.3 **Operations' role in gaining the first and securing the second sale**		
Phase		**Principal contributor(s)**
Gaining	the first sale	Sales and marketing – customer relationships, advertising and selling Operations – creating a business's reputation through successfully meeting customer needs
Fulfilling		Operations – meets customer needs
Securing	the second sale	Operations – meeting customer needs results in repeat orders

> **KEY IDEA**

Operations contributes to gaining the first sale, and procures the second sale

Managing technology

The operations manager is responsible for managing the technology involved in delivering the service or making the product. The degree of technology will differ from sector to sector and one organization to the next, but, in many situations, the level of technology involved can be quite low. Irrespective of the level, the operations manager needs not so much to understand the technology itself, but instead (and more importantly) to understand how well the technology in place or being proposed can meet the service or product specification (what the service or product comprises) as well as the other dimensions (such as low costs underpinning price or quick turnaround underpinning delivery speed) that make up the sale. In this way, operations managers use technology to provide services or make products for a company's markets, but the technical expertise is provided by support staff rather than operations managers themselves.

Using the common denominators of time and money

In order to run a business, managers need to be able to 'compare like with like' – to find a way of expressing the activities involved that everyone can understand. Many activities use money as the base. So, for example, sales are expressed in terms of their monetary value and not in terms of the number of services or products sold. Using a restaurant as an example, we can see why this makes sense: if a restaurant measured its level of activity by the number of meals provided, it would take no account of the number or type of course selected and served, and an output of 20 sandwiches would appear equivalent to an output of 20 three-course meals.

Money, however, is not always the best way of comparing like with like. Operations typically uses time as a more appropriate common denominator by which to express its activities. The reason is that the monetary value of the services and products provided does not adequately relate to the operations task involved. Returning to our restaurant, for example, it takes longer to produce a lasagne than to prepare a fillet steak, but the menu price for each would be the reverse. And as operations needs to assess, for example, the level of capacity needed at different times of the day and week, it has to work out the number of hours involved to meet forecast sales and what this means in terms of different types of staff.

Linking the thinking and doing ends of a business

The operations function forms the interface between the 'thinking' end (strategic direction) and the 'doing' end (meeting the needs of customers) of a business. Without action, strategic discussion and debate has little value: translating strategy into action is fundamental to the ongoing success of a business, and operations has a key role in this. Operations managers must develop and implement a strategy for the operations function as part of the corporate task of identifying and agreeing strategic direction – and then they must ensure that they meet these requirements in those markets in which a company chooses to compete. It is essential, therefore, to link the top and bottom of a business and so create the coherence and cooperation essential for the success of the enterprise.

Managing complexity

The perspective that best captures the essence of the operations tasks we have been discussing is that operations concerns the management of complexity. The decisions operations managers make have significant implications for investment, costs and people. The challenge of the job comes from the number and range of tasks and decisions to be completed, the interrelationships between these and their fundamental nature in terms of the business.

> **KEY IDEA**
Operations concerns the management of complexity

Inputs – the materials, staff, energy and other 'ingredients' necessary to provide a service or make a product

Outputs – the services or products produced by a delivery system or manufacturing process

This mix results in a demanding job that requires that, on the one hand, the fast, day-to-day pace of the short term is supported and delivered while, on the other hand, the long-term direction is secured – and all this within the context of providing appropriate interface and cooperation within the overall business. Add to this the essential need to manage the service delivery systems or manufacturing processes and the interface with customers through the key resource of people, and the outcome is a job that is fascinating in its challenge and complex in its execution.

Inputs and outputs

Taking a step back from the detail of the operation manager's role, we are now in a position to take an overview of the operations function. Broadly speaking, we can say that operations concerns the transformation process that involves taking **inputs** and converting them into **outputs** (with the support of the various specialist functions closely associated with this basic task). Figure 1.4 provides a simplified overview of what is involved in this transformation process.

> **KEY IDEA**
Operations concerns the transformation process that involves taking 'inputs' and converting them into 'outputs'

Figure 1.4 **Overview of the o**

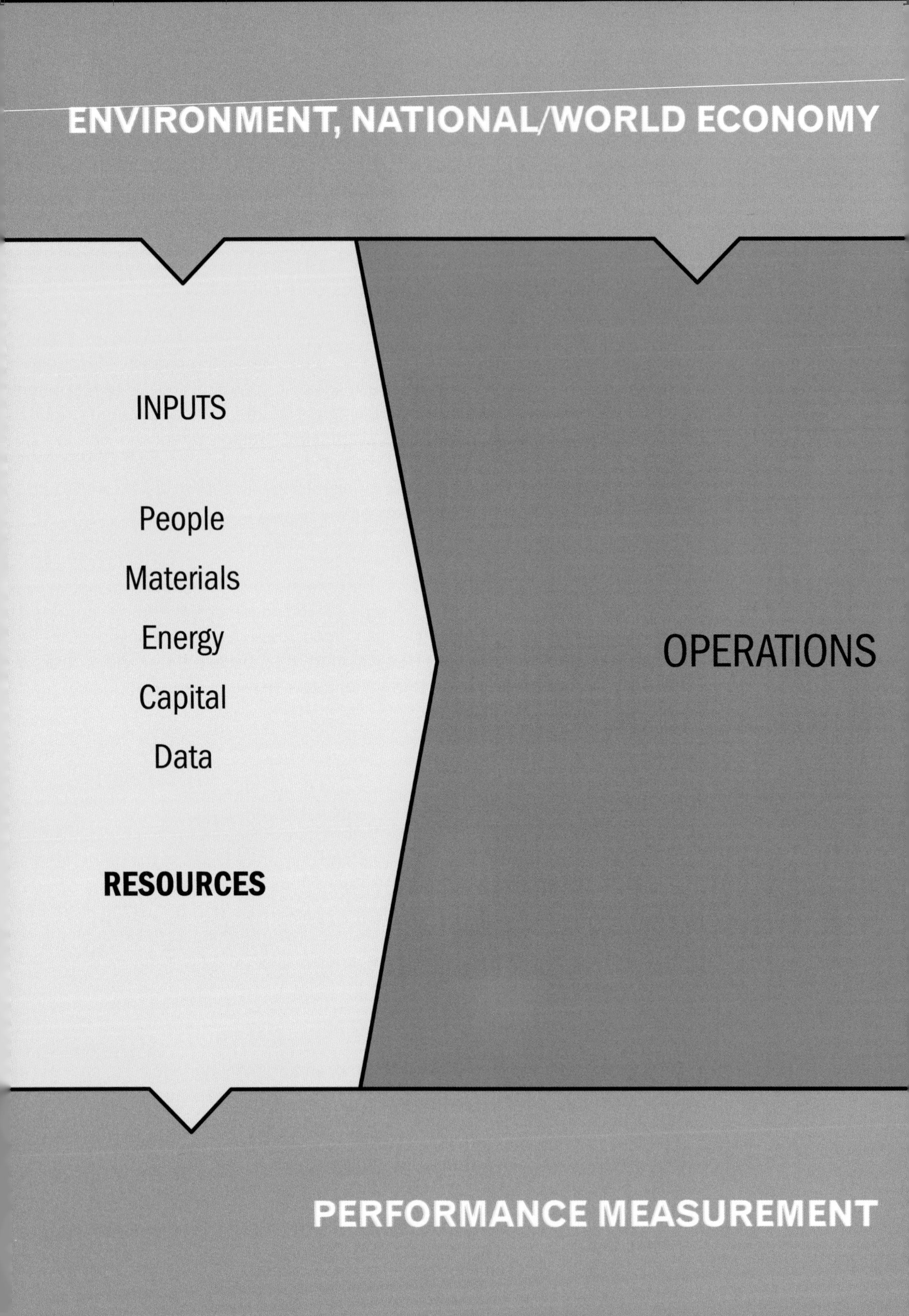

ENVIRONMENT, NATIONAL/WORLD ECONOMY

INPUTS

People

Materials

Energy

Capital

Data

RESOURCES

OPERATIONS

PERFORMANCE MEASUREMENT

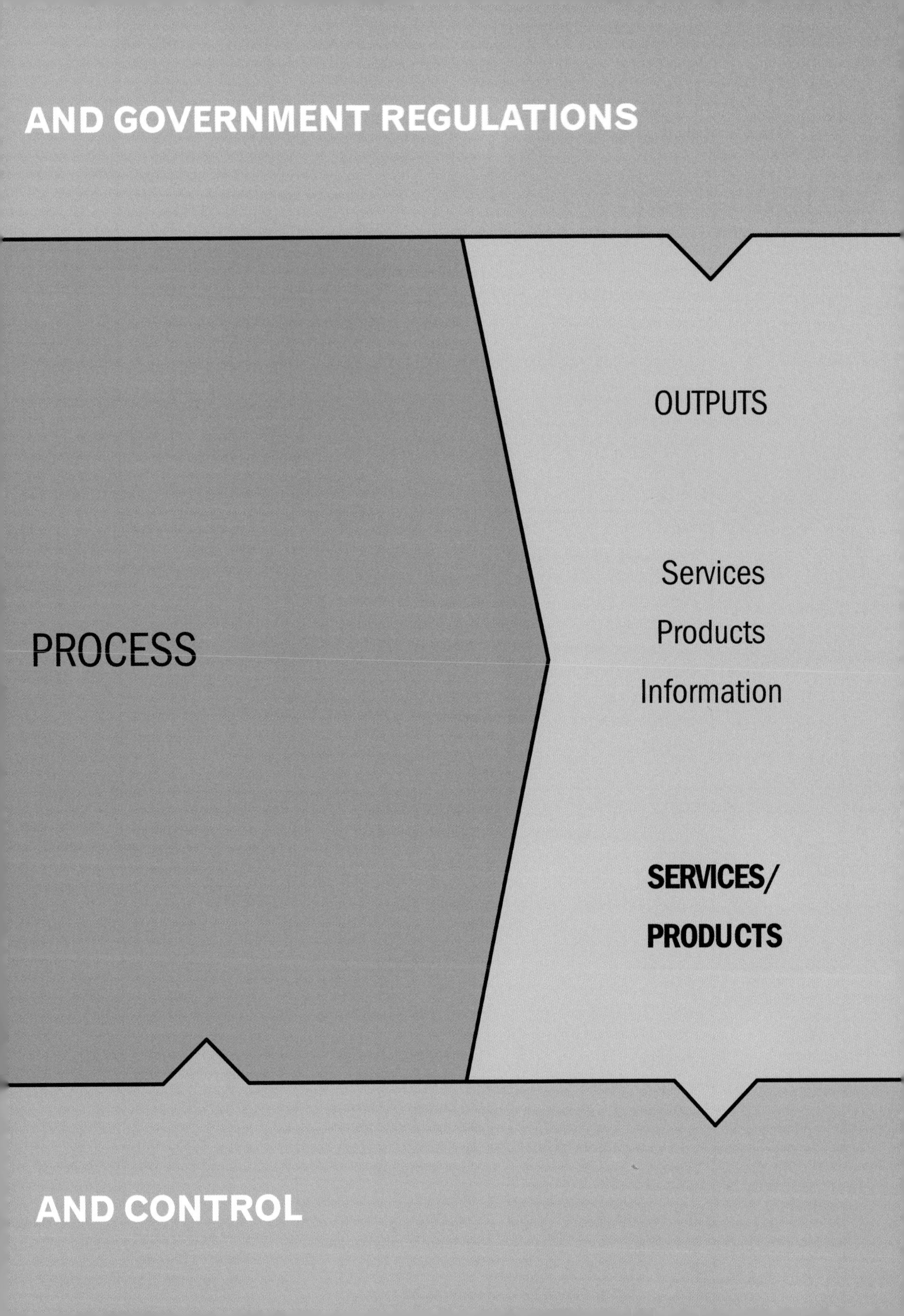

AND GOVERNMENT REGULATIONS

PROCESS

OUTPUTS

Services
Products
Information

SERVICES/
PRODUCTS

AND CONTROL

Figure 1.5 An overview of the operations process in a selection of organizations				
Sector	Organization	Inputs	Delivery system/process	Outputs
Services	Call centre	People Telephone systems IT equipment and support Buildings and furniture Rest and refreshment areas Washroom facilities Maintenance Energy	Receiving calls Processing requests and queries Updating records Staff scheduling Mail services	Customer queries, information requests and transactions completed accurately, within acceptable timescales and with appropriate levels of service
	Bank branch	People Banking procedures Processing equipment Buildings and furniture Rest areas Washroom facilities Meeting rooms Office areas Stationery Energy	Commercial transactions Updating records Processing requests and queries Providing general and specific advice Technical services IT support Equipment maintenance	Completed personal banking transactions Completed business banking transactions Provision of regular, or on-demand, up-to-date personal and businesses information and financial advice
	Metro or underground	People Tracks, trains and carriages Signalling and other support systems Traffic flows Passenger procedures Ticket offices and machines Staff rest areas Washroom facilities Maintenance Energy	Train schedules Ticket purchasing Passenger processing equipment/procedures Train maintenance and cleaning Station maintenance and cleaning Security	Trains provided in line with schedules reflecting the demand profiles throughout the day and evening Customers transported to their destinations safely and on time
Manufacturing	Pharmaceuticals	People Buildings and equipment Chemicals Packaging Utilities and energy	Drug formulation/mixing Equipment setting Liquid, tablet and capsule preparation Packaging Warehousing Distribution	Range of drugs prepared, packed and delivered in line with customers' orders and schedules
	Oil refining	People Docking facilities Crude oil and other chemicals Equipment Process monitoring Buildings Energy	Receipt and storage of crude oil and other chemicals Refining processes Distribution Equipment monitoring and maintenance	Refining crude oil into various products and distributing to customers in line with schedules
	Ice-cream products	People Equipment Food ingredients Packaging Buildings Energy	Material storage Mixing Packaging Equipment maintenance Warehousing Distribution	Range of products prepared and packed in line with customer schedules and to meet the variable pattern of seasonal demand

Some organizations provide services such as medical care, the processing of information and requests, banking facilities and retail sales, while others produce physical items such as furniture, building materials and stationery. The operations task, however, is common to all the diverse range of services and products that make up a national economy. To illustrate this, Figure 1.5 gives examples from both the service and manufacturing sectors.

The mix of sectors in different economies

National economies are made up from a mix of three key sectors:

- Primary sector: agricultural (producing food, feed and fibre)
- Secondary sector: industrial (production of products including fuels and fertilizers)
- Tertiary sector: services (economic activity not resulting in ownership).

As economies develop, the balance between these different sectors changes, as illustrated in Figure 1.6. The differences in the split across the three sectors reflect the general activities associated with the individual countries involved. For example, the relatively high percentage of gross domestic product (GDP) in the Chinese and Norwegian industrial sectors reflects a growth in manufacturing, and the North Sea oil and gas explorations, respectively. Similarly, the high percentage of GDP in the industrial sector for Singapore signals its role as a major manufacturing nation. On the other hand, the growing size of India's service sector GDP has been fuelled by the subcontracting of banking and other service activities from countries such as the US and the UK. However, the overall change from 2001 to 2008 shows a broad pattern: the service sector continues to grow as a percentage of GDP in most developed countries.

Figure 1.6 **Percentage of gross domestic product (GDP) by sector for selected countries, 2001 and 2009**

Country	Percentage of gross domestic product by sector					
	2001			2009		
	Agriculture	Industrial	Service	Agriculture	Industrial	Service
Australia	3	26	71	4	26	70
Belgium	2	24	74	1	22	77
Canada	2	27	71	2	26	72
China	15	51	34	11	47	42
France[a]	3	26	71	2	19	79
Germany	1	31	68	1	27	72
India[a]	24	28	48	17	28	55
Italy	2	30	68	2	25	73
Japan	1	31	68	2	22	76
Norway[b]	2	31	67	2	40	58
Singapore	0	33	67	0	28	72
Spain[b]	4	31	65	3	27	70
UK[b]	1	25	74	1	24	75
USA[a]	2	18	80	1	22	77

Notes: Agriculture – process of producing food, fuel and fibre by raising plants and animals.
Industrial – production of products (including fuels and fertilizers).
Service – economic activity not resulting in ownership.
[a] Data for these countries is for 2002.
[b] Data for these countries is for 2000.
Source: CIA – The World Factbook.

Printed with the permission of J Sainsbury Plc

Store managers of large companies are crucial appointments. When handed the keys to their own store, managers take on a task that is characterized by big numbers, typically with up to 700 staff, weekly sales revenues of £1 million and 200,000 customers entering the door in an average week. Store managers hold a pivotal role in the retail sector. Buyers can source products at competitive prices, and distribution can be fine-tuned to efficiently meet the varying patterns of demand, but the key to customer retention is what happens inside the store. It is customers' experiences while shopping that affect whether or not they come back. Layout, presentation, queue lengths, availability and, above all, service throughout the delivery system are the factors that most influence a customer's decision of where to shop.

According to many retailing experts, a 'good' store manager can increase the sales revenue of self-service outlets (such as supermarkets) by up to 5 per cent, while in stores heavily dependent on service (such as the electrical sector), the improvement can be as high as 15 per cent, and the best managers carry these increases down to the bottom line and vice versa. With stores' weekly sales of up to £1 million (and with the biggest stores in large national chains averaging well above this figure), the essential contribution made by store managers in driving improvements through frontline operations and into higher retail performance is fundamental.

Retailers agree that managing the operations units (the stores themselves) has all the ingredients of what makes a complex job. Staff management is fundamental, especially given the fast-moving environment, changing demand levels and long opening hours involved. Tied to this is the management of a sizeable budget that reflects the costs of running a large store. The job concerns managing a large investment in the form of the buildings, car parks and delivery areas, as well as the storage of products and their management in terms of waste and obsolescence. Knowing what goes on in both the store and the back office (including supply chain, logistics and inventory management) is essential to running the operation, as well as being good with customers and alert to actual and potential service issues.

Although overall the skill range may be similar, the type of store and its location will alter the task. Hypermarkets versus convenience stores, general retailing versus out-of-town shopping centres, self-service outlets versus those requiring a high level of personal service, rural location versus inner-city environment – place a different emphasis on the skills needed.

Attracting the right calibre of people is difficult, as the long, unsocial hours and weekend working are unattractive dimensions of the job. But on the plus side, the job is people-centred, rich in content, and full of energy, and buzz and addresses real problems, the solutions to which are fast and rewarding.

Questions

1 What makes the store manager of a retail company a classic example of an operations manager?

2 From the facts given here, assess the size of the operations task and its impact on corporate financial performance.

3 How is the store manager a key link in the supply chain?

Although it is useful to separate activities into agriculture, industrial and service sectors in order to help identify trends, each sector is in reality dependent on and interacts with other sectors to form part of a 'total' economy. Each sector is an integral part of one economy in its own right, but its performance will often also have an impact on other sectors. Arguments suggesting that developed nations can rely on the tertiary sector (services) as a way of sustaining standards of living or improving below-average trade performance are without foundation. For example, a large part of many service sales is made up of a product provided by activities in the primary and/or secondary sectors (for example, foodstuffs or IT equipment).

The operations management role, no matter what sector is involved, is similar in terms of its overall aim, the nature of the task and its central importance. Growing foodstuffs, extracting minerals, making products and providing services are parts of the basic task of any business and central to its continued success. Therefore, whether or not you are or intend to be involved in operations management, it is essential that you understand the concepts and approaches involved, the interfaces this function has within a business and its key role in helping to grow sales and meet an organization's short- and long-term financial goals.

Variations in the operations management role

So far in this chapter, we have looked in detail at the operations manager's role and at the main tasks that the operations function will perform in all organizations. Now we shift the focus to look at how and why the operations function might vary in different types of organization.

Variation in complexity

The level of complexity within the operations function will vary depending upon several factors, including:

- The size of an organization and the associated service/product volumes
- The range of services and products sold
- The technology levels embodied in both the services/products themselves and the processes used to provide them
- The extent to which the services and products are made in-house
- The nature of what is processed.

> **Customer surrogates** – when the item being processed represents the customer; for example, where clothes are being cleaned, the clothes represent the customer within the service delivery system

Most of these factors are fairly self-explanatory: for example, it is easy to see how managing operations for a business with only one service or product would be simpler than for a business with hundreds. However, the final factor – the *nature* of what is processed – benefits from further investigation. In a service organization, the operations function may process customers, **customer surrogates** or information, while in a manufacturing organization the operations function would make products. Which of these makes up the business will have a significant effect on the design and management of the operations delivery system. As Figure 1.7 illustrates, the presence of the customer in the system will impact its design and the operations management task involved, an aspect that is examined more fully in Chapter 4. The examples given in Figure 1.7 have been chosen to illustrate these differences, whereas in reality the operations function must often process a combination of customers, information and products. For example, car servicing will involve contact with the customer as well as processing the automobile (the customer surrogate), updating the vehicle's records, and invoice preparation and payment (information). Similarly, purchasing furniture will involve advising the customer, completing the relevant paperwork for the invoice and guarantee (information), as well as the product itself.

Figure 1.7 **Examples of service and product processing**			
Sector	**What is processed**	**Examples**	**Customer involvement in the process or delivery system**
Service	Customers	Beauty salons, hospitals, health farms, physiotherapists and restaurants	Present in the delivery system
	Customer surrogates	Garages, repair shops and dry cleaning outlets	Detached from the delivery system or process
	Information	Tax accountants, passport offices, lawyers, computing centres and insurance	
Manufacturing	Products	Chemicals, furniture, motor vehicles, personal computers, food and pharmaceuticals	

This variation in the nature of what is processed has significant implications for operations management, and we now examine these in more detail.

Variation in output – services versus products

You will have noticed throughout this chapter that we have referred repeatedly to the output of the operations function as 'services' and 'products'. We turn now to look at these two ideas in more detail, and to investigate their consequences for the operations function.

Products are tangible items (that is, you can touch them) purchased by individuals or organizations for subsequent use – for example, an iPod or a piece of sheet metal. Services are intangible items (that is, you cannot touch them) that are consumed at the time of provision, with a customer taking away or retaining the benefits of that service – for example, a carwash or a night at the cinema. However, in many situations, what is provided or produced by an organization can be a mix of both services and products. In some instances, there will be a heavy accent on service, and in others the reverse. To help illustrate this, Figure 1.8 shows a range of items sold and gives an idea of the mix between the service and product content provided. The purpose, however, is to illustrate that what we buy is a mix of both a service and a product, and the mix will differ depending upon the offering.

> **KEY IDEA**

The operations output can be in the form of services (intangible) or products (tangible)

Take, for example, the difference between 'regular car maintenance' and 'breakdown maintenance' shown in Figure 1.8. The 'product' content in a breakdown is typically less than for regular maintenance, whereas the 'service' content is more – if you break down, a skilled mechanic *comes to you*, thus offering a greater proportion of 'service' in the 'service/product mix' than for regular service maintenance, when you take your car to a garage. Similarly, a high-quality restaurant will offer a higher service element than a fast-food alternative.

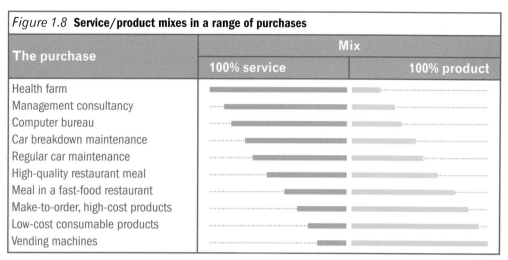

Figure 1.8 **Service/product mixes in a range of purchases**

The purchase	Mix	
	100% service	100% product
Health farm		
Management consultancy		
Computer bureau		
Car breakdown maintenance		
Regular car maintenance		
High-quality restaurant meal		
Meal in a fast-food restaurant		
Make-to-order, high-cost products		
Low-cost consumable products		
Vending machines		

Note: The purchase mix represented here is meant as a **broad indication only**; others may consider the balance to differ from that shown.

But what does all this mean for the operations function? Well, broadly speaking, its aim remains the same (its objective is always to make the products or provide the services that are sold), but the nature and characteristics of the operations function vary significantly depending on whether it is required to make a product, process information on behalf of a customer, provide a service for a customer or some combination of these. Embodied in these alternatives are different characteristics that either facilitate or restrict what operations can or cannot do in the processing task. For example, in services the opportunity to store capacity is limited. If a retail outlet (say) is not busy, the assistants' time cannot in some way be transferred to a future time period when customers are waiting. In manufacturing, however, a company may decide to make products in times of low demand to sell in a future period when sales are higher. Similarly, in a service organization, the presence of a customer necessitates the system to respond as quickly as possible, whereas in a manufacturing company the product eliminates the need for an immediate response (as the customer is not physically present), which allows the process to be managed to best meet the output and efficiency targets set by the business.

Such differences are fundamental and are investigated in more detail in subsequent chapters. This section is designed to alert you to the key points so that you get a better feel for the types of issue that operations has to manage in one type of organization compared with another.

Serving customers, processing customer information and making products all have different features and different sets of requirements. Figure 1.9 gives an overview of some key dimensions that are then briefly explained.

Figure 1.9 **Aspects of customer, information and product processing**

Aspects	Processing		
	Customers	Information	Products
Nature of the offering	Intangible	⟶	Tangible
Level of customer involvement in the operations process	High	⟶	Low
Operations capacity	Perishable	⟶	Can be stored
Organizational arrangements	Front office	⟶	Back office
Quality control	Level of server discretion	⟶	Highly specified
Typical competitive environment	Sheltered	⟶	Traded

Compare a cup of coffee provided by a vending machine with one provided in the lounge of a good hotel:

- The vending machine offers convenient, 24-hour, fast delivery of coffee. The product specification is controlled by the service delivery system, and hence the product range offered is limited: coffee is provided in a number of combinations (for example, regular or decaffeinated, with or without milk and sugar) and in a disposable cup. The price is likely to be low.

- On the other hand, coffee provided in the lounge of a good hotel involves significantly different service factors – better choice, superior coffee (in terms of higher-specification beans), better presentation, comfort and probably a slower,

'more leisurely' service, albeit delivered at a higher price.

In the former coffee provision, the ratio of products to service in the total package mix would be considerably higher than in the latter.

Questions

1 What operational factors might contribute to the fact that the hotel coffee is more expensive?

2 Now think about the last cup of tea or coffee you drank. How did it compare with the two scenarios outlined above?

Lecturers: visit www.palgrave.com/business/hillessential for additional resources

Take-away – what customers take away from their experience of a service, including the recollection of how well they were served

Nature of the offering

The services received by customers are considered to be intangible and are consumed at the time of delivery. The recollection of how well they were served forms part of the customer's **take-away**. On the other hand, the processing of customer information or the making of products changes the nature of the offering to one that is tangible, with the outcome being retained for use following delivery. These features place different sets of demands on operations: in each case, operations must ensure customer satisfaction – but what this entails can be very different depending on the nature of the offering. In the case of services, the delivery system must create the features that make up a customer's view of good service/experience, whereas in the case of a product, product quality (design and being made to specification) is typically a principal factor influencing customer choice and satisfaction.

Level of customer involvement in the operations process

As services involve customers, then, by definition, they are involved in the operations process and central to its design. In fact, service delivery systems are often designed to use customers to deliver part or all of the service and are thus an integral part of the delivery system design (for example, getting money from cash machines, and selecting, paying for and taking food to a table in a self-service restaurant). On the other hand, information is processed and products are usually made without the customers being present – it is not essential that customers are involved, and indeed operations can be more easily managed where customers are not involved in the service delivery system or manufacturing process. In instances such as self-assembly furniture, companies design the process to involve customers in the final build stage in order to reduce transport (as flat packs take up less space) and assembly costs. In this way, making the furniture has no customer involvement, whereas delivery from the store and final assembly is provided by the customer.

Operations capacity

Services are consumed by the customer at the point of provision. This means that the capacity in the process (for example, an empty seat on a passenger airline, or an unbooked appointment in a hairdressing salon) is perishable – that is, it cannot be held over to another time or stored in the form of inventory. In contrast, a typical manufacturing company can make products ahead of demand: for example, ice-cream can be made and stored during times of lower demand, which means that ice-cream-making capacity does not go to waste and that high demand (for example, during the summer months) can be met when necessary. For this reason, a manufacturing company producing a tangible product typically finds it easier to handle the imbalances that occur between the levels of demand and capacity.

Information-processing and customer surrogate businesses also have some opportunity to control the point at which tasks are completed. For example, information-processing tasks can be pulled together, handled as a total and then scheduled to be completed at the most suitable time, thus enabling demand to be spread in line with available capacity, or to accumulate volumes to help lower processing costs. Similarly, the timing of a vehicle or other repair can, to some extent, be managed to better meet the scheduling needs of a business. Even so, the length of time over which scheduling alterations can be made in a service organization will normally be limited in scale compared with manufacturing. With products, inventory can be made, if required, ahead of time and independent of demand profiles, whereas information-processing will invariably be an integral part of the overall service or procedure for a customer. The processing task can only commence on receipt of relevant data and needs to be completed to fit in with a customer's own requirements.

Take, for example, a data-processing unit that does work on behalf of a high-street bank. The processing unit updates the transactions of the bank's customers and then sends them their bank statements. The necessary data will be delivered to the processing unit from the bank on a given day each month, with agreed lead-times for completing the updates and sending out statements to the bank's customers. Within this time frame, the unit is able to schedule the job to best fit its own total workload. Similarly, a garage can schedule the work within its repair shop on a given day around factors such as the skills available, spare part deliveries and the efficient use of staff.

> **KEY IDEA**
Services are consumed by the customer at the point of provision, whereas many products can be made in advance and stored

Organizational arrangements

As Figure 1.9 above shows, the operations process is largely, and often totally, separated from the customer at the product end, whereas in the service sector customers are often involved in the provision. In a service company, the delivery system is, where possible, split between the front office and back office. The front office interfaces with customers and, for example, handles requests or provides a given service. However, systems and procedures are designed so that certain tasks are undertaken in the back office and, in that way, processing can be delayed until a more convenient time and activities cumulated in order to gain **economies of scale** and so justify investment as part of the way to reducing costs. Being separated from customers in the back office also allows procedures and tasks to be undertaken without making essential responses to customers' immediate requirements.

Quality control

The presence or absence of customers in the system also brings the aspect of server interpretation into the delivery of a service – known as **server discretion**. As a server typically interfaces with customers in the delivery of a service, there are elements of the delivery that are open to a server's interpretation, such as personal manner, approach and advice or assistance offered. As a result, it is more difficult to control quality as it is more difficult to establish service levels and to measure performance against these. For example, think of the variation in service you might receive from two different waiters in a bar – they might both deliver the same drink to you in the same time and at the same price, but their individual manner might make your overall experience quite different. In the provision of products, the making and purchasing events are separated, so the issues of quality control and measuring performance against a product's specification are more easily and objectively managed, making it easier to control how a product is made.

Competitive environment

The tangible nature of products enables the work and supporting technologies that go into making them to be easily transferred, in product form, from the place of manufacture to markets throughout the world. In this way, products are referred to as being **traded**. As a result, the manufacturing sector has been increasingly competitive from the latter half of the 20th century, highlighting the truly global nature of these markets. Many services, on the other hand, are classed as being **sheltered**, highlighting the fact that the extent of competition is restricted by the geographical boundaries of such markets – the 'you do not go to Hong Kong for a Chinese takeaway' syndrome. For example, individual retail outlets compete only with other high-street outlets within their own town or city.

In recent years, however, the format of competition for many service firms has changed. One source of this change has been the increasing use of technology. Online services for the purchase of items such as books, clothes, banking, holidays, flights and theatre tickets has increasingly moved many service sectors into the 'traded' category, with a resulting increase in competition. The role of operations in such instances has needed to reflect these new dynamics and business conditions, reinforcing its core contribution to the continued success of a business.

Critical reflections

Few operations managers would consider their role to be other than demanding, challenging, absorbing and satisfying. They would also tell of its frustrations and complexity; this is inevitable given the large number of variables and the many diverse and complicated short- and longer term objectives involved.

To manage such a task effectively requires a range of executive qualities, as outlined earlier in the chapter. To this specific list need to be added the more general attributes of diligence, intellect, experience and energy. Completing the day-to-day tasks requires much physical effort. To manage the operations function effectively and efficiently, operations managers have to be able to understand the whole, take it apart, fix the parts required and put it back together again. They need to be able to instigate appropriate initiatives and developments through others, to manage high levels of complexity and to provide support for their customers' many different needs. All this requires both intellect and experience, the former to appreciate the issues and perspectives involved, and the latter to be alert to potential problem areas. Figure 1.10 underlines this point: as you will see, management concerns the higher levels of learning, from application through to evaluation.

Figure 1.10 The levels of learning

Increasingly higher levels of learning	Levels of learning	Description
	Evaluation	Appraise, compare, conclude, contrast, interpret and explain
	Synthesis	Classify, compile, design, modify, reorganize, formulate, reconstruct and substitute
	Analysis	Select, discriminate, illustrate, separate and distinguish
	Application	Demonstrate, relate, use, complete and prepare
The task of management	Understanding	Explain, extend, generalize, infer, summarise and estimate
	Knowledge	Know, identify, list, name, outline and state

Source: Adapted from Benjamin S. Bloom et al. *Taxonomy of Educational Objectives,* Allyn & Bacon, Boston, MA. © Pearson Education 1984.

The operations manager's task is a classic example of these demands, a fact gaining increasing recognition not least because of the success that some developed nations have had as a result of placing great emphasis upon the management of the operations function. For example, by the early 1980s, it was becoming clear that Japanese success was based upon a greater investment not in processes but in management, particularly operations. Similarly, the successful growth of international retailers such as Wal-Mart and IKEA has been built on world-class operations capability. Some believe that the managers needed to convert operations into 'a competitive resource may have to be the best rounded and most intellectually able of all corporate managers'.[2] The competencies identified included 'a knowledge of technology ... as well as every business function ... a thinking style that includes the ability to conceptualize as well as analyse complex trade-offs ... [and] managers who are architects of change not house-keepers'.[3]

Recognition of these operations management qualities is a prerequisite for both the service and manufacturing sectors. Those nations that failed to carry out the operations tasks effectively in their manufacturing industries have stood by and watched this sector diminish dramatically in a few years. Next on the list are parts of the service sector. Passenger airlines, data-processing, call centre provision, banking and other parts of the financial services sector have already experienced the full weight of global competition. It will not abate in these sectors and is already surfacing elsewhere. The sound management of operations has a key contribution to make in the success of companies, sectors and hence nations.

This chapter has illustrated in general terms the crucial role of operations management for organizational success, with the aim of setting the scene for the rest of the book. The next chapter, on operations strategy, completes this overview. The rest of this book then reviews the essential tasks involved and some of the important perspectives that need to be understood by an operations manager.

Summary

- The operations process transforms inputs into outputs that the organization then sells in its chosen markets. Figure 1.4 overviews this core task, while Figure 1.5 provides examples from both the service and manufacturing sectors.

- As operations typically accounts for 60–70 per cent of the people, assets and costs within an organization, its sheer size makes it a demanding management task. In addition to undertaking these activities, operations comprises a wide range of functions and support roles, examples of which are given in Figure 1.2.

- Most companies deliver a mix of both services and product, as illustrated in Figure 1.8. Where an organization chooses to position itself on this service–product mix continuum will influence its competitive position and the operations task involved.

- While most offerings are a combination of services and products, there are important distinctions in managing operations in the service and manufacturing sectors. These are outlined and overviewed in Figure 1.9.

- Most of the people within a typical organization work within the operations function and reflect a wide range of jobs, skills and personal needs. A critical part of the operations role is to manage the operations process through people in such a way as to meet the short- and long-term needs of the business, as well as the development needs and personal expectations of those involved.

- Operations has a significant strategic contribution to make in retaining and growing market share. It is responsible for meeting the requirements of the sale and this, in turn, affects whether customers purchase a second time (see Figure 1.3).

Study activities

Discussion questions

1 What is operations management? What are the key elements of the operations task? Illustrate your answer with examples.

2 Identify an operations system in your own life. What are the inputs, operations process activities and outputs involved?

3 Select two service and two manufacturing businesses of your own choice. From an operations perspective, what are the similarities and differences that exist?

4 Select two functions other than operations within a service or manufacturing business. For each, identify three links to operations and explain the key dimensions of the activities involved and how they would assist operations to complete its tasks and responsibilities.

Assignments

1 Analyse the operations function in the university or college department in which you are registered or in the company in which you work in terms of:

- The key operations responsibilities
- The size of the operations task
- The operations function in the context of the rest of the university/college department or organization
- Four factors that illustrate the complexity of the operations task. Give reasons for your choice.

2 Consider the following processes that you frequently encounter:

- Enrolling on a course
- Buying lunch
- Buying a ticket for a concert or the cinema.

Identify the inputs, operations process and outputs involved.

3 Look through McDonald's website (**www.mcdonalds.com**) and list the dimensions that concern operations. How many outlets are there throughout the world, and how do you think the company ensures effective control over the operations task in order to maintain its desired standards within the service delivery system?

4 Make a list of the top 10 companies in the Fortune 500 (**http://money.cnn.com/magazines/fortune/fortune500/**) from 1965, 1985, 1995 and 2005. Compare these with the current list. Identify the fundamental differences and give reasons for these changes.

Exploring further

Ford, H. (1988) *Today and Tomorrow*. Cambridge MA: Productivity Press. This is a reprint of Henry Ford's 1926 book, and its direct style and insights into business are well worth the effort of reading it. The approaches that Henry Ford developed have been acknowledged as the basis of Japanese approaches today. The text is fun to read, and you could benefit from looking at Chapters 1–4, which provide a general context for business as a whole and operations in particular.

Hill, T. (1998) *The Strategy Quest: Releasing the Energy of Manufacturing Within a Market Driven Strategy: a Dynamic Business Story.* Available from AMD Publishing, 'Albedo', Dousland, Devon PL20 6NE, UK; e-mail: amd@jm-abode.tiscali.co.uk; fax: +44 (0) 1822 882863. This book (written as a novel) describes how an art business and manufacturing organization restructure themselves to meet the changing demands of their customers.

Hill, T. (2005) *Operations Management: Text and Cases*. Basingstoke: Palgrave Macmillan. The text provides a useful supplement to this book by offering a more comprehensive explanation and further examples (including long case studies) showing how service and manufacturing companies have applied these concepts.

Meredith, J.R. and Shafer, S.M. (2007) *Operations Management for MBAs*, 3rd edn. New York: John Wiley & Sons. This book includes a useful, easy-to-read opening chapter setting out the activities and dimensions of operations management as a function, within organizations and in an increasingly global economy.

Notes and references

1 Lawrence, P.A. (1983) *Operations Management: Research and Priorities*. Report to the Social Services Research Council, April, p. 14.

2 Meyer, R. (1987) 'Wanted: a new breed of manufacturing manager'. In *Manufacturing Issues 1987*. New York: Booz Allen, pp. 26–9.

3 Meyer, R. (1987) 'Wanted: a new breed of manufacturing manager'. In *Manufacturing Issues 1987*. New York: Booz Allen, p. 28.

Giles Chamberlain, the Production Manager of the Playhouse Theatre, set out for work on Monday morning. Over the weekend, he had drawn up a list of tasks to look at that day that would help reduce the ever-increasing production costs. 'I really need to find new suppliers for our high-cost and high-volume materials,' he thought. 'I also need to speak to Lois (Production Administrator) to work out how to plan the production of our shows better so we can reduce the overtime and casual labour costs. Better planning would also allow us to order in materials earlier, rather than paying the high prices we currently have to in order to get them in the next day. I also need to speak to Susan (Deputy Stage Manager) to create a proposal for some new stage facilities that would help reduce the designers' workload, and discuss with Fred (Head of Carpentry) how we can create modular stage designs to reduce timber costs and make the sets quicker to build.'

By the time Giles had reached the theatre, he had decided he should look for some new suppliers first and then speak to Lois, Susan and Fred. As he entered the building, Ian (Stage Manager) called him to explain that he needed more casual labour than planned due to the changes agreed last Friday for the forthcoming play *Joseph and the Amazing Technicolour Dreamcoat*. They discussed the proposed increases, and Giles asked Ian to advise him on the outcome and to let his secretary, Mary, know the costs involved. In the conversation, Ian also reminded Giles of several items that needed either purchasing or progressing from suppliers.

As he entered his office, Giles found on his desk some invoices and the time sheets for the casual labour employed the previous week. He checked the wage claims, made one or two notes and authorized those without queries for payment. He then checked the invoices and telephoned Fred, Jim (Head of Electrics), Martin (Head of Sound) and Jennifer (Head of Wardrobe) to confirm that the items and quantities on the invoices had been received. Neither Jim nor Jennifer answered, so he made a mental note to ask them later in the day. He then made several phone calls to either purchase or chase the materials requested by Ian before calling Mary to ask her to come up to his office. While he waited, he called the local Fire Officer to check on an issue raised by Assistant Director Matt last week. Following the discussion, he checked his file containing details of the local fire regulations and marked the appropriate section. Just then, Mary arrived. He discussed some administrative details with her and handed over the signed invoices and authorized casual-labour time sheets. Mary gave him the morning mail and explained one or two points.

At this point, Giles grabbed a coffee and then went down to the stage area to check with Ian on the progress of the alterations for the current production *The Sons of Light*. 'There's a problem fitting the rostrum onto the stage,' explained Ian, 'but Fred's working on an idea to get around it.' Giles went with Ian to meet Fred, and together they came up with another idea, Giles staying and watching until a satisfactory solution had been reached. Before leaving the stage area, he also checked the casual-labour time sheet queries with Ian and asked him to get overtime authorized in future to help control production costs. He then went to see Jennifer to discuss current wardrobe production costs and a proposed trip with Charles (Head of Design) to buy new costumes for the future production of *The Play What I Wrote*. After that, Giles discussed costs, costume resale policies and budget limits for the new costumes, and checked out an invoice query he had identified that morning. Returning to his office, he made a few notes on the points agreed that morning and went to lunch.

After lunch, Giles found a note on his desk saying that his meeting with Jason (Theatre Director) would have to be put back to 3.30 pm. He called a supplier to order a smoke gun for a future production and, while he was on the phone, Mary came in with some letters for him to check and sign. Having cleared the letters, Giles looked through his mail from earlier, made some notes, prepared his replies and then asked Mary to come to his office at about 3.00 pm. As he got up, he received a call from a company enquiring about a shower unit it had lent to the theatre for a production earlier in the year.

On leaving the office, Giles bumped into Gerald (Head of Scenic Paint) who asked him to order some paints he needed urgently. Giles agreed to do this and went down to the stage area to check that the problem he had discussed earlier with Ian and Fred was now resolved. Ian asked if he could use the theatre's large van to pick up some props for the next production. Giles agreed and then went over to see Jim about some queries on invoices for electrical equipment and consumables. Giles then continued on to the carpentry shop to discuss the props and scenery deadlines for the next production with Fred, who gave him some urgent tool and timber purchase requisitions.

As Giles returned to his office, Lois called to ask if he could meet next week with the agent of a touring company that was due to put on a show at the theatre the following month. Just then, Mary entered the room to let him know it was soon time for his scheduled 3.30 pm meeting and asked if he could call in to see Matt (Assistant Director) about an employee later that afternoon.

Giles met with the theatre's director Jason at least twice a week to discuss a number of issues. Today, he updated Jason on the progress of the current production, the rehearsal plans for the next two productions and the forward plans for both in-house and touring shows. Like most meetings, this one lasted about 45 minutes, and Giles left with a list of points to check or confirm in the next 24 or 48 hours, which would then be discussed at the next meeting.

He then called in to see Matt to check through the employment terms and conditions for a new employee starting next week and discussed the fire regulation query. Next he talked to Paul (Head of Props), who explained that the shower unit had been broken during the production and had been thrown away some weeks previously. Giles clarified exactly what had happened, went back to his office and phoned Martin and Jim, asking them to come to his office. He then called the company about the shower unit, explained the problem, asked the price involved and agreed for them to send an invoice for the replacement cost. When Martin and Jim

arrived, he asked them about the special sound and electrical effects required for the next two productions and made a note of the expected completion dates in order to update Jason later. Giles then telephoned Charles (Head of Design) asking him to come up to his office.

Between Jim and Martin leaving and Charles arriving, Giles phoned the artistic paints supplier and made an appointment with an agent for the one-man show booked in three weeks' time. Then Charles arrived to update Giles on the design progress for the next three future productions: *The Irresistible Rise of Arturo Ui*, *The Miser* and *Oliver Twist*. As a result of this discussion, Giles decided to meet everyone involved in these productions to ensure they could meet their deadlines. He then went back to the stage area to supervise a trial costume fit for the next production and discuss the new deadlines with the heads of the departments involved. Just as he was leaving the stage area, the Front of House Manager came over to ask if Giles could arrange cover for two people for tomorrow's matinee and evening performance as one was on holiday and the other was ill. Giles agreed to do this, and went back to his office to make notes following the afternoon's discussions.

He glanced at his watch and saw it was 6.40 pm. 'Time to go home,' he thought. 'Phew, that was a busy day! Too busy, in fact … I managed to get all the day-to-day tasks done but didn't have time to look at the some of the longer-term issues. Everyone thinks I'm doing a good job, but I'm not really sure what that is. It all seemed so clear this morning, but now I am not so sure.'

Questions

1 What do you think of Giles Chamberlain's day?

2 Comment on the situation described in the case study and be prepared to propose any changes that you think would be beneficial.

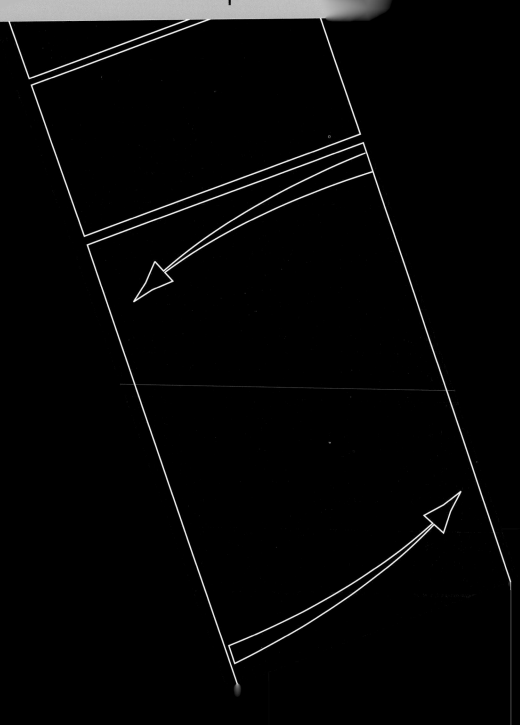

After completing this chapter, you should be able to:

- Appreciate how, in large organizations, strategy has evolved into three levels – corporate, business unit and functional

- Distinguish between an executive's day-to-day and strategic roles

- Identify how business unit and functional strategies interface with each other

- Appreciate why the critical first step in developing a functional strategy is agreeing the order-winners and qualifiers for the different markets in which a business competes

- Understand the strategic mix within most organizations of being both market-driven and market-driving

- Develop and implement an operations strategy

Chapter outline

Introduction

What is strategy?

The evolution of strategy within a business

- Levels of strategy

Developing a strategy

- Understanding customer requirements

- Understanding markets

- The process of strategy development

Implementing an operations strategy

Critical reflections

Summary

Introduction

Faced with the pressures of increasing competition, businesses need to coordinate the activities of their principal functions effectively in order to perform at their best in their chosen market(s). This involves developing a unified business strategy that embraces all parts of the organization. As a large function in most companies, and one that delivers the services and products sold to customers, operations has a key role in the development and implementation of a strategy. This chapter will define strategy in relation to the organization and explore the levels within a business at which strategy must be implemented, the relationship between strategic and day-to-day tasks, and the key step of understanding markets in the strategy development process. It will then go on to look at how operations can contribute to developing a successful strategy and the steps involved.

What is strategy?

To help appreciate what strategy means, it is useful to reflect on the meaning of the word itself. Derived from the Greek word *strategos*, a general, from *stratos*, army and *aegin*, to lead, strategy originally concerned the art of planning and directing the large military movements and operations of a campaign or war. The transfer of the word to business activities is understandable and appropriate, the market becoming the theatre of competition.

As in a military context, strategy in an organization involves deciding what to do (direction) and how to do it (implementation). Direction concerns choosing the markets in which to compete and the customers to target; it also involves identifying the criteria that must be met by the services or products in order to compete and win orders in chosen markets. Implementation involves deciding how to meet the required criteria for relevant market(s) by prioritizing where and how to spend the key resources of time and money.

So strategy concerns developing the capabilities of an organization to reflect the competitive needs of its customers and markets, recognizing, as on the battlefield, that its competitors are also planning to do the same. Now let's first look at the levels at which strategy development takes place, before going on to address customer and market needs in more detail.

> **KEY IDEA**
> Operations strategy concerns developing the capabilities of an organization to reflect the competitive needs of its customers and markets

The evolution of strategy within a business

As companies grow, they cope with the greater level of complexity that comes with size by splitting their total business activity into parts that are called **functions**. As organizations grow further, they invariably broaden the range of markets in which they compete. To cope with this growing complexity, organizations will typically arrange these different activities into separate **business units**, each made up of relevant functions such as operations, sales and marketing and finance. For example, within a bank, business units might include corporate banking, retail banking, financial markets, mortgages, pensions and insurance – each will serve a different market or a similar set of markets or market

Functions – the subdivisions of an organization that together make up the total activities of a business unit, for example sales and marketing, operations and IT operational tasks

Business units – the different parts of a whole organization, with each business unit serving a specific market or markets segments. One outcome of this is that strategy development now takes place at three levels – corporate, business unit and functional.

Levels of strategy

For most businesses, strategy needs to be developed in a different way at each of the three levels:

- *Corporate* At this level, companies decide where to invest or **divest** in terms of the overall business mix they wish to develop both today and in the future. Such decisions relate to where to allocate investment funds and the buying and selling of parts or all of the company.
- *Business unit* For each business unit, identifying the current and future markets in which to compete is an essential strategic task and one in which all relevant functions have to be involved. It is in these debates that functional differences need to be recognized and strategic direction needs to be decided. In this way, appropriate decisions on the markets to compete in are taken at the business rather than the functional level. On the basis of the markets it has identified, the business as a whole discusses and agrees which customers it wishes to gain and retain, with which to grow (as well as the **competitive factors** involved in retaining and growing these customers), and the increased market share that would result.
- *Functional* After the markets and customers have been agreed and the competitive factors involved in retaining and growing market share have been identified, functional strategies aim to:
  - Assess how well each function currently provides those competitive factors for which it is solely or jointly responsible
  - Agree their relative importance in chosen markets
  - Assess the gap between the provision of these factors and the level required to retain and/or grow the company's share of the market
  - Establish how to close the gap (the investments and timescales needed)
  - Implement the resulting plan.

The role of functions in supporting the needs of customers and markets differs from market to market in terms of their scope (the aspects involved) and level of importance. Thus, working within the context of the business as a whole, functions will agree priorities, the levels of investment involved and the timescales needed to complete the process. Figure 2.1 provides some examples of functional strategic responsibilities.

Figure 2.1 **Examples of functional strategic responsibilities**	
Function	**Examples of criteria for which it is solely responsible**
Research and development	Product and service design[a]
IT	System developments
Marketing	Brand name, customer relationships and pricing
Operations	Delivery reliability, quality conformance, price (in terms of cost reduction) and delivery speed

Note: [a] In a service company, the design function is typically part of marketing's strategic responsibility.

Functional strategy

Within each function, executives must balance their **strategic tasks** against their 'operational' or **day-to-day tasks**. The area of operational tasks within operations management is covered by the rest of this book but, in simple terms, these involve managing and controlling those wide-ranging tasks necessary to provide services or make products and

Divest – to sell all or part of a business

Competitive factors – factors such as price, delivery speed, delivery reliability and specification that will influence the purchases customers make

Delivery reliability – providing a service or product by the agreed delivery date

Strategic tasks – involve developing a functional strategy in line with those needs of agreed markets for which that function is solely or jointly responsible

Day-to-day tasks (or operational tasks) – involve managing and controlling the range of activities that fall within the function executive's area of responsibility as well as the crossovers between functions. It is important to note that 'operations' and 'operational' are two distinct ideas. Whereas operations is a function whose task is to provide services or make products, operational is a term applied to the tasks carried out by functions, and means 'day-to-day'

deliver them to customers. However, there is an equally essential role that concerns developing an operations strategy to support the needs of agreed markets and, although this is part of the same executive task, it is different in its orientation. Within operations management, the strategic role is to contribute to the debate relating to markets and agree on the markets in which a business should or needs to compete in terms of retaining customers, growing market share and entering new markets (this is something we will look at in more detail later in the chapter). Operations then needs to develop and invest in the delivery systems and infrastructure to provide those competitive factors for which it is solely or jointly responsible, for example price and delivery speed. In this way, operations' capabilities are guided by **strategic requirements** (the needs of agreed current and future markets) and so help to provide competitive advantage.

Whereas operational tasks require internal efficiency, strategic tasks need to be oriented to achieve external effectiveness – or, put another way, the operational role is to do things right, and the strategic role is to do the right things.

Use of resources

Undertaking either strategic or day-to-day tasks involves using key resources in terms of time (staff) and money (costs and investments). It is the reasoning behind a decision and the end goal that determine whether the use of resources is day-to-day or strategic:

- The use of resources is *day-to-day* if they are used to deliver services or make products, schedule customer requirements, record activities, monitor costs, supervise staff and manage the daily tasks of a business. Similarly, improving activities, procedures or systems to reduce costs by making these areas more efficient is also a day-to-day task.
- The use of resources is *strategic* if they are used to maintain or improve a function's performance so that a service or product more adequately meets customer expectations or gives it an advantage over its competitors (and thereby influences a customer's decision to buy).

Let's look at an example of where the agenda involves using resources to reduce cost. The intent will be:

- *Day-to-day* if the benefits of the cost reduction are retained in the business and used to improve profits
- *Strategic* if the benefits of the cost reduction are passed on to customers in the form of a reduction in price.

Now we've looked at some of the issues that affect strategy on a functional level, let's move on to look at strategy across a business unit.

> ### > KEY IDEA
> The use of the key resources can be either day-to-day or strategic in its orientation depending on the:
> - Agenda – for which aspect of the day-to-day or strategic tasks are the resources to be used?
> - Intent – are the resources being used to maintain or improve efficiency (the day-to-day task) or to maintain or improve competitiveness (the strategic task)?

Business unit strategy

Functional strategies are integral to the business units of which they form a part and, as a result, these two levels of strategy need to interface with each other. To help explain this interaction between functional and business unit strategy, let's go back to the origin of the word strategy. How would a general prepare his army to fight the battle? He would know his own and his enemy's (competitor's) strengths and develop a plan to engage the opposing forces. Just as with organizations, the Greek general would also divide his army into different units, for example archers, chariots and foot soldiers. As with functions in a business, this would lead to specialist skills and capabilities being enhanced. But, to win a battle, the different parts of his army would need to work from the same plan, and their roles and activities in battle would need to be agreed and coordinated. These principles can be transferred to our business situation – the same need to interface the different aspects of strategy and ensure cooperation and coordination between the parts (functions) is as essential for the success of the business as it would have been for the Greek army.

But businesses are whole entities and not just a number of different parts or functions. Therefore, it is essential to rebuild the parts we are describing back into a whole, and nowhere is this more critical than at the strategic level within a firm. As Figure 2.2 illustrates, the heads of the functions within the company will normally be part of the strategy development group, and it is this group's remit to set strategic direction.

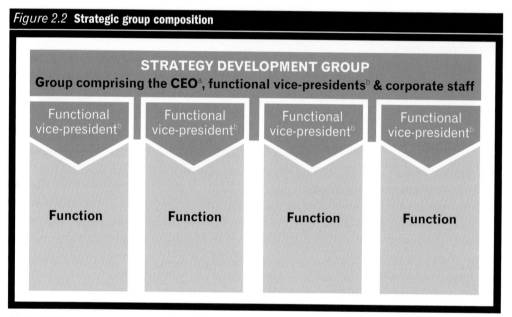

Figure 2.2 **Strategic group composition**

Note: [a] CEO means corporate executive officer, also known as 'managing director'. [b] Vice-president is the term for the head of a function and is also known as 'director'.

As we mentioned earlier in the chapter, discussion and agreement on current and future markets is an integral part of strategy development. This first step requires functions to discuss their views on markets (something we will look at in more detail later in the chapter), address and resolve differences and agree on what is best for the business overall. The outcomes of this debate will be major inputs into developing a business unit strategy, and ideally the process to be followed would be in line with that outlined in Figure 2.3.

> **KEY IDEA**

Discussion and agreement on current and future markets, the customers to gain, retain and grow, and the competitive factors involved is a decision that needs to be taken collectively by all functions in a business

However, the reality is often far from what is shown in Figure 2.3. Despite the importance of developing strategy across a business unit, many current strategy approaches reinforce corporate misunderstanding and promote differences and rivalry between functions. Functional dominance in developing corporate strategy is a typical source of such problems. The result is that key functions tend 'to treat one another as competitors for resources rather than coming together to serve external customers'.[1] In many organizations, 'business unit strategy is developed as a series of independent statements. Lacking essential integration, the result is a compilation of distinct, functional strategies

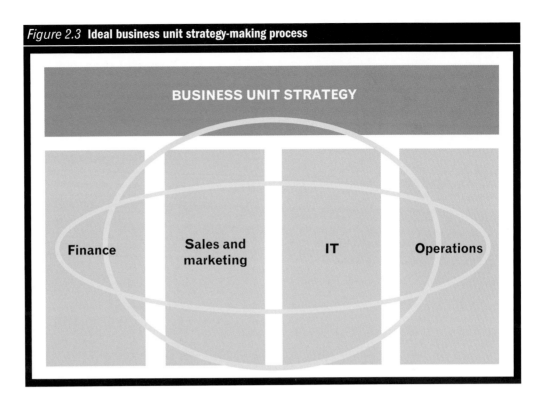

Figure 2.3 Ideal business unit strategy-making process

that sit side by side, layer on layer in the same corporate binder. Integration is not provided if, in fact, it was ever intended.'[2] The outcome, rather than being similar to that represented by Figure 2.3, may therefore be more like that shown in Figure 2.4.

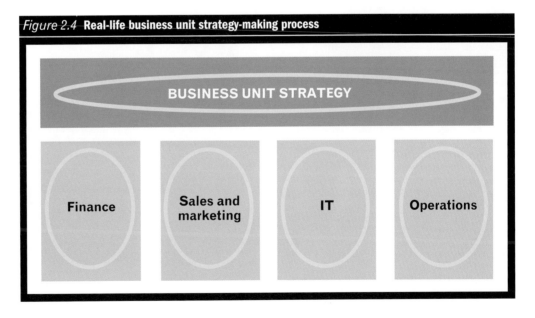

Figure 2.4 Real-life business unit strategy-making process

The two key functions of operations and marketing tend to develop independent strategies because of their differing views on several issues, which are discussed in the next section. At this stage, it is important to note that 'marketing' and 'markets' are not the same thing. Whereas marketing is a function within an organization, the market is made up of the various businesses competing to sell services or products.

Linking strategy across functions – marketing and operations
The importance of linking the marketing and operations functions is as vital as it is logical. They are, after all, two sides of the same coin. Together they constitute the basic task in

'**Strategy** concerns **direction** and **coordination**'

any business – the sale and delivery of services and products. On the surface, it would seem simple to unite their efforts to meet the needs and expectations of customers, but the reality is often far removed from what should be the desired goal. This is well illustrated by Figure 2.5, which lists the different, often opposing, views held by operations and sales/marketing on a range of issues.

Figure 2.5 **Operations and marketing perspectives on key issues**			
Issues		**Perspectives and goals**	
		Operations	**Sales and marketing**
Services/ products	Range	Restricting range enhances volumes, helps reduce cost and simplifies control	Customers typically seek variety. Restricting range reduces segment coverage and sales revenues
	Standardization versus customization	Lack of change reduces uncertainty and room for error. Limiting server discretion (see Chapter 1) maintains cost and throughput targets	Customization is often important, particularly in **mature markets**. Server discretion personalizes service, often at little cost, and enhances customer retention
Costs and profit		Measured on meeting cost budgets. Resists orders that increase costs. Has no control over pricing	Sales revenue is the key performance measure. Profit implications are not part of the decision or evaluation. Higher costs are not part of its budget considerations
Productivity improvements		Reduce unit costs	May cause a decline in the provision of quality conformance
Location of facilities		Considerations relate to costs and the convenience for suppliers and staff	Customers may find it unattractive, undesirable and, for a service business, inaccessible
Managing capacity		High utilization of capacity has an effect on costs and assets. Pressure to manage capacity and thereby keep investment as low as possible	Service/product may be unavailable when needed. Quality compromised in high demand periods
Job design		Oriented to minimizing errors and waste. Simplify tasks and use technology where possible	Employees are oriented to operations task and not customer need. Restricts the ability to meet changing requirements as they occur
Queues		Optimize the use of available capacity by planning for average throughput	Increases **customer lead-times**. Customers facing long lead-times or queues may go elsewhere

Mature markets – refers to the stage in the life of a service or product where demand starts to level off and where the range of services and products promoted by competitors is similar. To enhance sales, companies often differentiate their service or product offerings by customizing items to specific customer needs or preferences

Customer lead-time – the length of time a customer expects or is prepared to wait for a service or product from the point of making an order

As you can see from Figure 2.5, there are inherent tensions, concerns and rivalries that characterize the marketing–operations relationship, but the question is, how can these be solved? The way forward is to resolve interfunctional differences not at the level of the function, as is often the case now, but at the level of the business. Given the critical nature of strategy development, what then needs to happen to bring the parts back together in order to forge a unified business unit strategy? The first and most critical step involves all functions, including marketing and operations, agreeing on which markets to focus their attention. The next section of this chapter deals with the process of developing a strategy, beginning with the first critical step of understanding customer and market requirements.

Developing a strategy

Strategy development is an interactive process linking all parts of a business with one another and with the objectives set within a given period. However, it is important to remember that core to this is the markets in which a company competes, as shown in Figure 2.6.

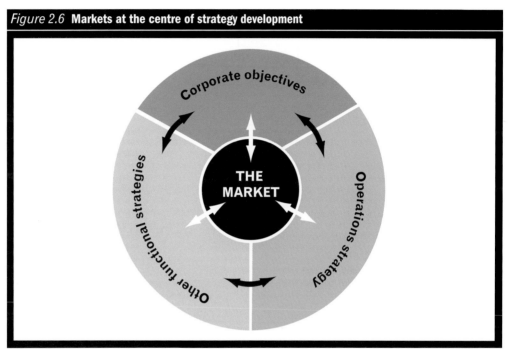

Figure 2.6 Markets at the centre of strategy development

Note: The phrase 'corporate objectives' here refers to the objectives set at the level of the business unit.

Satisfying the needs of the market is an important priority for any business and, as a result, understanding the needs of the customers and the market is vital in order to formulate strategy. Let's look at each of these in turn.

Understanding customer requirements

When customers purchase a service or product, they buy a combination of:

1 The service/product itself (see Figure 1.8), which has a specification (what it comprises)
2 A number of related criteria such as:
   • Price – it matches or betters an acceptable price, or the purchase price set by competitors
   • Delivery speed – it meets its customers' lead-time requirements
   • Quality conformance – the service/product is provided to the stated specification (see point 1 above)
   • Customer relationships – the company/staff have established relationships with customers
   • Delivery reliability – the service/product is delivered on time.

In some instances, the specification of the service/product may be the only or the dominant factor influencing a customer's decision to buy – for example, with a custom-made wedding dress, an expensive automobile or choice of restaurant. But, in most instances, the purchase is made on the basis of the specification together with a mix of related criteria such as those listed above, and is illustrated in Figure 2.7. The criteria and their relative importance in securing the sale will differ from one service/product to another and from customer to customer.

Figure 2.7 **The purchase: the make-up of customer choice**							
The purchase	**The service/ product specification**	**Examples of related criteria**					
		Price	**Delivery speed**	**Quality conformance**	**Customer relationship**	**Delivery reliability**	
The business task	Meet/better the design of competitors	Reduce costs	Shorten lead-times	Meet the specification	Develop customer relations	Deliver on time	
Function responsible	Marketing for services, research and development for products	Operations	Operations	Operations	Sales and Marketing	Operations	

> **KEY IDEA**

Customer purchases are rarely made solely on the basis of the specification of a service or product, but are often also influenced by a mix of other related criteria, such as quality conformance, delivery speed and price

Order-winners and qualifiers

One way to classify the criteria that are important to customers when purchasing services or products is to divide them into order-winners and qualifiers:

• *Qualifiers* These criteria get a service or product onto a customer's shortlist and keep it there. They do not in themselves win orders but provide the opportunity to compete. Conversely, the failure to provide qualifiers at an appropriate level will lead to a loss of orders. In this way, qualifiers are order-losing in nature, as a failure to provide a qualifier results in not being on the list – so the opportunity to compete is not in place. In such situations, competitors do not win orders from a rival; instead, the rival loses orders to its competitors.

• *Order-winners* Gaining entry to a market is, however, only the first step. The task then is to know how to win orders against competitors who have also qualified to be in the same market. With qualifiers, you need to match customers' requirements (as do competitors), whereas with order-winners you need to provide them at a level better than that of your competitors.

Having determined which criteria are relevant, as well as the relative importance of these as order-winners or qualifiers, providing them will form the strategic task of different functions (see Figure 2.7).

Market-driven and market-driving strategies

Before we look at methods for understanding markets in more detail, it is important to understand the difference between **market-driven strategies** and **market-driving strategies**, as well as how they relate to some of the criteria that affect a customer's purchasing decisions.

Examples of market-driven strategies, necessary to compete in a chosen market include:

• Meeting the delivery lead-times that customers require or expect (such as keeping queue lengths in a bank to, say, three minutes or less, or delivering a product within 24 hours)

Market-driven strategies – aim to provide the criteria that enable the company to compete in its chosen markets

Market-driving strategies – involve proactively seeking ways to change the competitive norms and hence create a situation where a company can influence its market position in relation to those of its competitors

- Making products to specification (such as a new car made without faults)
- Delivering a service or product in line with the promised date.

Market-driving strategies allow organizations to improve on current norms to gain a competitive edge. The way to do this can be either a market-based or a resource-based approach:[3]

- *Market-based* Here, companies proactively identify where market advantage could be gained by outperforming the current norms on one or more relevant order-winners and qualifiers, and then allocating resources to achieve this.
- *Resource-based* The emergence of resource-based competition continues the theme of being more proactive in arriving at appropriate strategies. Again, the emphasis is to be knowingly proactive in seeking ways to change the competitive norms – to change the rules of what is wanted for market advantage. Here, the approach is to exploit the potential of existing resources and capabilities in order to outperform current norms on one or more order-winners or qualifiers. However, it is also essential to ensure that the competitive advantages that result from consciously looking to exploit existing resources or create **synergies** within the organization are, in fact, what customers need and would be willing to pay for should there be additional costs.

Synergies – the potential for actions or resources taken or used together to result in a greater outcome than the sum of the individual parts

For most companies, their current and future markets will be targeted through a mix of both market-driven and market-driving strategies. Much of what a company sells, the customers it sells to, the markets in which it competes and how it competes will be similar today to what it was yesterday, and will be the same tomorrow. But being aware of the need to proactively seek ways to drive markets and exploit resource-based opportunities is an essential element of the strategic task in times, like today, when markets are increasingly different and competitive. For this reason, most companies will need to have a strategy that is a mix of the market-driven and market-driving approaches, as illustrated in Figure 2.8.

Figure 2.8 **Market-driven and market-driving strategies**			
The strategic mix	Market-driven		A strategy based on understanding current and future markets and recognizing how the competitive drivers in these markets are time- and market-specific. This will differ depending on whether it relates to maintaining the company's share, growing its share of the market or entering new markets
	Market-driving	Market-based	A proactive approach to identify where advantage can be gained by outperforming current norms in one or more drivers and then investing in appropriate resources and capabilities
		Resource-based	Exploiting the potential of existing resources and capabilities to outperform current norms on one or more competitive drivers

As there will typically be several markets served by a business, the relevant order-winners and qualifiers to retain and grow the existing market share, change the rules (become market-driving) and enter new markets will differ from market to market as well as from each other. The strategic role of functions (including operations and marketing) is to agree the markets in which to compete and the relevant qualifiers and order-winners in each market today and in the future, and then to develop and implement a strategy to support those criteria for which they are solely or jointly responsible. In that way, the company becomes market- (as opposed to marketing-) driven. But how do functions go about improving their understanding of markets in order to agree where and how to compete?

Understanding markets

As well as understanding customer purchasing choices, understanding the markets within which services and products are sold is vital to making decisions over strategy. Markets are the essence of a business, the very reason for its existence, and consequently you can never know too much about them. Identifying differences, supporting these insights with clear explanations and descriptions, and verifying them with supporting data is essential. Without this clarity, insufficient and inadequate insights are provided on which to build functional strategies. One outcome is that, without adequate discussion, understanding and agreement, each function's investment and development priorities will tend to be in line with what they think is best to improve overall performance. As a result, the essential link between market needs and functional strategies does not exist.

Current approaches to market analysis

Current approaches to market reviews usually embody a number of characteristics that contribute to the general nature of the outcomes and tend to lead to the provision of statements that lack essential meaning. The result is descriptions of markets that imply a similarity that does not exist.

For example, markets are often only looked at and described from a marketing point of view. Where this is so, segment descriptions are typically based on factors such as geographical regions (for example, Europe, South East Asia and North America) or sectors in which customers operate (for example, food and financial services). Although this has a sound rationale from a sales and marketing viewpoint in terms of, for instance, arranging promotional and sales activities and the approach to technical literature and support, the assumption is carried forward (because it is implied) that such segments are coherent wholes in terms of the way a company needs to compete. Reflection will show that this is both an unreal and an inaccurate conclusion. Although, from the viewpoint of marketing, Europe/South East Asia/North America or food/financial services, for example, are coherent segments, from an operations point of view there will be different sets of demands from groups of customers within these marketing segments, and hence these will constitute different markets. Case examples 2.1 and 2.2 illustrate this point.

With growing competition, markets are becoming increasingly different rather than increasingly similar as competitors seek to gain customers by changing their offering and hence increasing the number of segments they reach. The only way to uncover this essential difference is to dig deep. Approaches that fail to do this result in statements about markets that are broadbrush in nature and inadequate in terms of the insights they provide.

This inadequacy is further compounded where general phrases are used to provide market descriptions, for example words and phrases such as 'customer service', 'delivery' and 'quality'. Each can be defined in more than one way:

- 'Customer service' – this can mean any number of factors and is, in fact, the desired outcome of a strategy and not the strategy to achieve the desired outcome.
- 'Delivery' – is this to be measured in terms of speed (short lead-times) or reliability (being on time)?
- 'Quality' – does this refer to superior design or providing the service/product to the design specification on a more consistent basis (quality conformance)?

Once there is more than one meaning, misunderstanding and a failure to clarify will follow. The result is that generalities will mask critical insights, and essential clarity will be replaced by unhelpful ambiguity (see, for example, Cases 2.1 and 2.2). Where this is the case, the result will be that the key, first step of clarifying and agreeing markets – the basis on which to link corporate direction and relevant functional support – will not be provided. As a consequence, coordinated strategic direction is not in place,

CASE 2.1 MARKET POSITIONING OF BOTTLED WATER

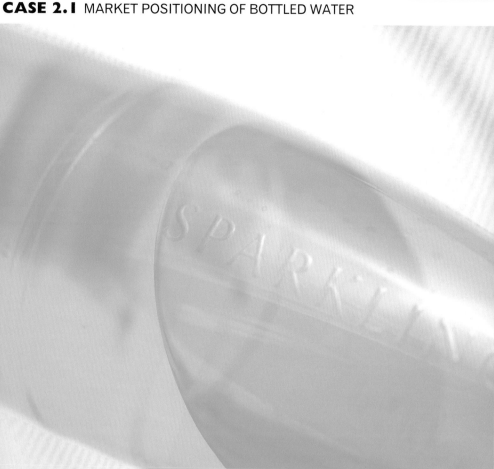

Imagine that you are the CEO of a manufacturing company. One of your customers is a company that produces and sells bottles of mineral water, and your organization has been employed to provide the labels to go on the bottles. Into which segment would your sales and marketing department place the customer for whom you are producing these labels?

The likelihood is that this customer would be placed in the 'beverage' or 'soft drinks' segment (that is, the sector in which your customer operates). From a marketing perspective, this makes sense, but from an operations point of view, the kind of product to which your customer attaches the label is actually of little consequence. Instead, the key issues for operations relate to factors such as the level of price sensitivity, the length of delivery lead-times and the size of demand peaks throughout the year. By segmenting markets based on the sector in which a company's customers operate, the implication is that all cus-

tomers in this beverage segment are equally price-sensitive, require similar delivery lead-times and have similar demand profiles throughout the year. As you can see, taking the view of only one function gives insufficient insight and leads to unfounded assumptions – and these will result in inappropriate strategic decisions.

Questions

1 Why would marketing place this customer in a 'beverage' or 'soft drinks' market segment?

2 Why is operations' view of customers focused on qualifiers and order-winners such as price sensitivity, length of delivery lead-times and size of demand peaks?

3 How would you use both perspectives to arrive at an overall strategy?

Lecturers: visit www.palgrave.com/business/ hillessential for additional resources

A major UK electricity distributor segmented its customers into large businesses, small- and medium-sized enterprises (SMEs) and residential customers on the basis of the relative size of sales revenue per customer account. The marketing strategy was to grow sales revenue and so the distributor's efforts were directed towards increasing its large business customer portfolio as the best way of meeting this objective. However, with the sales revenue growth that followed came a noticeable decline in profits as a percentage of sales. A data review revealed that profit margins in the large business segment were, on average, more than 40 per cent lower than for SME customers, and also less than that for residential custom-ers. Marketing's successful drive to increase sales revenue had also led to a lack of effort to retain, let alone grow, SME customers. The outcome was an increase in overall sales revenue but a decrease in profit percentages.

Questions

1. List side by side the market dimensions used above by marketing and operations.

2. How would you use both perspectives to arrive at an operations strategy?

interfunctional rivalries are reinforced, and the approaches used to develop strategy do not deliver the very essence of what is required or intended.

Market analysis – the approach to follow

It is essential to be clear about what the markets are. Companies are typically in multiple markets, and the debate on markets needs to identify, and provide a clear understanding of, the differences that exist between them. Several steps can be taken to secure these insights:

1 *Avoid general words and phrases* With markets at the core of a business, one needs to consciously and rigorously avoid using general words and phrases to describe them. Each dimension of a market review should be expressed on its own, and a single definition needs to be associated with each word or phrase used. In this way, each competitive dimension put forward as being relevant can be discussed separately and its relevance assessed. One classic example of this is the phrase 'customer service', highlighted earlier. Although we know that this is a desirable objective, the answer to the question of what it means is not self-evident as the term embodies a number of potential meanings. Using 'customer service' to describe the competitive nature of a market thus confuses rather than clarifies.

2 *Long lists denote poor strategy process* Discussing how a company competes in its markets will typically lead to a long list of factors. The intention seems to be to leave nothing off the list, thereby covering all aspects. But nothing could be further from the truth. This phase of the strategy process concerns distilling the very essence of how a company has to compete. A shorter list provides increased clarity.

3 *Separate out order-winners and qualifiers* A further step to improve a company's understanding of its markets is to separate relevant competitive criteria into order-winners and qualifiers. There are, however, some key points to remember here:
   - Qualifiers are no less important than order-winners – they are different. Both are essential. With qualifiers, a company needs to qualify and requalify at all times in order to stay on a customer's shortlist. If you are not on the shortlist, you cannot compete.
   - Order-winners and qualifiers are time- and market-specific – they will differ from market to market and will change over time within any given market.
   - The relevance and importance of order-winners and qualifiers will typically be different in order to retain market share, grow a company's share in existing markets or enter new markets.
   - The relative importance of individual qualifiers and order-winners will change when moving from being market-driven to being market-driving.
   - As highlighted earlier, not all criteria will be either a qualifier or an order-winner. Some criteria do not relate to some markets.

4 *Weight qualifiers and order-winners* To improve clarity still further, it is essential to weight qualifiers and order-winners in the following way:
   - *Qualifiers* It is adequate and appropriate to limit the classification of qualifiers to two categories – qualifiers (denoted by Q) and order-losing-sensitive qualifiers (denoted by QQ). The latter is intended to alert a company to the fact that failure to provide criteria that are considered to be 'order-losing-sensitive' will lead to a rapid loss of business.
   - *Order-winners* The appropriate step here is to allocate 100 points across all the order-winners within a market. This forces the different levels of relevance to be exposed and provides an essential step in identifying which are more important. It is essential, therefore, to avoid procedures in which stars (for example) are allocated as a way of indicating importance, as this approach avoids the key step of determining the relative importance of one criterion against another. In approaches such as allocating stars, any level of importance can be attributed to any criterion.

What is gained from understanding the market?

After gaining an understanding of market and customer needs, and identifying the relevant qualifiers and order-winners, the strategic task of functions can be developed. Clarity in terms of recognizing the market helps to identify the most appropriate direction (which qualifiers and/or order-winners need to be provided), emphasis (the target) and resource allocation. For example, the greater the order-winner weighting, the more emphasis and importance it is given. Similarly, as qualifiers indicate a need to match competitors' norms, any gaps between a company's performance and the market norm need to be closed quickly, especially where a qualifier is order-losing-sensitive in nature.

To illustrate this point, let's take the role of price in a particular market:

- When price is an order-winner, a company competes on price. The higher the weighting, the more emphasis is placed on reducing costs, which, in turn, allows a company to be more competitive on price while sustaining its profit margins.
- When price is a qualifier, a company needs to be price competitive (that is, by being at an acceptable level within market norms). For example, highly skilled specialists who win business primarily on the uniqueness of their skill sets will be able to pitch their fee rates at the top end of the acceptable range for their sector. In such instances, there will be limits on how high they can set their fees (because of the order-losing nature of failing to qualify by setting fees at an unacceptably high level) and this will, in turn, relate to the level of their skills compared with those of their competitors. Here, the key task regarding costs would be to control them within the agreed budget rather than seeking to lower them as a strategic objective. Acceptable profit margins would be created by the high level of price and not by cost reduction.

Having agreed the markets and relevant qualifier/order-winner mix and weightings, then, as mentioned earlier, the steps in developing functional strategies are to:

- Assess how well the relevant qualifiers and order-winners are being provided
- Identify the gap between the provision of a criterion, its relative importance and the level required to retain or grow a company's market share
- Work out how to close the gap – in terms of the level of investment and timescales
- Implement the plan.

In order to illustrate this, Figure 2.9 outlines some typical areas for review and the type of improvements to make against a list of possible operations-related qualifiers and order-winners.

The process of strategy development

Now let's look in more detail at how the step of understanding markets fits into the whole process of developing a strategy. Functional strategies relate to investing and developing in ways that support the needs of markets in terms of being both market-driven and market-driving. As shown in Figure 2.6, the role of functional strategies is to contribute to meeting agreed business objectives. The form and size of the contribution will vary from market to market, but the strategic development process is similar for all functions:

- *Phase 1 – understand the markets*, ensuring both a market-driven and a market-driving approach while maintaining an ongoing, rigorous review throughout this first critical step. The outcome here is for the functions within the business to agree which markets/

Figure 2.9 Translating qualifiers and order-winners into actions

Relevant qualifiers and order-winners	Typical areas for review and improvement
Price	Reduce costs in all areas, particularly regarding materials and overheads, which can make up to 70–90 per cent of total costs
Quality conformance	Provide services or make products to specification. Build quality into the process and delivery system rather than checking conformance after the event. Improvements here also impact costs
Delivery reliability	Assess on-time delivery performance by service/product and customer. Review current approaches to meeting orders – this will involve discussions on the extent to which services and products can be or are made-to-order, and the role of activities and investments such as scheduling and inventory in meeting these requirements
Delivery speed	Review the elements of the operations process with the purpose of reducing the lead-time of the various steps making up the service delivery system or manufacturing process
Service/product range	Review the process capability and staff skill base in relation to current and future service/product range requirements. Identify and supplement capabilities in line with current and/or future needs
Demand spikes	Assess current capacity provision in terms of the ability to rapidly increase output in line with known or anticipated changes in demand. Approaches include short-term capacity and inventory-holding alternatives
New services/products – time to market	Identify the elements of lead-time within the new service/product development process for which operations is responsible. Assess the tasks involved and the opportunities to reduce the work content, bring forward the start times in relation to the overall procedures, and identify the possibility of completing part or all of the task in parallel (rather than in sequence) with other elements of the process
Meeting specific customer needs	Assess current approaches to identify how standard services and products can be modified in line with specific customer requirements and the impact on costs, lead-times, quality conformance and the overall schedule

customers to gain, retain and grow, as well as the order-winners and qualifiers that need to be supported and provided to achieve these outcomes. This is a business-based activity involving all functions to ensure that:

- All insights and perspectives on markets are identified and discussed
- The outcomes are agreed at the level of the business and not the level of the function
- The mix of roles in implementing strategy and the resources needed and timescales involved are agreed
- All functions are pointing in the same strategic direction
- Frequent discussion about markets and customers is necessary, and must be underpinned by data and not fuelled by opinion. Without this, outcomes are based on unsubstantiated arguments and, in such scenarios, functions typically compete for their own perspective to be the one adopted by the business overall. Deflecting rather than embracing insights that provide a fuller picture is often both the intent and the outcome.

- *Phase 2 – translate* these reviews into strategic tasks. For example, if price is an order-winner, the task is to reduce costs; similarly if on-time delivery is a qualifier, improving the reliability of meeting customer due dates is the task. A more comprehensive list of such factors will be given in a later section.

- *Phase 3 – check* that what is currently provided matches what is required in a market-driven scenario or for the new level in a market-driving scenario.

- *Phase 4 – develop a strategy* (the prioritizing of investments and developments) to close the gap where the level of provision falls short of what is required, or to achieve the new level of performance in a market-driving scenario.

- *Phase 5 – implement* the necessary investment and development priorities. In this way, companies are better able to coordinate functional contributions, with markets appropriately providing the common agenda for all.

> **KEY IDEA**
Sound strategy development requires:
- All functions to be involved
- Frequent and regular discussion
- Individual functional performance measures to be set in a business context

Using this development process, companies are better able to coordinate functional contributions, with markets at the centre of all strategy decisions. As we have already learned, two functions that are central to this task are operations and marketing. The framework given in Figure 2.11 outlines the key strategic decisions that need to be made, as well as how links can be made between operations and marketing strategies through the market. The framework has five columns, each representing a step in strategy development.

Column 3 is related to analysing and understanding the market and lies at the centre of the framework. The arrow going from left to right represents the need to link corporate objectives and marketing strategy to the market, while the arrow going from right to left represents the need to link the operations strategy to the market. In this way, how a company competes in its markets and how it may wish to drive the market is at the centre of the debate. This allows functions to discuss current and future markets, how competitors behave and their potential responses in the future, alternative ways of competing in these, the constraints, developments, investments and timescales involved and how the company can coordinate its strategic efforts to meet the agreed objectives for the business as a whole. As Figure 2.10 illustrates, this is an interactive approach and needs to be an ongoing process forming an integral part of the senior executives' roles.

Before going on to look more specifically at the process of developing an operations strategy, let's take a look at the case of supermarket Aldi as an example of successful integration of marketing and operations strategies.

Figure 2.10 The interactive, ongoing nature of the strategy

CORPORATE OBJECTIVES	MARKETING STRATEGY	HOW DO YOU QUALIFY AND WIN ORDERS IN THE MARKETPLACE?	OPERATIONS STRATEGY	
			Delivery system choice	Infrastructure choice

Price leadership strategy – the strategy employed by organizations to compete principally on the basis of offering the lowest price in the market

The advent of the warehouse model for distributing food and dry goods provides a good example of companies competing on a **price leadership strategy**.

For Aldi, the German-based food chain, this has been successful because it has supported its chosen price leadership strategy with a clear integration of marketing and operations that cooperate to provide low costs. The basis of these retail offerings is a no-fuss concept. The design is simple, making it easy to shop – wide gangways, bare floors, inexpensive lighting (basic, bright and abundant), basic displays (often with the manufacturer's origi-

nal packaging) comprising warehouse-style racking and sturdy wire mesh cages, and limited support staff keep costs down. Of the product range on offer, Aldi keeps a limited (typically about 25 per cent of the range offered by traditional supermarket competitors), mainly own-label range of goods. Next time you are passing an Aldi outlet, step inside and analyse for yourself the marketing and operations features that help keep costs and prices down.
www.aldi.com

CORPORATE OBJECTIVES	MARKETING STRATEGY
Sales revenue growth	Service/product markets and segments
	Range
Survival	Mix
Profit	Volumes
Return on investment	Standardization versus customization
Other financial measures	Level of innovation
Environmental targets	Leader versus follower alternatives

HOW DO YOU QUALIFY AND WIN ORDERS IN THE MARKETPLACE?	OPERATIONS STRATEGY	
	Delivery system choice	Infrastructure choice
Price		Function support
Quality conformance	Choice of various delivery systems	
Delivery: speed reliability		Operations planning and control systems
	Trade-offs embodied in these choices	
Demand increases		Quality assurance and control
Colour range	Make-or-buy decisions	
		Systems engineering
Service/product range	Capacity: size timing location	
		Clerical procedures
Design leadership		
		Payment systems
Technical support	Role of inventory in the delivery system	Work structuring
Brand name		
		Organizational structure
New products and services – time to market		

Notes:
1 Entries in each column are to provide examples and are not intended to be a definitive list

2 Although the steps to be followed are given as finite points in a stated procedure, in reality the process will involve statement and restatement, as several of these aspects will impinge on each other.

3 Column 3 concerns identifying both the relevant order-winners and qualifiers.

Developing an operations strategy

The objective of using the framework in Figures 2.10 and 2.11 is to develop an operations strategy for a business. Let's now outline the steps involved in more detail. Although they are presented here in a sequential form, they will in fact constitute an ongoing set of discussions, with statements and restatements of corporate objectives and functional strategies making up the outcome of the process.

1 *Corporate objectives* These are set by the business as a whole and typically take the form of targets, for example sales revenue growth, profit, return on investment and other financial measures. They may well include non-financial objectives such as environmental targets.

2 *Marketing strategy* This is developed by the marketing function to meet the relevant corporate objectives. It is typically concerned with approaches to growing sales in existing markets and strategies to enter new markets.

3 *How do services and products qualify and win orders in the marketplace?* Addressing this question constitutes the core step in the development of functional strategies, in which the executive group (see Figure 2.2) debates and agrees markets (to include both the market-driven and market-driving dimensions) and the qualifiers and order-winners involved. This step will be expanded on in the next few sections.

4 *Operations strategy: choice of delivery system* Part of the strategic task of operations is to develop one or more delivery systems to provide the services and products involved, as well as underpinning the qualifiers and order-winners (for example, price, quality conformance and on-time delivery) that form part of the sale.

5 *Operations strategy: choice of infrastructure* The other strategic task of operations is to develop the relevant aspects of infrastructure (for example, organizational structure, procedures and controls) that form part of how it meets the qualifiers and order-winners for which it is responsible.

Take a look at Case 2.4, which provides an example of how operations strategy is used to support the rest of the supply chain.

Implementing an operations strategy

The reality of implementing a functional strategy is to translate the order-winners and qualifiers for which that function is solely or jointly responsible into relevant actions. Translating from order-winners and qualifiers into actions is a straightforward step. Implementation, on the order hand, is typically far from easy, as highlighted in Figure 2.12.

Knowing which approach to follow for the best results and then making the developments happen is a capability that management needs to have.[4] What to do and how best to do this are addressed throughout the different topics covered by this book. The place to start in terms of operations strategy is linking the strategic tasks (the relevant order-winners and qualifiers) to courses of action. Figure 2.9 above gives an overview of some typical areas to be revised and improved.

> **KEY IDEA**
> Understanding markets is difficult. Identifying actions to take (solutions) is easy. Making it happen is difficult

Operations strategy – an illustration

Let's now look at a short illustration of what is involved in the approach to and outcomes of operations strategy developments. Figure 2.13 is the outcome of a major UK bank's full and extensive analysis of one key customer segment – recruiting students at the beginning of their study course and retaining them at the end.

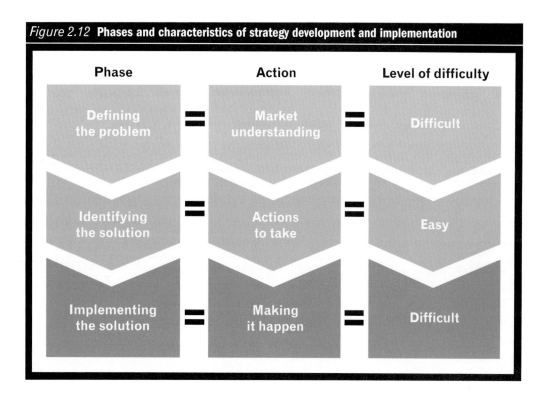

Figure 2.12 **Phases and characteristics of strategy development and implementation**

Phase		Action		Level of difficulty
Defining the problem	=	Market understanding	=	Difficult
Identifying the solution	=	Actions to take	=	Easy
Implementing the solution	=	Making it happen	=	Difficult

Based on a recognition that many customers stay loyal to a bank unless there is a serious mishap, recruiting customers is an important aspect of retaining and growing a bank's market share. There are a number of key times at which potential and/or existing customers make or can make a decision about which bank to use, two of these being:

1 At the time of going to college or university
2 At the point of leaving college or university and starting a job.

Figure 2.13 **Student banking qualifiers and order-winners in two key phases**

Criteria		Recruitment-non-customers	Retention
Ease and speed of opening an account		QQ	–
Influencers	Negative	QQ	QQ
	Positive	60	–
Location of	ATMs	Q	–
	Branches	10	20
Overdraft facilities	Level permitted	QQ	QQ
	Cost	Q	25
	Flexibility in terms of permitted level	20	40
Staff	Empathy to students	Q	Q
	Providing dedicated banking managers	10	15

Notes: Order-winners have a weighting, the total of which is 100.
Q, a qualifier; QQ, an order-losing-sensitive qualifier.
–, aspect not relevant.

Benetton Group – Photo: Glenn Dearing

Benetton is perhaps the most widely known brand in the world in the segment of Italian affordable fashion. After the death of his father at the end of the Second World War, Luciano Benetton first worked in a clothing store in Ponzano Veneto (a small town 30 km north of Venice) and then started a small business with his younger brothers Carlo and Gilberto and sister Giuliana, producing sweaters in bright, unconventional colours and selling them door to door. In 1965, they formed the Benetton Group. Three years later, the first innovative store (using the same room for displaying, selling and stocking the products, with a wide range of bright colours and affordable prices) was opened in Belluno, Italy, and more soon opened their doors in other major European cities. Today, Benetton sales originate from 6,300 shops in over 120 countries.

INNOVATION AND OPERATIONS PROCESSES

Creativity and innovation are strongly emphasized with the help of 300 designers coming from several countries and travelling around the world in search of ideas and trends. About 1.5 per cent of sales revenue goes into researching and developing new materials (for example, very light cashmere at affordable prices), spinning, weaving and dyeing technologies and computer-aided design techniques, occasionally in partnership with multi-national companies and universities.

Up until the early 2000s, Benetton's retail was entirely based upon a licensor–licensee relationship channelled through more than 80 agents who were paid a commission of around 4 per cent of total sales in their region, supervised by seven area managers. The store owners entered agreements with agents, without any written contract with Benetton. No license fee or royalty was paid by franchisees, but they were committed to stocking and selling only items supplied by Benetton, which operated on a no-return basis upon orders from agents about eight months in advance.

This system became increasingly unsuitable to manage the changing 'fast fashion' trend, very popular among young generations who were better served by competitors such as Zara and H&M, which owned their shops and offered up-to-date designs at affordable prices with up to 12 different collections a year (compared with the two collections offered by Benetton at comparably higher prices). Franchisees became increasingly unhappy about their earnings, and Benetton felt a decline in margins and profitability. As a result, from the early 2000s, Benetton took a new market approach to the core wholesale business, introducing directly operated stores.

THE SUPPLY CHAIN

To further adapt to the fast-changing nature of its markets, Benetton moved in 2003 to a much more flexible 'dual supply chain', aimed at ensuring an almost continuous collection of new designs with fast adaptation to changing market trends. Key to their success is the short time to market for new styles and the quick delivery in response to high sales. One (sequential) chain from design, to research and development, to operations, to sales is matched by the other (integrated) chain, which maximizes the speed of coordinated interconnections between these basic stages of the production and distribution process.

Five kinds of collections stretch from an extreme of six to eight months before the season to the other extreme of one to two weeks before it. These fast feedback, short **operations lead-times** and quick deliveries better met market needs while cutting inventory and asset investments.

Operations lead-time – the time taken by operations to provide a service or make a product

© Alex Hill and Terry Hill 2011

MANUFACTURING

The production of garments takes place in 10 factories located in Italy and nine others across Europe and Asia. These operate both with vertically integrated processes and through outsourcing of labour-intensive tasks (such as stitching, finishing and ironing), while more strategic tasks (like cutting, weaving, dyeing, quality control and logistics) are kept within the company's own factories. Outsourcing includes many Central Eastern European suppliers and has been recently directed to more than 200 contracting and subcontracting Asian suppliers from China, India and East Asian countries such as Thailand and Laos. Today, about 50 per cent of production is carried out by third-party suppliers. Wool, cotton and other raw materials are purchased by about 180 suppliers worldwide.

MODERN OPERATIONS FACILITIES

Logistics has traditionally been a crucial function within Benetton's approach to production and distribution planning. A fully robotized logistics centre in Castrette (Italy), with an electromagnetic propulsion system for moving pallets, has been built on a 30,000 square metre site. The plant has a total capacity of 800,000 boxes (in which materials, part garments and completed garments are moved through the manufacturing process) and is able to handle 120,000 incoming and outgoing boxes a day, operated by just 28 staff. This centre works with two hubs in Shenzehn and Mexico City, for the Asian and American markets, respectively.
www.benetton.com

Questions

Review the above example and consider the following questions:

1 What do you see as the order-winners and qualifiers in Benetton's markets?

2 Identify the key ways in which operations supports these market requirements.

At these points, there is or can be a more conscious decision about where to bank, so recruiting and/or retaining these customers (and their future worth to the bank in terms of revenue from banking and other products) becomes an important dimension of retaining and growing the company's share in the personal banking segment.

The outcome of this major bank's discussions is shown in Figure 2.13, and some comments can be made here:

- When opening an account, potential customers (who bank elsewhere or are new to banking) may choose from a number of providers – any failure to make this process easy and quick can lead to a bank not qualifying when this decision is taken.
- Influencers include features such as family's/friend's advice or preferences, with cash and non-cash incentives on the one hand, and horror stories on the other. Negative influencers can be order-losing in nature, while positive ones at the point of beginning a course have been identified as the most significant order-winner.
- Location of ATMs at convenient sites was perceived to be a qualifier when a student but was not considered a factor with the greater mobility that comes with working. Being able to get to a branch when necessary was, on the other hand, seen as having an order-winning, albeit small, role in both instances.
- Overdraft facilities were seen as a significant factor at both points, more so in the work phase of a person's life.
- Dedicated help from staff was considered important at each stage as a person moved towards greater independence.

The criteria listed in Figure 2.13 are the sole or joint responsibility of several functions of the company and would need to be reflected in each function's development and investment priorities. Figure 2.14 highlights those criteria which operations have to support.

Figure 2.14 **Operations actions arising from Figure 2.13**	
Criteria	**Some key aspects of operations' performance and development that may result**
Ease and speed of opening an account	Simplifying the account-opening process, advising any checks ahead of time to avoid delays and revisits, and monitoring the success rate of discussions and applications
Overdraft facilities	Although principally a decision taken by several functions, clear explanations and an understanding attitude on the part of operations would form part of managing this key dimension
Staff	Allocating staff, ensuring that the background details and history of customers are known, together with an understanding approach, would be key operations' tasks

Critical reflections

Developing an operations strategy involves a number of phases, the first of which is the most critical; it is one in which operations must be involved, ensuring that its perspectives on and insights into customers and markets are taken into account and form part of the discussion and agreement. Being proactively part of and contributing to the ongoing debate about markets, agreeing the order-winners and qualifiers involved in current and future markets, and being party to market-driving opportunities comprise the first critical step.

Operations helps gain the first sale while also securing the second

An important strategic task for operations concerns its role in retaining customers. As Figure 2.15 shows, although sales and marketing will have the principal role in gaining the first sale, fulfilling the order or contract and thereby securing repeat business principally falls within the remit of operations.

Figure 2.15 Operations' role in gaining the first sale and securing the second					
Task	**Gaining the first sale**		**Fulfilling the order or contract**		**Securing the second sale**
Function(s) responsible	Sales and marketing	Through customer contacts and relationships, advertising, promotions and selling	Operations	Operations fulfils a mix of requirements such as meeting the service/ product specification, delivering on time and supporting the relevant degree of price sensitivity	Operations	Operations – as a consequence of fulfilling an order and meeting customers' needs, customers typically return and repeat their purchase. If operations fails to meet customer orders and needs, it is likely that customers will go elsewhere – and may tell others!
	Operations	Creating a good business reputation based on past performance in meeting customer orders and customer needs leads to existing customers recommending a business to others				

Let's explain with an example. Wishing to eat out one evening on some special occasion and not knowing where to go, you ask a friend for suggestions. The restaurant suggested is duly booked, but the reality of the evening doesn't match your expectations – your table isn't quite ready, the service is slow, and the food is nothing special. So next time you wish to celebrate, where will you go? While your first visit to the restaurant arose from it being recommended (the reputation it had established), any subsequent visits will be based on your own experience of the delivery of the service. In this way, how well a service is delivered results in:

- Creating the reputation (the equivalent of a brand name) that leads to customers' recommendations to others (the first sale)
- Customers returning to repeat-buy (the second sale).

As operations is central to creating the customer experience (the reputation) and repeat purchases, its critical role in the selling process cannot be overemphasized.

Market- or marketing-led?

Markets are the common denominator of functional strategies. With markets analysed in depth and agreement reached on the current and future directions to follow, the strategic task in operations is to develop the capabilities to support relevant order-winners and qualifiers. However, as highlighted earlier, companies do not always keep in sharp focus the critical difference between being market-led and being marketing-led. Substituting the business (market) perspective with a functional (marketing) perspective will invariably lead to distorted strategies and eventually to the company losing out. Unfortunately, in many businesses, marketing is increasingly characterized as having the perceived role of creating ideas, with the rigour of testing whether the business will fit the market being left to others. This trend not only trivializes the important functional perspective of marketing, but also detracts from its fundamental strategic contribution.

Moving to a business-level strategic debate

Choosing in which markets to compete is a business decision and not a functional decision. Whatever the strategic mix between being market-driven and market-driving, markets lie at the very centre of strategy development, interconnecting corporate objectives with their delivery and connecting functional strategies, as illustrated earlier in Figure 2.6. In this way, markets form the agenda for the development of all functional strategies and help ensure that differences and alternatives are resolved at the level of the business and not the level of the function.

Companies need to continuously seek to line up their functional strategies with market needs, and one of the major players in delivering strategy is operations (see Figure 2.15). The critical nature of its role reflects the increasing importance of those order-winners and qualifiers for which it is jointly or solely responsible. As shown in the case examples given throughout the chapter, getting it right in operations results in a sizeable and sustainable advantage. Although it is not the only strategic player, in most organizations the role of operations will be important, and in many it will be central to the continued success of the overall business.

Summary

- As companies grow, clusters of similar activities are separated out and managed as functions. Typical functions include accounting and finance, sales and marketing, human resources, IT, operations, and research and development. The principal reasons for this are to make it easier to manage the corporate complexity that follows growth, while also allowing for the development of specialist skills.

- Functions have a dual role: they must undertake the day-to-day management of the areas for which they are responsible while also developing strategies to support agreed markets. The latter role has been the subject of this chapter, and the former is addressed in the rest of the book.

- To cope with further growth and increasing complexity, organizations are split into different business units in which relevant functions are provided and developed. The outcome is strategy at three levels – corporate, business unit and functional.

- Operations, like other functions, contributes to the strategy debate about which markets to compete in, which customers to retain and with which to grow, and the order-winners and qualifiers that relate to these choices.

- Once markets have been agreed and the way to compete has been identified, the current level of support for relevant qualifiers and order-winners is assessed. Any gaps form the basis of a function's strategy, which specifies targets, investments and timescales.

- Operations needs to be proactive in encouraging discussion of the market, as changing operations is typically expensive and involves long lead-times.

- Throughout the chapter, examples of how organizations have successfully developed operations strategies in support of chosen markets have been provided. These examples illustrate how an operations strategy works, while the end of chapter questions cover issues raised throughout this section. Have a go at answering some of these as a way of checking your understanding.

Study activities

Discussion questions

1 Why should all functions within a company, including operations, participate in business-level strategic planning?

2 In the early 1970s, when the Japanese entered the European colour television market, they took market share partly on the basis of providing higher levels of quality conformance. Explain how the improvement of this factor worked in terms of gaining sales. In the period of the early 1970s, was quality conformance an order-winner or a qualifier in the European colour television market? And which is it in today's market? Explain your reasoning.

3 Why would delivery reliability typically be designated an order-losing-sensitive qualifier (QQ) for a carton company supplying packaging to a food company?

4 Why are operations-related considerations becoming more important in formulating business strategy? Describe one example from both the manufacturing and the service sector (other than those given in this chapter) that illustrate how they have gained competitive advantage from operations.

5 Many companies fail to appreciate the fact that the most critical orders are the ones to which a company says 'no'. Explain.

Assignments

1 Identify the order-winners and qualifiers for the following enterprises:

- A private hospital company

- A company hiring cars for business or leisure

- A pharmaceutical company – for generic and patented products

- A furniture removal company.

2 What would constitute the operations strategy for the four organizations reviewed in Question 1?

3 Search the Internet to find a European company with operations in China. What is the stated rationale for this decision? Do you think any other factors are involved?

Exploring further

Journal articles

Gouillart, F.J. and Sturdivant, F.D. (1994) 'Spend a day in the life of your customers'. *Harvard Business Review*, **72**(1), pp. 116–25. The article argues that a senior executive's instinctive capacity to empathize with and gain insight from customers is the single most important skill that can be used to direct a company's strategic posture approach. Yet most top managers retain only limited contact with consumers as their organizations grow, relying instead on subordinates' reports to define and feel out the market for them. To get a true sense of the market, senior executives should consider the wants and needs of every step in the distribution chain, right down to the end user of a finished product.

Gulati, R. (2007) 'Silo busting: how to execute on the promise of customer focus'. *Harvard Business Review*, **85**(5), pp. 98–108. Shifting from selling products to selling solutions (packages of products and services) is a strategic alternative that many business need to consider. However, many companies are not structured to make that shift. Knowledge and expertise often reside in silos, and companies often have trouble effectively harnessing these resources. The article identifies four key sets of activities that need to be in place for this to successfully occur.

Heracleous, L. and Wirtz, J. (2010) 'Singapore Airlines' balancing act'. *Harvard Business Review*, **88**(7), pp. 145–9. Singapore Airlines (SIA) is widely regarded as an exemplar of excellence both in its service standards and as one of the civil aviation industry's cost leaders. SIA executes its dual strategy by managing four paradoxes: achieving service excellence cost-effectively, fostering centralized and decentralized innovation, being a technology leader and follower, and using standardization to achieve personalization. The results speak for themselves – SIA has delivered healthy financial returns, it has never had an annual loss and, except for the initial capitalization phase, the Asian airline has funded its growth itself while paying dividends every year.

Kumar, N. (2006) 'Strategies to fight low-cost rivals'. *Harvard Business Review*, **84**(12), p. 104–12. Successful price warriors, such as the German retailer Aldi, are changing the nature of competition by employing several tactics: focusing on just one or a few consumer segments, delivering the basic product or providing one benefit better than its rivals do, and backing low prices with superefficient operations. This article discusses the various approaches to competing against cut-price players.

Mittal, V., Sarkees, M. and Murshed, F. (2008) 'The right way to manage unprofitable customers'. *Harvard Business Review*, **86**(4), pp. 95–102. Customer divestment (whereby a company stops providing a product or service to an existing customer) was once considered an anomaly. However, it is fast becoming a viable strategic option for many organizations. The article reports its findings from interviews with 38 executives from 32 companies in a variety of industries, including IT, manufacturing, health care, finance and professional services. The research results identified four common reasons why businesses terminate relationships with end-users.

Books

Fitzsimmons, J.A. and Fitzsimmons, M.J. (2000) *Service Management: Operations, Strategy and Information Technology*. New York: McGraw-Hill.

Hill, A. and Hill, T. (2009) *Manufacturing Operations Strategy: Text and Cases*, 3rd edn. Basingstoke: Palgrave Macmillan. The text provides a useful supplement to *Essential Operations Management* by outlining an in-depth approach for developing and implementing operations strategy within manufacturing organizations.

Hill, T. (1998) *The Strategy Quest. Releasing the Energy of Manufacturing Within a Market Driven Strategy: a Dynamic Business Story.* Available from AMD Publishing, 'Albedo', Dousland, Devon PL20 6NE, UK; e-mail: amd@jm-abode.tiscali.co.uk; fax: +44 (0) 1822 882863. This book (written as a novel) describes how an art business and manufacturing organization restructure themselves to meet the changing demands of their customers.

Notes and references

1 Schneider, B. and Bowen, D.E. (1995) *Winning the Service Game.* Boston, MA: Harvard Business School Press, p. 200.

2 Hill, T. (1998) *The Strategy Quest.* AMD Publishing, p. vii. Available from AMD Publishing, 'Albedo', Dousland, Devon PL20 6NE, UK; e-mail: amd@jm-abode.tiscali.co.uk; fax: +44 (0) 1822 882863.

3 See, for example, Gagnon, S. (1999) 'Resource-based competition and the new operations strategy'. *International Journal of Operations and Production Management*, **19**(2), pp. 135–8; Grant, R. (1991) The resource-based theory of competitive advantage: implications for strategy formulation'. *California Management Review*, **33**, pp. 114–22.

4 These approaches and the issues involved are dealt with in greater depth in the following books by Terry Hill: *Manufacturing Strategy: Text and Cases*, 3rd edn. Burr Ridge, IL: McGraw-Hill/Irwin, 2000; *The Strategy Quest*, see note 2; see also Hill, A. and Hill, T. (2009) *Manufacturing Operations Strategy*, 3rd edn. Basingstoke: Palgrave Macmillan.

THE STORY

Apple Computer Inc was founded in 1976 by Mike Markkula (the businessman), Steve Wozniak (the technical genius) and Steve Jobs (the visionary wanting to change the world through technology). In 1978, they launched Apple II, and three years later they were the industry leader with a 16 per cent market share. But then IBM entered the market. Although its computers had a less secure operating system, slower processors and looked grey and bland, they were easier to clone than Apple computers. Other manufacturers started making cheap IBM-compatible computers, and Apple's market share fell to 6 per cent by 1982. To try to regain its share, Apple launched the Macintosh (Mac) com-puter in 1984, but the lack of compatible software limited sales and its market share continued to fall. In 1985, the company was in crisis. Jobs was moved out of an operational role and left later that year to set up another company called NeXT Software.

The following 12 years were turbulent times as Apple went through three different CEOs, lost market share and made a loss of US$1.6 billion in 1997. In that year, the board of directors decided to reappoint Steve Jobs as CEO, and he quickly started to turn the business around. He was still idealistic about design and technology, but his years away had made him more realistic and collaborative. As a result, he invited Microsoft to invest in Apple, developed iPod and iTunes products for Windows, fitted Macs with Intel chips, outsourced operations, developed supply chains and ventured into retailing.

Jobs persuaded Microsoft to invest US$150 million in Apple and commit to develop core products such as Microsoft Office for the Mac. He then consolidated its product range from 15 to three lines and launched the iMac, with a distinctive translucent case available in various colours. It was a success and sold 6 million units over the next three years. Jobs continued to restructure the business by outsourcing the Mac product manufacturing to Taiwanese contractors, stopping sales through smaller retailers, expanding sales through national chains and launching the Apple website selling products directly to consumers. As result, inventory reduced significantly and the cash released was reinvested in research and development, as shown in Figure 1.

Four years later, Apple introduced a new operating system called Mac OSX and launched the iPod, its first non-Mac product. Although sales were slow for the first couple of years, it now has 70 per cent of the portable media player market. A number of different models are available, and every year a new generation of each model is launched that is typically lighter, has more features and costs less than the previous version. Since then, Apple has introduced other non-Mac products such

as iTunes, Apple TV, iPhone and iPad. In 2007, it began using Intel chips in its Mac products, allowing them to run Windows-based software. Alongside this product development, it continued to invest in software applications such as iLife (iPhoto, iTunes, iWeb and iMovie), video editing (Final Cut Pro) and the Safari web browser, now also available for Windows.

TODAY

All these developments refocused Apple on developing cutting-edge, easy-to-use products, which are updated every 12–18 months. It has also transformed its operations, particularly through the introduction of its retail stores in 2001. These new stores broke every rule of traditional retailing – they were much larger than necessary and encouraged customers to linger by offering free Internet browsing and providing extensive product training rather than just sales help. The stores showcase Apple products and create an enjoyable experience. Each store has a simple, intuitive and logical layout and is split into four sections: products, music, photos and accessories. There are a number of free services such as the 'Genius Bar' to solve customer technical problems and the 'Design Studio' to help customers create photos and design graphics. Regular workshops and presentations are held in theatre-like sections of the store to train customers on aspects such as the Mac operating system, editing home movies and recording music. In 2003, the stores became profitable, and by 2007 Apple was

Figure 1

Gross margin and research and development (R&D) as a percentage of sales for Apple, Dell and Hewlett-Packard (1997–2009)

Performance	1997	2000	2003	2005	2006	2007	2008	2009
Gross margin (%)								
Apple	21	28	29	30	30	34	36	40
Dell	23	21	19	18	17	19	19	18
Hewlett-Packard	38	31	29	25	26	24	24	24
R&D/sales (%)								
Apple	12	5	8	4	4	4	4	4
Dell	1	2	1	1	1	1	1	1
Hewlett-Packard	7	5	5	3	3	3	3	3

Sources: Apple, *Annual Reports* (1997–2009), Apple Computer Inc. Web; Dell, *Annual Reports* (1997–2009), Dell Corporation; Hewlett-Packard, *Annual Reports* (1997–2009), Hewlett-Packard Company Web. August 16, 2010.

the fastest growing retailer in the world with 197 stores drawing over 100 million visitors a year.

As well as managing its physical supply chain, Apple has also developed a digital supply chain through iTunes. This has been a huge success, and in 2008 and 2009, AMR Research identified it as the best supply chain within Fortune 500 companies. Such an achievement shows that Apple have made significant supply chain developments and moved away from a 20th-century production efficiency mentality toward a new era of value that is based on ideas, design and content. In 2007, it delivered US$2 billion sales of inventory involving few or no iTunes products. This not only significantly improves cash flow, but also creates a platform for selling its higher margin iPod and iPhone products. Rather than using traditional distribution channels, it is able to deliver music, movies, television shows, music videos, games and publications instantly and directly to customers through its online iTunes store. This has revolutionized not only the sectors within which it competes, but also how we fundamentally think about supply chains. The numbers and types of products being supplied through iTunes are increasing all the time, and the possibilities seem endless.

THE FUTURE

In early 2007, Apple changed its name from Apple Computer to Apple Inc to signify its growing focus on consumer electronics rather than computers. Some analysts feel that its move into consumer electronics has made it more competitive as customers value its easy interface and simple design, but others feel it is losing its focus. Apple faces tough competition from the likes of Microsoft and Dell in the computer market, and diversification could cause the company problems. The recent iPhone launch has also moved it into sectors with highly competitive markets, with companies such as Nokia, Motorola and Samsung providing much more competition than Apple's rivals in the iPod market. Continually developing products and moving into new markets puts huge stress on all parts of its business, and some analysts have argued that Apple's operations and supply chains may not be able to keep up with its surge in growth.

Questions

1 How does Apple compete in its major markets: Macs, iPods and iTunes?

2 How has operations designed its supply chain to support these markets?

3 What must Apple do to maintain its competitive position in the future?

Sources: Booth, C. (August 18, 1997) 'Steve's job: restart Apple'. *Time*. Available from: http://www.time.com/time/magazine/article/0,9171,986849,00.html (retrieved August 2, 2010).
Friscia, T., O'Marah, K., and Hofman, D. (May 28, 2009) The AMR research supply chain top 25 for 2009. Available from: www.amrresearch.com

Lecturers: visit www.palgrave.com/business/ hillessential for additional resources

Introduction

Growth and success are to a large extent based on an organization's ability to introduce new services or products and develop existing ones. Although a natural market may exist for some essential needs (for example, food and clothing), for others a market has to be created. In either case, most organizations have changed from the ad hoc approach to the planning of new services/products that they used in the past, to one that is an organized activity involving a process from generating ideas through to market launch. Here we examine the procedures involved and some of the important issues to be considered for both new and existing services and products.

This chapter will first outline the phases of the **research and development (R&D) process** from generating ideas through to the final design. It will then address key issues and considerations in service/product design, including life cycles, portfolio analyses and design contributions to help support different service/product market segments. Finally, it will cover the role of operations techniques and approaches to improving design, including standardization, modular design, Taguchi methods, quality function deployment (QFD), value analysis, simultaneous engineering and variety reduction.

Designing and developing services and products

Introducing new services/products and developing existing ones is the lifeblood of organizations. However, the task involves more than just initiating new ideas, although that is where it typically all begins. The procedure also involves checking ideas and alternatives against two criteria:

- Is there is a demand – will customers buy the service/product or is there a need for it (for example, health care in the public sector)?
- Can what is proposed be done – can the service be delivered or can the product be made?

The task of designing and developing services/products involves generating ideas, setting financial targets, providing detailed **specifications** and checking what will be involved in providing the services/products in question. Ideas come from internal or external sources depending on an organization's allocation of resources (for example, research spending), its approach to stimulating and taking up contributions from its employees, and its attitude towards the degree of risk it is prepared to take, for example whether it chooses to be a leader or follower in its chosen markets. One thing is for certain – in many markets, service/product design can have a telling impact on the success of an organization, as Case 3.1 illustrates.

The research and development process

The objective of R&D activity is to bring about technological change and innovation within both the services/products and the processes by which they will be produced. The total cycle of events to achieve this embraces programmes classified as being either long term or tactical.

Long-term programmes

Long-term programmes comprise activities concerned with both fundamental and applied research. Although it is convenient to highlight this split when defining what is involved, in reality the distinction between fundamental and applied research is often blurred:

Research and development (R&D) process – the procedures used to develop new knowledge and ideas, or how to use existing knowledge or ideas, on which service, product, process and system designs are based

Specification – a detailed statement of the required features and elements (such as materials, parts, information, user groups or speed of delivery) that make up the service or product design

Long-term programme – a plan or schedule of tasks to be completed that are considered to need a long time to undertake. The meaning of the phrase 'long term' will vary from one business to another but usually refers to longer than one year

Asahi Breweries, Japan's biggest beer company, is still revered as the company that transformed the Japanese beer industry by launching its 'Super Dry' beer towards the end of the 1980s. Developed in 1987, the country's first *karakuchi* (dry) beer became an overnight success. In 2008, the company held in excess of 50 per cent of the Japanese lager market, selling almost four times the amount of the next most popular brand, Kirin Ichiban.

One of the secrets of Asahi's success was that its taste had been developed to suit the Japanese market. As such, it was a new type of beer and the first new beer since the 1950s. Furthermore, Asahi Breweries was the first company in Japan to offer beer in cans, and the first to sell beer in 3 litre containers.

In the 1990s, Asahi Breweries began exporting, first to China, which consumes over 25 billion litres of beer a year, and later to the UK and then the rest of Europe.

More recently, Asahi Breweries has stopped exporting to the UK and continental Europe and instead started brewing within the region. In 2000, Asahi started to brew Super Dry in the Czech Republic, and in 2005, the UK's oldest brewery, Shepherd Neame, signed an agreement with Asahi to brew its beer for the UK market. In 2009, the company announced its aims to increase overseas sales to 30 per cent of its total sales by 2015.

www.asahibeer.co.jp/english/

Questions

1 Is the role of design (that is, developing the beer specification in terms such as taste, strength and colour) an order-winner or a qualifier in the Asahi Super Dry example?

2 Explain the reasons for your view.

Lecturers: visit www.palgrave.com/business/hillessential for additional resources

- *Fundamental research* studies the basic relationship between cause and effect, with the aim of increasing knowledge, making discoveries and establishing new applications that may eventually be used on a commercial basis.
- *Applied research* is concerned principally with practical applications and solutions to practical problems. It relates to classifying and interpreting basic knowledge from fundamental research activities in order to facilitate problem-solving. The financial return on this research investment is quicker and more assured than it is for fundamental research.

How much to spend on long-term research programmes is a corporate-level decision, with organizations deciding to adopt either an offensive or a defensive strategy, or lying somewhere in between by making a moderate R&D commitment – for instance, contracting out research or licensing other organizations' existing service/product designs.[1] An offensive strategy brings with it a relatively large commitment to spend on research, with the objective of being a leader in service/product innovation within a given market. A defensive strategy usually limits the amount of research spending to a minimum and will be largely directed towards developing existing knowledge in order to enhance services/products in a particular market or in response to customer requirements.

The following categories are often used to help to explain these alternative strategies:[2]

- A *'first-to-market' posture* focuses on cutting-edge research that leads to the introduction of new technologies ahead of a company's competitors.
- A *'fast-follower' posture* requires a quick response to technical innovation by industry pioneers and may include modifying the technologies involved.
- A *'me-too' approach*, on the other hand, is aimed at imitating widely available technologies by introducing close substitutes for them.
- A *'late-entrant' approach* is concerned with making incremental changes to existing technologies for limited applications.

Now look at Case 3.2 as an illustration of one approach.

Other strategic approaches also exist, such as providing a service under a franchise or manufacturing under licence. In the former, all aspects of the service/product would typically be specified by the franchiser. For example, in a franchised fast-food restaurant, the purchase and supply of foodstuffs would be centrally controlled, the layout, decoration, fixtures, fittings and uniforms would be specified, and the working arrangements to be followed would be laid down in advance. In that way, the franchiser would maintain a tight control over service/product specifications and their provision. In manufacturing under licence, the products involved are produced under licence agreements that specify the materials and components to be used and the method of manufacture to be followed.

Tactical programmes

After the strategic activities just described come the tactical steps in developing a service or product. **Tactical programmes** cover all stages throughout the development of a service/product, including its launch. They are concerned with the functional aspects of design and address basic questions covering:

- What will it do?
- How will it do it?
- How will it be made or provided?
- What maintenance and repair needs will there be?
- How will it be distributed?

Maintaining a link between market need, technology, development, design and the operations delivery system is essential if a service is to be provided or a product produced profitably, and all the steps in the process must be addressed.

In 2010, Microsoft, the world's largest software company, announced that whereas most of its rivals were cutting back, it planned to spend US$9.5 billion on research and development – not only a huge amount in itself but, according to Kevin Turner, Microsoft's chief operating officer, US$3 billion more than any of its competitors was aiming to spend. This commitment to R&D has been a significant feature in Microsoft's strategy throughout its history.

Microsoft set up its R&D division in the early 1990s and has consistently increased its annual spending on this area – in fact, it more than tripled its budget between 1998 and 2010. Bill Gates stressed the worthwhile and essential nature of Microsoft's continued commitment to high levels of research expenditure, explaining that customers underestimate the software's potential and outlining his belief that the industry and the market 'are going to be stunned at the advances we make'. Clearly, Microsoft intends to maintain its position in cutting-edge technology as it supports its belief in the significance of software in the future.

www.microsoft.com

Questions

1 In which category of R&D strategy would you place Microsoft?

2 Explain your choice.

The approach to development involves defining a service/product by a procedure of checking successive designs until the required specifications have been met as economically as possible. This usually involves testing several designs to evaluate their feasibility in terms of functionality and cost. The following section looks at these steps in detail.

The design and development process

The first step in designing and developing a new service/product or modifying an existing one is generating ideas. But good ideas do not necessarily indicate successful outcomes – a significant amount of development work is required before a service can be provided or a product produced and made available to customers. These steps are described as the design and development process for the service/product and are outlined in Figure 3.1. Before discussing these in some detail, it is important to make two observations about the figure:

- The *process is not sequential* – although the process outline shows the steps as following on from each other, parts of several stages will, in fact, be completed in parallel to one another. This allows for a reduction in development lead-times and so enables the final designs to be introduced earlier.
- *Reiteration* – the steps involve much reiteration throughout as questions are posed at each stage and these often take the proposal back one or more steps in order to clarify and resolve the fresh issues raised.

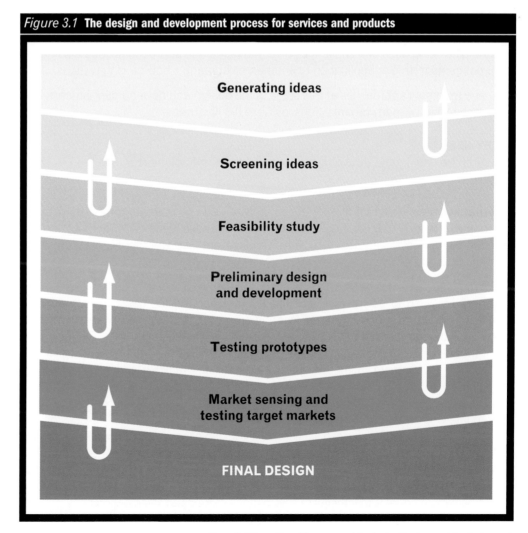

Figure 3.1 **The design and development process for services and products**

Generating ideas

Screening ideas

Feasibility study

Preliminary design and development

Testing prototypes

Market sensing and testing target markets

FINAL DESIGN

Generating and developing ideas

Generating ideas is a key step in this process, especially as maybe only 1 or 2 per cent of ideas lead to the introduction of successful services or products. Ideas for new services/ products can arise from a variety of sources within and outside a firm.

Internal sources from within the company are an important provider of ideas and include:

- *Employees* Companies stimulate ideas in several ways. For example, suggestion schemes (where prizes of various values are awarded for useable ideas) and including the generation of ideas as part of employee evaluations have long been effective ways of getting ideas on the table.

- *R&D* An investment is made in staff and other resources to generate ideas.

- *Market research* This is the systematic process of talking to customers to identify needs and ideas. For example, part of the procedure used by Asahi Breweries when launching its Super Dry beer (see Case 3.1) was to visit pubs, restaurants and parks asking drinkers what they wanted from a beer. As well as confirming that people mainly wanted something to drink with food, the company also received a resounding message: people wanted a beer that was *nodogoshi* (easy to drink) with a somewhat dry bite. So, Asahi Super Dry was launched to meet these characteristics. A new taste was developed, and a success story was born.

- *Sales force* By remaining alert to potential customer needs and systematically record-ing and evaluating customers' comments and discussions, sales staff can add to the stream of ideas at this stage in the design and development process.

- **Reverse engineering** Taking existing services and products (those of competitors as well as the company's own) and analysing them to check the design concepts and principles being used can challenge current thinking and approaches and helps trans-fer concepts from one application to another, so creating a source of new ideas.

> **Reverse engineering** – the process of analysing an existing service or product (often made by a competitor) to understand what it is made of, how it has been made and how it works, with the purpose of improving existing designs or designing new services or products

The need to rethink approaches at this stage in the design and development process has been recognized by many organizations, as Case 3.3 illustrates.

> KEY IDEA

During the design and development process, organizations need to use both internal and external sources to generate ideas

---

External sources are equally important as, and sometimes more important than, inter-nal sources in terms of producing ideas and relate to those ideas generated outside the firm, for example by customers, legislative requirements, environmental pressures and technological advances:

- *Customers*[3] There has been a marked change in the last 30 years regarding the sources of and approach to new service/product design. Gone are the days when the role of researchers was to come up with services and products that customers were encouraged to buy. Although this still happens (see, for example, the bullet point on 'Technological advances' below), it is now recognized that customer involvement (such as through focus groups or involvement in the design process, as with vehicles and housing) brings consumer-led ideas into the design arena. For example, recognizing the changing life-styles of their customers, banks have altered the way they provide many of their services from late weekday/Saturday branch opening on the one hand to online services on the other. In this way, customers can access many banking services more when it suits them. Another example is the growing awareness among consumers in developed economies of the need to eat healthily, which has resulted in changes to the range of food on offer. Vegetarian options are now typically included, while many fast-food restaurants include non-beef main courses together with a wide range of fruit and salad options.

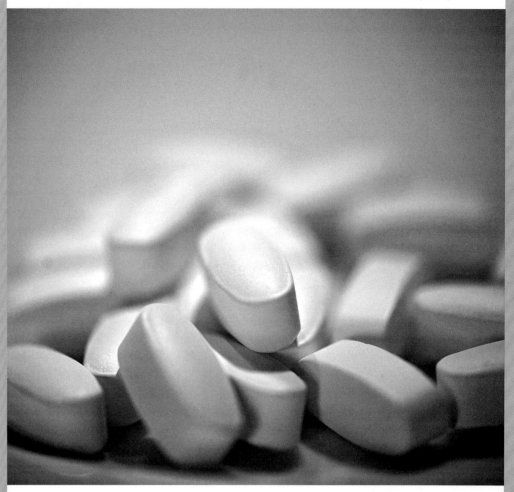

© Alex Hill and Terry Hill 2011

During the 1990s, the pharmaceutical industry, where new product introduction is a key factor for success, saw 'a quantum leap in the mechanics of drug research' that promised 'to revolutionize pharmaceuticals in the way PCs reinvented the computer industry.' During this period, GSK (a leading healthcare company) started to use 'combinatorial chemistry', which creates tens of thousands of new molecules – the building blocks of new medicines – within a few hours, compared with conventional chemistry that results in an average of some 40 new molecules a year. Linked to this was a robotized screening station that evaluates a compound's effectiveness against specific disease-causing genes at the rate of 50,000 a week and, in the process, allows new compounds to be developed in a cost- and time-effective way on an industrial scale.

However, in more recent years, GSK has overhauled its R&D system. Andrew Witty took over as CEO of GSK in May 2008, promising to move away from the industrial-scale drug discovery processes of the 1990s. The upheaval was radical, but there have been qualitative and quantitative benefits. The focus has been on developing smaller scientific teams that take a more lateral approach to problem-solving.
www.gsk.com

Question

Describe the fundamental changes in approach adopted by GSK. What are the advantages?

Source: Moore, D.D. (1996) 'Glaxo accelerates pursuit of new medicines; Glaxo lab initiates a high-speed chase in the drugs industry'. *Wall Street Journal*, Europe, December 6, pp. 1, 5.

Lecturers: visit www.palgrave.com/business/ hillessential for additional resources

- *Legislative requirements* Government legislation invariably requires organizations to adapt and change, often necessitating new services and products to meet new requirements. For example, the European Commission's year-on-year higher targets for waste management continue to affect packaging design and stimulate change to meet future needs, while legislation concerning issues such as noise and pollution has led to product design changes such as active noise cancellation in turboprop aircraft. The pressure to control vehicle emission levels and the growing production of battery-driven vehicles also illustrate the impact of legislation on design.

- *Environmental concerns* Concerns and pressures from the 'green lobby' and environmentally aware consumers are encouraging change, often independent of government action. For example, more than 500 German companies have signed up to the Duales System Deutschland (DSD), which has established the infrastructure needed to recover and reuse packaging waste. At an estimated set-up cost of £3.5 billion and annual running costs of £0.7 billion, DSD has arisen in response to growing consumer awareness about waste. These recycling targets are influencing European standards, and the impact on packaging and waste collection services is already widespread.

- *Technological advances* Technology shifts have far-reaching effects on service and product design. In some instances the changes revolutionize design, whereas in others they provide a plethora of new offerings. For example, advances in touch-screen technology have had a significant impact on the design of mobile phones and other electronic devices such as Apple's iPad. This has, in turn, prompted the development of software and applications or 'apps' that incorporate this touch-screen technology. Enhancing services/products by integrating new technologies is also widespread. For example, the US courier firm Federal Express interlinks stages in the service system by using computers to monitor and track packages throughout its delivery system. On receipt of a customer call, a Federal Express operator enters the details onto a computer. This information is then radioed to a courier and displayed on a hand-held computer terminal. After pick-up, the package is logged into the company's central computer in Memphis, Tennessee. With the use of industrial bar codes, packages can be tracked in the system, and customers can access these details at any time on request.

Screening ideas

The purpose of screening ideas is to eliminate those which do not appear to have high potential and so avoid the costs incurred at subsequent stages. Proposals, supported by graphics, models and an outline specification, are then judged against a set of criteria to enable each design to be evaluated overall. To provide greater insight, organizations often score each dimension of each idea on a 0–10 scale and then apply weights to each of these dimensions. The resulting aggregate score helps when deciding which ideas to progress and which to terminate.

Feasibility study

The next step is to complete a more detailed check on the ideas still being considered. This part of the process is called a feasibility study and will look at a whole series of dimensions that relate to a service/product idea and its intended markets, for example:

Service and product development
- Development lead-time – how long should it take to develop a service or product from idea to provision?
- Uniqueness of design
- Anticipated length of its life cycle – how long will the sales levels of a service/product be sufficient to justify keeping it on the sales list?

Market(s)
- Relevant order-winners and qualifiers
- Selling price

- Sales volumes over time
- Level of existing and future competition
- The stable or seasonal nature of sales forecasts.

Operations
- Ability to support relevant order-winners and qualifiers
- Capacity needs
- Potential process investments.

Financial
- Capital outlay
- Return on investment
- Cash flows.

Preliminary design and development

This stage of the process involves developing the best design for a new idea. Here, the outline of the new service/product will need to be specified in much greater detail. Many trade-offs will have to be made concerning features, costs and producibility. Reconciling these – often conflicting – demands is a difficult task and one that needs to be resolved at this stage.

Prototype – an initial design of a service or product made to help evaluate a new or existing design option

Testing prototypes

The physical embodiment of the functional and aesthetic requirements of a service or product is known as the **prototype**. Using this step in the process serves many ends. In addition to illustrating the aesthetic dimension, it serves to check the functionality of the idea, its robustness and the operations implications of providing it. In this way, the prototype tests the specification of the service/product, its physical or other dimensional properties and its use under actual operating conditions.

Market sensing and testing target markets

The previous section explained the need to test the functionality of an idea and undertake the continuous and critical task of checking prototypes. At the same time, potential demand must also continually be assessed. That the idea works and can be reproduced is one side of the coin, but whether customers will buy it is the other. For example, a national retailer or fast-food chain could trial a new range of clothes or a new line of meals in selected outlets and, if successful, would then launch it throughout the rest of the business. In the same way, product prototype-testing is a way of verifying the technical performance and sales potential of a new idea. Test marketing in a selected geographical area is a similar approach to that outlined above for services. Throughout this process, screening and testing is a continuous activity aimed at checking and rechecking in order to reduce uncertainty before large capital investments are committed.

Final design

Prototype testing often identifies necessary changes to the initial design, and these will be incorporated during the final design phase. At this stage, specifications will be completed (something we will look at in more detail later in the chapter), and the essential tasks of marketing plans, material supply, operations tasks and associated investments will be confirmed.

The decision

As mentioned earlier, the design process is characterized by reiteration and a non-sequential nature. Steps into the unknown embody uncertainty, and the rigours of the design and development process are intended to flush out questions essential to arriving at a viable design. The final decision on whether or not to go ahead rests with top management, and levels of investment, corporate profile and reputation, and the strategic direction of the firm are invariably central to these decisions. Rejection stems from a combination of experience, judgement and placing a decision in the context of other investment opportunities. Approval commits a firm's efforts and resources one way and to a course of action whose success may not be measurable until months, even years, later.

Developing new services/products is the lifeblood of organizations. They typically require substantial resources, and their introduction is a key factor in terms of market share and sales revenue growth. At the same time, companies need to review their existing services/products and ensure the best use of the resources necessary to support them. We will now look at the issues involved and the approaches needed for reviewing this task.

Reviewing the service and product mix

All organizations have a range of services or products at a given time. To be competitive, it is necessary to have a set of these that is complementary, relates to the organization's strategic decisions on issues such as growth and market share, and takes account of tactical considerations such as completeness of the range, process capability and distribution costs. Furthermore, the mix is always changing as new services/products are necessary for survival and growth. It is essential, therefore, for an organization to review its service and product mix as a whole. When undertaking such a review, three important factors need to be considered:

> **Service/product life cycle** – the process of introduction, initial growth, maturity and eventual decline in sales that a service or product typically undergoes as it moves into and then out of its market

- The development and introduction of new services/products is both risky and costly.
- Services/products tend to follow a **life cycle**.
- Some services/products are or have the potential to be more successful than others – so service/product portfolio analysis is necessary.

The issues around the first point have been addressed earlier. Here we look at service/product life cycles, service/product portfolios, and designing services and products to meet the needs of different market segments.

Service/product life cycles

The extent and rate of new service/product introductions can make a significant impact on a business. However, of equal concern in these decisions is the life cycle pattern that is anticipated or experienced once the service/product has been introduced. Market pressures mean that designs can never remain static, and continuous endeavours are made to increase the fit with customer needs while scrutinizing the relationships between the cost of provision and the specification that has been provided for the service/product. Despite the attention that most organizations give to this, many services/products enter the market and are then quickly phased out due to a lack of sales.

> **KEY IDEA**
> Assessing where services/products are in their life cycle helps when forecasting sales revenue

Figure 3.2 outlines the phases through which a service or product may go as it moves into and out of its market.

New services/products are required to replace those already in the cycle, no matter how extended the timescale may be. The phases detailed in Figure 3.2 are as follows:

- *Introduction* Initially, the sales pattern of many services/products shows a slow rate of growth. Market awareness is low, and the service/product has not yet been accepted. The concept is often new, and initial teething troubles are usually experienced. This makes for low sales with slow growth.

- *Growth* In the growth phase, the market has been conditioned to the service/product. With acceptance comes a rapid growth in sales resulting from promotion, increased dependability, past sales and often a lower selling price.

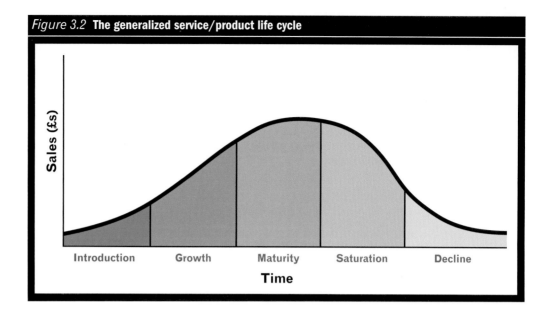

Figure 3.2 **The generalized service/product life cycle**

- *Maturity* At the maturity stage, there is increased overall demand as a service/product becomes well known and established within its market segment. However, the rate of sales increase for a company begins to slow due to competitors entering the market. It is also here that companies may use increased levels of customization as a way to help stimulate demand.

- *Saturation* In the saturation stage, most of those who want the service/product have typically now bought it. Market demand is, therefore, restricted to the need for replacements plus a small quantity of new sales. Service/product promotion is often used more extensively here, not to publicise the item but to differentiate it from its competitors.

- *Decline* In the decline phase of a product's life cycle, sales continue to fall off, invariably at a rapid rate. The introduction of competing services/products, either as improvements or substitutes, accelerates the decline to the point where the product/service becomes obsolete.

Reporting current and forecast sales for services/products in terms of their life cycle stage provides insights into the spread of sales by phase, future sales patterns and the levels of new services/products that need to be targetted in the future. Also, different strategies are more relevant to one cycle stage than another. For example, an applications-oriented strategy is appropriate in the mature stage by increasing the level of customization through offering modifications to existing services/products in order to serve particular market segments, whereas an emphasis on reducing costs and keeping designs fixed is most appropriate in the saturation phase of a typical cycle.

Service/product portfolio analysis

Portfolio analysis provides another way of helping companies to look forward and decide on how to allocate resources. As shown in Figure 3.3, services/products can be separated into four classes, with the market share held by an organization being measured horizontally, and the growth rate within the market being measured vertically.

Services/products are then placed throughout or across two or more of the four segments to illustrate their relative positions against these two dimensions. The resulting 'portfolio' of services/products serves as part of the basis for determining how to appropriately allocate or concentrate corporate resources, particularly R&D funding. These quadrants are explained below:

Figure 3.3 **Service/product portfolio analysis**

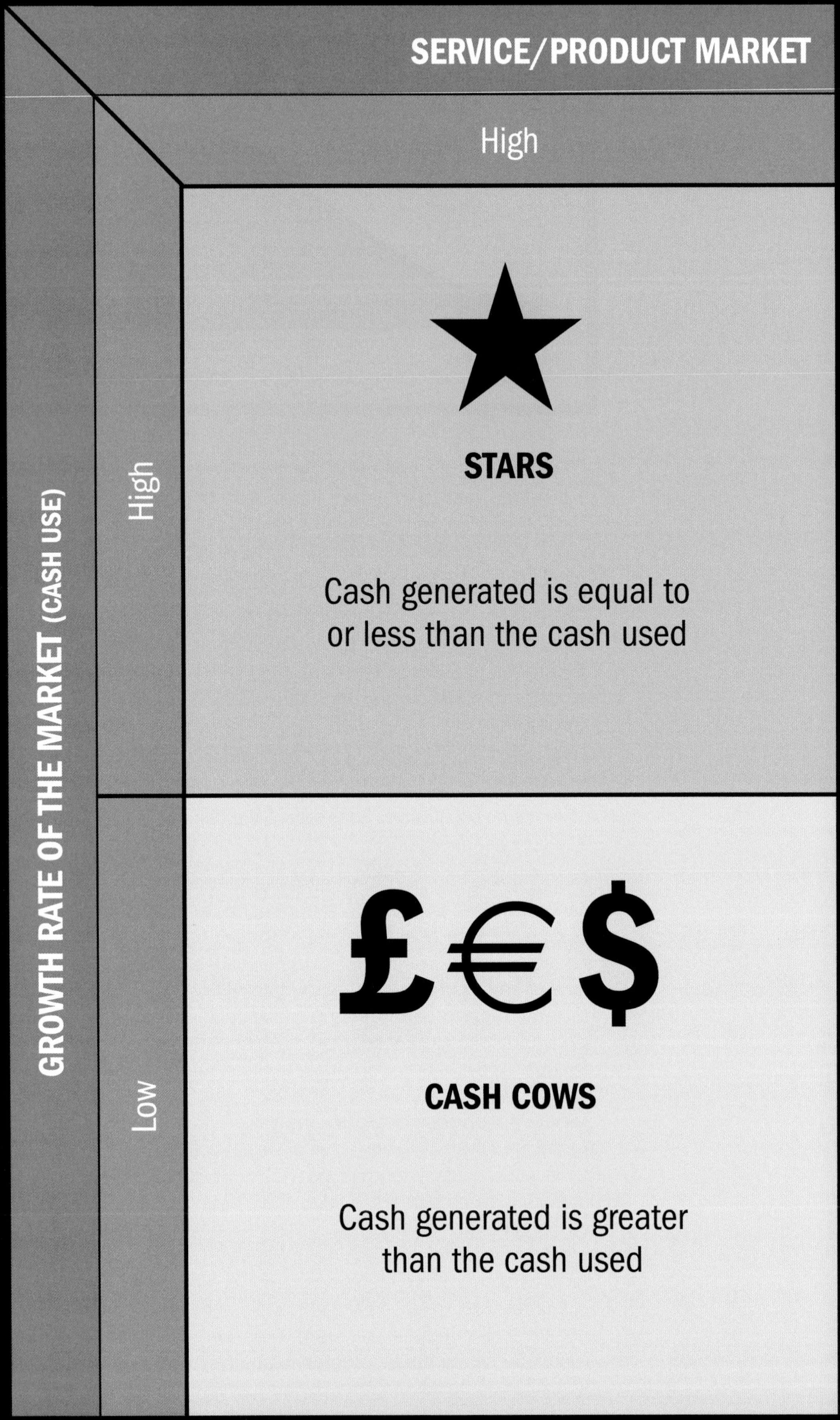

SERVICE/PRODUCT MARKET

High

GROWTH RATE OF THE MARKET (CASH USE)

High

★

STARS

Cash generated is equal to
or less than the cash used

Low

£€$

CASH COWS

Cash generated is greater
than the cash used

SHARE (CASH GENERATION)

Low

?

DILEMMAS

Cash generated is less
than the cash used

PETS

Cash generated is less
than the cash used

- *Dilemmas* – services/products that hold a small percentage of a high-growth market. In order to maintain or improve its position, an organization will have to allocate more cash than the services/products generate. Although the environment is favourable, current performance is questionable, thus requiring close examination and often remedial action. Consequently, it will be uncertain whether a service/product will in the future become a star or a pet.

- *Stars* – services/products with a high market share (typically market leaders) in a high-growth market, but they are often in a position where the cash generated is, at best, equal to (and often less than) the cash needed. Stars will eventually become cash cows if they hold their market share; if they do not, they will become pets.

- *Cash cows* – services/products that hold a high percentage of a low-growth market and are in the latter half of their life cycles. These are the principal generators of funds. The cash cow can be 'milked' to generate more cash than can be profitably reinvested. However, they can in no way be forgotten: they have to be managed efficiently, new developments within a service/product range have to be made, and customers have to be carefully tended, with the emphasis on cash flow rather than building market share.

- *Pets* – also known as cash traps, cash dogs and cash coffins, describe services/products for which individual market share is low and market growth is low. They leave no cash surplus for investment elsewhere and often absorb cash surpluses created by other services and products. As a rule, they should be deleted from the range.

An organization that has analysed its services/products in this way is then able to look at its current or proposed mix of cash and profits. This will help it to ensure the continuity of a suitable service/product mix by addressing a series of corporate issues, including for which markets to aim and the degree of support required, particularly with regard to decisions on research and operations investment.

> **KEY IDEA**
  Service/product portfolio analysis helps to pinpoint those services or products with the greatest potential in terms of revenue and cash generation

The service/product portfolio analysis is essentially static but is a useful selection technique to help organizations understand their current position more fully and reposition their service/product portfolio in the future. The analysis has two primary functions: to aid resource allocation and cash management by pinpointing those services and products with greatest potential, and to maintain a balance within the current mix. On the other hand, the service/product life cycle is a dynamic model with associated market-related strategies built in. Thus, combining the two analyses allows companies to assess their service/product mix on both dimensions and this, in turn, provides further insights to help determine decisions such as investment priorities and where best to harvest existing services or products.

So far, we have looked at the introduction of new services/products, the design process and the need for organizations to review what they currently offer. Now we turn our attention to the key task of developing a specification and the role that operations has in this part of the design process.

Developing a specification

As we learned earlier in the chapter, developing a specification is an important part of the process of service/product design and development. It is self-evident that services/products need to be defined in terms of what they comprise. What is equally important, however, is to identify within the development process those aspects of the design that will later affect other functions tasked with selling and providing the service/product. As highlighted in Chapter 2, the need to link decisions made within functions to one another is essential and, because of this, the development of a specification (what a service/product comprises) has to be detailed from several perspectives. For example, the design of services/products and the design of the service delivery systems or manufacturing process to provide them are interlinked. The following sections will explore the factors that must be considered when developing a specification.

The inherent nature of services and products

The physical nature of products brings with it an inherent need to specify what a product encompasses when it is being developed. Services, on the other hand, are less tangible, so the task of defining what a service comprises needs to be a more specific undertaking. If this is not recognized, the rigour necessary to define a service may not be applied and the required detail may not be provided.

In manufacturing, products and end-customers are invariably detached from each other in the system, for example through inventory or the wholesale and/or retail stages in the total supply chain. With services, however, the provider and customer are often linked at the point of provision. The result is that the opportunity to interpret what is meant by 'service' also lies at the point of provision. It is necessary, therefore, for organizations to determine the level of server discretion allowed in the service delivery system. This relates what a service comprises and the extent to which a server can vary the service offering.

Developing a specification to reflect the service/product mix

Most offerings comprise a mix of service and product, and Figure 1.8 provided some examples of this. When detailing a specification, it is useful to identify the nature of the service and the nature of the product within the mix. One way to highlight the corresponding roles of the service and product elements in the mix is to ask whether this is a service within which there is a facilitating product (that is, the offering is predominantly a service but includes a product that contributes to influencing customer choice), or whether this is a product that also involves a facilitating service. This helps to clarify the mix and identify which elements are an integral part of the specification and which elements will enhance the offering in the eyes of the customer.

Figure 1.8 reminds us that what is purchased is a combination of services and goods and that the mix will vary – for example, purchasing a television set compared with tailored kitchen units requiring installation, or a meal provided by a high-class restaurant compared with one from a fast-food outlet.

The explicit and implicit benefits of the offering

When developing a specification, it is useful to separate the elements of the specification into explicit and implicit dimensions.[4] When customers purchase services or products, they perceive that they are receiving one or more explicit services. For example, a bank provides the explicit service of money transactions, a hotel provides food and accommodation, and a hairdresser the styling of hair. Customers may choose from a range of quality levels related to the provision of a service, and this will typically influence their selection of which organization will provide it for them.

In addition, the offering may also include a range of implicit dimensions: for example, security and privacy within a banking system; the level of attention, promptness and recognition of a regular customer on the part of hotel staff; and the magazine and drinks provision and levels of cleanliness within a hairdressing salon. In fact, in some markets the implicit services may be more important in influencing a customer's selection than the explicit service that lies at the core of the purchase. But no matter what the relative importance of the explicit and implicit dimensions is, recognizing those differences helps in developing a specification and in signalling in detail what the organization's offering should involve.

The supporting structural facilities

Developing a specification also involves determining the support facilities that are required. These reflect the nature of the service/product provided and customers' perceptions of what this entails. Typical examples include the quality of buildings, reception areas, meeting rooms, furniture, fittings and equipment, appropriate decor, level of maintenance and general upkeep, delivery vehicles, and the appearance and technical know-how of after-sales support staff.

Techniques for improving design

The final section of this chapter outlines the operations techniques and approaches used to help improve the design process in the overall context of a business:

- Standardization
- Modular design
- Mass customization
- Taguchi methods
- QFD and the house of quality
- Value analysis
- Simultaneous engineering
- Variety reduction.

Standardization

To help enhance volumes, designers, where possible, use the same components, ingredients or materials to provide a range of offerings. For example, the same chassis may be used in more than one car and, similarly, the same engines in more than one model. In the same way, suppliers of pre-packed food use much the same packaging from one item to another, while fast-food restaurants use the same containers, food items and disposable packaging wherever possible. In doing so, the volume of the standard item is increased, which helps reduce costs. Thus, the concept of standardization helps to provide a range of options while enhancing the volumes of parts from which the end services/products are built. The concept can be applied to components, materials, processes and delivery systems with great effect.

Modular design

The use of modules as standard building blocks in designing and providing services and products is an extension of the concept of interchangeable parts. Using common sets of parts enhances volumes, lowers costs and reduces inventory levels, as Case 3.4 illustrates.

Mass customization

The increasingly competitive nature of today's markets has heightened the need to provide customers' requirements without imposing prohibitive prices and lead-times. Widening choice requires a delivery system that is flexible in terms of meeting the broader range on offer. Ever since General Motors (GM), by offering choice and alternatives, took world leadership in the car industry from Ford and its 'no-choice' strategy in the 1920s, the automobile sector has offered a wide range of options along many dimensions. The result is that the potential number of different car configurations (engine types and sizes × colours × options) for most models runs into six figures, and they are all assembled using the same process. This approach to broadening the options on offer continues to spread to other markets.

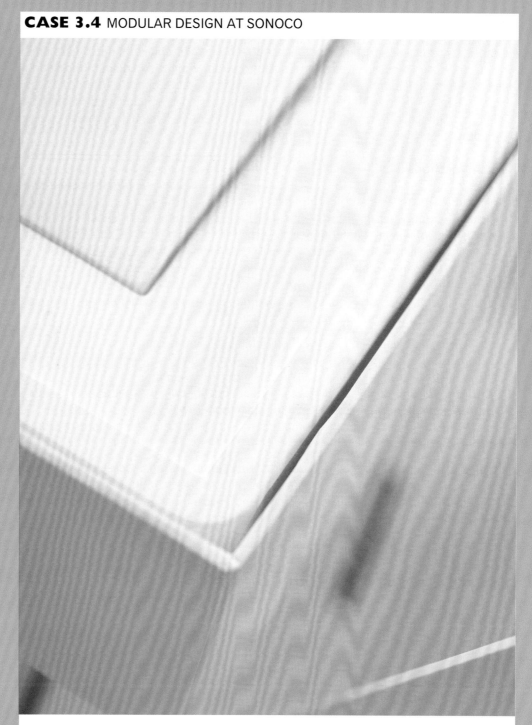

Offering modular services in support of products enabled the industrial products division at Sonoco, a large US packaging company, to customize its packaging of support services 'to meet more precisely the requirements of its spectrum of customers'. The concept of offering only essential services as part of the **sales package** and then offering modular services at set prices enables companies such as Sonoco Products, Baxter Healthcare Corporation and power and automation company Asea Brown Boveri (ABB) to tailor their packages to customer needs and keep their prices lower.

www.sonoco.com

Question

How is modular design used by Sonoco and others?

Lecturers: visit www.palgrave.com/business/hillessential for additional resources

Sales package – the mix of services and/or products that make up a sale

© Alex Hill and Terry Hill 2011

The proliferation of faster, smarter and more affordable computers, software and telecommunications allows more choice or customization on a mass (that is, high-volume) scale. Aspects of modular designs and interchangeable parts offer choice to customers and, with the necessary process investment in place and an organization geared to meeting these offerings, customizing a standard product is a viable option. Whereas mass customization is not in itself new (the GM strategy having been launched in the late 1920s), its application to a wider range of product offerings is, and the phrase 'mass customization' is intended to herald this growing phenomenon.[5]

Taguchi methods

The approach to design developed by Japan's Genichi Taguchi[6] received considerable attention in the early 1990s and now forms an integral part of the approach to design. His principle is simple: instead of constantly using effort to control a process in order to assure consistent quality conformance, it is better to design the service/product to achieve desired levels of quality conformance in the first place despite the variations that will occur in the service delivery system or production process. Based on his work in manufacturing, Taguchi's approach uses statistically designed experiments to optimize design and operations costs. This approach requires a service/product to perform to its specification in extreme conditions, such as:

- *Above-average demand* – the ability of operations to increase capacity
- *Absenteeism* – staffing plans to provide short-term cover
- *Dietary needs* – a range of options to provide alternative menus
- *Weather shifts* – alternative activities to meet changeable weather patterns
- *Unexpected demand* – plans to meet early customer arrivals
- *Working conditions* – developing products to withstand harsh climates or extreme patterns of use.

This approach brings the service delivery system/manufacturing process and service/product design together to agree the parameters so as to meet a range of conditions and build these into the specification. In so doing, it moves to a more proactive approach that emphasizes the prevention of defects and enables organizations to meet design specifications more consistently and achieve higher levels of quality conformance, a key factor in many of today's markets.

Quality function deployment and the house of quality

Two dimensions that affect the success of the design effort are the extent to which a service/product design meets customers' needs, and how well an organization can produce or deliver the design. **Quality function deployment** (QFD) is a way to evaluate how well the service/product design and the operations process meet or exceed customers' needs. Using competitors' offerings as an additional part of the assessment helps organizations to identify both where they need to improve and also the service and product features and activities that are non-value adding.

> **Quality function deployment** – a formal system to ensure that the eventual service or product design meets the needs of customers while eliminating wasteful features and activities that do not add value or contribute to meeting these needs

----

> **KEY IDEA**

Quality function deployment links customers' needs to operations requirements

----

QFD had its origins in the US tyre manufacturer Bridgestone Corporation and Mitsubishi's Kone (Japan) shipyards in the late 1960s. Professor Yoji Akao of Tamagawa University and Shigeru Mizuno gave QFD its name in the late 1970s and popularized the concept of formalizing customer inputs into service and product design procedures. The complete QFD approach involves a sequential set of matrices (Figure 3.4) through which the links between the customer's needs and the technical, component/material and operations requirements can be identified and maintained.

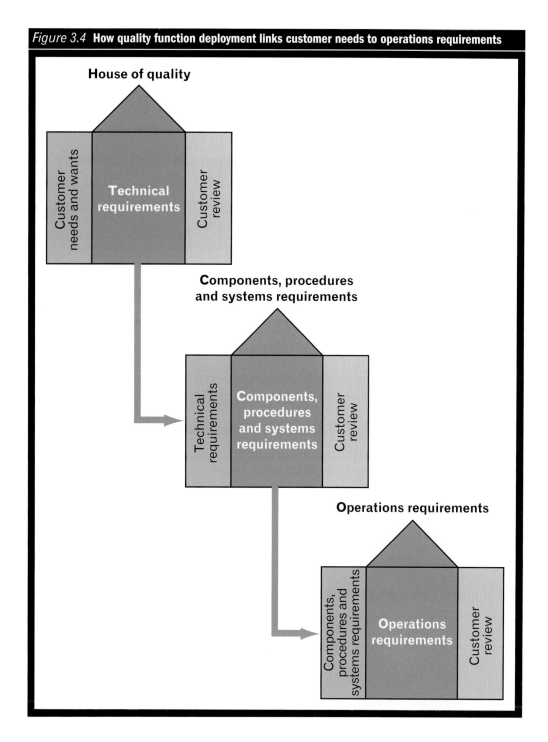

Figure 3.4 **How quality function deployment links customer needs to operations requirements**

House of quality

Customer needs and wants

Technical requirements

Customer review

Components, procedures and systems requirements

Technical requirements

Components, procedures and systems requirements

Customer review

Operations requirements

Components, procedures and systems requirements

Operations requirements

Customer review

The most commonly used phase of QFD is the stage 1 matrix, often called the 'house of quality'. Figure 3.5 illustrates the general steps involved and will be used to show how the approach is applied, in this instance to a fast-food restaurant:

1   *Establish customers' needs and wants* as well as the characteristics and attributes of the services/products involved. Furthermore, the relative importance of these must be established and the weighting agreed as a percentage, as shown in Figure 3.5.

2   *Establish customers' 'view of competitors'* – how well does this restaurant satisfy customers' needs compared with its competitors' outlets? In Figure 3.5, three competing restaurants are compared, with OP (own performance) representing this outlet and A, B and C representing the competitors' facilities. Giving a score of 1 as the best

Figure 3.5 Using the quality function deployment matrix: the house of quality

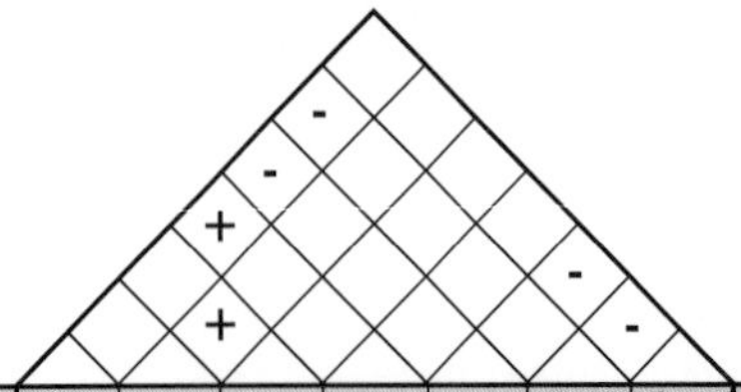

Customers' needs and wants		Weights %	Increase grill area	Increase server staff at peak times	Increase server stations	Increase kitchen staff at peak times	Decrease average time food is stored	Decrease maximum time food is stored	Decrease process steps – main meal	Best 1	2	3	4	Worst 5
Decor & layout		5									OP B	A&C		
Menu variety	Child	5	+			+					OP C	A&B		
	Adult	10	+			+				C		B	OP A	
Service speed		30	+	+	+	+	-	-	+	C		OP A	B	
Food	Tastes good	15	+	+	+	+	+	+	+		OP C	A&B		
	Served warm	10	+	+	+	+	+	+	+	C	A	B	OP	
	Ingredients	5									OP C	B	A	
Low price		20	-	-		-	-	-			OP	A&B		C

Technical evaluation of competitors		m²	#	#	#	mins	mins	#	Comments
Own performance (OP)		2.5	5	5	7	6	9	8	
Competitors	A	2.4	5	5	7	6	8	6	
	B	2.7	5	5	8	6	7	6	
	C	3.0	6	7	8	4	7	5	
Target technical specifications		2.9	6	7	8	4	7	5	

and 5 as the worst, category comparisons can be made, which will reveal areas that potentially need improving.

3 *Identify the technical requirements* necessary to provide for customers' wants and needs. For example, fast service may be achieved, in part, by making food ahead of time or reducing the process lead-time involved. Measuring the factors that affect these and other dimensions is completed as an input into Step 5 below.

4 *Look for links between the technical requirements and their effect on different customers' needs and wants* – these are then recorded in the body of the house of quality with a + or − sign indicating the extent to which a technical requirement

would potentially improve or harm relevant service/product attributes. For example, consider the technical requirement 'Decrease average time food is stored' in Figure 3.5. Although decreasing the average storage time of food is potentially harmful to service speed (the chance of being out of stock increases and customers will have to wait; therefore, both are given a minus [–] sign), it potentially helps the attributes 'food tastes good' and 'food served warm' (and, therefore, both are given a plus [+] sign). Obviously, if we changed this technical requirement from 'decrease' to 'increase' average time food is stored, the + and − signs would be reversed.

5 *Complete technical comparisons* – check the extent of your technical provision against that of your competitors. Filling in the actual figures involved – as in Figure 3.5 – or using a scale of 1–5 will help comparisons and assessments. For example related to the technical requirement 'Decrease process steps – main meal', the number of steps currently undertaken in 'Own performance' is 8, whereas for 'Competitors' A, B and C, it is 6, 6 and 5, respectively.

6 *Evaluate the trade-offs for different design features* – in the 'roof' section of the house of quality, information is recorded relating to the trade-offs of different design features by using + and − signs. This highlights the effect of changing the extent of one requirement on the other technical dimensions in the process. In Figure 3.5, you will see a + sign recorded between the first and fourth technical requirements. This highlights the need for both these requirements in order to increase menu variety and improve delivery speed. There is, however, a − sign between the first and fifth, and first and sixth, technical requirements: whereas increasing the grill area will help to improve service speed, decreasing storage times will have the reverse effect.

Value analysis

In most industries, the ratio of purchases to employment costs is typically around 3:1. It makes sense, therefore, for companies to give time and attention to reducing material costs so as to secure the significantly higher potential benefits and savings.

The purchasing bill is made up of two elements: the price of the materials, components and services purchased, and the amount of materials, components and services used. Whereas the former is the concern of the purchasing function of the company (which will to some extent be influenced by world markets, competition and usage volumes), the latter is influenced by service/product design (the specification itself) and how well these purchased items are utilized. There are several approaches to checking the amount of materials, components and services used, which we will now review.

An important, but often underused, technique to help provide this systematic approach to reducing the cost of a service/product without impairing its function is value analysis. Each product, component or service is methodically examined with the purpose of minimizing its cost without reducing its functional value.[7] The process can be successfully applied to services, products and overhead costs.

Value analysis, like other methods of continuous improvement, aims to reduce costs. However, its orientation is different. Continuous improvement methods (discussed in detail in Chapter 12) tend to accept the service/product as a given and instead concentrate on the way it is provided or made. Thus, the principal aim is to reduce aspects such as staff costs, the number of rejected items, wastage and lead-times. Value analysis, however, considers the functions that the components, services/products or overhead activity are intended to perform. It then reviews the present design in order to provide these functions at a lower cost, without reducing the value – that is, the specification of a service/product meeting a given customer requirement or overhead activity will be maintained, and it will continue to be met by any proposed changes.

'**Good design** involves identifying what is **critical** and taking everything else away'

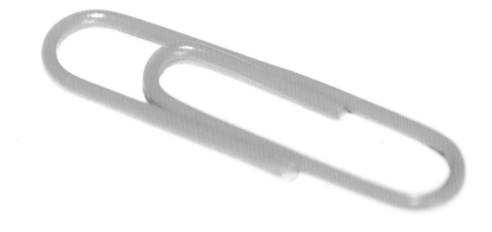

When analysing value, three aspects need to be taken into account:

1 Design of the service/product or overhead activity
2 Purchase of materials or services
3 Service delivery system/manufacturing process methods.

> **KEY IDEA**
Value analysis is a systematic approach to reducing costs without reducing the service/product specification

Value analysis procedure

Value analysis has two parts: (1) selecting those responsible for completing the analysis, and (2) the procedure to be followed.

The make-up of those responsible for completing the analysis work should be quite wide-ranging. The classic structure is to have a group made up of a full-time specialist (the value analyst) and representatives from design, purchasing, costing and operations. However, other group compositions have proved equally successful, and can also, in the case of many Japanese companies, include groups constituted under the title of 'quality circles'. In each instance, prerequisites for applying value analysis successfully are that those concerned must be trained in the procedures involved and that corporate goodwill is demonstrated at all points throughout the process, including time to complete the tasks, access to cost and other data and liaison with outside suppliers. Eight steps are involved:

1 Select the service or product.
2 Gather information about it.
3 Analyse its function and its value for money.
4 Generate alternative ways to provide the same function through speculation and brainstorming.
5 Assess the worth of these ideas.
6 Decide what is to be done.
7 Implement the decisions.
8 Evaluate the results.

In Step 4, it is essential to use someone with experience (the value analyst) and carefully select the group involved. The selection should avoid the potential problems of seniority and provide a wide range of disciplines within the group. This stage is key to applying the technique successfully and needs to be handled with care.

The items selected are usually known to be of high cost, and use of the 80/20 rule (that 20 per cent of the material or service items account for 80 per cent of total costs – see Chapters 9 and 10 for a fuller explanation of this rule) will help in the procedure.[8] However, it is important not to select a service/product that is nearing the end of its life cycle, as value analysis is not a prop to help non-viable services/products become viable, although it can form a legitimate part of extending the life cycle of existing services/products.

Value analysis consists of taking each part of a service/product and looking in detail at its function. Every feature, tolerance, hole, degree of finish, piece of material or part of the service is vetted to ensure that none of these is adding to the total cost without providing a useful function. The sources of savings from value analysis come principally from reducing activities, steps in the process and material costs:

- Eliminate parts (for example, components, transactions or steps in a service system) without reducing the functional qualities involved.
- Combine the functions of two or more components or services by redesign.
- Reduce tolerances that are unnecessarily tight and make for higher operations costs.

Simultaneous
engineering –
overlapping the
stages in the design
process (that is, they
are undertaken partly
or wholly in parallel
with other stages)
in order to reduce
the time taken to
introduce services
or products into the
market and cut costs

- Extend the concept of standardization.
- Simplify the service delivery system or manufacturing process and consequently reduce staff costs.

Simultaneous engineering

The speed with which services and products can be designed and introduced into a market directly affects sales revenue and profit. **Simultaneous engineering** is an approach to reduce design lead-times. It involves all relevant functions within a business (for example, design, marketing, IT and operations) as well as suppliers. Its purpose is to undertake tasks, partly or wholly, in parallel rather than sequentially. Receiving ideas and contributions from functions early in the process reduces time-consuming redesigns and delays, and teamwork encourages co-ownership of the design and a greater commitment to making a service/product succeed. Jobs are also enriched, and creativity is stimulated. Because everyone is communicating with everyone else throughout the design process, the quality of the service or product increases, service/product lead-times are dramatically shortened and service/product costs are cut. The principles underlying what happens are shown in Figure 3.6.

To achieve reductions similar to these, companies use a number of approaches:

- *Contracting out activities* Using external resources for one or more of the stages increases the available capacity and reduces delays. Possible tasks range from design, marketing and IT through to prototype development, initial launch and public relations.
- *Increased use of suppliers* As explained in Chapter 11, suppliers are increasingly being asked to take on several phases during the design and introduction of a service/ product as part of the supplier package. This reduces the overall demand on a company's own design team and shortens the total time involved.
- *Teamwork* Forming service, product and process teams stimulates ideas, speeds up the process and eliminates problems.
- *Combining or eliminating stages* Combining or eliminating stages by re-examining existing procedures rigorously tests current practices and reduces lead-times throughout.
- *Overlapping stages* As illustrated in Figure 3.6, identifying opportunities to begin the next phase before the current stage is complete moves the overall procedure away from a sequential process to one in which some activities (in part or in total) take place in parallel, which means that overall lead-times dramatically reduce.
- *Incremental versus breakthrough innovations* In the past, breakthrough innovations have often been the desired goal of designers. These are harder to come up with, involve longer lead-times in all phases of the design process and experience a higher failure rate. Switching the emphasis to incremental improvements and introducing clusters of these at the same time still gives rise to significant improvements but involves shorter lead-times to their introduction.
- *Using standard parts and modular designs* Earlier, we looked at the principles and benefits of using standard parts and components and modular approaches to designs. A further design lead-time advantage is also made available where 'common' parts are introduced into new designs, with corresponding benefits.
- *Using new technologies* Employing technologies such as computer-aided design (CAD) and computer-aided engineering (CAE) reduces lead-times within the overall process as well as eliminating stages. For example, CAE takes CAD designs and subjects them to stress, load and vibration tests to assess their strength and reliability, thus eliminating later elements in the design and development process.

Variety reduction

The approaches and techniques listed so far have addressed issues relating to the design process itself. Variety reduction, on the other hand, is a quantitative appraisal of the range of current services and products provided. The process questions whether

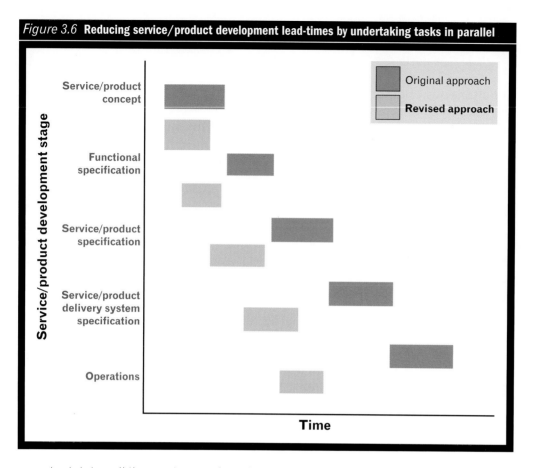

Figure 3.6 Reducing service/product development lead-times by undertaking tasks in parallel

or not retaining all the services and products currently on offer is best for the business as a whole.

In any service/product range, some items will generate more sales or more profit, or contribute more to fixed costs, than others. Consequently, checking the contribution (selling price – variable costs = contribution) that they make can lead to a cut-back on the items that are uneconomical and provide some control over the future variety in the range.

The first step in the process is to arrange all the services or products on offer in a list, with highest total value of sales at the top and lowest at the bottom. This often reveals that about 20 per cent of items account for about 80 per cent of the total sales revenue – the '80/20 rule' described earlier (see Chapters 9 and 10 for a fuller explanation). As you can see in the example in Figure 3.7, the top six of the 24 products shown account for about 74 per cent of total sales, whereas the bottom 15 products account for only 17 per cent. In addition, the top six account for some 76 per cent of the total contribution, whereas the bottom 15 (or 62 per cent) contribute only £375,000, that is, about 13 per cent.

The next step is to check the relative performance of the items with a low percentage of sales revenue over the last three or four years to determine whether the individual trend is going up, staying the same or going down. Further checks are then made on the stable and downward-trend items to see if their contribution can be improved by reducing variable costs and/or increasing the selling price. If this action does not bring about the required changes in terms of the percentage contribution to selling price, the company should consider phasing out the service/product.

The advantages of variety reduction include leading to:

- Longer average production runs, with less downtime through fewer changeovers
- Potential savings in plant and equipment requirements

Figure 3.7 **Product analysis by annual sales revenue**

Product reference number	Sales revenue (£000)	Percentage of total sales	Total variable costs (£000)	Total contribution (£000)	Percentage of total contribution
054-19	2480	19.5	2128	352	12.7
303-07	2134	16.8	1684	650	23.4
691-30	1720	13.5	1372	348	12.5
016-10	1440	11.3	1028	412	14.8
418-50	980	7.7	676	304	10.9
402-50	620	4.9	580	40	1.4
155-29	428	3.8	390	92	3.4
900-01	360	2.8	240	120	4.3
308-31	308	2.4	220	88	3.2
341-17	280	2.2	212	68	2.4
540-80	260	2.0	200	60	2.2
701-91	232	1.8	160	72	2.6
650-27	220	1.7	202	18	0.6
712-22	192	1.5	140	52	1.9
137-29	180	1.4	152	28	1.0
003-54	172	1.4	168	4	0.1
541-21	140	1.1	122	18	0.6
543-61	136	1.1	112	24	0.9
305-04	96	0.8	86	10	0.4
097-54	88	0.7	86	2	0.1
323-34	72	0.6	68	4	0.1
542-93	68	0.5	62	6	0.2
386-07	44	0.3	36	8	0.3
440-18	20	0.2	19	1	–
Total	**12,724**	**100.0**	**7463**	**2781**	**100.0**

Notes: Contribution = selling price – variable costs.

Further analysis could be enhanced by grouping like products together and showing the product group totals for columns 'Percentage of total sales' to 'Percentage of total contribution' inclusive.

The '80/20' relationship implied in the rule is only an indication of the size of the actual figures involved. Thus, in the example here, 25 per cent of the products account for 74 per cent of sales, illustrating clearly the concept of a relatively small number of products accounting for a high percentage of the sales revenue.

- Lower inventory, resulting in less investment and reduced inventory control and space costs
- Less sales effort and less need for after-sales service
- Easier operations planning and day-to-day scheduling of tasks
- Appropriate reallocation of capacity (particularly scare resources) to the overall benefit of the business.

Loss leader – a service or product offered at below cost to attract customers

The disadvantages of this approach include a reduced service/product range on offer and the danger of cutting out services/products that serve as **loss leaders**. Thus, it is the net corporate effect of variety reduction that needs to be considered and on which such decisions should be based. Case 3.5 highlights some of the issues.

Few products have resisted standardization as much as the humble door lock. In Europe alone, several hundred thousand types are on sale – a product range diversity that reflects the fact that doors and buildings have evolved in different ways in different countries over several centuries.

Today, demand for security is growing, and prospects for lock sales are good. Assa Abloy (the Swedish lock master with worldwide sales of SEK 35 billion) is now number one worldwide, with 6 per cent of total sales. Its growth (in 2010 it was over 10 times larger than it was in 1994) has been partly generic and partly achieved by taking over other businesses – in recent years Assa Abloy has bought out more than 20 lock companies worldwide. The company is represented in Europe, the Middle East, Asia, the Americas and the Pacific rim, with strong market positions in emerging markets such China. Despite this international spread, products sold in more than one country account for only 25 per cent of sales.

Where possible, Assa Abloy tries to capitalize on the potentially higher volumes involved – for instance, all exit bars for its fire and emergency doors are made in one plant in France – but this tends to be the exception rather than the rule. As a result, it has 40 manufacturing plants around the world, each mainly supplying its own domestic market.

www.assaabloy.com

Questions

1 Why are some product ranges less open to variety reduction than others?

2 Why is the company less able to introduce standardization into its product range even though sales are growing?

Lecturers: visit www.palgrave.com/business/ hillessential for additional resources

Critical reflections

All organizations have a range of services or products at a given time. To be competitive, it is necessary to have a set that is complementary, that relates to the organization's strategic objectives (such as growth and market share), and that takes account of tactical considerations (such as completeness of range, process capability and distribution costs). Furthermore, the mix is always undergoing change, as organizations continuously introduce new services/products in a never-ending bid to meet customers' requirements and grow sales. On the one hand, developing and introducing new items is typically expensive and risky and involves long timescales, while, on the other hand, new services and products are necessary for survival and growth.

> **KEY IDEA**
   New services and products are the lifeblood of a business

Attitudes and norms concerning the level of innovation and the introduction of new services and products are affected by internal and external forces. Decisions to invest in R&D or to seek to exploit developments in technology will vary from industry to industry and company to company, often markedly so. In product-based companies, the tradition of investing in R&D and actively seeking to introduce new products has noticeably increased over the past few decades. This varies from superficial modifications (for example, in markets such as customer durables, there have traditionally been regular 'facelifts' to existing models/products) to major product changes.

A review of service industries also highlights changes over the past decade in what is on offer. Protected for a long time by geographical distance, commercial legacies and legal constraints, many service industries have remained conservative and insensitive to the needs of their customers. They have competed in what are known as 'sheltered markets' (see earlier in the chapter). However, the impact of deregulation, advances in data-processing and increased global competition in many areas of the service industry have moved many sectors into what are known as 'traded markets'.

For instance, deregulation and advances in data-processing have had an enormous impact in the travel industry. Whereas 20 years ago high-street travel agents commanded a prime position (as a sheltered market), the advent of online selling has moved much of the industry into a traded market, bypassing high-street outlets and, in some instances such as airlines, bypassing travel agents altogether. In the same way, the limited competition that banks always enjoyed changed with alterations to the trading rules, the opening up of financial markets, investments in data-processing and the entry of non-finance organizations (for example, supermarket chains, other retailers and a wide range of other business) into credit sales, personal loans and the like. One outcome has been a dramatic alteration in the basis and form of competition in the finance sector.

A tough business lesson that top managers need to draw from the history of progress is that most services, products and technologies will be replaced, and most efforts to replace them will fail. This is somewhat a game of Russian roulette in which companies need to participate if they wish to grow and prosper with high stakes and high uncertainty. But the level of change can also be minor and yet have a major impact in a market. Case 3.6 illustrates how an undramatic change to existing, well-established markets can result in a major shift in success.

While cost-cutting, rationalization and restructuring are key components of any corporate agenda, companies need to recognize the key role of innovation in their quest for growth. In part, this stems from recognizing that improved efficiency is no substitute for growth. Organizations that have for some time pursued activities to reduce costs often

CASE 3.6 INCREASING THE FRESHNESS OF BREAD IN SUPERMARKET BAKERIES

A small change in existing specifications can often be enough to make a significant impact. For example, increasing the freshness of the bread they provided enabled supermarkets not only to match local high-street outlets, but even to outperform them. Bread technology now enables doughs to be held for several days without deterioration. This enables in-store supermarket bakeries to produce bread several times each day, thereby increasing product freshness. In addition, the introduction of part-baked breads to be oven-finished at home has opened up a new dimension to fresh bread provision.

Students: www.palgrave.com/business/hillessential provides learning resources for this case

experience anxious times as they have difficulty in moving back towards an innovative culture. Many are stressing innovation as a corporate goal, while others (for example, 3M, Elf Aquitaine, Siemens and British Airways) are introducing innovation schemes as a way to further stimulate these essential activities. But the area of innovation is as difficult to embrace as it is essential for continued success. Some pointers to these issues and ways forward include the following:

- Encouraging more creativity only addresses part of the problem. Much of the difficulty lies in establishing a clear link between innovation and corporate success.

- One common mistake is to believe that innovation can compensate for competitive disadvantages elsewhere.

- There is a need to move away from a preoccupation with R&D to the totality of innovation, in terms of scope and organizational style. Innovation is potentially in everyone and everywhere.

- Using customers is essential. One third of the toy company Hasbro's annual sales come from new products. To ensure this trend continues, Hasbro goes to great lengths to keep its designers in touch with children, and to this end it has built a crèche (known as the 'fun lab') for 25 children next to its R&D department.

- The task is to generate good services and products on a continuous basis. A culture of innovation is essential for this to happen. Ways of encouraging and incorporating the need to spend time on creating ideas has to become part of the corporate culture. 3M allows designers to spend up to 15 per cent of their time on any research project they wish – the Post-it note pad had bottom-up origins. Other organizations need to break down the status quo that traditionally goes with innovation – they need to create a culture that encourages and develops innovation in order to bring everyone and their ideas on board.

Summary

- The introduction of new services/products and the development of existing ones is the lifeblood of organizations. For this to become an integral part of how companies grow and prosper, they need a way to generate ideas and then translate them into reality.

- Although breakthroughs will always gain the spotlight, most companies will typically sell today what they sold yesterday, and will do the same tomorrow. This does not imply, however, that they do not need to 'think outside the box'. On the contrary, nothing could be further from the truth. The key is more to do with where to focus attention, and for many companies this means thinking differently about what they currently provide and the markets in which they currently compete.

- With ideas being the spark that ignites developments, companies are realizing that they also need to seek views from less traditional sources. Key among these are the staff who provide the service or make the product, and the customers who buy it. Breaking the mould of past approaches is difficult, but in today's competitive world it is essential.

- While the first step of the process is vital, getting an idea to a market reality is critical. For much of the time, this part of the process changes from being one of inspiration to one based on hard work. Systematic checking and rechecking involves much time and effort.

- Finally, although new services/products create tomorrow's success, a company needs to get the most out of today's offerings. On the scale of being inherently interesting, generating ideas is at the top, with developing existing services/products much lower down. However, on the scale of what affects corporate success and prosperity, the order is often the reverse. The attraction of stars and the mundane nature of cash cows often results in an imbalance of time, attention and recognition. Keeping all the corporate balls in the air is an essential element of successfully managing the process for the design and development of services and products.

Discussion questions

1 Select a service and a product that are at different points of their life cycles. Explain their progress to date, where they are now and what you expect will happen in the future.

2 The section 'The service/product mix' explained that a service or product can be expressed as a combination of dimensions (that is, 'a service within which there is a facilitating good', 'the explicit and implicit dimensions of an offering' and 'the supporting structural facilities'). Analyse the following businesses in line with these dimensions:

   • A supermarket

   • A high-street post office

   • An upmarket restaurant.

3 Give one example of the use of standardization and modular design for both a service and a product of your choice.

4 A major German shoe company launched a new range of tennis shoes. There were two styles, one for men and one for women. Within each of these two styles there were six colour combinations, and the shoe sizes ranged from size 7 to 14 for men and 4 to 9 for women. (Note: the sizes available do not include half sizes.) How many shoes would a store have to stock to have one pair of each shoe within both ranges?

Assignments

1 Apply the value analysis principles to a service or product and see if you can identify opportunities for cost reduction without reducing value.

2 Complete a review of two fast-food restaurants of your choice using the quality functional deployment approach. In this task, use the outline in Figure 3.5 but check, where possible, the detail for:

   • Customers' needs and wants, and weight the resulting percentages, as in Figure 3.5

   • Technical requirements

   • Customers' ratings for each restaurant.

3 In what types of organization might new ideas have:

   • A low mortality rate (that is, they last for a long time)?

   • A high mortality rate (that is, they last for a short time)?

   Explain your choice with supporting arguments and details.

4 Give two examples (with supporting details) of the impact of technology on:

   • A service

   • A product design.

5 Since markets for services typically have lower entry barriers than product markets, why do overseas companies not start with services when they first begin to compete in foreign markets?

Exploring further

Journal articles

Dougherty, D. and Murthy, A. (2009) 'What service customers really want'. *Harvard Business Review*, **87**(9), p. 22. This article argues that while superior customer service is a key to future growth, managers need to understand the extent to which consumers' expectations have shifted.

Hansen, M.T. and Birkinshaw, J. (2007) 'The innovation value chain'. *Harvard Business Review*, **85**(6), pp. 121–30. The challenges of coming up with fresh ideas and realizing profits from them are different for every company. This article provides a framework for evaluating innovation performance entitled 'the innovation value chain'. The article illustrates how smart companies (such as Intuit, P&G, Sara Lee, Shell and Siemens) modify the best innovation practices.

Shankar, V., Berry, L. and Dotzel, T. (2009) 'A practical guide to combining products and services'. *Harvard Business Review*, **87**(11), pp. 94–9. Many firms are trying to combine products and services into innovative offerings to boost revenue and profit by attracting new customers and by increasing demand among existing ones as a result of offering them superior value. The findings are based on an analysis of more than 100 winning hybrid solutions from a variety of business-to-business (B2B) and business-to-customer (B2C) companies.

Books

Akao, Y., ed. (2005) *Quality Function Deployment: Integrating Customer Requirements into Product Design*. Cambridge, MA: Productivity Press. Using a wide variety of case studies, charts and diagrams, this book looks at how quality function deployment can be used to design services and products to meet customer demands.

Hill, T. (2005) *Operations Management: Text and Cases*. Basingstoke: Palgrave Macmillan. This provides a useful supplement to the current book by offering a more comprehensive explanation and further examples (including long case studies) showing how service and manufacturing companies have applied these concepts.

Notes and references

1 This explanation of design strategies was put forward by R.J. Schonberger in *Operations Management*, Plane, TX: Business Publications, 1981.

2 Zahara, S.A., Sisodia, R.S. and Das S.R. (1994) 'Technological choices within competitive strategy types: a conceptual integration'. *International Journal of Technology Management*, **9**(2), pp. 172–95.

3 For example, see Thomke, S. and von Hippel, E. (2002) 'Customers as innovators: a new way to create value'. *Harvard Business Review*, April, pp. 74–81.

4 These concepts were first introduced by Sasser, W.E., Olsen, R.P. and Wyckoff, D.D. in *Management of Service Operations: Text, Cases and Readings*, Boston, Allyn & Bacon, 1978, pp. 10–11.

5 Articles giving different perspectives on mass customization include: Berman, B. (2002) 'Should your firm adopt a mass customization strategy?' *Business Horizons*, July–August, pp. 51–60; Feitzinger, E. and Hau, L.L. (1997) 'Mass customization at Hewlett-Packard: the power of postponement'. *Harvard Business Review*, **75**(1), pp. 116–21; Gilmore, J.H. and Pinell, B.J. (1997) 'The four faces of mass customization'. *Harvard Business Review*, **75**(1), pp. 91–101; Salvador, F., Forza, C. and Rungtusanathan,

M. (2002) 'How to mass customize: product architectures, sourcing and configurations'. *Business Horizons*, July–August, pp. 61–9; Zipkin, P. 'The limits of mass customisation'. (2001) *Sloan Management Review*, **42**(3), pp. 81–7.

6 References include Noori, H. (1989) 'The Taguchi methods: achieving design and output quality'. *Academy of Management Executive*, November, pp. 322–6; Taguchi, G. and Clausing, D. (1990) 'Robust quality'. *Harvard Business Review*, January–February, pp. 65–75.

7 Value analysis is defined in British Standard BS 3138 as 'a systematic interdisciplinary examination of factors affecting the cost of a service or product, in order to devise means of achieving the specified purpose most economically at the required standard of quality and reliability'.

8 This refers to the principle put forward by Vilfredo Pareto (1848–1923) that a few items in any group contribute the significant proportion of the entire group. Pareto was an Italian sociologist and economist who used this law to express the frequency distribution of incomes in society. Chapter 10 provides another example of its application.

DYSON

Since launching the first bagless vacuum cleaner in 1994, Dyson has grown to achieve sales of £64 million by 2008, with 32 per cent of the US market and 46 per cent of the UK market (Figure 1). It has achieved its market leadership through a constant focus on engineering and innovation, but how did it get this to happen? According to Sir James Dyson, it is all about having 'the ability to first grasp that creative moment and then having the scientific aptitude to bring that idea forward.'

CREATING THE RIGHT ENVIRONMENT
By creating an innovative environment, Dyson hopes to encourage its employees to think creatively. The inside of the offices of its factory in Wiltshire, UK, is painted in bright colours such as lilac, purple and lavender, and its employees all sit on £400 Vitra chairs. The shop floor is also bright, airy, air-conditioned and very clean. Staff are well paid and encouraged to wear casual clothes. James Dyson believes that a suit is like a biker's leathers or a fireman's

Figure 1
Dyson's performance (1996–2008)

£million	96	98	00	02	04	05	06	07	08
Sales revenue	56	63	56	71	60	59	59	61	64
Gross profit	3	3	3	7	8	10	5	7	8
R&D	0	0	1	2	4	4	4	7	2

Source: Dyson, *Annual Reports* (1996–2008).

protective kit – it is merely protection – whereas he would rather that the qualities of his employees shine through in what they did rather than what they wore. To encourage creativity in its workforce, the company employs young graduates, recruited straight from university with no experience at all. 'They haven't learnt it all by heart,' Dyson says. 'They're not institutionalized. Engineering requires free-thinkers.'

COMMUNICATING EFFECTIVELY

The business is managed using a flat, informal structure and open-plan offices that encourage people to talk to each other. A daily meeting with employees is held to discuss how well the business is performing and what its competitors are up to. There are also 'feedback sessions' twice a week to highlight problems and identify solutions, and a suggestion box is provided for employees who are uncomfortable talking in front of a large group.

MAKING TINY, STEP-BY-STEP CHANGES AND EMBRACING FAILURE

Although the company is known for vacuum cleaners, digital motors and hand dryers, it is also working on plenty of other inventions. The company approach to innovation is to seek out items that do not function or perform properly and to think about how they could be improved. Engineers are encouraged to follow Edison's design approach. Instead of spending ages planning and sketching, they build prototype after prototype, making tiny step-by-step changes until they get it right. The term 'innovation' is often associated with a 'Eureka' moment, but to Dyson it involves constant experimentation and making mistakes. Error and failure are acknowledged as an important and positive part of the design process, leading to new and exciting developments. In fact, along with the usual appraisal methods, employees are also assessed on their ability to take risks and their willingness to make mistakes.

THINKING ILLOGICALLY AND NURTURING IDEAS

Employees are encouraged to think differently, as Dyson believes that most people in the world think in straight lines because they have been taught to think logically. He also believes that ideas are often fragile and ephemeral when they have just been generated; therefore they need to be nurtured to help them grow strong.

WORKING AS A TEAM

Teamwork and collaboration are vital to the design process at Dyson, as individuals must bring together their different areas of skill to solve problems and create an integrated product. The graphic designers and engineers are located in the centre of the factory, and team members rotate between projects to share expertise and cross-fertilize ideas. Ideas can come from anyone. For example, someone in the customer service department came up with the idea of putting Dyson's helpline number on the handle of their vacuum cleaners. Dyson sees himself as part of the team, and for him a vital part of his job is communicating with his employees in their working environment, and making sure that all staff, not just engineers, are working creatively. 'I don't mean I go around like a policeman,' he says, 'more just encouraging creativity.'

Questions

1 How does Dyson encourage innovation and creativity within its business?

2 Visit **www.dyson.co.uk** and use Figure 3.1 and the text that follows to identify and evaluate the stages of Dyson's design and development process.

3 What lessons can other businesses learn from Dyson's approach to design and development?

Sources: Dyson, J. (2005) James Dyson on Innovation. *Ingenia*, **24**, pp. 31–4.
'Sir James Dyson: Britain needs to copy the French and love its engineers'. *Telegraph*, July 27, 2010. Available at: www.telegraph.co.uk (retrieved August 3, 2010).
James Dyson at the Design and Technology with Science Show. *Journal of Design and Technology Education*, **5**(1), pp. 16–19.
Wallis, I. (April 1, 2004). 'James Dyson'. Growing Business. Available at: www.growingbusiness.co.uk/james-dyson.html (retrieved August 3, 2010).

Delivering Services 4

Learning objectives

After completing this chapter, you should be able to:

- Recognize the technical and business requirements that need to be met when delivering services

- Identify the distinctive characteristics of service operations

- Identify the difference between categories of service and types of service delivery system

- Explain the approach to the overall design of service delivery systems

- List the key phases in the detailed design of service delivery systems

- Give examples of the impact of IT on the design of service delivery systems

Chapter outline

Introduction

Factors affecting service delivery design

- Characteristics of service operations

- Understanding how services differ

Designing the service delivery system

- Phase 1 – the point of customer interface: back office or front office?

- Phase 2 – the delivery system

- IT-based service delivery system designs

- Further aspects of service delivery

Critical reflections

Summary

Introduction

As explained in Chapter 1, transforming inputs into outputs is central to the operations management task, and the system used for delivering services or products is a vital part of this transformation process. In this chapter, we will look at how the characteristics of services affect the design of service delivery systems, the different methods available to an organization for delivering services to customers, the task of choosing and designing a service delivery system, and the development of IT-based designs. In the next chapter, we'll go on, in a similar way, to look at the process of making and delivering products.

Factors affecting service delivery system design

> **KEY IDEA**
>
> As services differ, so will the designs of their delivery systems

The service delivery system will (as you might imagine) often involve different designs, depending on the type of service that is being delivered. We'll explore how particular aspects of services affect service delivery system design in a moment but, as an introduction, let's look at how two more general aspects of services impact the design – the complexity of the offering itself and the characteristics of the market in which the service is sold:

Technical requirements – the tangible and/or intangible features that make up the technical dimension of a service/product sale

Business requirements – the order-winners and qualifiers that make up the business dimension of a service/product sale

- *Service complexity* This will directly affect the number of steps needed to complete the delivery of the service. In many organizations, the provision of a service is completed as a single step (for example, borrowing books from a library, buying a newspaper or paying in a cheque at your local bank), whereas the processes involved to meet the needs of different patients in a hospital will be made up of several steps and combinations of steps. The design of the service delivery system will, therefore, reflect this complexity.
- *The market* A delivery system must provide the following dimensions to meet market needs:
  - The **technical requirement** – what the service comprises. For example, bread needs to be baked and cheques need to be processed. Completing these tasks requires appropriate technology (in the form of skills and equipment) within the delivery system – in these instances, a baker and ovens, and skilled staff and cheque-processing equipment, respectively.
  - The **business requirement** – how operations decides to provide a service will reflect the volumes involved and the order-winners and qualifiers to be supported.

In order to gain an idea of how market requirements might affect a business in practice, consider how the approach to service delivery might differ between a village bakery and a large bakery company that bakes and delivers bread throughout a city and its suburbs, with several sites around the country. Both businesses must consider:

- The *technical requirements* that comprise the specifications (recipes) of the bread to be made. These will include the types and quantities of ingredients, and the processing and baking cycles for the range of breads in order to provide the desired taste and texture of the products.
- The *business requirements* that comprise the order-winners and qualifiers that, along with the technical dimension, make up the sale. These will include quality conformance (making bread to the specification), the price and the availability of the products on the shelf.

All these requirements are dealt with by operations. In addition, factors such as location, which will be decided by another function in the business, must be taken into account.

In order to deliver the product/service, operations needs the support of technical experts such as systems and IT specialists. For example, the large bakery would have engineering specialists to maintain the equipment and be on hand to respond to technical problems. Similarly, operations managers in call centres would not themselves meet the technical requirements of the systems used by their staff but would look to specialists to fix any technical problems and undertake technical developments.

Operations managers use the necessary system technologies together with other inputs, particularly staff capabilities, to meet a market's needs and the cost profiles and profit targets of the business. Working hand in hand with technical specialists, a key role of operations managers is to choose and develop the service delivery systems that best meet customers' needs. Each delivery system has trade-offs (things it can do well and less well), and these need to be understood by a business and form part of making these key investment decisions.

Characteristics of service operations

Before discussing alternatives, let's look at the characteristics of services that have to be taken into account when designing delivery systems. These include the service/product mix, the intangible nature of services, the simultaneous provision and consumption of services, the time-dependent nature of service capacity (that is, the fact that service capacity cannot be held over for use at a later time), the role of customers in the delivery system and managing services across a range of sites. The extent to which these characteristics will affect the design will, as you would expect, differ from one service offering to another.

Service/product mix

Earlier in the book, we highlighted two important dimensions of services, and it is important to bear these in mind when discussing delivery system design:

- Customer purchases are a mix of both services and products. As Figure 1.9 illustrated, the ratio between these two elements within the mix will vary. In some instances, there will be a heavy accent on services, in others, the reverse.
- The service component of the mix is a package of explicit and implicit benefits performed within a supporting structural facility. The need to identify these three elements was highlighted in Chapter 3, where these terms and concepts were explained.

Customers receive impressions about an organization through their experience of the way a service is delivered. These impressions will affect repeat business and will be created by how well the specification (the technical dimension) and its delivery fit with a customer's expectations, together with the experience a customer has within the service delivery system itself.

Intangible nature of services

Whereas products are tangible (a customer is able to see, feel, inspect and even test a product before purchase), services are not. This presents a problem for both providers and customers. While customers rely on a firm's reputation, recommendations or just 'pot luck', the provider needs to develop a delivery system for the service dimension of the package such that existing customers will purchase again and new customers will be attracted by factors such as reputation and recommendation.

Simultaneous provision and consumption of services

The simultaneous provision and consumption of most services means that **inventory** cannot be used as a way to help absorb fluctuations in demand. Whereas manufacturing

> Inventory – also known as stock, comprises the inputs (materials) into the delivery system or manufacturing process, part-finished items (services or products) within the service delivery system or manufacturing process and outputs (finished items) to be sold or supplied to customers

Decouple – one role that inventory provides is to separate two consecutive elements of a delivery system from each other, a role known as decoupling. This allows the two parts of the delivery system involved to work independently of one another

companies can use inventory as a way of transferring capacity by making products in one time period to be sold in a later time period, most service companies cannot do this. In a manufacturing firm, inventory also serves as a convenient boundary line separating the management of the internal process from the external environment of the market. The result is that inventory can be used to cushion the process at both ends: it **decouples** the system from the suppliers by holding materials and parts at the beginning of the process, and from fluctuations in customer demand by holding finished products at the end. The manufacturing process can thus operate as a closed system and, as a consequence, at a level of output that is deemed most efficient for the overall business. Services, on the other hand, operate in the front-office phase as open systems, and are thus exposed to the full impact of variations in market demand.

As customers are often part of the service delivery system, the design has to be able to handle variations in customer demand effectively. It does this by a combination of varying capacity (for example, the number of staff serving customers) and allowing varying queue lengths to form in order to help absorb changes in the number of customers entering the service delivery system.

Time-dependent capacity

Linked to the last point is the fact that capacity in a service firm is time-dependent. If a hotel room, passenger airline seat, or space on either a container ship, goods train or truck is not used at the time it is available, that capacity is lost for ever. Similarly, if a restaurant cannot seat you for dinner, that sale is lost for ever. Therefore, a service firm has to find ways to handle the fact that unused capacity is perishable (and thereby expensive), while insufficient capacity will lose sales.

Capacity also involves a complex set of issues, as decisions on how much is needed have to be made during the different phases of a delivery system. These design issues include not only how much capacity there needs to be in terms of structural facilities (for example, teller windows in a bank) and staff, but also the shape of the capacity, for example the hours worked and mix of part- and full-time staff in a bank, and which aircraft sizes are needed to best meet the demand profiles of a passenger airline's routes.

> **KEY IDEA**
>
> Services are provided and consumed at the same time. Having too much, therefore, results in unused capacity that cannot be stored for future use, while having too little capacity means that the sale is lost

Customers as participants in the service delivery system

In most service firms, the customer forms part of the delivery system and is often actively engaged in the system itself. The popularity of supermarkets, self-service stores, Internet purchasing and online banking illustrates this phenomenon. From the firm's point of view, the customer provides capacity within the system that helps lower costs and also helps some aspects of the operations management task. For example, where customers undertake part of the role of a server, staff costs and the need to plan staff capacity at this phase of the delivery system are both reduced.

Customer management

Relating to the last point, the design of the delivery system is such that customers and staff are linked. Customers are not just onlookers: their presence creates a dynamic that needs to be managed. For example:

- The supporting structural facilities (such as decor, furnishings and cleanliness) need to meet customer expectations.

- Staff need to be conscious of their roles, how they affect a customer's experience and sense of participation, and the lasting impression that they make (see Case 4.1).
- The level of server discretion (the extent to which staff are permitted to customize the offering) within the service specification needs to be identified, agreed and managed.
- The social dynamics of the customer experience, from entering to leaving the delivery system, need to be accommodated by and accounted for within the system itself. The approach adopted to meet these dimensions needs to form part of the service delivery system design, part of the people skills development and part of the operations management task.

People skills

In service organizations, some staff deal directly with customers, and the customer–server interface often combines both selling and serving. Consequently, the people skills that staff need to develop as part of the delivery system often have a significant effect on a customer's perceived value of the service.

Part of the skill set essential to staff who serve customers is an effective use of the levels of discretion they are allowed to exercise. Developing skills for when they can respond, within agreed limits, to varying customer requests or preferences enables staff to customize the service to better meet customers' needs at little or no extra cost.

Effective services are reproducible

One of the reasons for the emergence of large service companies lies in the improved method of reproducing service delivery systems. Franchise companies (for example, fast-food chains) are classic examples of this. Here, there is control over key elements of the offering and delivery system, such as the physical layout, internal and external decor, range of offerings, purchasing of inputs (for example, food ingredients), service delivery system design, training and equipment, and this is routinely checked by the franchiser. This approach allows companies to expand using the same model and tried and tested approach.

Site selection: proximity to the customer and multisite management

Whereas products are shipped to the customer, in many companies the service provider and customer must physically meet for a service to be performed. As a consequence, many service organizations are made up of small units of capacity sited close to prospective customers. Either the customer comes to the facility (as in a restaurant, retail store, hairdresser or hospital) or the service provider goes to the customer (as in a mobile library or ambulance service). Of course, there are exceptions (such as distance learning), especially with the growing use of IT systems (for example, telephone and Internet banking, online shopping and airline, holiday and theatre ticket sales).

Travel times and costs are thus reflected in the economics underpinning the selection of sites, with many small units of capacity bringing the added task of multisite management. The resulting challenges for an organization include gaining consistency across multiple sites as services are performed in the field, so to speak, and not in a controlled factory environment.

Lack of patents on services

Firms that design their own products have the advantage of patents and licensing agreements to protect them, but the intangible nature of services is more difficult to protect using these legal formats. Although some protection of a service may be afforded by copyright and trademarks, the most effective way to guard the service idea or concept is through designing robust delivery systems that meet the needs of customers and that respond to and proactively lead change and development. Reproducing a comparable delivery system often provides an effective barrier against competition.

CASE 4.1 TIPPING AS A MEASURE OF CUSTOMER SERVICE

Tipping is not a trivial business. For staff, it often represents a substantial portion of their income, while for the organization it provides a tangible measure of the customer's satisfaction with the service provided. Research on what makes customers tip at the end of a service encounter, such as a meal in a restaurant, highlights certain aspects of customer management that can have a general application elsewhere. Some of the key findings include the following:

1 Interacting with a customer throughout the delivery of a service For example:
 • Making initial eye contact and then reinforcing this contact throughout the service encounter
 • Personalizing the service – introducing oneself by name works better than a badge, while even gestures such as writing 'thank you' or drawing a cartoon on a bill together with one's name help personalize the service
 • Smiling warmly and genuinely when greeting a customer and being pleasant throughout
 • Making additional and discreet visits not related to tasks in order to check that all is well and nothing extra is required.

2 Speed of service – there are four occasions when speed of response is important:
 • Delivery of the menu and pre-dinner drinks
 • Taking the food order

 • Delivery of the food
 • The payment process from presenting the bill to conclusion.
But the key is to gauge the optimum speed rather than the maximum speed, and this relates to trying to understand the level of speed a customer wants. Getting the timing right is an essential part of the overall service specification, and the clues are not hard to spot.

3 Goodwill gestures Providing symbols of goodwill such as a complimentary aperitif, bite-size, pre-meal nibbles, a truffle with the bill or an overtly generous measure of pre- and post-dinner drinks all help to create an impression of goodwill and good value.

To an extent, tips reflect fulfilling customers' expectations about the quality of the food and service provided. Getting these right leads not only to satisfied staff, but also to satisfied customers and repeat business.

Questions

1 What makes up the total service offering for a customer during an evening meal at a restaurant?

2 How would the examples here translate into customer management in a boutique or hairdressing salon?

Lecturers: visit www.palgrave.com/business/ hillessential for additional resources

Understanding how services differ

Understanding how services differ is an important prerequisite when designing delivery systems, especially in organizations that offer a range of services that typically require different delivery systems. Here, we will highlight several key differences between services.

The role of technology in service provision

A company needs to select the delivery systems that it will use to provide the services it sells. In part, this concerns the technical dimensions of the items involved, for example:

- A restaurant will need to prepare food in line with the menus on offer and customers' requirements. It will, therefore, need the equipment and skilled staff to undertake the food preparation involved.
- A computer services bureau will need the hardware and skilled staff to enable it to process customers' information requirements.

While the need for appropriate equipment and levels of skilled staff is obvious, a suitable mix and suitable levels further depend on the volumes of sales involved. As we saw in the earlier example of a village baker and a large company bakery, the lower the sales levels, the less justification there is for investing in equipment and processes to complete the task. Figure 4.1 illustrates this point while also giving examples of the mix of equipment and staff in a range of service businesses.

Figure 4.1 **Range of operations requirements within the service delivery system**		
Predominant base	**Level of automation and people skills**	**Examples**
Technology	Automated	Cash dispensing
		Ticket machines
		Vending machines
		Mechanized car washing
	Monitored by unskilled/semi-skilled people	Photocopying
		Dry cleaning
		Gardening
		Tree surgery
		Taxi firm
	Operated by skilled people	Air traffic control
		Computer time-sharing
		Data-processing
People	Unskilled	Cleaning services
		Security guards
	Skilled	Catering
		Vehicle maintenance
		Appliance repairs
	Professional	Lawyers
		Management consultants
		Accountants

The nature of the services to be delivered

The services to be processed by the operations system are different not only in themselves (for example, fast-food and high-quality restaurants provide a different service and product mix, as illustrated in Figure 1.9), but also in terms of the nature of what is involved. The key dimensions that make up these differences are listed below and illustrated in Figure 4.2.

- The complexity of the service to be provided (that is, the number of steps to complete it)
- What is processed in the delivery system – customers, customer surrogates, products, information or some combination of these.

Figure 4.2 **The nature of service processing**

Nature of the service	Examples
Customers	Hairdressing, passenger airlines and health care
Customer surrogates	Car maintenance and repair, dry cleaning and furniture restoration
Products	Retail outlets and vehicle purchases
Information	Mortgage applications, insurance claims and tax advice

Categorizing services

The key dimensions that help to classify services are provided in Figure 4.3. This shows why the system design to deliver a professional service needs to be different from that used in a retail bank or supermarket. Such differences, therefore, need to be taken into account when designing the service delivery system. For example, volumes, levels of service variety and the degree of customization will differ significantly and will need to be catered for within the delivery system design.

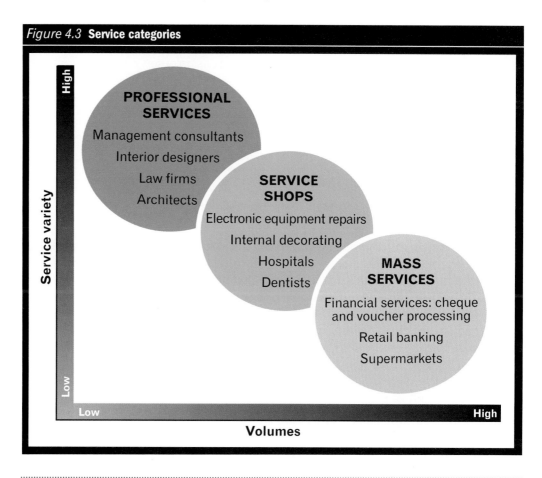

Figure 4.3 **Service categories**

> **KEY IDEA**
> A delivery system processes either customers, customer surrogates, products, information or some combination of these

Complexity of the service

Many customer-based services are relatively simple in terms of the operations process involved and can be delivered as a single-step transaction, for example the front-office process in a retail bank or a take-away food restaurant. Other services, however, need multi-step process provision. For example, whereas a 'dry cut' in a hairdressing salon is a single transaction, a cut and blow-dry requires two or more processes depending upon what is involved. Similarly, the delivery system to provide dinner at the Ritz in London will involve many more steps than having dinner at McDonald's.

Volumes

We've already introduced the idea of the impact of volumes when designing service delivery systems. Figure 4.3 shows the relationship between different categories of services, levels of volume and service variety. The key factors concern the non-repeat or repeat nature of the service offering and the volumes involved. The design of the delivery system will then need to reflect these fundamental dimensions.

Order-winners and qualifiers

Service delivery system design needs to reflect the order-winners and qualifiers for which operations is responsible. These comprise the business dimension of the offering, and the system design needs to be built around this as well as the technical aspect of the service specification.

Designing the service delivery system

Now we've got an idea of the features that characterize services, let's take a closer look at service delivery system design. We'll first deal with aspects of the overall design and then go on to look at the phases involved in the more detailed design of service delivery systems.

Figure 4.4 provides a way of analysing and developing the overall design of a service delivery system. The principal phases are:[1]

- *The market* The market provides the external context in which the service delivery system needs to be set, and is where the process of design and development starts. Identifying volumes and the relevant order-winners and qualifiers to retain and grow the company's share in chosen markets, together with the service mix and design specifications, are the requirements to be met when designing the system.

- *The service encounter and service experience* The service encounter (where and what is delivered) and the service experience (the reality of the service delivered) are the essence of the delivery system. But, as shown in Figure 4.4, each dimension needs to take into account both customers' expectations and what the service delivery system has been designed to provide. For example, the service encounter needs to determine customers' expectations of what will be provided, which, in turn, needs to be set against what the delivery system has been designed to provide (the operations standards that the organization has set). Similarly, the reality of the service delivered (the service experience) needs to match customers' perceptions with operations performance. In this way, customers' needs and the reality of provision will be in line with one another.

  Where customer's expectations exceed what the delivery system has been designed to provide, organizations need to work to adjust customers' expectations. Unless this happens, even though the delivery system meets the specification set, it will fall short of what is expected, and customers will be dissatisfied.

- *Retention* One aim of the service delivery system is to help retain and grow market share. The delivery system design, therefore, needs to monitor its level of success while determining what to do to recover failure situations. As Figure 4.5 shows, although failure impacts on retention rates, a recovery of the service by satisfying customers' complaints can help to counteract the loss of repeat business when customers are dissatisfied and complain.[2]

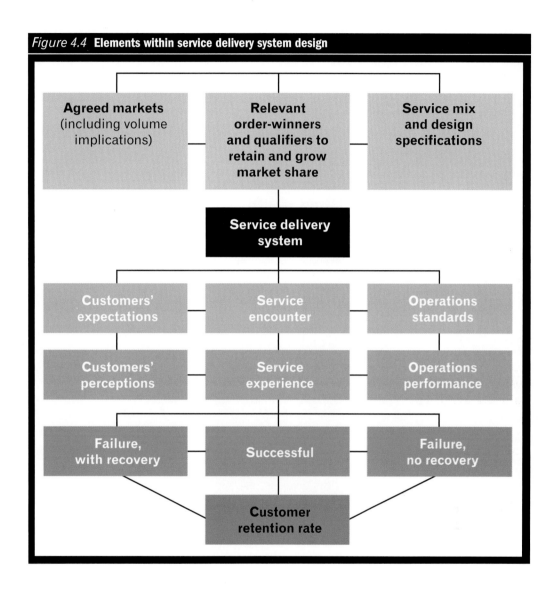

Figure 4.4 **Elements within service delivery system design**

Figure 4.5 **Repurchase intentions of dissatisfied customers**

Level of service recovery	Percentage of customers who will buy again by level of complaint	
	Major	Minor
Complaint not resolved	19	46
Complaint resolved	54	70
Complaint resolved quickly	82	95

Designing the detail of a service delivery system involves two principal phases:

- Phase 1 – addressing the issue of the delivery as a whole. This includes decisions about how and where a system will deliver the service and the point of customer interface.
- Phase 2 – the design of the delivery system itself.

'**Organizations** must clearly understand **customer** needs to **deliver** services effectively'

Phase 1 – the point of customer interface: back office or front office?

For a service to occur, the customer will at some point interface with the delivery system. But at what point and for how long a customer is involved are important factors when designing the service delivery system. The phase of a delivery system where customers are present is referred to as the 'front office' (or sometimes 'front of house'), and the phase where they are not present is known as the 'back office' (or sometimes 'back of house').

In some instances (for example, a hairdresser and a restaurant), customer involvement is not the subject of a decision. Here, the service can only be provided with the customer present. In other instances, how long a customer is involved in the delivery system's front office is, to some extent, a matter of choice. In some circumstances, a company may decide to limit the front-office service provision to what is essential, and complete as much of the service as possible in the back office. For example, paying a bill at the local high-street branch of your bank has both front- and back-office elements. In the front office, the bill and payment are presented and checked by the teller, processed and set aside. The remainder of the transaction is completed in the back office. Similarly, taking garments to be dry cleaned involves the front-office tasks of the customer explaining what is required, payment and the issue of a receipt. The cleaning takes place in the back office, with the garment then being later collected from the front office.

What, then, are the characteristics of the back office and front office that influence the design of the service delivery system?

> Line of visibility – marks the separation between the front and back offices. The 'line' is often, but not always, physical in nature (for example, a wall or partition)

Back office

As we've just mentioned, the key distinction between back office and front office is that, in the former, the activities take place without the customer being present or involved. For this reason, the separation of the front and back office is sometimes referred to as the **line of visibility**, highlighting what parts of the delivery system a customer can and cannot see. Some of the advantages of completing work in the back office include:

- *Easier scheduling* Undertaking tasks in the back office means that the system does not need to respond immediately to customer demands; this allows completion of the work to be planned for when it best suits the system itself. For example, choosing to delay completing the work means that scheduling what to do and when to do it can occur in line with staff availability, when it best fits in with other work priorities and so on.

- *Higher processing volumes* Similarly, delaying completion allows the back-office system to accumulate volumes of work so that tasks can be undertaken more efficiently as all the work can be done at the same time. Furthermore, in a bank, for example, back-office tasks such as cheque clearance and bank statement preparation can be accumulated still further by bringing together the demands of many high-street bank branches. Using regional or even national centres for these tasks creates even higher volumes that justify more process investment, leading to lower overall processing costs.

Front office

On the other side of the 'line of visibility' is the front-office portion of the system, in which customer contact occurs. The characteristics inherent in this part of the system include:

- *Structural facilities* As the customer is present in this part of the system, the structural facilities need to reflect the organization's standards and meet customers' expectations. Ambience, decor, staff presentation and speed of response need to reflect the company's desired image and its customers' expectations.

- *Lead-times* As customer contact occurs here, the system needs to be able to meet the service specification while having sufficient capacity to meet the service targets related to queuing (the time a customer waits), the length of time it takes to deliver the service and the costs of having too much capacity.

- *Ease of customer use* The design must make it easy for customers to interface with the system as customers will then be encouraged to use the organization's preferred method of delivering the service, for example getting cash from an ATM instead of inside the bank branch.

To help illustrate how organizations split delivery systems into front and back offices, Figure 4.6 gives some examples, while Case 4.2 provides two examples of how companies have changed the front office/back office mix in order to influence customer perceptions on the one hand, and improve service provision on the other.

Figure 4.6 **Examples of front- and back-office activities in selected service organizations**

Part of the delivery system	Illustrations		
	Passenger airline	**Hotel**	**Supermarket**
Front office – direct customer contact	· Reservation and booking changes · Check-in · Departures and arrivals lounges · In-flight attendance · Flight transfers · Airport information desk	· Sales agents · Reservations · Reception · Concierge · Restaurant and bar staff · Switchboard	· Checkout · Fish, cheese and deli counters · Tobacco and sundry sales · Dry cleaning counter · Restaurant and café
Back office – no customer contact	· Aircraft maintenance · Flight preparation · Accounts · Refunds · Administration · Self-check-in system maintenance	· Administration · Accounts · Human resources · Kitchen	· Warehouse · Shelf provisioning · Bakery · Dry cleaning · General cleaning · Maintenance · Administration

Phase 2 – the delivery system

Earlier, Figure 4.3 introduced the principal ways to categorize services as 'professional services', 'service shops' and 'mass services', which provides a useful starting point. But, in reality, many organizations provide a range of services that fall into more than one of these categories. For example, within a law firm, house conveyancing (the steps to transfer the legal ownership of a property from the seller to the buyer) involves a set of standard procedures typically completed by junior staff. The process is known, and there are well-documented steps to be followed, with clear guidelines and pre-printed forms containing questions that need to be answered by third parties as well as internal staff themselves. At the other end of the spectrum, there will be one-off, non-repeat, complicated cases requiring technical and legal advice in a specialist field. Clearly, these two tasks do not fall within the same service category.

Similarly, the services in a hospital range from refreshment facilities through reception to surgery, postoperative care and rehabilitation. There will be outpatient clinics, accident and emergency provision and ambulance services that range from paramedic tasks at the scene of an accident to routine collection services for disabled or elderly patients. Although categorized as a service shop, the full scope of services provided by a hospital will need to be allocated to all three broad categories.

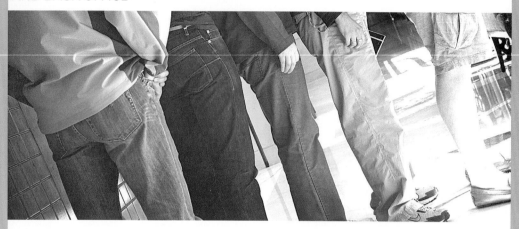

INFLUENCING CUSTOMER PERCEPTIONS AT ROYAL BANK OF CANADA

Royal Bank of Canada believes that customers' perceptions are a critical factor in service provision. The bank considers that, when queues form, customers' attitudes to waiting are affected by both the server's attitude when they are eventually attended to, and the fact that, when they are waiting, they have judged the service in terms of the level of staff attendance shown in the front office. Thus, if bank staff are doing jobs other than attending to customers, and the queues are long, customers' attitudes to the bank's overall regard for service provision are affected. Thus, the bank's aim is to transfer as much paperwork as possible to head office or the back office.

www.rbc.com

CHANGING THE POINT WHERE CUSTOMERS INTERFACE WITH THE DELIVERY SYSTEM

An electrical repair shop recently changed the customer interface point in the delivery system. Whereas previously the customer explained the repair needs to those in the front office, the customer now takes the repair to the back office and discusses the problem with the person who will complete the repair. Everyone gains. The repair person can now ensure that all pertinent questions are covered, and the customer is able to discuss the repair both before and after the service has been completed. This, of course, has long been the arrangement in many good quality dressmakers and tailors.

Questions

1 How do these two examples differ?

2 What are the benefits and disadvantages of the alternative approaches in the two examples?

Lecturers: visit www.palgrave.com/business/hillessential for additional resources

Non-repeat services – unique services that are not provided in the same format more than once; the term also applies to services where the gap between one provision and the next is too long for the gains of repetition (resulting from investing in the system to reduce costs) to be realized

It therefore follows that, as services differ, so will their delivery system designs. This section describes the different systems and the types of service they are used to support. The key characteristics underpinning these differences are the non-repeat or repeat nature of a service, the range of volumes involved in the latter, and whether the delivery system is designed as a single-step or a multi-step process.

Non-repeat services

As the name implies, services in this category are unique (known also as 'specials') and will not be provided in the same format a second time. Examples include interior design, legal advice for a business merger or takeover, financial advice for a stock exchange placement, executive development by one-to-one coaching and the design and installation of tailor-made IT systems.

Providers of **non-repeat services** sell their skills and capabilities to meet a customer's specific needs. In this way, the service specification is determined by the customer, with changes to what is required often being made throughout its delivery. Order-winners such as having a unique set of skills (being the best), referrals and repeat business are characteristic of the way this type of market works. Although customer orders will not be price-sensitive, the price for a service will need to be competitive (that is, in an acceptable price band) but one that yields high margins. For non-repeat services, price is a qualifier (prices have to be competitive by being in the acceptable price band) and not an order-winner. On the other hand, where price is an order-winner, a company will compete on price, with services and products typically yielding lower margins.

The delivery system used for non-repeat services involves one person or a small group of skilled people providing all the service. The provider's role will include helping to identify what is required, determining the best process to follow and undertaking all the other steps involved through to and including implementation of the service. As the service will not be repeated, the opportunity to invest in the delivery system is not available and could not be justified, given the volumes involved. What is transferred from one service provision to the next is the provider's capability and skill base, and the experience gained from providing other one-off services in the past.

Repeat services

Most organizations provide services that are deemed standard (that is, they have been provided before) rather than special. The repeat and higher volume nature of standard services signals a need to consider a different delivery system designed to take advantage of these characteristics. The volumes involved, however, can range from low to very high, and this factor will be reflected in the design of the service delivery system used.

To illustrate this, let's take a transcontinental air flight. At the extremes, there will be first-class and economy cabins. Although all passengers are travelling to the same destination and both classes of seat are repeat service offerings, the delivery system will show marked differences. Check-in arrangements, pre-boarding lounge facilities, carry-on luggage allowances, cabin staff to passenger ratios, the range of food, drinks and beverages, the level of customization provided, choices of in-flight entertainment, and disembarkation and luggage collection priorities will all differ, and the design of the service delivery systems will reflect these differences.

Earlier, Figure 4.3 provided other examples of **repeat services** and illustrated the different volume levels associated with these offerings. Where volume is higher, factors such as service variety, level of price sensitivity and degree of customization will change, as shown in Figure 4.7. Higher volumes justify the higher levels of process investment necessary to support the associated order-winning nature of price. Where possible, work is deskilled, with the process investment completing more of the task; this, in turn, will result in lower staff costs in terms of both skill levels and work content. Figure 4.7 summarises some of the principal factors in delivery system design that reflect the non-repeat/repeat nature of the service offering and the levels of volume involved.

Now, take a look at Case 4.3, which gives an example of an unusual service delivery system design in the field of eye surgery.

Single-step or multi-step process

A key decision in the design of a system concerns the number of steps to be taken in delivering the service. A **single-step design** implies that the complete service is delivered as a single transaction – for example, getting cash from an ATM or purchasing a newspaper from a shop. In a **multi-step delivery system**, the first part of the design process is to break down the service into a number of steps. How many steps there are will depend on the complexity of the service involved. The activities in each step that make up the total service will then be determined. These will be done separately, by different staff and normally in different parts of the system. Splitting the task into a number of smaller steps is a form of investment in itself, and is one way to help undertake the task more efficiently by accumulating similar activities from a range of services and completing these in the same part of the delivery system (for example, the pharmacy and X-ray functions in a hospital). This also provides the potential for staff specialization and process investments.

Consider, for example, customers entering a service delivery system such as a hospital. The patients (that is, the customers) will initially go to reception and staff will process them, such as by recording relevant details. Patients will then go to the next step in the process (for example, to see a specialist consultant) and, having waited, will go through that stage of the treatment. They will then go through the next steps in the same way until the total service has been completed. A similar example is provided in Figure 4.8 (p. 126), which outlines the steps in two delivery systems in a dental surgery.

With information-processing, the procedure is again broken down into a number of steps, the total of which completes the whole process. As in the hospital example, the documents go from step to step, with each step typically involving waiting time, a single set-up or preparation stage, and processing of all the documents at the same time. This waiting between steps allows processes to work independently of one another (decoupling) and hence more efficiently, while the processing of all the documents at one stage reduces the number of set-ups involved and increases the volume processed for any one step at any one time.

Now let's address the question of why organizations choose a multi-step rather than a single-step delivery system design. The factors to be taken into account include the following:

- *Delivering the service involves a range of staff skill levels* When delivering a service comprises a range of skill levels, organizations seek to keep costs low by allocating the activities and tasks involved to staff with the relevant skill sets. If a hospital were set up as a single-step system, the health-care specialist would record a patient's details, undertake the consultation, complete the X-ray, check to confirm the nature of the broken limb, apply the plaster and make the next appointment. But the delivery of such a service is much more suited to a multi-step design in which the various tasks are performed by different staff who specialize in different areas to deliver different parts

Repeat services – services that are provided more than once. The level of repetition may range from low volume (which makes delivery system design more like that for non-repeat services) through to very high volume

Single-step delivery system – when a service is delivered using a single step

Multi-step delivery system – when a service is delivered using two or more steps

CASE 4.3 SERVICE DELIVERY AT THE MOSCOW SCIENTIFIC INSTITUTE FOR EYE MICROSURGERY

For most of us, our perception of hospital surgery is one of delicate and sensitive operations. In reality, though, many surgical approaches are routine and comprise a series of standard steps and procedures. One surgeon who took this dimension to an extreme was the prominent Russian eye surgeon, Dr Svyatoslav Fyodorov. In his Institute for Eye Microsurgery (which has continued to operate in his name since his tragic death in an accident in 2000), the surgical treatment for myopia (short-sightedness) is a procedure called radical keratotomy. During this, patients lie on moving theatre tables, six surgeons perform their part of the operation, and then each patient moves on to the next stage. Surgeons check the previous step(s) in the surgical process, perform their own step, and then the process continues onwards. TV screens, microphones and headsets enable visual and voice contact to be maintained throughout between the surgeons.[3]

http://eng.mntk.ru

Question

What advantages and disadvantages does this approach bring compared with alternative approaches?

FACTORS REFLECTED IN SERVICE DELIVERY SYSTEM DESIGN	
Service variety	
Level of customization	
How orders are won?	typical order-winners
	typical qualifiers
Volumes	
Delivery system	design
	level of flexibility
Ability of delivery system to cope with	service change
	new services
Dominant factor of utilization	
Prior knowledge of the operations task	
Level of process investment	
Staff skill levels	

NON-REPEAT SERVICES	REPEAT SERVICES	
	Low volume	High volume
Wide	→	Narrow
High	→	Low
Design, response to change	→	Price
Price	On-time delivery and quality conformance[a]	
Low	→	High
General and unspecified	→	Specified and dedicated
High	→	Low
High	→	Low
High	→	Low
Staff	→	Process
Not well defined	→	Well defined
Low	→	High
High	→	Low

Note: [a] The qualifiers 'On-time delivery and quality conformance' are typical of all markets, as shown ab

Figure 4.8 Patients visiting a dental surgery – an example of a multi-step delivery system

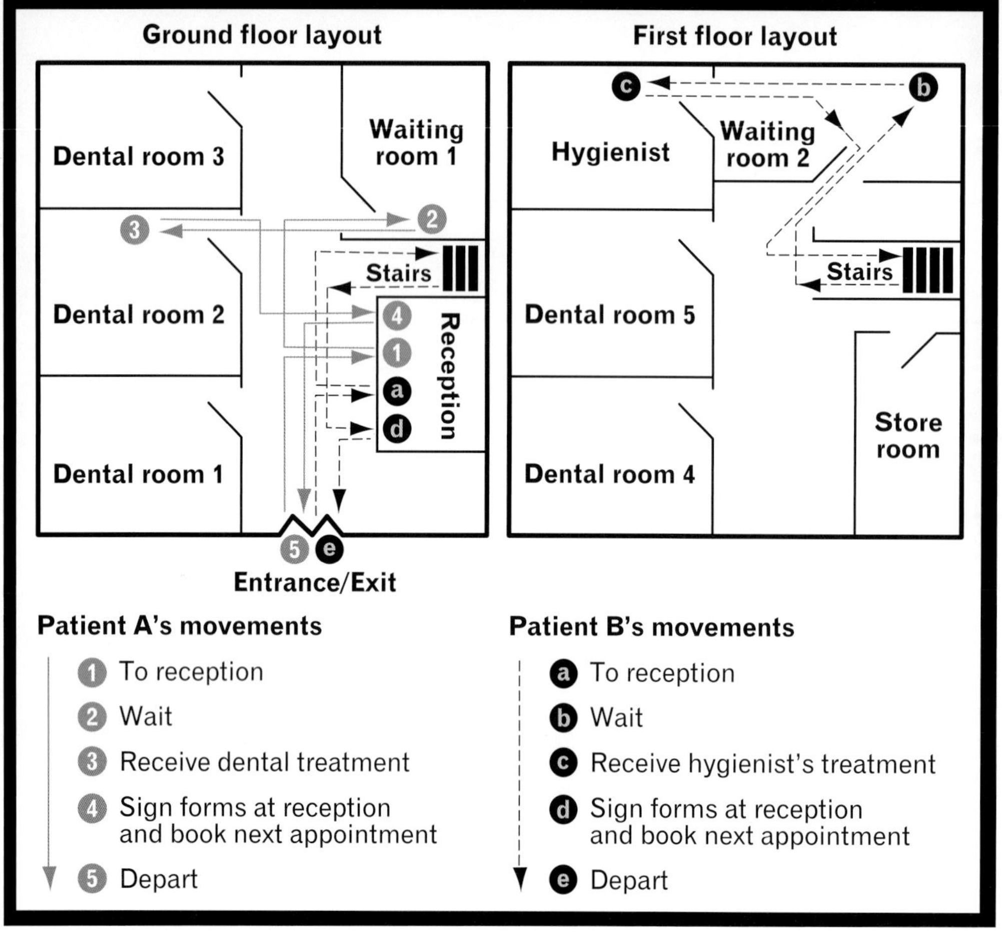

Ground floor layout

Dental room 3

Waiting room 1

③

②

Stairs

Dental room 2

④

①

ⓐ

ⓓ

Reception

Dental room 1

Entrance/Exit

⑤ ⓔ

First floor layout

ⓒ

ⓑ

Hygienist

Waiting room 2

Stairs

Dental room 5

Dental room 4

Store room

Patient A's movements

① To reception

② Wait

③ Receive dental treatment

④ Sign forms at reception and book next appointment

⑤ Depart

Patient B's movements

ⓐ To reception

ⓑ Wait

ⓒ Receive hygienist's treatment

ⓓ Sign forms at reception and book next appointment

ⓔ Depart

of a service. Thus, health-care specialists restrict their involvement to their area of specialism, with other tasks being completed in a more cost-effective way in terms of staff skills, and with each step of the process being provided by specialized and more effective procedures and approaches to completing the tasks involved. By processing customers step by step, the capacity at each step in the process is used and reused to meet the different requirements of different customers, with volumes justifying process investment and leading to a more overall cost-effective provision.

- *The service specification is complex* Where services are relatively simple, they lend themselves to being delivered by a single-step system. Where services are more complex, companies typically provide them in a multi-step format. One reason is that matching the task requirement to the appropriate skill set is easier to schedule.

- *Volumes can be enhanced* Using a multi-step design to provide a number of services brings together similar steps from two or more services to be completed in the same function or area. The higher volumes that result provide scope for cost reduction by creating the opportunity to invest in the process, develop specialist skill sets and match each step in the service to the required skill levels and salary grades that go with these.

Now look at Case 4.4 to reflect on the choices that need to be considered.

IT-based service delivery system designs

When designing delivery systems, many organizations have used developments in IT to rethink approaches. Such developments have not only reduced costs and lead-times within systems and procedures, but also enabled organizations to redesign many of these delivery systems, as the following examples illustrate.

Source: Barclays Bank PLC

If you go into the local high-street branch of your bank and want to collect foreign currency, pay cash into your account and discuss your account details, you will have to use three different, single-step delivery systems to meet your needs. Each of these will only deal with a limited number of the total range of services the bank provides. On the other hand, if you go into a post office, you will stand in one queue, and all the services you require will be delivered by the one teller.

Question

What is the fundamental difference in service delivery design in these two examples?

Lecturers: visit www.palgrave.com/business/hillessential for additional resources

Automated banking

Banks are continuing to cut costs by automating more of their services. For example, ATMs are now the principal way to get cash from your bank account. Increasingly, banks are adding video displays selling insurance and providing details on loans, as well as screens offering share quotations. In parts of Europe and the US, fully automated bank branches are replacing traditional set-ups, offering all the usual range of services but without bank tellers, and in the UK automated machines for depositing cash and cheques have become commonplace.

Teleworking

Since the early 1980s, companies have been extending the practice of using computers and telephone links so their staff can work away from their offices. 'Home offices' are an established part of this growing trend, while companies are making increasingly heavy use of telecommuting, a policy that allows employees to work in the office one or two days a week and spend the rest of the time with clients and working from home. Jack Nilles, the 'father of teleworking', coined the phrases 'teleworking' and 'telecommuting' in 1973 while leading a research project at the University of Southern California into the impact of IT at work.[4]

Teleworking brings benefits including productivity increases of 20 per cent or more, reduced office space requirements and lower staff turnover levels. In addition, benefits to a nation's economy are significant. It is estimated that traffic congestion costs the UK economy more than $100 billion in lost productivity annually, while London commuters waste more than 10 hours per week going to work. In the US, clean air legislation is obliging large firms to reduce their commuter workforce. And by 2008, 17.2 million employees in the US worked some of their time remotely. Whereas in the late 1970s there were very few teleworkers, by the first part of this century the figure had grown to 30 million worldwide, and it is predicted to reach 200 million by 2016.

E-commerce

The Internet has the capability to personalize a service as it can be tailored itself to every one of its millions of users. Similar benefits at the retail end of the spectrum have also been realized through company intertrading that covers dealings with suppliers as well as customers. Corporate intranets can be linked in order to provide a safe, secure, manageable, business-to-business environment, with e-commerce becoming an integrated part of the customer–supplier partnership. Dealing with customers and suppliers through e-commerce has profound implications for the way companies operate and, as more users gain access to the Internet, the need for organizations to incorporate relevant technologies into the design of their delivery systems is crucial. Here are some examples of online service developments.

Travel booking

Since its early days, online travel booking has grown rapidly. The European online market is forecast to continue to grow by 20–30 per cent a year, compared with single-digit growth for the travel industry as a whole. Part of this growth has been boosted by the no-frills passenger airline phenomenon and the pressure from companies such as Ryanair and EasyJet to force customers to book online; their success here has encouraged more traditional airlines to move to increase their online bookings.

Call centres

Whether the vendor is a PC manufacturer providing a helpdesk for users, a gas or electric distribution company answering queries or a financial services company handling account and general enquiries through to mortgage and personal loan applications, call centres have become the preferred solution.

The advances in computer telephony integration have enabled call centres to replace traditional service departments by linking the telephone to a computer that routes calls to the most appropriate agent, prompts the agent with caller data (known as 'screen popping') and leads the agent through a script to produce answers to thousands of different questions. Call centres cut staff costs compared with multisite arrangements, in terms of both the number of staff required and the opportunity to locate call centres in lower wage rate areas. With call centres, customers are offered free or low-rate telephone calls to encourage their use, and international centres allow customers to call a local number, the system then transferring them to an overseas agent who speaks their own language.

In addition, some companies (for example, Dell) transfer calls from one region to another (for example, mainland Europe to the UK or Ireland and then to the eastern seaboard of the US, and so on) as a way of efficiently handling the times during a 24-hour period when the number of calls in a particular region is low. For example, bookings and enquiries for Radisson Hotels in Europe and the Middle East are handled by the Group's call centre in Dublin from 7 am to 7 pm. The operation handles more than 1,000 calls daily, with 22 incoming telephone lines (all freephone) operated by 25 staff speaking 11 different languages. From 7 pm, the service switches to operations in the US.

Grocery shopping

After its first tentative steps, online grocery shopping is gaining ground. Competitors in the field have, however, chosen different ways to provide this service. Ocado, the UK's first e-grocer, has taken a warehouse-based approach. Its dedicated picking and delivery system is based at its depot in Hatfield, north of London, which is the size of seven soccer pitches, or about 20 average supermarkets. Others using the warehouse model include Coborns Delivers in Minneapolis, GreenGrocer.com in Australia and Carrefour, Europe's biggest retailer, based in France.

Tesco (the UK's largest supermarket), among others, has taken a different approach. It developed its own technology to enable it to use store-based picking – a low-investment route to this new type of shopping. This approach is now gaining ground in the US, with Safeway, California's biggest supermarket group, being one of the early adopters. In 2003, Tesco's Internet food sales was close on £500 million. By 2008/09, food and non-food Internet sales had risen to £1.9 billion, up 20 per cent from the previous year. Using this model, Tesco estimates that it can service up to £3 billion of sales through its existing stores. On the other hand, Sainsbury's (a large UK supermarket) has chosen a hybrid model, with a warehouse in north London but most sales done through store-based picking. In 2008/09, food-only sales exceeded £500 million, with 100,000 orders per week.

Now take a look at Case 4.5 for a further illustration.

Further aspects of service delivery

This section introduces some additional issues that organizations need to consider when developing the overall design of their service delivery systems.

Enhancing services

Companies basing their approach on service differentiation employ several strategies to enhance the service they are providing. One way is to bring the intangible aspects of a service to the attention of a customer by making them tangible. By doing this, parts of a service package that may go unnoticed by the customer now become a visible part of the provision. For example:

- Maid service in a hotel bedroom can include collars placed on toilets with phrases such as 'Sanitized for your personal use', end-folded toilet paper and folding down the bed in the evening, with a personalized note and guest room checklist duly completed.

Shopping for plants at the online nursery Garden Escape offers many benefits – not only because the website lists unusual plants, but also because Garden Escape creates a personal 'store' for regular customers. Greeted by name on your personal page each time you visit, you can make notes on a private online notepad, tinker with garden plans using the site's interactive design program, and get answers from the Garden Doctor. As they are getting such a personalized service, many customers rarely go elsewhere.

www.burpee.com

Question

What are the advantages of shopping on the Internet? Do you see any problems?

- Prompt service is also made tangible in one of several ways – many hotels guarantee an in-room breakfast that will be provided free of charge if it is not delivered within 10 minutes of the requested time. Domino's Pizza promises to deliver an order to your home within 30 minutes (in normal demand times) or 40 minutes (peak demand times), or the pizza will be replaced or the customer's money refunded. In practice, this means that if a delivery is late, customers will be asked to pay for the pizza(s) but not (for example) the soft drink(s) or dessert(s). Furthermore, if a delivery is considered very late (20 minutes or more), the whole order is offered free of charge. The Domino's Pizza replace or refund policy also applies to its quality guarantee.

- A car wash given free with a routine service or paper covers left inside the vehicle demonstrates to customers the level of care taken by the company when providing the core element of the service.

Customer participation in service delivery

When designing the delivery system, organizations need to decide the extent to which customers will or will not participate in the creation of the service. The degree of customer involvement in the system affects many factors, including the provision and management of capacity, service levels, staff training requirements and costs.

Employing the do-it-yourself concept in service delivery systems has been gaining ground over the last several decades. Various examples can be given of service industries increasingly using this approach:

- *Supermarkets* control over 80 per cent of the gross retail market and sell principally on a self-service basis.
- *Fast-food outlets* form a growing part of overall restaurant provision.
- *Telephone services* are principally based on subscriber dialing, with almost all telephone calls now being made by customers.
- *Petrol stations* use self-service as the basis for providing fuel, screen washing and oil, water and tyre pressure checks.
- *Online shopping* is a major provider in the retail industry. It requires a customer to complete the selection, application and payment parts of the procedure, with the business providing fast delivery once the transaction is fed into the service system.
- *Financial services* provide a growing range of products through self-service delivery systems from ATMs, general banking, insurance, mortgages and personal loans.

The reasons for the growth in these sectors vary; Figure 4.9 summarises some factors that relate to their success, while Case 4.6 provides an illustration.

Figure 4.9 **Success factors of self-service approaches**						
Success factors	**Selected service sectors**					
	Super-markets	**Fast-food outlets**	**Telephone services**	**Petrol stations**	**Online shopping**	**Financial services**
Faster service	✓	✓	✓	✓	✓	✓
Lower price	✓	✓	✓	✓	✓	✓
Improved product quality	✓	✓				
Increased product variety	✓				✓	
More convenient	✓	✓			✓	✓
More customer control within the delivery system	✓	✓	✓	✓	✓	✓

The downside of supermarket shopping is queuing to pay. To speed up this part of the delivery system, retailers are looking for ways to involve customers in this last step of the process. For some time now, the facility has been available for self-scanning your purchases as you go and then paying at a designated checkout. Similarly, self-check-outs are gaining popularity and are now well established throughout major supermarket stores. With these, the system uses visual and voice commands to talk customers through the process. Bar codes are swiped in the normal way, while for loose items such as vegetables and fruit, price by weight details are stored on a database. If an item does not register properly, the voice system asks the customer to scan it again.

Lack of pre-registering and ease of use appeal to those who simply wish to shop and go. With the average person in the UK spending two hours in queues every week (even with Internet banking and shopping), user-friendly forms of self-service are gaining ground.

www.ncr.com; www.safeway.com; www.sainsbury.co.uk; www.optimalgrp.com; www.marksandspencer.com; www.waitrose.com

Questions

1 Why are supermarkets introducing self-checkout systems?

2 Consumers recently ranked self-check-out technology as second only to cash machines in terms of the self-service they were most likely to use. Why?

Lecturers: visit www.palgrave.com/business/hillessential for additional resources

Critical reflections

Although how a company chooses to meet the technical specification of its service offerings will affect the design of its delivery systems, operations managers must also ensure that their design decisions:

- Are aligned to the order-winners and qualifiers of its chosen markets
- Reflect the internal requirements of the organization, such as capacity utilization, control of costs, queue lengths and the interface with customers
- Incorporate IT and other development opportunities to help keep the business competitive and improve its ability to meet customers' requirements.

This chapter has emphasized how businesses must recognize the key differences that exist between services and then incorporate these differences into the design of their delivery systems. Organizations need first to recognize the fundamental differences in approach that result (Figure 4.10), check their desired position on relevant factors and then incorporate these approaches into their delivery system designs.

Figure 4.10 **Factors in reactive and proactive service delivery system design**

Factors		Service delivery system design	
		Reactive	Proactive
Delivery system design	objective	Streamlined and efficient	Customer-focused
	structure	Rigid	Responsive
	design premise	Events are consistent and unchanging	Change acknowledged and built into the design
	approach to service failure	Prevention	Recovery
	response to service failure	Not designed in the system	Integral part of system design
	role of server in quality conformance provision	Procedures specify server behaviour	Proactive response expected
Achieving quality conformance	systems design	Built into the system	Built into the staff
	error handling	Refer to another level	Dealt with on the spot
	level of recovery	Low and slow	High and immediate
	response to failure	Back-office management	Frontline staff
	quality objective	System has zero defects	Customer-centric
Staff	attitude	Lack of involvement	Part of provision and solution
	level of discretion	Low and not encouraged	High and encouraged
	attitude to failure	Part of failure	Part of recovery solution and then part of success
	level of motivation	Frustration leading to lack of interest	Part of service provision leading to becoming involved and motivated

What underpins the drive to develop delivery systems that meet the needs of customers is the impact they have on market share, retention and growth. Online retailers estimate that there is no overall profit on transactions until a customer has returned three or even four times. Similarly, as Figure 4.11 shows, keeping customers grows profit. Aligning delivery systems to markets is, therefore, a key task and requires a sound corporate understanding of what is needed and how systems are to be developed.

Figure 4.11 **Trends in annual profit per customer**

Sector	Annual profit/customer				
	1	2	3	4	5
Car servicing	100	140	280	350	350
Credit cards	100	250	283	290	309
Distribution	100	220	270	320	373

Note: Figures indexed on year 1.

Summary

- A key decision for any company is how to deliver its services in order to meet both the needs of its customers and the objectives of the business.

- Factors that must be taken into account are divided into the technical requirement (what the service specification comprises) and the business requirement (the order-winners and qualifiers for the chosen market). Together, these requirements form the service offering, which is experienced by the customer.

- Decisions about service delivery system design are influenced by the distinctive characteristics of the service and the features of the overall and detailed service delivery system design.

- The impact of IT and other developments on design alternatives has been described in the chapter, and examples have been provided to illustrate the continued impact on service delivery.

- Finally, the other issues to be considered in delivering services were explained, with examples.

Study activities

Discussion questions

1 Choose a service company that uses at least two of the delivery systems detailed in this chapter. Explain why a company would have made such choices.

2 Based on Figure 4.2, identify an organization that illustrates one of the examples given for each of the four types (customers, customer surrogates, products and information). Then provide an overview (two or three lines) to show what is processed (for example, customer and information).

3 Why is queuing often an integral part of a service system design?

4 For a service company of your choice explain:

- The service delivery system design

- How the company could reduce queues within the system.

5 Review the data in Figures 4.5 and 4.11. Why do the results seem to make sense?

Assignments

1 Envisage going to the emergency unit of your local hospital with a suspected broken wrist. List the key steps in the delivery system in which you would be involved. What type of system is used at each step?

2 Select a company (other than the examples provided in the chapter) to illustrate a:

- Non-repeat business
- Repeat business – low volume
- Repeat business – high volume.

For each, outline the service delivery used.

Exploring further

Journal articles

Dixon, M., Freeman, K. and Toman, N. (2010) 'Stop trying to delight your customers'. *Harvard Business Review*, **88**(7), pp. 116–22. The notion that companies must go above and beyond in their customer service activities is so entrenched that managers rarely examine it. The article studied more than 75,000 people interacting with call centre representatives or using self-service methods and found that over-the-top efforts made little difference: all customers really wanted was a simple, quick solution to their problem.

Books

Hill, T. (1998) *The Strategy Quest. Releasing the Energy of Manufacturing Within a Market Driven Strategy: a Dynamic Business Story.* Available from AMD Publishing, Dousland. This book (written as a novel) describes how an art business and manufacturing organization restructure themselves to meet the changing demands of their customers.

Rowley, J. (2002) E-business: *Principles and Practice*. Basingstoke: Palgrave Macmillan. This provides a comprehensive review of e-business, including the choice of technologies, website design, serving customers and e-business strategies.

Teboul, J. (2006) *Service is Front Stage*. Basingstoke: INSEAD Business Press/Palgrave Macmillan. This provides a classification of services and identifies the quality gaps that occur while emphasizing the need to meet customer requirements.

Notes and references

1 See also the approach to service delivery system design in Heskett, J.L., Jones, T.O., Loveman, G.W., Sasser, W.E., Jr. and Schlesinger, L.A. (1994) 'Putting the service–profit chain to work', *Harvard Business Review*, March–April, pp. 164–74.

2 See also Hart, C.W.L., Heskett, J.L. and Sasser, W.E., Jr. (1990) 'The profitable art of service recovery', *Harvard Business Review*, July–August, pp. 148–56; Reinartz, W. and Kumar, V. (2000) 'The mismanagement of customer loyalty', *Harvard Business Review*, July, pp. 4–12.

3 Smoland, M. and Cohen, D. (1987) *A Day in the Life of the Soviet Union*. London: Collins, pp. 66–7.

4 Jack Nilles' books include *Managing Telework*, published in 1998 by John Wiley & Sons, New York.

HISTORY

BA's origins go back to the birth of civil aviation following the First World War when, in 1919, it offered the world's first daily international scheduled air service between London and Paris. Since then, it has been through some turbulent times. It lost $1 billion in 1986, was privatized in 1987, was voted the world's best airline in 1989, but then started losing customers to low-cost airlines in 1992. To fight back, BA asked passengers and cabin crews what they thought of its service and how it could be improved. The feedback showed that service levels were considered acceptable but predictable. To rectify this, BA redesigned cabins and services based on the principle 'If you don't do it on the ground, why do it in the air?' It introduced new seats, increased the hand baggage allowance, created more in-flight storage space and introduced higher quality food such as pastas and salads. Passengers were encouraged to design their own service specification – for example, they could sleep as long as they wanted on overnight trans-Atlantic flights without being woken for breakfast and were encouraged to 'raid the larder' that offered a range of snacks. The aim was to create a comfortable atmosphere in which passengers could, in part, design their own service.

Customers responded well but BA didn't stand still. In 1999, it launched its 'Putting People First Again' programme, in which all 62,000 employees underwent intensive customer service training to improve the level of service given and make passengers' end-to-end journeys as smooth as possible. Executive lounges were increased and redesigned with discrete 'zones' to suit customer needs or moods, including a combiz centre (business centre), world wine bar, library, larder, cappuccino and juice bar, sanctuary and terrace. Passengers flying from the US east coast to Europe could also have dinner before take-off. Arrival lounges were introduced at Heathrow, Gatwick and Johannesburg where customers could shower, have their clothes pressed, breakfast and make telephone calls before starting their day. These were all significant improvements, but the revolution came with the introduction of beds into business class in March 2000. Customers could now turn their seat into a flat 1.83 m bed at the click of a button, and the number of seats in each cabin was reduced to give 30 per cent more personal space. It seemed that BA had the business traveller market all wrapped up, but the competition had other ideas.

BATTLE FOR THE SKIES

Competition for business class customers increased significantly in the early 2000s, but its intensity varied depending on the regulatory environment, route, number of competitors and whether these were state-owned/state-supported or not. At one extreme, some international routes had regulated fares and BA only competed with state-owned competitors. At the other end, on internal European flights, any European airline could operate on any route and set whatever fares it wished. Strong competition in the European market led to consolidation between airlines trying to reduce costs, while the quality and number of competitors increased in Asia and the Middle East. Despite these developments, it was actually BA's old UK rival, Virgin Atlantic, that took away its coveted 'Best Business Class' Business Traveller Award in 2006 after a $312 million investment in cabin seat configuration, flat beds, four complementary limousine journeys per return flight and number of in-flight services such as a bar, a massage and a place to sit and have a meal. Not only did Virgin offer a superior service to BA's, but it was also often less expensive.

In 2008, BA achieved a 10 per cent gross profit for the first time ever, through improved operational performance and new services, but then came the economic downturn. Falling business traveller sales and increasing oil prices contributed to the company making a record loss of £600 million in 2009 (equivalent to 2 per cent of its sales revenue), when oil prices had risen to a record high. The company received mixed responses to its Club World service and was hampered by cabin crew strikes in 2009 and 2010. Its loyal customers have been happy with what BA has done, but some critics feel it is still lagging behind the competition. For instance, Singapore Airlines spent $310 million upgrading its fleet in 2009, and its new business class flat bed now has memory stick ports allowing passengers to fly without their laptops. The question asked by many analysts has been, how can BA reduce its costs and maintain sales in these tough economic times within such a competitive and constantly changing market?

BACK TO THE DRAWING BOARD

To work out how to improve its service, BA again surveyed business class passengers who had flown with them in the previous five years. It found that space, comfort, privacy, control and storage were most important. Using this feedback, it launched its new Club World service in 2007 by investing $184 million in new seats, audio-visual services on demand with 50 films, 60 hours of TV and 50 hours of music, touch-screen TV screens, noise-cancelling headphones, a laptop plug socket and a storage drawer. A more extensive and flexible food menu was also introduced, with a range of hot and cold snacks and drinks in the Club Kitchen, which replaced the 'raid the larder' concept.

Major IT investments were also made to improve customer service and lower costs. All employees were given company e-mail accounts, and an Employee Self Service (ESS) extranet site was created allowing administration tasks to be completed online. The 'ba.com website' was also updated, enabling customers to compare products, buy tickets, reserve hotels, hire cars, book tours, manage bookings, check in and print boarding passes before arriving at the airport. By 2008, 80 per cent of customers were booking e-tickets using 'ba.com', and 70 per cent were managing their bookings before flying. Almost 250 self-service check-in desks were now also available across 43 airports, and agreements had been made with the airlines in the One World Alliance (a group of airlines that work with each other around the world) to move to 100 per cent e-ticketing in 2009.

Customers responded well to these improvements, but then Heathrow Terminal 5 opened. This new terminal was meant to be the jewel in BA's crown, offering smoother check-in, fewer queues, less waiting around, a huge range of eating, drinking and relaxing options and the world's largest complex of premium passenger lounges. Despite three years planning and more than $600 million investment, passengers experienced long delays, and for the first months of the terminal's operation, baggage often did not arrive at its destination. What was meant to be a great success turned out to be a huge disaster and tarnished BA's reputation. Even loyal customers were forced to look to BA's competitors for alternatives.

THE FUTURE

British Airways has worked hard to improve the operational performance and customer experience at Heathrow Terminal 5. It has started introducing its first new, long-haul aircraft since 2001, which are substantially quieter, greener and more efficient than before. It has set its sights on becoming the world's leading global premium airline, which seems like a risky strategy when premium industry sales fell by 19 per cent last year. In line with this strategy, however, BA is starting to roll out its new first-class cabin, along with lounge upgrades in line with those at Terminal 5. BA's most critical hub is still Heathrow, where it owns over 40 per cent of the available landing slots. However, the decision by the new UK government not to build a third runway means it needs to keep looking elsewhere. As a result, BA launched a 100-seat business class-only flight in October 2009 from London City airport to New York, but many analysts have argued that it is still too soon to know whether this will be a success, and that controlling and reducing costs will also be critical given the global economic slowdown, increasing oil prices and ongoing cabin crew strikes.

The move back into profit (£158 million in the first six months of 2010) was based on structural changes and reducing non-fuel costs by 1.6 per cent but this is undoubtedly going to be a long haul in what is a very competitive market.

Questions

1 How has BA responded to increasing competitive pressure in the business class market segment?

2 Outline BA's service delivery system for business class passengers.

3 How well does this meet the needs of business class customers?

Lecturers: visit www.palgrave.com/business/ hillessential for additional resources

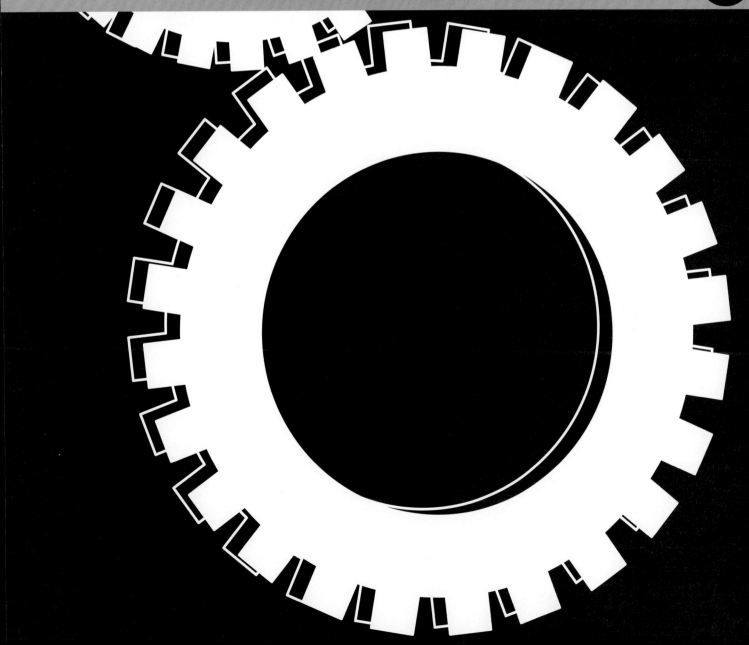

Making Products 5

Learning objectives

After completing this chapter, you should be able to:

- Recognize the technical and business requirements when making products

- Describe the manufacturing process decision and how it is influenced by the volume of demand

- Define the different types of manufacturing process – project, jobbing, batch, line and continuous processing

- Identify the difference between categories of product and types of manufacturing process

- Appreciate the key business implications of the types of manufacturing process

- Explain why hybrids such as cells may be introduced

Chapter outline

Introduction

Factors affecting manufacturing process design

- Categories of product

- Types of manufacturing process

Designing the manufacturing process

- Implications of process design

Hybrid processes

- Cells

Critical reflections

Summary

Introduction

The last chapter looked at delivering services, and this chapter does the same for manufacturing. First, we'll look at the factors involved in making products, including product categories (from special to mass products), the complexity of a product and the volumes involved. We'll then go on to define the different types of process (from project through to continuous processing) before looking at cells, a hybrid that mixes two of the other process types.

Factors affecting the design of the manufacturing process

Manufacturing companies sell products, and operations is responsible for making them. A key task for the operations function is selecting the appropriate manufacturing process for the product (the technical fit) while at the same time meeting the order-winners and qualifiers of the market into which it is sold (the business fit). These two factors are interlinked as the choice of manufacturing process will directly influence how well order-winners and qualifiers such as quality conformance, price, delivery speed and on-time delivery are provided.

The manufacturing process is the method of transformation or conversion (refer back to Figure 1.4) of inputs (materials, people skills, processes, and so on) into outputs (the products). In turn, the design of this process will need to cover two related but distinct dimensions.

- The *technical requirement* comprises the technical steps that need to take place in order to transform the inputs into products. For example, packaging for food products will need to be produced on printing machines and then cut to size using slitting machines. Plastic containers, on the other hand, need to be produced by loading the appropriate tooling (a mould designed to provide the shape and detail of the product) onto a machine and then injecting material under pressure to fill the cavity within the mould – a process known as injection moulding.

- The *business requirement* involves deciding on the appropriate manufacturing process to meet the requirements of both customers and the market, for example which printing and slitting machines and which injection moulding machines would best suit the volumes, order-winners and qualifiers for food packaging and plastic containers sold to customers, respectively.

> **KEY IDEA**

Designing the manufacturing process to make products needs to meet both the technical requirement and the business requirement

Categories of product

When manufacturing a product, the starting point is to determine the steps involved in making the product and the order these steps should follow. However, the type of product to be made will itself affect the design of the manufacturing process. For example, the process for making a Formula One racing car will differ from the process for making a high-volume line of cars such as a Ford Focus. Although both are automobiles, the associated volumes, range of colours and options and other market factors require a different response in terms of the manufacturing process. Figure 5.1 divides products into three categories, which reflect some of the key differences to be taken into account. Let's look at how some of these factors affect the manufacturing process.

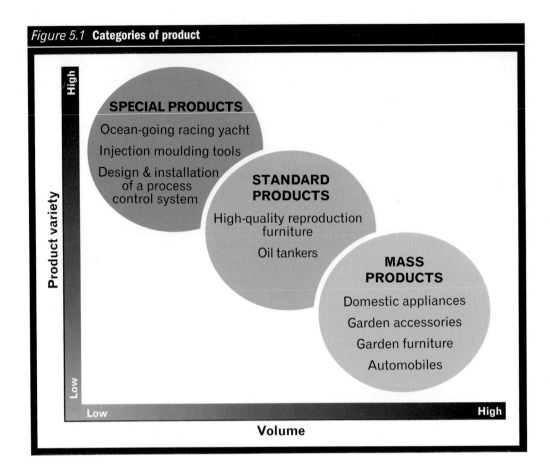

Figure 5.1 **Categories of product**

Product complexity

As you might imagine, the complexity of a product can vary dramatically. A plastic screw top for a soft drinks bottle is much simpler to make than a decorated coffee mug, and a jet engine is a much more complex product to make than a coffee mug. In fact, the number of steps to make the Rolls-Royce Trent 700 and 1000 engines for the Airbus 330 and Boeing 787 passenger aircraft, respectively, runs into hundreds in each case. As the product complexity increases, the number of steps and different processes involved will also increase, and this will have an impact on the process design.

Volumes

Figure 5.1 shows the important relationship between the three categories of product and the volume of items to be produced. As you will see from the list of process types below, this factor is central to the choice of process design.

Types of manufacturing process

There are five classic manufacturing process designs (project, jobbing, batch, line and continuous processing), together with a number of hybrids (processes that are a mixture of two of the classic process types). This section explains these classic processes and provides examples to illustrate the differences between them.

> **KEY IDEA**

There are five classic processes (project, jobbing, batch, line and continuous processing), together with a number of hybrids

---

Project process

Organizations selling large-scale, complex products that cannot be physically moved once completed will normally provide them using a **project process**. Examples include civil engineering contracts to build reservoir dams, housing, roads, tunnels and bridges. It can involve the provision of a unique product (for example, the Sydney Opera House or the Gotthard Base Tunnel, a 57 km rail tunnel in Switzerland), or a standard product such as estate housing. The former examples are made to unique, specific requirements, while the latter are of a standard design with limited options. But, in each instance, the resource inputs will be taken to the place where the product is to be built.

When a product has to be made on site, the choice of using a project process is forced upon an organization. This process incurs costs and, as resources need to be moved to and from the job as it progresses, is, therefore, not an efficient way of working. Because of this, companies try to produce as much as possible of the product off site and then transport these parts to the site. For example, concrete sections and timber framing for buildings will be made off site and assembled or arranged on site as required. Overall, the improved process efficiency of making components off site outweighs the additional transportation costs of getting the parts to the site. Figure 5.2 summarises the main points here.

Figure 5.2 **Project process – key characteristics**	
Products	Made or provided on site as they are too large or too difficult to move after completion. Examples include building reservoir dams, tunnels, roads, bridges and houses
Process	Resources to make the product are brought to the site, allocated for the duration of the project and then reallocated once their part of the task is complete or at the end of the job

Jobbing process

If products are transportable, companies use another process to make them. The **jobbing process** is designed to meet the one-off (that is, unique) requirements of customers where the product involved is of an individual nature and tends to be of a smaller size (and, therefore, transportable) than that provided by a project process. Product examples include a purpose-built piece of equipment (for example, injection moulding tools), hand-made, built-in furniture to meet specified customer requirements, a customer-designed and specified control unit, and hand-crafted shoes and clothing. Jobbing requires that the person making the product interprets the design and specification of the job, applying high-level skills in the conversion process.

Normally, one person or a small group of skilled people will be responsible for completing all or most of the product. It is a one-off provision, which means that the product will not usually be required again in its identical form or, if it is, the demand will be very low, with either irregular or long periods between one sale and the next. Figure 5.3 summarises the main points of this type of process.

Figure 5.3 **Jobbing process – key characteristics**	
Products	Special (that is, will not be repeated) products. Examples include the design and installation of a control system, a purpose-built piece of equipment, handmade, built-in furniture and hand-crafted shoes and clothing
Process	One person or a small group of skilled people do everything, including interpreting the product specification, clarifying issues with the customer and ensuring that what is made meets the specification

Batch process

Most organizations provide products that are deemed standard (that is, they have been provided before) rather than special. The repeat and higher volume nature associated with standard products signals the need to consider a different process designed to take advantage of these characteristics. A **batch process** is one alternative. As the product has been provided before or will be provided again in the future, it makes sense to invest in the process in order to simplify, automate and reduce costs. The level of investment will relate to the repeat nature and the total volumes involved. This investment can range from recording and establishing the best way to complete a job through to making a substantial investment in equipment to reduce costs.

When using a batch process, the first task is to break the job down into a number of steps. How many steps there will be will depend, in part, on the complexity of the product involved. When a product is simple, it might be completed in one step. A more complex product will require several steps (known as a multi-step process), as with the example given in Figure 5.4.

Here, a repeat customer order is received for a particular label (say), and the details are passed to operations. The order will be planned in line with the customer's delivery requirements. The details on the order will specify the label and the quantity required. The cylinder and plates for printing the label and the type and quantity of paper (in this instance, a large roll) will be issued to the printing area. This order will then be in a queue and, in line with the production schedule, the cylinder and plates for the job and the roll of paper will be loaded onto the designated printing machine (in our example in Figure 5.4, P2). The printing stage will be completed, and the printed roll of paper will go into an area awaiting the next stage. The part-completed material is now classed as **work-in-progress inventory**.

The next stage (slitting and collation) will have its own schedule of work, and the order in our example will be loaded, in line with this schedule, onto an appropriate slitting and collating machine. Here, the roll of paper will be cut or slit (depending on what is required by the customer). Again, the order will go into a work-in-progress area awaiting the packaging stage.

All batch processes are designed to be used and reused by a range of products, and this enables a company to invest in equipment in order to reduce costs. The downside of a process being used by a range of different products is that each change requires the process to be reset, known as a 'changeover', and these changeovers are costly, first, because of the skilled staff time to make the change, and second, because there is a loss of output during each changeover as no products can be made on the machine in question. Figure 5.5 summarises the main points of this type of process.

Line process

If volumes are sufficiently high, the company can justify investing in a process dedicated to the needs of a given range of products. As with batch processing, the product is split into a number of steps and the process is arranged to complete these, step after step and in a line, hence the name. Products are then processed, with each product passing through the same sequence of operations. The result is that operation 1 is completed on the first product, which goes immediately to operation 2. Meanwhile, operation 1 is being completed on the next product and so on. The line has also been designed to cope with any item within a given range and, therefore, an essential characteristic of line is that, in order to produce another product within the given range, the process does not have to be stopped and reset; that is, there are no set-ups. Examples include the production of domestic appliances and motor vehicles. Figure 5.6 (p. 148) provides a summary of the key characteristics of a **line process**.

Batch process – having broken down the products into different operations, the quantity to be produced is taken to process where the first operation is to be undertaken. The process is made ready/set up, and the whole order quantity is completed. The part-made product(s) typically goes into work-in-progress inventory, awaiting the next step in the process

Work-in-progress inventory – part-finished items (services or products) in a process

Line process – the making of products is separated into steps. The line process is then designed around a series of sequential processes to complete these steps and through which all items pass

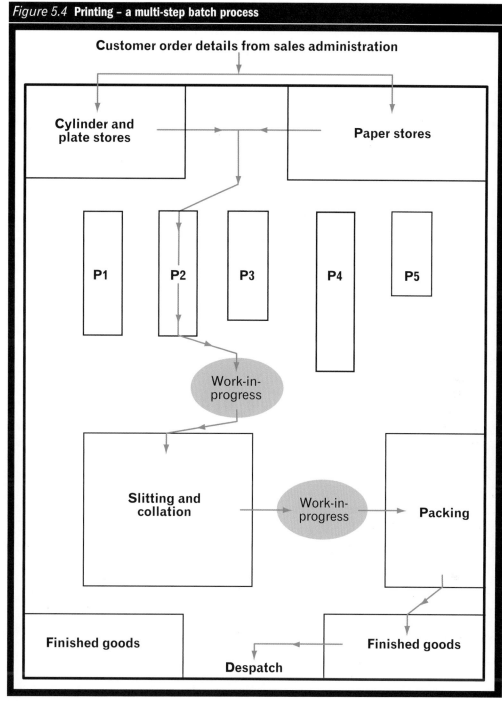

Figure 5.4 Printing – a multi-step batch process

Customer order details from sales administration

Cylinder and plate stores

Paper stores

P1   P2   P3   P4   P5

Work-in-progress

Slitting and collation

Work-in-progress

Packing

Finished goods

Despatch

Finished goods

Notes: 1 The 'P' in P1 to P5 is an abbreviation for printing machine.
2 (———▶) Movement of a typical order.

Figure 5.5	**Batch process – key characteristics**
Products	Standard, repeat products, the volume demand for which justifies the process investment. Examples include machined parts, injection moulding and printing
Process	Having broken down the products into different steps, the order quantity to be made is taken to the process where the first operation is to be undertaken. The process is made ready/set up, and the whole order quantity is completed. The part-made product typically goes into work-in-progress inventory awaiting the next process, which will complete the second step. When available, that process is made ready, the order quantity is processed and so on until the whole product is completed

'**Organizations** must clearly understand **customer** needs to **make** products effectively'

Figure 5.6	Line process – key characteristics
Products	Standard, repeat, high-volume (mass) products. Examples include motor vehicles and domestic appliances. It is not found in many manufacturing sectors today as the volumes required to justify the investment are not typical of current markets
Process	Products are separated into different steps. These are met by a series of sequential processes through which all items in a selected range pass. As far as the process is concerned, all the products are the same, and, therefore, the line does not have to be stopped and reset between one product and the next. However, the line can only cope with the predetermined range for which the process has been designed. Widening the existing range would require additional (often substantial) investment

Continuous processing

With **continuous processing**, one or several basic materials are processed through successive stages and refined into one or more products (for example, petrochemicals). Unlike a line process, the costs of stopping and starting up at the end of a working day are very high (often prohibitive) so the process will have been designed to run all day every day with minimum shutdowns for tasks such as major maintenance work. Materials are transferred automatically from one part of the process to the next, with the staff tasks being predominantly ones of system monitoring. Closing down and restarting such a plant would take several days, due to the complex process and safety requirements involved. Figure 5.7 provides a summary of the key characteristics.

Continuous processing – materials are processed through successive stages, with automatic transfer of the products from stage to stage. The costs of stopping and restarting are typically so high that the process is not stopped – hence the name continuous processing

Figure 5.7	Continuous processing – key characteristics
Products	Standard, very high-volume (mass) products. Examples include oil refining and some petrochemicals
Process	Materials are processed through successive steps, with automatic transfer of the product from step to step. The costs of stopping and restarting are typically so high that the process is not stopped, hence the name – continuous processing

Designing the manufacturing process

Figure 5.8 summarises the different types of manufacturing process, including the category of product to which they are most suited (look back at Figure 5.1 for an overview of product categories). You will see that the transition from special through to mass products given in Figure 5.1 corresponds, in general, to the type of process used. We'll now explore how the manufacturing process is designed and tailored to the type and volume of the product to be produced.

1 Project for special and standard products As shown in Figure 5.8, both special and standard products can be made using the project process. For example, a new estate of 120 houses comprising six designs would, for the builder, be a standard product – that is, the house specifications would be known, the method of build would be decided ahead of time, and any possible options for the basic design would be fixed. However, the houses would need to be built on site as they could not be moved. On the other hand, a large country house built to a unique design would, for the builder, be a special product, although it would again need to be built on site.

2 Project and continuous processing are specific to certain product types Typically, a project process would be used only when a product has to be built on site. Setting up and dismantling a site, and moving equipment and people to and from a site, increases costs

Figure 5.8 Manufacturing processes and their relationship to product categories

Process type	Product		Process description
	Category	Examples	
Project	Special	• Sydney Opera House • Øresund bridge connecting Denmark and Sweden • Gotthard Base Tunnel in the Alps	Products that cannot be physically moved once completed use a project process. Here resources (materials, equipment and people) are brought to the site where the product is to be built. These resources are allocated for the duration of the job and will be reallocated once their part of the task is completed or at the end of the job
	Standard	• Estate housing • Prefabricated industrial and warehouse units	
Jobbing	Special	• Ocean-going racing yacht • Injection moulding tools • Formula One and Indy racing cars • The design and installation of a process control system	Once a product can be moved, companies will choose to make it in-house and then despatch it to the customer. Jobbing is the name of the process that is used for special (that is, unique) products that will typically not be repeated. Here, one person or a small group of skilled people will complete all of the product. Often the provider is required to install and commission the product as part of the order
Batch	Standard ↓ Mass	• Business cards • Golf tees • Wheel rims • Packaging • Plastic bottles	The repeat and higher volume nature of standard and mass products requires a process designed to take advantage of these characteristics. Batch, line and continuous processing are the alternatives, but which one to use depends on the volumes involved. Batch can be appropriately used for low through to high (mass) volumes. As how to make the product is known, the steps involved are also known and products move from step to step until completed. Batch is chosen for standard products with volumes insufficient to dedicate processes. Thus, different products share the same processes by setting and resetting each time. Consequences of this include waiting between steps and the prioritizing of jobs using the same process
Line	Mass	• Domestic appliances • Cans of Coca-Cola • Automobiles • Pet food • Mobile phones	Higher volumes mean that processes can be dedicated to the needs of a given range of products. Whereas in batch a process has to be reset each time a new product is to be made, in line the process does not have to stop as it has been designed to make the range of products required without being reset. The steps to make them are sequentially laid out in a line, and a product goes from step to step until completed. Although the range of products will vary, in terms of the process they can be made without stopping and resetting the line. Unlike with continuous processing below, stopping a process at the end and restarting it at the beginning of a shift, day or week is not expensive
Continuous processing	Mass	• Petrochemicals • Oil refineries • Some chemical plants	For some products, the high volumes involved are best handled by continuous processing. In addition to high volumes, the nature of these products will need to be of a type that is transferable through piping or in liquid form. Continuous processing is similar to line in that it handles mass products without being stopped and reset. Its distinguishing feature is, however, that stopping and restarting the process is lengthy and expensive, and consequently it is designed to be run continuously, hence its name

and makes the management task more difficult compared with making a product in-house. As a consequence, project is typically used only where the product has to be made on-site.

Similarly, the use of continuous processing is limited. The products best suited to this process would be high volume, with the physical characteristics that would allow them to be moved from step to step in the process using pipework, such as in the refining of oil and the production of petrochemicals.

So, the appropriate use of a project process and continuous processing is restricted (as shown in Figure 5.9), and most organizations choose from jobbing, batch and line processes for their business needs.

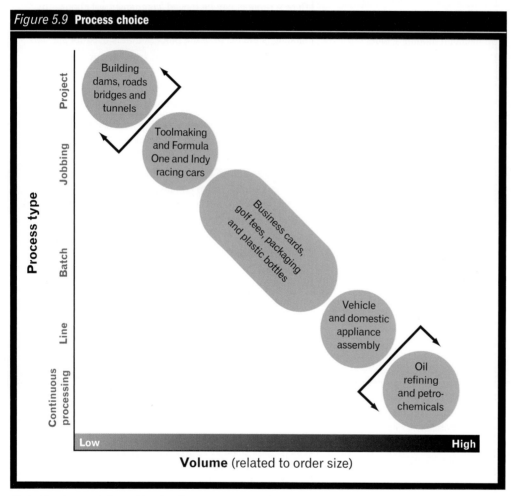

Figure 5.9 Process choice

Note: The elongated shape of batch reflects the range of volumes (from standard to mass) that this process covers.

3 *Combinations of processes* Companies often use more than one process type to meet the overall needs of their business. The reason is that different processes best meet the different needs of a particular product or part of a product. For example, building the 120 new houses we discussed above would use a combination of processes:

- *Project* to meet the overall requirements of bringing resources to and from the site, with one person having the overall management responsibility for undertaking this task to ensure the effective use of resources and to meet the cost budgets involved.

- *Batch* would typically be used to meet several phases of the work. For example, once the footings had been completed on a number of houses, the concreting of the ground floor areas for these homes would be completed one after the other. Other phases in the building of several houses would similarly be completed one after another (for example, roofing, glazing, electrics, plastering, bathroom fitting and kitchen installation). In this way, a builder would take advantage of the increased volume associated with completing the same phase on several houses one after the other, thus looking to reduce costs and make the management task easier. So all roofing tiles for several houses would be delivered to the site at the same time, as would the materials for the glazing, electrics and other phases. In addition, contractors to complete each phase would be less costly as they would have several consecutive days (even weeks) of work, which would, in turn, reduce their costs.

- *Jobbing* Where specific alterations or additions to a standard design are requested and agreed, they will be completed using jobbing as the appropriate process. Here, skilled staff such as bricklayers and joiners would receive drawings, interpret these and be fully responsible for fulfilling the specification(s) and checking the results.

4 *Jobbing, batch and line* These are the processes from which most companies choose, and again they often select more than one to best meet their needs, as illustrated in Figure 5.10.

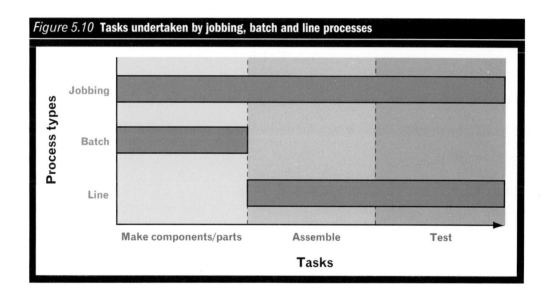

Figure 5.10 Tasks undertaken by jobbing, batch and line processes

This shows that companies typically make components or parts in batch processes, while using a line process to assemble products. For example, the body panels for a Honda Civic will be made on a press. This will be set to make the left body panel, stopped and reset to make the right body panel, and so on. However, Honda uses a line process to assemble and test cars.

5 *Process flexibility* One recent trend is to assess and seek to improve the 'flexibility' and 'agility' of a manufacturing process. Although these terms can be useful, they are often employed in too vague or general a way, without taking into account their many different meanings. It is important to understand that a manufacturing process can be flexible in a variety of different ways. Each type of flexibility has its own strategic relevance (that is, provides a different market advantage) and will determine where investment is focused. Achieving an improvement in any of the following areas will result in more investment, so knowing the costs and benefits of each needs to form part of the decision of where and how to improve flexibility.

- *Introduction of new products* The flexibility of the operations process in terms of handling the introduction of new products is vital to the long-term success of any business, as operations is one of the functions that plays a key role in this task.

- *Handling a range of products* Most, if not all, companies produce a range of products and product options. Even Ford with its Model T car and 'any colour as long as it's black' approach of the 1920s was soon replaced by General Motors and its willingness to provide choice. The process flexibility to handle variety is, in most markets, a key factor in the successful growth of a business as it reflects the nature of today's demand.

- *Handling a range of volumes* As explained earlier, the level of volume is typically not high enough to justify dedicating processes to a given range of products. For this reason, batch is the most commonly used process as it is designed to be used and reused by a range of products. One key feature that results is the ease (that is, how long it takes to change a process from making one product to making another product) with which a process can cope with different levels of volume. The volume requirements of products will differ not only from one to the next, but also over time. How quickly a process can be changed from making one product to another will directly affect the loss of potential output while the process change is taking place. Hence, the shorter the changeovers, the more flexible the process is regarding this dimension.

- *Meeting demand peaks* If the demand for a product is seasonal, having the flexibility to ramp up the manufacturing process in order to cope with sudden increases in demand is vital to the success of such a business.

The key factors then in managing the need for flexibility are to:

- Specify what type of flexibility is required – this brings clarity to an analysis and prevents confusion in communicating within a business

- Identify where the investment needs to be made – this helps to ensure that the investment is appropriate to what is needed and that unnecessary investment is kept to a minimum.

....
> **KEY IDEA**
Use the words 'flexible' and 'agile' with care as they have many different meanings and, therefore, can be misleading
....

Now have a look at Case 5.1.

Implications of process design

Investing in the means to make products takes many forms. It can range from investment in process equipment through to the task of determining how best to make a product and preparing the necessary process details, procedures to follow and supporting information. But no matter what form the investment takes, switching the making of a product from one type of process to another will invariably be costly. For this reason, companies choose the process they judge best, with the intention of not changing their decision and thus avoiding future additional investment.

Figure 5.11 illustrates and reinforces the point that there is not typically a transition from one process to another. Organizations do not, for instance, choose project and later replace it with jobbing; similarly, companies rarely move from jobbing to batch and then line. However, as Figure 5.11 illustrates, some marginal transitions may take place between jobbing and low-volume batch, low-volume batch and higher volume batch, and high-volume batch and line, but these are unusual and not the norm. You will notice in Figure 5.11 (as earlier in Figure 5.9) that batch is depicted as an elongated shape, highlighting the fact that batch covers a wide range of volumes and other factors, as the next section explains.

No one is ever likely to build another car plant like Volkswagen's Wolfsburg plant in Lower Saxony, Germany – which is capable of producing 750,000 vehicles a year – or another Toyota city, near Nagoya in Japan. Most new factories are now built to make around 200,000 cars a year, and some believe that many future plants could be a quarter of this current size.

To create the volume required to justify these new plants, the process is designed to handle a wider product range. For example, Ford's truck assembly plant at Rouge in Dearborn, Detroit (which was opened in 2004) makes light trucks and sport utility vehicles and can handle three basic platforms (the chassis and underpinnings of a vehicle) and nine different model variations built on these. The mix scheduled to be made will depend on which models are most in demand.

www.volkswagen.de; www.toyota.com; www.ford.com

Questions

1 The process type used at Ford's assembly plant at Rouge is line. Why?

2 Why would you classify the Rouge plant as inflexible (see Figure 5.12)?

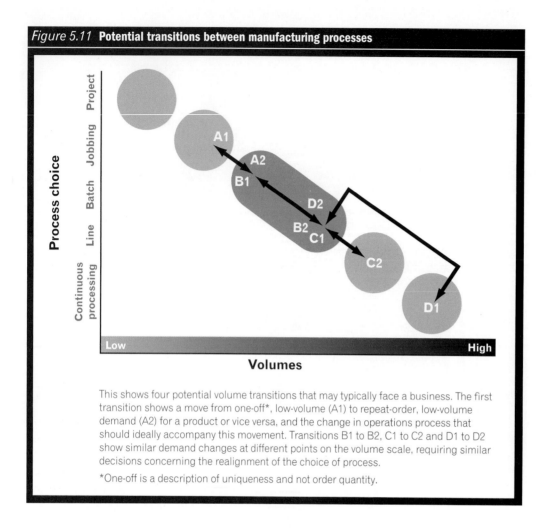

Figure 5.11 Potential transitions between manufacturing processes

Process choice (vertical axis): Project, Jobbing, Batch, Line, Continuous processing

Volumes (horizontal axis): Low → High

This shows four potential volume transitions that may typically face a business. The first transition shows a move from one-off*, low-volume (A1) to repeat-order, low-volume demand (A2) for a product or vice versa, and the change in operations process that should ideally accompany this movement. Transitions B1 to B2, C1 to C2 and D1 to D2 show similar demand changes at different points on the volume scale, requiring similar decisions concerning the realignment of the choice of process.

*One-off is a description of uniqueness and not order quantity.

As implied throughout the chapter, each process is associated with different characteristics and alternative sets of trade-offs (things a process can do well or less well). To illustrate these, Figure 5.12 provides an overview of some of the factors involved, and recognizing and understanding these forms part of the decision on which process to buy. You will note in Figure 5.12 that the format used to reflect the elongated shape depicting batch in Figure 5.11 is that of an arrow. In this way, the wide range of volumes and other characteristics that the batch process covers is again appropriately depicted. Finally, the format of Figure 5.12 also reflects the specific nature of the type of businesses in which project and continuous processing would be used.

Some comments on Figure 5.12 will help to explain the trade-off alternatives and different characteristics that go hand in hand with each type of manufacturing process. The first part of the table illustrates the fact that as the choice moves to the right, high volumes justify more dedicated processes, which, by their nature, are less flexible and less able to cope with the introduction of new products or changes to existing products. In essence, it is the process that makes the product here, which, in turn, requires a high level of prior knowledge in order to design and develop it. One outcome is that process utilization become more important than the utilization of staff as the process is, in fact, the key resource.

You will note that three of the last four dimensions in Figure 5.12 do not conform to the arrow principle. Regarding waiting time, there can be some occasions in the project process when one group of skilled people has to wait for another aspect of the job to be completed. But in all other processes, except for batch, the waiting time between one part of the system and the next tends to be low. In jobbing, the skilled person is always moving the job forward, whereas with line and continuous processing, the product moves automatically from one part of the system to the next. In batch, on the other hand, because products use the same processes, priorities need to be determined and, as a consequence, some products will have to wait.

This need to prioritize means that day-to-day scheduling is most complex in batch. Once materials are brought to a line or continuous process, on the other hand, the scheduling of products through the system is straightforward. With jobbing, the person making the product schedules the work, but the unknown (as all products are new) brings with it a level of complexity. In project, the building of a product on site, the uncertainty of resource and material supply, together with potential problems of weather, leads to scheduling difficulties.

Finally, process layout is functionally based in both jobbing and batch processes, and is product-based in line and continuous processing.

Hybrid processes

In many markets, manufacturing capacity is growing faster than demand. The excess capacity that has resulted will continue as newer industrial nations such as China and India keep growing. One outcome is that the emerging competition is driving product offerings to become more different, and companies have responded by developing processes to reflect these changing demands. Line processes are often developed to produce a relatively wide range of products, with a marked increase in the level of investment necessary to make this increased variety. In addition to investing directly in the process itself, companies may also choose to rearrange or use existing processes in a different way in order to provide the required set of trade-offs. Processes that are redesigned or created by mixing original processes are known as **hybrid processes**.

Cells

Let's look at one of the more common examples of these hybrid processes – **cells** or cellular manufacturing.

As a company choosing batch processes will be providing standard products, the only practical alternative to a batch process is line. Companies tend to choose batch rather than line on the basis of volume: where products do not have sufficient volumes to justify dedicating processes, as in a line process, a batch process is used. As explained earlier, these processes are designed to allow products to share processes and thus make more sense of the utilization/investment equation. However, batch processes embody trade-offs, and companies may look to change some of these. Cells are a hybrid process that, although still batch in origin (as the process will still have to be stopped and reset to handle a product change), are, in fact, a mix of batch and line, and offer changes in terms of some key variables. First let's discuss what cells are, and then we'll review the key trade-off changes that result.

Figure 5.13 shows the functional layout of a batch process (similar processes are grouped together in the same geographical area; it might also be helpful to take a look back at Figure 5.4, which illustrates a similar arrangement). Now, the rationale underpinning cells is that grouping products together and treating them as being the same leads to an increase in volume (the volumes of all the products under consideration can be added together and the aggregate viewed as a whole). This then allows processes to be allocated to these products for their sole use. What happens in cells is that the necessary processes, in terms of both capability and capacity (that is, they are able to provide the

FACTORS		TYPICAL
		Project
Process	nature	General purpose
	flexibility	Flexible
Level of process investment		Variable
Ability of the process to cope with	product changes	High
	new products	High
How are orders won?	typical order-winners	Capabilities
	typical qualifiers	Delivery on time Price
Operations volumes		Low
Set-ups or changeovers	number	Many
	expense per	Variable
Dominant utilization		Predominantly people
Prior knowledge of the	operations task	Variable
	material requirements	Known at tendering stage
Level of waiting time in the process		Varies
Difficulty of the day-to-day scheduling task		Complex
Process layout		Fixed position
Operations key strategic task		Respond to product & scheduling changes

CHARACTERISTICS OF MANUFACTURING PROCESS ALTERNATIVES

Jobbing	Batch	Line	Continuous processing
General purpose →→		Dedicated	Dedicated
Flexible →→		Inflexible	Inflexible
Low →→		High	Very high
High →→		Low	Nil
High →→		Low	None
Unique capability →→		Price	Price
Price / Delivery on time and quality conformance			Delivery on time, quality conformance
Low →→		High	Very high
Many →→		None in the life-time of the process	None in the life-time of the process
Inexpensive →→		Prohibitive	Prohibitive
People →→		Process	Process
Known but often not well defined →→		Well defined	Well defined
Some uncertainty →→		Well defined	Well defined
Low	High	Low	Low
Complex	Very complex	Easy	Easy
Function	Function	Product	Product
Respond to product and schedule changes →→		Low cost	Low cost

product requirements in terms of both its technical and demand dimensions) are allocated to the sole use of these products; this 'dedication' is justified by the enhanced level of volume that results (Figure 5.14).

Figure 5.13 **Batch layout**

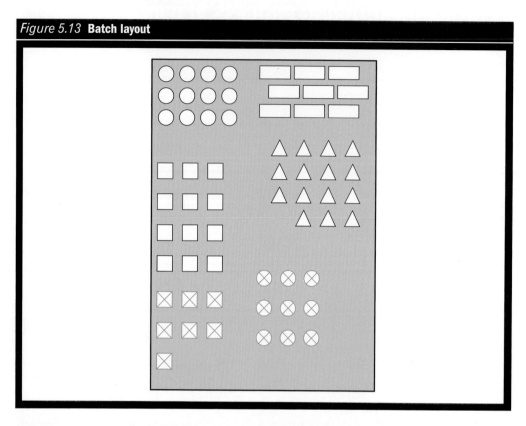

Figure 5.14 **Cellular layout**

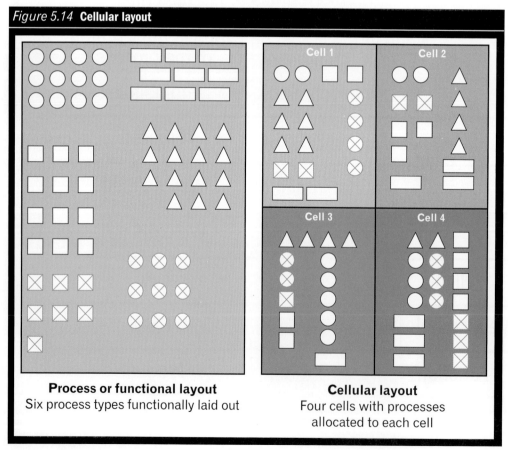

Process or functional layout
Six process types functionally laid out

Cellular layout
Four cells with processes
allocated to each cell

Compared with a batch process, this rearrangement brings with it changes in certain key dimensions, for example:

- Process waiting time is reduced.
- Work-in-progress inventories are lower.
- The day-to-day scheduling of operations is made easier.

These positive changes result from the hybrid process shifting towards a line process (although still being on the batch process dimension), as shown in Figure 5.15. The production process will be laid out within a smaller physical area and handle a reduced range of products. This will, in turn, simplify the day-to-day scheduling task and enable lead-times and work-in-progress inventory to be reduced, as the waiting time between processes is more easily managed.

Figure 5.15 **The position of cells relative to batch and line processes**

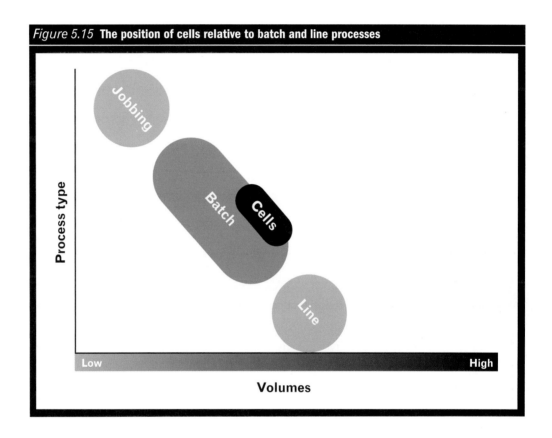

Just as these 'gains' come from moving the hybrid process towards a line process, cells, compared with batch, also incur certain disadvantages associated with their repositioning on the process continuum. Compared with batch, cells:

- Are less flexible
- Result in a lower utilization of equipment, which may lead to additional process capacity having to be purchased.

Both these are characteristic of a line rather than a batch process.

> **KEY IDEA**
  Cells are a commonly used hybrid process

Critical reflections

Operations makes the products that a company sells. To be competitive, products need to meet customers' needs (the design must be right) and must be made to that design (known as quality conformance, and a prime task of operations). But when customers choose to buy a product in the first place (and make a repeat purchase where that would take place), they are influenced by aspects such as variety, price and availability.

As operations fulfils most of the wide-ranging set of factors that affects sales, how it chooses to make products will have a significant impact on sales revenues and profits. The different sets of trade-offs that result from the alternative ways of making products need to be explained to the business and need to be a key factor in the decision-making procedure. However, given that demand changes over time but manufacturing processes will only change with further investment, which process is chosen needs also to reflect the life cycle of a product.

Operations, therefore, needs to provide these key business insights in the debate about markets and customers. As the provider of the products, how it makes them is a key factor in the short- and long-term success of a business.

Summary

- A key role in operations is to determine how best to make the products an organization sells to its customers. In the context of the business, 'how best' means selecting manufacturing processes that can meet both the technical dimensions and the market needs (the order-winners and qualifiers) of its customers.

- Meeting the technical characteristics leads to certain, often predetermined, choices – commercial bread-making requires ovens of a given size, plastic mouldings need injection moulding machines and so on. While this is a key issue, alternative process technologies normally form part of the role of engineering and other technical functions. Operations must use these technologies to make products in line with the needs of a company's chosen markets.

- Operations has to choose the type(s) of manufacturing process to best meet customers' demands. This chapter has described the process choices and their associated trade-offs.

Study activities

Discussion questions

1 Select one simple (involving one or two steps) and one more complicated (three or more steps) batch process in manufacturing companies of your choice. Explain how they work.

2 What are the essential differences between the following processes:

Project   and   jobbing

Jobbing   and   batch

Batch   and   line

Line   and   continuous processing?

3 When assembling a car, there will be five tyres (four plus a spare) for each vehicle. Why is it that tyre-making uses a batch process, whereas the car itself is typically assembled using a line process?

4 Why is waiting time an integral part of a batch process design? Illustrate with two examples.

Assignments

1 Visit the website of a major petrochemical company. Find information on one of its oil refineries and explain:

   - How it handles the product range that is processed in the particular plant

   - How often the plant is shut down and why.

2 Select a business/organization (other than the examples given in this chapter) to illustrate the five types of process – project, jobbing, batch, line and continuous processing. For each example, briefly explain how the process works.

Exploring further

Journal articles

Holweg, M. and Pil, F.K. (2001) 'Successful build-to-order strategies start with the customer'. *MIT Sloan Management Review*, **43**(1), pp. 74–84. The article outlines a true build-to-order strategy in which managers systematically improve the value chain's flexibility in three areas: process, product and volume.

Takeuchi, H., Osono, E. and Shimizu, N. (2008) 'The contradictions that drive Toyota's success'. *Harvard Business Review*, **86**(6), pp. 96–104. Toyota Motor Corporation's unorthodox manufacturing system – the Toyota Production System (TPS) – enables it to make the best automobiles at the lowest cost and to develop new products quickly. As described in the article, TPS is a 'hard' innovation that allows the company to keep improving. But Toyota has also mastered a 'soft' innovation that relates to corporate culture: Toyota believes that efficiency alone cannot guarantee success. Some key contradictions that Toyota fosters and how other companies can learn to thrive on contradictions are discussed in this text.

Books

Ford, H. (1988) *Today and Tomorrow*. Cambridge, MA: Productivity Press. Originally published in 1926, this book outlines Henry Ford's ideas on manufacturing and the impact that these still have. Even influential Japanese ideas such as just-in-time have been influenced by Ford's ideas. Similarly, using low-cost, high-quality manufacturing to win markets inspired many Japanese companies to do the same.

Hill, A. and Hill, T. (2009) *Manufacturing Operations Strategy: Text and Cases*, 3rd edn. Basingstoke: Palgrave Macmillan. The text provides a most useful supplement to the current book by outlining an in-depth approach for developing and implementing operations strategy within manufacturing organizations.

Hill, T. (2005) *Operations Management: Text and Cases*. Basingstoke: Palgrave Macmillan. This provides a useful supplement to this current book by offering a more comprehensive explanation and further examples (including long case studies) showing how service and manufacturing companies have applied these concepts.

Hill, T. (1988) *The Strategy Quest. Releasing the Energy of Manufacturing Within a Market Driven Strategy: A Dynamic Business Story*. Available from AMD Publishing, 'Albedo', Dousland, Devon PL20 6NE, UK; e-mail: amd@jm-abode.tiscali.co.uk; fax: +44(0) 1822 882863. This book (written as a novel) describes how an art business and manufacturing organization restructure themselves to meet the changing demands of their customers.

BACKGROUND

Pret A Manger was described by *The Times* newspaper as having 'revolutionised the concept of sandwich making and eating'. Sinclair Beecham and Julian Metcalfe, two university friends, founded Pret in 1986. They saw an opportunity in London to introduce a sleek, healthy, fast-food concept as an alternative to the hamburger–fries–shake menus around at the time. Since opening its first store, Pret has been hugely successful, expanding rapidly both in the UK and more recently elsewhere in the world. Rather than franchising its stores (an approach used by McDonald's, for example), Pret owns and manages all its stores so as to control the brand and ensure that all the stores deliver consistently high standard products and service. The company is passionate about serving fresh food and goes to extraordinary lengths to avoid the chemicals, additives and preservatives common to so much of the 'prepared' and 'fast' food on the market today. This is reflected in the 'Passion Facts' found in their shops and on their packaging, which documents their continual search for what they feel are Pret-quality ingredients.

STORE ENVIRONMENT

One of the things that makes Pret stand out from its competitors is its industrially chic store decor. Each outlet is a very crisp clean environment consisting of reflective brushed aluminium walls and floors. All the equipment used, from refrigerated cases to cash registers and coffee brewers, has that stainless steel, modern look. There are a few touches of colour here and there that add to its overall distinctive nature, including a yellow wall and orange ceiling with suspended, exposed pipes as well as the burgundy Pret star logos found on entrance mats, packaging and menu boards.

PRODUCTS

Pret sells a variety of items including sandwiches, baguettes, wraps, sushi, salads, yoghurt pots, cakes, deserts, crisps and a range of bottled beverages, brewed coffees and teas. The menu offered in the morning for breakfast differs slightly from the lunch menu, although the majority of the items offered are the same. Up to 30 types of food are offered in each store. Of the menu items available, about 12 are 'standards' and the rest can change on a daily basis. Indeed, about 70 new items are typically introduced annually into each store.

Pret keeps its menu exciting and innovative by constantly introducing new products and flavours. Even though probably only one idea in every 20 makes it through its testing process, a new product goes on sale in Pret's UK outlets on average every four days. Existing products are continuously being improved. For example, the recipe for the chocolate brownie has been improved 33 times over the last few years. Each change is miniscule but, the company believes, detectable.

MAKING AND DELIVERING PRODUCTS

Fresh ingredients are delivered to each shop every morning, and all the sandwiches, wraps, baguettes, deserts and salads are made one by one in each shop each day. A set number of products are assembled at the beginning of the day and stocked in the shop front, from where the customers select and pay for their meal (Figure 1). This stock level is then replenished during the day in line with demand. The aim is to continually meet the company's high quality and freshness standards. As a result, if any of the products assembled that day have not sold by the time the store closes, they are given away to local charities rather than being stored and sold the following day.

Service in the shop is fast and friendly, with members following strict service guidelines, such as serving every customer within 90 seconds. The challenge of providing the customer with a fast, efficient and professional service is exciting, and there is a buzz among the staff. To ensure that this happens, store managers tend to spend about 80 per cent of their time on the shop floor and hold team meetings twice a day so it is clear what each member needs to do.

PEOPLE

Key to Pret's success is the way it recruits, motivates, trains and develops its staff. It aims to offer staff a fun and open working environment, reward, recognition, training, development and career opportunities. As a result, staff turnover is less than 60 per cent of the industry average and it has won a number of awards, including being voted 10th in The *Sunday Times* '50 Best Companies to Work for in the UK', while *Fortune* magazine rated it as one of the top 10 places to work in Europe. One company initiative involves sending all managers into an outlet every 3 months to familiarize themselves with the daily operation of their stores. This encourages staff to have a good knowledge of how products are made and the way in which customers are served. The hope is that this will result in better decisions in other parts of the business, as well as helping managers get to know their team and the business in which they work.

THE FUTURE

With its ambitious plans for expansion over the next few years, Pret is continuing to refine the formula that led to its current success. Key to this will be not only the suppliers and outlets it selects, but also, more importantly, the people it recruits. The company typically receives over 5,000 jobs applications each year, encouraged by the training and incentives that it has on offer. Continuing to use the right recruitment policies to create a culture where people want to stay will be important in sustaining the company's success. Its recent introduction of a delivery service is also helping it meet the needs of young professionals who want a fast and efficient service with a variety of high-quality products. As these customers are typically very busy and short of time, a delivery service is often a more convenient solution for them. The challenge is maintaining the Pret experience even when customers do not actually come into the store.

www.pret.com/about

Figure 1

A typical Pret A Manger delivery system in the kitchen and the store front

Kitchen

Fresh ingredients are delivered to each store on a daily basis. Chilled foods are placed into a back-of-house (back-office) walk-in cooler, while a small number of frozen goods, including part-baked croissants, baguettes and cookies, are stored in a reach-in freezer. Staff in each outlet begin food assembly at 7 am and refresh the food supply throughout the day as needed.

In a large outlet, 10 stainless-steel preparation tables and refrigerated ingredient display units are arranged so that employees can assemble fresh ingredients into sandwiches (making on average 1,500 a day), and then wrap and package them in boxes (carrying the Pret logo and a message saying 'handmade in Pret today' and listing natural ingredients) for presentation in refrigerated display units located in the store area. Sandwiches are made at designated tables with assembly instructions and photos showing how each ingredient should be positioned. Desserts and salads are also assembled here.

In the kitchen, there are also coffee brewers, a bean grinder, a tea brewer and a countertop slicer for cutting meats and vegetables. The only product heated on the premises is soup. Soups are delivered to each unit in 1 gallon sealed plastic bags and then heated in a 10 gallon electric steam-jacketed kettle before being taken out to the shop front and placed in tureens for holding and serving.

After preparation and assembly, all items are taken to the front-of-house (front office) for display. Refrigerated items, including bottled beverages, are place in one of five floor-to-ceiling refrigerated cases that have been positioned side by side near the entranceway.

A set number of products are assembled at the beginning of the day and stocked in the store front. The store manager is responsible for making sure inventory is then replenished during the day in line with demand. This also includes items such as sushi, drinks, juices and yoghurt pots that are brought in pre-assembled and stored in the kitchen before being moved into the store front.

Store front

In the store front, customers help themselves to the products they want and take them to the counter to pay. All products apart from hot drinks and soup are stored in the shop front and replenished from the kitchen in line with demand. When customers come to the counter to pay for their products, they can then order hot drinks or soup, which are then either made or served to order.

A centrally positioned serving counter with up to eight cashiers positioned shoulder to shoulder offers customers a quick and efficient service. The aim is to serve customers in 90 seconds or less.

Behind the serving counter, there is typically a reach-in refrigerator for storing milk, two tea dispensers, a drip coffee dispenser, two coffee machines, two soup tureens and a convection oven for baking croissants, cookies, tomatoes, almonds and pine nuts.

Products made in the oven are placed either into take-out bags or onto 12-inch aluminum round trays. Seating is available at larger units with up to 72 stools with aluminum bases and vinyl cushions placed at bar counters lining the walls, and at round tables with marble tops.

© Alex Hill and Terry Hill 2011

Questions

1 In which market does Pret A Manger compete?

2 How does its delivery system help it meet its customers' needs?

Lecturers: visit www.palgrave.com/business/hillessential for additional resources

Introduction

This chapter addresses the two issues of location and layout – where best to position a facility or outlet, and how best to lay out the processes, equipment and staff used in providing the services or making the products. Choosing the best location and layout is crucial, as both will have a direct impact on the sales and profit margins of a business. The factors that will be affected by location and layout include ease of serving customers, speed of service provision, level of customer support and costs of delivery, all of which influence both sales and profits.

In the first part of this chapter, we'll look at the process of choosing a location, including the levels at which a decision needs to be made, general factors (such as the origin of existing decisions, political constraints and need for market access) and specific factors influencing location decisions (including existing infrastructure, proximity to markets and suppliers, staff availability, costs and government policies). Finally, some of the techniques used in making these decisions (weighted factor and centre of gravity method) are described.

The second part of the chapter addresses layout – the task of how best to arrange the processes, systems and staff used. First, background factors such as existing space, health, safety and aesthetics are discussed. Second, the basic types of layout (fixed position, process or function, and service or product) are described, together with those for hybrid delivery systems. The final section looks at detailed layout design, the approaches used for each of the basic types of layout and how to analyse queues and waiting times.

Choosing a location

The location of any business or organization must be chosen carefully in order to secure the best net gains both now and in the long term. Choice of location can affect initial as well as future development costs, the resulting trading costs when providing services or products to customers, sales revenues and the extent to which a facility is able to provide agreed levels of customer service.

No matter what the facility, whether it be a hospital, an office, a retail outlet, a warehouse or a manufacturing plant, the decision of where to locate is significant in terms of three factors:

- The size of the investment
- The fixed nature of the choice – the organization will have to live with the choice for a long time or prematurely incur the costs of relocation
- The uncertainly of the future – the pros and cons on which the site selection was made may well be less relevant in the future.

Much time and effort needs to be put into identifying and assessing the key variables on which these decisions are based as the size and binding nature of the investments involved mean that relocation is hard to justify. In fact, many organizations are, in reality, committed indefinitely to a location once it has been chosen.

> **KEY IDEA**
Once chosen, many organizations are committed indefinitely to a location

In order to secure the best net gains for an organization, the following factors need to be taken into account when deciding upon a suitable location:

- Investments and costs – the initial investment and any later site or facility investments, and the trading costs (including supply and distribution) that will be incurred when providing services or products to customers
- Sales revenues – the impact on sales revenue includes whether customers can easily see, recognize and access the site, factors that will influence both initial and repeat sales, particularly in the service sector.

Levels of decision

The location of an outlet or facility might involve decisions concerning which continent or region, which country, area or city, and finally which office block, business park, shopping centre or street to choose. Depending on the type of outlet, the number of decision levels and the importance attached to the factors determining choice at each level will change. For example, the factors that Disney's management considered when deciding where to locate a new theme park in Europe would have been at all levels and embraced more parameters than (say) Burger King's decision on where to locate its next outlet in Stockholm. While Disney would place great importance on factors such as staff availability, transport infrastructure, proximity to potential customers, climate and level of government support, for Burger King's local management factors such as local customer density, location of competitors, zoning and building regulations, space availability and ease of access would have been more important.

Not only do the number of levels involved differ, but the factors to be taken into account will also change for each decision to be made. Let's first look briefly at each possible decision level and afterwards review the factors that organizations may have to take into account when deciding where to go.

> **KEY IDEA**

   The number of levels and factors involved in selecting a location differs decision by decision

Choosing the continent or region

For many larger organizations, there is an increasingly regional dimension to deciding where to locate a facility. In more recent times, many service companies have also been locating in different regions. For some companies (for example, hotel chains such as Holiday Inn, coffee outlets such as Starbucks, accountancy firms such as PriceWaterhouseCoopers and retailers such as IKEA), the prime reason is access to new markets. For others, the main reason is to lower costs – for example in 2011, an estimated 3.3 million call centre jobs in the financial services industry were relocated from the US to India, Malaysia, China and other Asian countries, as were over 2 million jobs from Western Europe. And for some organizations (for example, management consultancy companies such as Accenture and McKinsey & Company), the reason is a combination of market access (via a local presence) and a less expensive service provision, with local consultants commanding lower salaries and requiring lower living costs than expatriate staff brought in from the country where the company is based.

Choosing the country

In many instances, the choice of country is an integral part of the regional decision. For example, where the prime aim is to access markets, the regional and country choices are typically part of the same decision. In other instances, however, they will be a separate issue. Disney's decision to build a theme park in Europe was only the first step. While choosing Europe may have involved selecting from only a very few options, deciding on the best country in Europe would have involved considering a whole range of alternatives before choosing from several viable alternatives to arrive at a shortlist of two (France and Spain being the two alternatives in question). Similarly, choosing France ahead of Spain would have meant carefully judging the relative importance of a number of variables, while weighting the relevant criteria over the timescales involved.

Choosing the area or city

For Disney, the decision of choosing France over Spain still left a long way to go. Similarly, choosing northern France still left the decision of which area or city would best meet corporate objectives. Again, trade-offs between factors such as climate, availability of staff and density of potential customer catchment areas would have come into play. Analyses would have then been made, and models used to provide options and identify one or more possible optimal locations. A whole range of parameters, as discussed in the next section, would have been used to model the alternatives, and different scenarios would have been considered to test the impact of changes in key variables at alternative sites.

For companies whose locations comprise smaller sized outlets, this level of decision is often more straightforward, with the 'which site?' decision becoming the one that needs greater care and being the more difficult to make.

Choosing the site

Selecting the actual site takes into account other considerations. This is the domain of the micro-scale decision that deals with the precise location within a city centre, regional centre, business or industrial park, or the site in relation to major roads, rail links, airports or seaports. At this level of detail, a whole range of factors come into play, as discussed in the following sections.

Background factors influencing location decisions

Before looking at the specific factors to be considered when deciding on a location, we will begin by recognizing that although the choice of where best to locate should, as with other management decisions, be set against objective criteria, reality is often a major factor in determining what is and is not feasible. This section now looks at six factors; in the list below, 1 and 2 are of general nature, 3 and 4 result from recent technology changes and globalization trends, while 5 and 6 are of an economic nature:

1   *The origin of existing locations* Many organizations are located where they are now as a result of decisions made in the past, with the cost of changing to a more suitable location not being justifiable. Over time, as organizations grow and the investment to meet that expansion also grows, the cost of relocation can often become prohibitive compared with extending an existing site. As a result, organizations stay where they are.

2   *Politically based constraints* Countries wish to develop their own industrial and service sectors in order to create the wealth essential for national prosperity. To this end, one step being taken by governments is to require **multi-national corporations** (MNCs) to build facilities locally in order to reduce imports and create value-adding activities. Joint ventures are an increasingly common way of meeting these requirements. Such arrangements dictate the location and often the size of facilities as MNCs seek to increase their global presence. These pressures relate not only to developing nations as marked balance of payment deficits can result in governments of more developed economies putting pressure on foreign competitors to locate their facilities locally. This is one reason why Japanese car makers have located plants in the US and Europe and are continuing to increase the capacity of these over time.

3   *Technology developments* Technology is not specific to a location and, in that way, is redefining what makes a location feasible. Advances in technology and electronic communications are undermining the emphasis once placed on key factors such as

Multi-national corporations – companies that manage operations or deliver services or products in more than one country

'Many
organizations
never change
location'

proximity to customers. The opportunities that these technologies provide have already changed the pattern of location in several industries.

4 *New countries are opening up* Areas of the world that had for decades been closed to outside investments due to political dogma and/or social or economic instability have now opened up. Notable examples were parts of South East Asia in the 1980s and China and Eastern Europe in the last 20 years. Being close to new markets, low labour costs and the opportunity for companies to take over existing, often not well-managed, facilities have driven many recent location decisions.

5 *Market access/local presence in large consumer markets* There is no more clear-cut example of how large markets are attractive locations for businesses than the recent and continuing investments in North America and Europe. This is primarily because of market access. The US is a very large market in its own right, and the North American Free Trade Agreement (NAFTA) – which aims to remove barriers to trade and investment between the US, Canada and Mexico – has swelled the consumer base by over 40 per cent, to some 460 million consumers in 2010. The opportunity to become direct participants in this highly competitive and innovative market was one reason why Honda and Toyota built plants and established joint venture agreements in the 1980s and have continued to expand these facilities through to the present day. This was also part of the rationale for BMW and Mercedes-Benz in building their first manufacturing plants outside Germany, locating them in South Carolina and Alabama, respectively. Similar patterns are also present in Europe, where the total market continues to grow as membership of the European Union increases. One outcome reflecting the growing importance of this combined market is the level of foreign direct investment within Europe. Since the mid-1990s, this has consistently been more than 40 per cent of the world total, although the continent was hit by the global recession in 2008, when the figure fell to 39 per cent as investors sought other locations in which to invest.

6 *Currency value fluctuations* As the relative values of currencies change, the impact on costs may force a company to rethink the location of its manufacturing plants, particularly those serving local markets. The most marked example of this is Japan. In order to enable them to remain competitive, particularly in export markets, a whole range of Japanese companies have moved the location of their manufacturing plants to regions to which they export. The motor industry examples above were also influenced by this factor. Other examples include electronics and consumer products companies.

The specific factors influencing the choice of where to locate can be broadly separated into those which relate to the higher level decisions of continent/region, country and area/city, and those which relate to the choice of the site itself. Let's first look at the factors affecting higher level decisions and then consider the factors affecting choice of site. The various techniques that can be used to select a site will then be discussed.

Factors affecting the choice of continent/region, country and area/city

When making the decision of which continent or region, country and area or city to locate in, the following factors need to be considered:

1 *A well-developed infrastructure* Ease of access to road and rail systems and sea and air links will often be high on a company's list of requirements, particularly where the inputs and outputs of the transformation process are high volume and bulky. Similarly, other aspects of infrastructure such as communication and power systems will be important factors in deciding where, in general, to locate. In addition, the availability of appropriate support services is an increasingly important factor. For example, the growing technology base, particularly the role of IT that characterizes many businesses today, places great emphasis on the need for local technical support.

2 *Proximity to markets* It makes sense for services and goods to be produced as close to their markets as possible. The benefits include lower distribution and provisioning costs and shorter distances, especially where aspects such as product freshness are involved.

3 *Proximity to suppliers* As well as the obvious cost implications of distance, being a long way from suppliers also incurs longer lead-times, introduces a higher level of uncertainty and reduces a supplier's ability to respond quickly.

4 *Hospitable business climate* The long-term nature of location decisions places the business climate high on the agenda. The combination of an environment of free trade, free thought and the opportunity to create wealth is key in attracting investors. For this reason, Europe and North America continue to attract a high percentage of global foreign investment.

5 *Availability of staff* Recent surveys of the factors cited by executives when making location decisions all point to a pool of suitable and sufficient staff as one of the most important. Concerns about the skill levels and flexibility of staff are high on the location agenda, while MNCs will also take into account the traditional attitudes to work (the work ethic) within different regions.

6 *Quality of life for employees* It is not enough that sufficient skilled staff are to be found in the region or area: a prospective employer must also be satisfied that facilities are or will be made available at a level that will retain staff. Schools, accommodation and social infrastructure all affect the quality of life for employees, particularly expatriates, whose skills and experience may be particularly critical in the earlier phases of a project.

7 *Variable cost structures* These remain a critical factor in location decisions and concern several dimensions that make up total variable costs:
   • *Staff costs* Locating in lower staff cost areas of the world such as Mexico, Eastern Europe, China and parts of the Asia Pacific region is often fundamental in the decision process. In the past, these decisions were often made by businesses using less skilled staff, but developments in IT and communications systems have extended this location alternative to businesses using more highly skilled people.
   • *Energy costs* Where the energy costs of processing are high, companies often choose to locate near to a less expensive source of power, such as hydroelectricity.
   • *Transportation costs* Incoming materials and the distribution of finished goods involve not only the actual costs of haulage, but also excise duties and tariffs, which may vary depending on the country of origin.

8 *Fixed costs and investments* These are the costs of getting started and also the fixed costs of doing business in a country or region:
   • *Investment factors* Governments can offer sizeable incentives to encourage companies to locate in a particular country or area, including financial assistance in the form of special grants, low-interest loans and tax allowances on building and material imports. For example, AMD, the US computer chip maker, confirmed that it would build a second chip plant in Dresden, Germany only after it had won $1.5 billion in German government-backed funding. The $2.4 billion plant began production in 2006 and now employs about 1,000 people. It is one of the biggest investment projects in the former East Germany since reunification in 1990.
   • *Fixed costs* These can include inducements in the form of low local rates bills, low rents and low employment taxes.

Now take a look at Case 6.1, which provides an illustration of some of the factors that influence location decisions.

Until the late 1990s, Noida, a suburb north of Delhi, was a sleepy haven for pensioners wishing to escape the hustle and bustle of India's capital city. Now it is a boom town, with shopping malls, multiplex cinemas and chaotic traffic reflecting its growth and the lifestyle that its well-educated workforce is demanding.

At the centre of Noida's rapid expansion is the office that houses Software Technology Parks of India (STPI), the quango at the centre of India's rapid IT growth. STPI is the licensing authority for companies wanting to export IT or IT-enabled services. Formed in 1991, STPI has been central to the rapid growth in India's IT exports, which now exceed $10 billion.

As well as its licensing role, STPI has pushed hard on developing the necessary IT infrastructure, including setting up broadband networks across the country. It now receives 10 applications per week from companies wanting to join the IT phenomenon. While it expects this rate to increase in the future, it is sure that it can still turn the paperwork around inside a month.
www.hyd.stpi.in

Questions

1 What are the reasons for the rapid growth in Noida's IT-based services?

2 Now analyse the case and relate the detail to each of the factors in the section of this chapter entitled 'Factors affecting the choice of continent/region, country and area/city'.

9 *Favourable government policies* In addition to investment and tax inducements, national and local government departments can affect the siting of a new business by how easy or difficult they make the process that the company has to go through. This includes the political stance towards:
   - *Environmental concerns* – the extent to which building and planning regulations embody stringent rules regarding all forms of pollution, including noise, toxic emissions, odour and the types and levels of effluent
   - *Political attitudes towards inward investment*
   - *Barriers and licenses* – individual countries and trading blocs may impose restrictions in the form of quotas or increased tariff levels for different importers. The task of overcoming or circumventing such restrictions often leads MNCs in particular to choose locations that reduce or even eliminate such disadvantages
   - *Easing capital movement restrictions* to allow companies to transfer money in and out of the country
   - *Government planning assistance* – including simplifying planning procedures and reducing the time taken for planning applications to be approved
   - *Making suitable land available* in terms of its amount and location.

10 *Being near to the customer* Customers, especially those requiring frequent deliveries of materials in a just-in-time context, increasingly require suppliers to build plants close by. In this way, deliveries can be made, sometimes several times a day, thus keeping inventories low. Also, being close to your customer signals commitment and provides reassurance, as Case 6.2 illustrates.

Factors affecting the choice of site

The final step is to decide the precise location within the chosen city centre, regional shopping centre, business park, industrial complex or street. At this micro-level, an array of factors specific to this particular decision come into play. To help review these, the different factors have been grouped under two headings: the site (addressed here), and the impact of site location on potential demand (discussed in the next section).

The factors affecting the choice of site comprise a whole range of issues, including:

- Adequate, off-street parking for both staff and customers
- The building's design related to, first, its external impact, and second, the internal arrangements in terms of the basic tasks involved and the front-office space where customers are to interface with delivery systems
- Attractive rental costs and local taxes
- The appropriateness of the existing space to the business's specific needs, including the amount of time and investment to bring it up to the required level
- Proximity to support services
- Room for future expansion and associated development costs
- High traffic volumes, which may be beneficial in terms of demand but may be an unwelcome factor in terms of customer access
- Being visible from the street or highway, which is particularly relevant where call-in trade is an important factor.

Impact of site location on potential demand

The factors here include the following:

- *High levels of customer traffic* in the area as this influences demand for a whole range of businesses such as hotels, restaurants and retailing.
- *Proximity to competitors*[1] When shopping for services such as banking, hotel accommodation, clothes, shoes, accessories and restaurants, customers prefer to be able to choose from a range of options – the concept of **competitive clustering**. For example, research has shown that hotels located in areas with many competitors nearby

Competitive clustering – where similar and/ or competing organizations site their facilities in the same geographical area in order to increase the overall productivity with which they work or increase overall sales for all involved

In 1947, Pierre Burelle, founder of Plastic Omnium, a parts supplier, published his strategic blueprint. It was a drawing of an automobile showing all the components then made of metal that he thought could be replaced by ones made of plastic. More than half a century on and guided by Burelle's earlier strategic vision, Paris-based Plastic Omnium is, through joint ventures, the world's biggest maker of plastic fuel tanks and the second largest supplier of bumpers for automobiles.

In 1987 the company had just four factories, three of them in France, but by 2009 the company had 94 plants in more than 25 countries. The key to this growth has principally been the company's willingness to build plants next to its customers' premises. It all began in 1990 when Plastic Omnium agreed to build a plant near to BMW's Munich assembly plant and, in that way, gain second-supplier status.

Since then, it has adopted the same location strategy many times over, for example with VW in Slovakia, and with General Motors, VW and others in Mexico. More recently, the focus has been on emerging markets in Asia, especially China. Of Plastic Omnium's €2.5 billion sales in the automotive sector in 2009, revenue from China doubled to €100 million, which represented 5 per cent of the company's total automotive revenue, and this is set to increase in the coming years as two new plants were opened in China in 2010.
www.plasticomnium.fr

Question

How has plant location been central to Plastic Omnium's rapid growth in the last 25 years?

Market saturation
strategy – where an
organization groups
multiple outlets
close together in
urban and other
high-traffic areas

experience higher occupancy rates than those in isolated locations. Furthermore, many budget hotels are located by motorways or major highway intersections to reflect the fact that their market is not the local population but business people and others on the move.

- **Market saturation strategy** In Europe and North America, this unconventional strategy is gaining ground. Examples include Benetton, the Italian clothing company, and Au Bon Pain cafés in the US. The idea is to locate the same outlets close to one another in the same area. For example, Au Bon Pain's US cafés are concentrated in Boston, Cambridge (Massachusetts), New York, Philadelphia, Miami, Pittsburg and Washington DC. As Figure 6.1 illustrates, the company's deliberate policy is to locate several cafés, all selling a wide range of gourmet sandwiches, salads, muffins, croissants, bread and soups, in the same area. As you can see, the pursuit of this strategy is a key factor in the company's location decisions.

Figure 6.1 **The location of most of Au Bon Pain's outlets (2010)**

Locations		Outlets
New York City		25
Boston		22
Washington DC		18
Chicago		17
Miami		15
Philadelphia		10
Cambridge (Massachusetts)		8
Pittsburg		8
Airports	Dallas Forth Worth	8
	JFK	6
	La Guardia	5
	Logan International	4

Before moving on to the next section, take a look at Case 6.3, which illustrates a growing phenomenon in call centre location, and review the case questions.

Site location techniques[2]

Although site selection is often based on opportunistic factors such as site availability and cost benefits, including government grants and favourable tax rates, undertaking a quantitative analysis brings an important perspective to the decision and helps to identify the optimal location based on the key benefits an organization is seeking. A number of approaches have been developed to help companies make location decisions. This section introduces the more commonly used techniques, but first let's look at the basic ideas on which they are built.

The objective underlying the optimal choice of location is to maximize the desired benefits, but which aspect of benefit an organization wishes to maximize will differ. In the private sector, the driver will typically be either maximizing sales revenue, in the case of retail outlets or restaurants, or minimizing costs, as with a distribution centre or courier service company. In the public sector, on the other hand, the drivers will reflect the needs of the community that a facility serves. For example, a hospital may be located to offer the easiest access to local people in terms of distance and availability of public transport.

© Alex Hill and Terry Hill 2011

HSBC, the world's largest banking and financial services corporation, cut 4,000 UK staff when it relocated work to India, Malaysia and China. The decision by the bank follows similar moves by other companies including BT, Goldman Sachs and Prudential. The jobs involved were principally processing work and telephone enquiries.

The number of offshore operations belonging to UK financial service companies grew from 200 employees in 1996 to about 250,000 by the end of 2010. HSBC was already running a number of global processing hubs in Hyderabad and Bangalore in India, and also in Malaysia, and much of the UK work was relocated to these sites. India, in particular, has emerged in the past decade as a new location for call centre operations, given its large number of well-educated, English-speaking young people and lower staff costs. By the end of 2010, about 10,000 (some 15 per cent) of HSBC's staff were in service centres in Asia.

www.hsbc.com

Questions

1 HSBC's chief executive is quoted as saying that such moves are essential to the bank's continued success and to help ensure job security for the bank's staff worldwide. Why?

2 Why does HSBC relocate work to its existing hubs in India and Malaysia?

Lecturers: visit www.palgrave.com/business/hillessential for additional resources

Each facility will approach the problem of where best to locate by assessing the various factors involved. For example, a company building a distribution centre will focus on the trade-offs between the building costs and operating costs of the centre and the transportation costs to its various sites. For a retail outlet, the trade-offs will include building and operating costs versus the attractiveness of different sites to potential customers and its potential impact on sales revenue. In the public sector, location decisions are often more difficult to assess as the factors involved are not as easily defined. However, two of the factors more commonly used to maximize the location benefits for a community are:

- Distance per visit – to minimize the average per-visit distance to a facility (for example, a hospital or health centre) for potential users
- The utilization level of the facility – to maximize the total number of visits to a facility by choosing a location that will make visiting it easier if the use of the facility is optional as, for example, in the case of a library.

The first task in location analysis is an accurate assessment of the spatial demand for a service, that is, the demand by geographical area. To establish this, the target population needs to be defined. For a distribution centre, the sites that the centre is intended to serve will be known. For a community health centre, on the other hand, the target population could be the total number of people it is intended to serve, broken down by groups to reflect the level and type of service to be provided (for example, family units and age groups). The area being served will then be split into smaller geographical units for which demand will be assessed, and from these a complete picture can be established of the spatial demand requirements for the whole community to be served by the health centre in question.

The second task is then to use one or more of the following techniques to evaluate how best to meet the demand requirements in terms of selected criteria. Of the various techniques and models that exist for locating facilities, the appropriate one to use will reflect the nature of the location problem on hand. Here, two more commonly used techniques are reviewed – the **weighted factor** and **centre of gravity** methods.

Weighted factor method – a method of determining the optimum location for a facility that involves allotting points (with proportionally more points being given for meeting the more important criteria) to each site on the basis of how well it meets the various criteria

Centre of gravity method – a method for determining the best site for a facility in which the outcome will be the location point that strikes the optimum balance between the set of variables involved

Weighted factor method

Consider the example of a chain of coffee and sandwich bars choosing between three potential sites in Copenhagen. The company's experience of what makes a good location has highlighted the factors that influence sales and the importance of these relative to each other. To assess each site, these factors are then scored on a scale of 0–10, and a weighted average score for each site is then calculated, as shown in Figure 6.2. The individual scores are multiplied by the weight (%) given to each factor, and the one with highest total is the best potential site based on this measure. For example, Site 1 in Figure 6.2 gets a score of 630, as shown below:

Site 1 = $(40 \times 6) + (20 \times 7) + (15 \times 5) + (10 \times 8) + (10 \times 6) + (5 \times 7) = 630$

In the example given in Figure 6.2, Site 2 is clearly the best potential location for the proposed coffee and sandwich bar as it has the highest score.

Centre of gravity method

Where the choice of site needs to be made in relation to a number of existing locations, the centre of gravity method provides a way to address the factors involved. As the name implies, the outcome will be the location point that strikes the optimum balance between all the variables involved.

The best way to explain this approach is to provide a worked example of the steps to follow. A German supermarket chain is planning to build a distribution centre to serve the Bavarian region where, over the last five years, it has built seven outlets. Until this time,

Figure 6.2 Weighted factor method of choosing a coffee/sandwich bar site

Factor	Weight	Site 1		Site 2		Site 3	
Closeness to office customers	40	6	240	8	320	7	280
Visibility from street	20	7	140	7	140	6	120
Nearness to metro station/bus stops	15	5	75	8	120	8	120
Closeness to tourist attraction(s)	10	8	80	5	50	5	50
Ease of access/width of sidewalk	10	6	60	8	80	6	60
Ease of parking for suppliers	5	7	35	7	35	7	35
Totals	100	–	630	–	745	–	665

it has supported these with a combination of approaches including direct supply and deliveries from its existing distribution centres located further north. Several ranges of product will continue to be delivered directly from producers, but the company's past experience has shown that a combination of direct supply and distribution centre supply works best. The location of the seven supermarkets is shown in Figure 6.3.

You will see from the figure that a reference grid has been superimposed on the map. The centre of gravity method identifies the lowest distribution cost location for the new centre by calculating the mean of X and Y. To add to this, Figure 6.4 shows the number of weekly van deliveries to each supermarket.

The information in Figures 6.3 and 6.4 is then combined in the following way in order to identify the optimum position for the new supermarket:

$$\text{Mean of X} = \frac{\Sigma X_i A_i}{\Sigma A_i} \quad \text{where } X_i = \text{site locations on the X axis}$$
$$A_i = \text{\# weekly van deliveries to each supermarket}$$

$$\text{Mean of Y} = \frac{\Sigma Y_i A_i}{\Sigma A_i} \quad \text{where } Y_i = \text{site locations on the Y axis}$$
$$A_i = \text{\# weekly van deliveries to each supermarket}$$

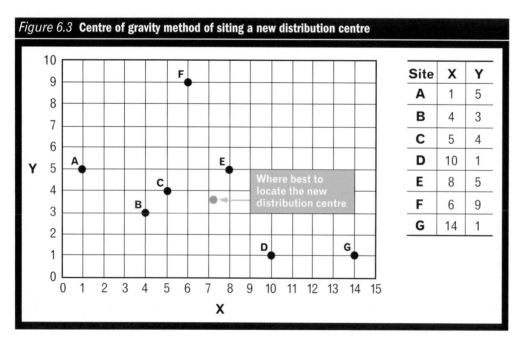

Figure 6.3 Centre of gravity method of siting a new distribution centre

Site	X	Y
A	1	5
B	4	3
C	5	4
D	10	1
E	8	5
F	6	9
G	14	1

Figure 6.4 **Number of weekly van deliveries to each supermarket**

Supermarket	# weekly deliveries
A	6
B	14
C	14
D	10
E	8
F	12
G	14
TOTAL	**78**

So, in this example:

$$\text{Mean of X} = \frac{(1 \times 6) + (4 \times 14) + (5 \times 14) + (10 \times 10) + (8 \times 8) + (6 \times 12) + (14 \times 14)}{78}$$

$$= 7.23$$

$$\text{Mean of Y} = \frac{(5 \times 6) + (3 \times 14) + (4 \times 14) + (1 \times 10) + (5 \times 8) + (9 \times 12) + (1 \times 14)}{78}$$

$$= 3.85$$

Now that we've identified the factors that influence the choice of location, and the methods for identifying the optimal site, let's move on to look at the process for deciding on a layout.

Choosing a layout

The following sections address the task of how best to arrange the delivery systems, processes and staff used in providing services or making products. First, we will review the general background factors to be taken into account in layout design. This will be followed by an overview of the basic types of layout and where and how each is used, together with an explanation of a hybrid layout (a mix between one basic type of layout and another) and a review of the techniques and approaches used in layout design.

Factors influencing layout

There are several background factors that will dictate some design parameters when laying out facilities. These include the nature of the organization's task, the available space, the need for flexibility in the future and health and safety. The relative importance of these will differ from one organization to another, but they will need to be incorporated into an organization's layout design.

The nature of the core task

The nature of an organization's core task will dictate some of the parameters involved in a facility layout. For instance, a supermarket will need to incorporate sufficient customer parking as well as adequate access for the delivery of goods. Similarly, it will have a stockholding area that needs to include cold storage facilities for fresh dairy, meat and fish products. The branch of a bank will need to incorporate an area for ATMs that can be accessed by the public when the branch is closed, cashier facilities inside the bank that afford sensible levels of security and areas that will provide privacy when customers are seeking advice on personal finances from banking staff. And so on.

Available space

The space available for a facility often comes with a mix of constraints including ease of access, building regulations, land costs and the actual area itself, and the facility design will need to accommodate all these. As an example, where land is at a premium (in terms of either availability or cost), a facility incorporating several floors will be a design prerequisite. For instance, while the classic McDonald's outlet is a single-storey, free-standing facility, in cities such as Stockholm, Copenhagen and Madrid, the outlets are designed with several floors.

Making space for future expansion and layout changes

Organizations are dynamic and need to adapt to future changes in terms of space requirements and the layout of facilities. It is important, therefore, during the design phase of a facility to take account of the possible need for change. The dimensions of such future changes may include:

- *Activity volumes* – for example, how many passengers would be handled by an airport in the future, or how many customers would be served in a retail outlet or accommodated in an upmarket restaurant if the businesses were a success
- *The range of services and products* to be provided
- *The nature of the services or products* on offer, for example whether a bank or a fast-food outlet will incorporate a 'self-service' or 'drive-thru' option in the future.

Health and safety

The increasing and appropriate emphasis on health and safety in the workplace has to be incorporated into the design of facilities, in terms of both staff and customers. Factors range from chemical and other pollution hazards and fire risks through to eliminating possible accidents in terms of flat walking surfaces, the width and depth of stairwells, the provision of handrails and adequate entrances and exits.

Now take a look at Case 6.4 to reflect on some of the background factors we have just covered.

Basic types of layout

The objective of a layout is to arrange the delivery systems, processes and related equipment, work areas, storage areas and staff needed to provide a service or make a product such that these resources operate at peak effectiveness and efficiency. This section looks at the three basic types of layout: fixed position, process or functional, and service or product. Some organizations seek to improve the level of effectiveness and efficiency of these basic types by mixing elements of each together. One hybrid form, as these new types are known, is discussed in the next section. The appropriate basic layout type reflects the service and product characteristics involved, as will now be explained.

> **KEY IDEA**

The three basic types of layout are fixed position, process or functional, and service or product

> Fixed position layout – a layout in which the tools, staff and equipment are brought to the product or service, which remains fixed in one location. This layout is necessary if, for example, the product is too large to be moved

Fixed position layout

Some services and products have to be provided or made where they are to be consumed or used because there is no other way for customers to access them or they are too large to move. Where the service needs to be undertaken on a customer's site (for example, a management consultancy assignment, or the regular or breakdown maintenance of a

CASE 6.4 CREATING SPACE ON PASSENGER JETS

When push comes to shove, more than 50 per cent of airline passengers cite elbow room as their first choice when it comes to extra space (having an empty seat next to them being the ideal). Economy seats are about 17 inches, or 42 cm, wide, the same as they have been for years. Making aisles dangerously narrow and putting fewer seats in a row and sacrificing revenue are difficult calls to make. But more elbow room is starting to influence an airline's choice of which aircraft to buy. Denver-based Frontier Airlines has cited the 7 inch (17 cm) wider interior as 'a big selling point' in ordering 20 Airbus 318s and 319s over the new-generation Boeing 737s.

As most airlines report, one of the biggest drivers for satisfaction is whether the seat next to a person is empty. When the number of seats filled crosses the 60 per cent line, customer satisfaction plum-

mets, while at a 70 per cent load factor, only 25 per cent of passengers view a flight as being satisfactory. The consideration of seat layouts on today's passenger jets has taken these issues on board – Continental Airlines specifically designed the coach-class seating layout in its new Boeing 777s in a way that increased the chance that passengers would have an empty seat next to them.

Questions

1 Why is elbow room on passenger airlines an increasingly important factor in the new millennium?

2 Why is legroom often easier to provide than elbow room in passenger jet design?

Lecturers: visit www.palgrave.com/business/hillessential for additional resources

computer system or a large piece of manufacturing equipment) or the completed product cannot be moved as this is not feasible (for example, with a roadway) or the product is too large (for example, a bridge or office block), the layout arrangement used is known as fixed position (see Figure 6.5). This requires staff, equipment, materials and other resources to come to or be brought to the place or site where the service is to be provided or the product is to be made.

As a consequence of the fixed position nature of this provision, the layout design requires the scheduling of materials, equipment, skilled staff and other resources at a site and the rescheduling of these to other jobs when their phase of the work has been completed or the job is finished. The consequence is that the capabilities and resources needed to complete a service or product are brought to and arranged on site, are managed on site and are then dismantled or redistributed during and at the end of a task. The layout, therefore, needs to:

- Reflect the space requirements of each part of the task while recognizing that the levels of activity will vary over the duration of the project
- Provide for the delivery and storage of materials
- Accommodate staff and equipment needs over the time it takes to provide the service or make the product
- Facilitate the movement of staff and equipment on site
- Minimize the total movement of resources on site.

However, fixed position layouts are complicated by a number of factors, including:

- Typically, there is limited space. When building an office block, the total site is limited in area and has to accommodate the various construction as well as support activities that are part of the building process. Similarly, when completing the maintenance programme on a large piece of equipment, the space available for accommodating the tasks restricts the optimum layout.
- The tasks that make up the service or product will vary in nature and volume during the provision, so the layout needs to accommodate these often sizeable differences .
- The steps involved are often uncertain, and plans change due to delays. Consequently, the schedule has to be rearranged, and the layout needs to be able to cope with changes such as these.

Process or functional layout

The term **process or functional layout** reflects the fact that the layout is arranged by putting similar processes or functions together in one area. The customers, information or products then move to the various process or functional groups in a given order. So whereas, in a fixed position layout, the resources (for example, staff and equipment) move to the point where the service or product is to be provided, with process or functional layouts the reverse happens – the resources stay still and the customers, information or products move to them in a given sequence. Once the service or product does not have to be provided or made on site, companies typically prefer to use a process or functional layout.

There are several advantages to this delivery system layout, including:

- Similar skills are located together, which allows for skill levels to be enhanced and experience to be transferred within the group.
- The utilization of processes, skilled staff and equipment improves as it is easier to access these total resources because they are grouped in the same area.
- A wide range of services and products can be accommodated.
- The delivery system can handle many customer requirements at the same time.

As indicated in Figure 6.5, a process or functional layout is used for both non-repeat (special) and repeat (standard) services and products; the examples that follow illustrate how the delivery system and layout would work for these types of service and product.

Process or functional layout – a layout that involves sets of capabilities (equipment or staff) of a similar nature or function being grouped together in one area; this allows a range of different services or products to be processed using the same process or functional groups

Non-repeat (special) services and products As these services and products are unique and will not typically be repeated, the skilled person or team undertaking the job will determine and then follow the best sequence of steps to complete the job, and then access the relevant processes, functions or other resources as appropriate.

For example, the analysis phase of designing and implementing an IT system would be completed by an information systems specialist. The consultant would access or compile the relevant data and complete the appropriate analyses to meet each phase of the assignment. When discussions with executives and staff were necessary, the systems consultant would typically meet with them in their own office, area or location. Similarly, analyses of the procedures, systems and facilities would be completed in the various functions or areas involved. In this way, the skilled person would take each phase of a job to the appropriate process, complete the work, move to the next process to complete the next step and so on until the job was complete. A further illustration of a company using a process layout to complete a non-repeat job is given in Figure 6.6 (p. 188).

This figure represents a tool-making company that builds unique tools, moulds and dies for customers. Having reviewed and discussed the details of a customer's drawing, a skilled toolmaker will complete the whole task of machining and building the tool to the required design. To do this, the toolmaker completes the machining requirements by taking the part-finished die from work bench to machine, and from machine to machine, to undertake each appropriate step until it is completed. Here, just as with the information systems consultancy described earlier, both product and skilled person move from process to process until the work is finished.

Now you understand what happens, why does a process or functional layout best suit these requirements? The principal reason is that this layout design enables any skilled person to access the resources (processes or people in a function) in any chosen sequence to complete the whole of a task. In the toolmaking example above, there will be several skilled toolmakers machining and building customer-specific tools, moulds or dies. With this layout, each can access a specific resource in the order that best meets the task at hand and, as the sequence of steps will differ for any particular product, the layout must facilitate the use of the various machines and other pieces of equipment to meet these various work patterns.

Repeat (standard) services and products As explained in Chapters 4 and 5, when services and products are completed more than once, the higher volumes and repeat nature mean that a different delivery system is more appropriate. What is processed (that is, customers, information or products) will determine the people skills and equipment required, but the layout of the delivery system will be designed on a process or functional basis (see Figure 6.5).

Examples of process layouts for delivering standard services and products include:

- *Hospitals* The functions in a hospital (for example, operating theatres, pharmacy, consulting rooms, reception area, X-ray facilities, wards and laboratories) are laid out functionally. That is, the facilities and staff who run the pharmacy services will be put together in one department, all operating theatres will similarly be located in the same area, and so on.

- *Printing companies* The activities in a printing company that comprise design, plate preparation, ink laboratory and stores, printing and post-printing tasks such as cutting and creasing, slitting, collation and packing will be brought together each in their own area, such that all designers and the relevant equipment are in the same department, similarly with plate preparation, and so on, as shown earlier in Figure 5.4.

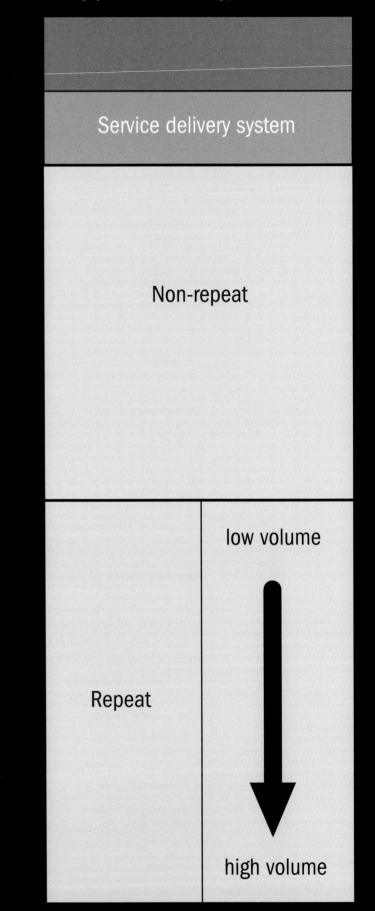

TYPES OF

Layout	Manufacturing process
Fixed position	Project
Process or functional	Jobbing Batch
Service or product	Line Continuous processing

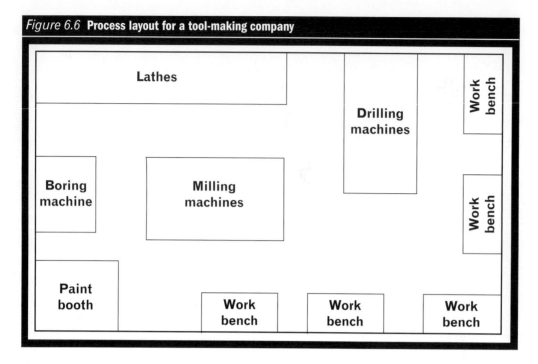

Figure 6.6 **Process layout for a tool-making company**

- *Supermarkets* The layout in a supermarket is based on similar merchandise (for example, bakery items, soft drinks, wines, cheese, cooked meats, fresh vegetables and cereals) being located in the same aisles, and similar activities (for example, check-outs) being positioned in the same area. Where merchandise and activities are positioned will also reflect the levels of demand, traffic flows, nature of the purchase and similar factors. But the reason for locating similar merchandise and activities in the same area is twofold: it is easier for customers to shop, and it is also easier for staff to replenish the shelves.

Now let's look at how the process or functional layout facilitates the delivery of the required services and products. First, with this type of layout, facilities are laid out with like kinds (functions, processes or merchandise) grouped together, which brings with it economies of scale and other gains, such as improving the utilization of the resources as all services or products can access and use them, keeping skill groups together, reducing operating costs and lowering investment (due to higher utilization and a minimization of unnecessary process, equipment and space duplication).

Second, the total service or product is often provided in two or more steps. In such instances, the task is broken down into the required number of steps, and each step is completed at a different process. This is achieved by the customer, information or product going to each function or process group in the appropriate order, the required step then being completed. In some service delivery systems, for example fast-food restaurants, the total requirement is provided as a single step. But the principle is the same as in a multi-step provision. The food preparation processes and counter service operation are laid out in their own area. The customer then goes to a server at the counter and is 'processed' (that is, orders, pays and is given the food).

To illustrate a multi-step process, let's imagine you need to go to hospital as you have injured your arm. You will typically be 'processed' by the hospital in the following way, with potential delays (queues) between steps, as shown in Figure 6.7:

1 Go to the hospital reception, queue and then provide your details.
2 Go to the orthopaedic consultant and wait for your turn. The consultant assesses that you may have a broken arm and asks you to go for an X-ray to confirm and provide details of the break.

3 You queue, and then your arm is X-rayed.
4 You return to the consultant with the X-ray pictures and wait. The consultant reviews the X-rays and instructs the plaster room on how the arm is to be bound and supported.
5 You then go to the plaster room, where first you wait and then your arm is treated.
6 Then it's back to reception to arrange your follow-up appointment.

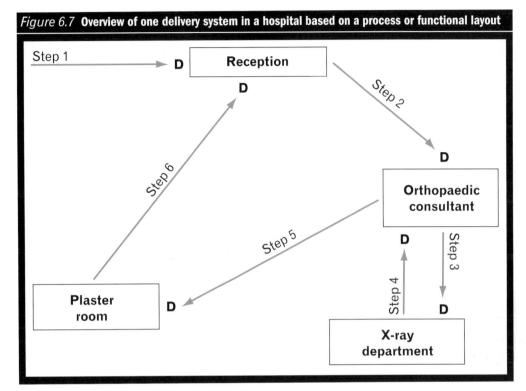

Figure 6.7 Overview of one delivery system in a hospital based on a process or functional layout

Notes: 1 Explanation of steps 1 to 6 is given in the accompanying text.
2 **D** indicates a delay (in this instance, a queue).
3 The hospital layout (not to scale) comprises corridors, rooms and waiting areas. Patients (the customers being processed) will move between departments using corridors, lifts and stairs.

As you will see from this, the processes or functions (in this instance, skilled staff and equipment) remain in place, and the patients (that is, the hospital's customers) move from function to function to be processed. This movement by customers, information or products is an underlying characteristic of this type of layout design. Furthermore, they will typically wait between steps for a process to become available. In this way, several of the advantages of this type of layout that were highlighted earlier will be provided. For example, utilization of skilled staff is enhanced as the layout design requires that patients wait (queue) to see them. As a result, these key resources do not have to wait for patients, and utilization is thereby increased. Also, this type of layout allows the hospital's delivery system to treat a wide range of requirements at the same time, with patients going through their own sets of steps. The system can therefore handle different customer needs requiring different combinations of skilled staff and equipment, with the amount of any resource required at each step being variable and unknown. These characteristics are those associated with low to relatively high volume, repeat (standard) services and products. Similarly, in our supermarket example, customers move from aisle to aisle selecting the food items they wish to purchase. This functional layout means that many customers can be served at the same time.

In manufacturing, the process layout and the way in which a product is completed follows the same format as in the previous examples. Similar processes are grouped together in the same geographical area (Figure 6.8). Products are broken down into a number of steps, and a product moves from process group to process group to be completed. So, looking at Figure 6.8, a product that required moulding, sonic welding, hot roll stamping and final assembly would go through the necessary series of steps with periods of waiting between one step and the next.

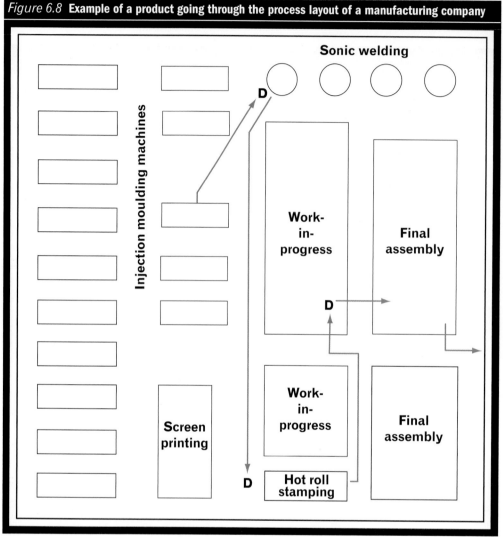

Figure 6.8 **Example of a product going through the process layout of a manufacturing company**

Notes: 1 **D** indicates a delay: a product here is waiting its turn to be processed.

2 ⟶ provides an example of one product's movements from injection moulding to sonic welding to hot roll stamping to work-in-progress to final assembly.

Finally, with functional layouts, the position of processes in the overall layout may reflect the flow of the services or products through the different steps or stages, but this will only be the case where the services or products involved all follow (at least in part) the same sequence. Hence, for the examples provided so far:

- For the printing company example given earlier as Figure 5.4, you will see, when you glance back at this figure, that the functional layout reflects the sequence involved. That is, all the products will start with cylinders/plates and paper stores, through printing and then to slitting and collation (if required), before going on to packing and finally to finished goods.
- Figure 6.8 is similar to Figure 5.4.
- Figure 6.6 on the other hand, does not reflect service/product flow as here the products will all take different routes and may, in fact, go back to earlier processes at some stage. This lack of similarity in process sequence is also well illustrated in the hospital example shown in Figure 6.7. As you can imagine, the sequence of steps for one

patient's treatment will differ greatly from that for another patient, and consequently patients' routes will differ.

Service or product layout

Like the last type of layout, this type is oriented around similar services or products, but the volumes will be higher, demand patterns will be more stable, and the services or products will again be standardized. Line and continuous processing use product layout in their manufacturing processes. As explained in Chapter 4, examples in the service sector are infrequent, with Dr Svyatoslav Fyodorov's eye microsurgery unit (see Case 4.3) being one of the exceptions.

Here the facilities are oriented in relation to the service or product. The first task is to determine the steps involved in providing a service or making a product, and then the process is designed to complete each step at a different work station. For example, an assembly line is designed with several work stations, and at each of these the parts making up the product are put together in a given order. To design a continuous processing system, for example to refine oil, the steps to complete this task are determined and the process is then designed to complete these in sequence. Both these examples illustrate the high volume and standard nature of the products involved (they all go through the same steps in the same sequence). As highlighted earlier, high volumes justify the dedicated investment, and the standard nature of the products means that the process design involves the same sequence of steps. Finally, this leads to the fact that both line and continuous processing need to be balanced. That is, the work performed at each work station must be balanced (that is, take the same amount of time to complete) with the work at all the other stations. While assembly lines tend to be paced (in terms of how long it takes to complete the work at a station) by people, continuous processing systems will be paced by the processing equipment.

Going back now to Dr Fyodorov's eye clinic. The radial keratotomy treatment for myopia (short-sightedness) described in Case 4.3 illustrates all the features of a service-oriented layout. The patients to be treated fit the medical specification for this treatment procedure, the eye operation performed is the same for each patient, the surgeons each complete their designated step in the total procedure, the patients, who lie on operating tables, are all then moved one step further, and so the process continues. At each step, the work involved takes a similar time to all the other steps, with the activities monitored on TV screens and the surgeons linked to each other through an audio system.

Cells – a hybrid delivery system layout

Given the increasing difference between markets, companies have responded by developing alternative delivery systems to reflect these changing demands. One widely used rearrangement is cells.

> **KEY IDEA**

> Cells (a mix of functional and service/product layouts) can better meet the needs of some businesses

As explained earlier, process or functional layouts are based on grouping similar processes or functions together in the same geographical area. Without sufficient volumes to justify dedicating facilities (staff and/or equipment) as with a service- or product-oriented layout such as line, process or functionally based layouts allow a range of services and products to share skilled staff and equipment, thus better balancing the utilization/investment equation. What cells do is mix the process or functional and service or product layouts to create a hybrid, as was illustrated earlier in Figure 5.14 and has been reproduced here as Figure 6.9.

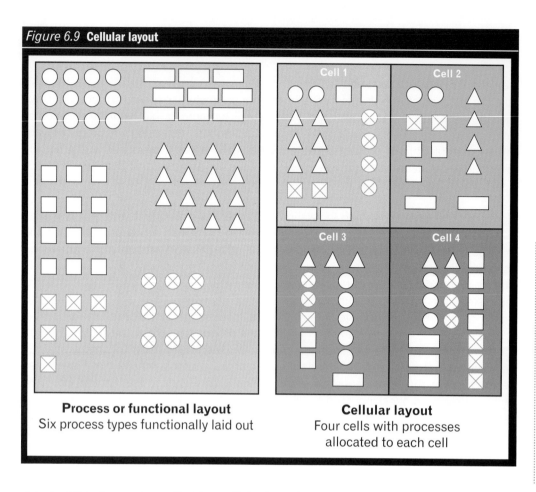

Figure 6.9 **Cellular layout**

Process or functional layout
Six process types functionally laid out

Cellular layout
Four cells with processes
allocated to each cell

Cell 1

Cell 2

Cell 3

Cell 4

Cellular layout – a mix of functional and service/product layouts in which the necessary staff/ equipment to provide a range of services or make a range of products are positioned in the same area. The work stations are grouped together according to the process requirements, and the relevant services and products are then processed in the 'cell'

A look at this figure shows that the **cellular layout** comprises processes allocated to one of four cells based on the skills and equipment required to make the products within a cell (thus reflecting the service or product layout principle). In addition, like skills and equipment in a cell are positioned in the same geographical area (thus reflecting the process or functional layout principle). Hence it is termed a hybrid.[3] The same use of the cellular layout is now gaining ground in the service sector, as Case 6.5 illustrates.

Detailed layout design

Having selected the appropriate basic layout, the next step is to design a detailed layout, the objectives of which are to decide:

- Where to position the staff, processes, equipment and other facilities involved in providing the services and products
- The position and size of other facilities that are not part of the delivery system, such as meeting areas, rest rooms and cafeterias
- The number and dimensions of other aspects such as entrances, exits, emergency routes, walkways, corridors, stairways and lifts
- The space to be allocated to each of the above.

Designing fixed position layouts

The techniques and approaches for addressing fixed position layouts are not well developed, and layout issues are often addressed on a somewhat ad hoc basis because of the level of uncertainty inherent in this type of service or product provision.

Even where the task has been completed before (for example, building set house designs on an estate), many variables are liable to change. Delays in material shipments, design alterations and adverse weather conditions are some of the factors that can create

A large US telecommunications company used to organize its call centre on a functional basis. Using three tiers of staff, customers' correspondence (including payment collections) and requests and queries by phone were initially handled at the Tier 1 level. Any issues that could not be resolved here would be passed to Tier 2 technicians who worked in the same call centre but in another function and reported to their own Tier 3 supervisor. There were frequently delays in transfers between Tier 1 and Tier 2 staff, and when Tier 2 technicians could not resolve issues, these would be passed back to the Tier 1 originators to give to their own Tier 3 supervisor, who would further investigate it and then give it back to the relevant Tier 1 staff to advise the customer. The passing back and forth between Tier 1 and Tier 2 staff could often happen two or more times. The result was that an issue requiring (say) half an hour to resolve could involve two or more days before a reply was given to the customer.

So the company decided to reconfigure its call centres. Now, cells have been formed to handle specified groups of customers, with both Tier 1 and Tier 2 staff contained within each cell, this being headed by a Tier 3 cell team leader. Hand-offs between Tier 1 and Tier 2 staff now occur within a cell, with the result that over 90 per cent of customer queries are resolved quickly and fall within a single team leader's span of control. Tier 3 cell team leaders are ultimately responsible for ensuring that every customer query is followed through to a satisfactory conclusion.

Questions

1 How did the original call centre structure result in delays?

2 How did the cell-based redesign reduce delays?

3 What other advantages or opportunities would a cell-based structure offer this company?

uncertainty. Add to this the limited space on site, the changing availability of this space as the work progresses (as, for example, an area may be available for material storage at one stage but then be designated as a roadway or site for a building at a later stage), the varying volumes of materials and storage areas required and the changing priorities as a job progresses, and this all creates uncertainty and affects layout decisions. Similarly, in a management consultancy assignment, the availability of suitable on-site office space at a client's premises and the changing need for and availability of consultancy staff throughout an assignment, particularly where the direction of the assignment changes, make what ought to be relatively simple layout decisions more complex.

These uncertainties seldom allow an optimum solution as the decisions are more often a temporary solution rather than being well thought out, and are handled on an ad hoc basis that reflects the position, progress and current dynamics of the task and situation.

Designing process or functional layouts

The objective is to arrange these processes or functions in line with the aspects and features of a detailed layout design listed at the start of this section. This procedure involves the following steps:

- Clarify the total space on hand and the costs of any possible extensions.
- Identify any constraints that exist, the possibility of reducing or eliminating these and the costs that would be involved.
- Determine the area required by the different facilities, processes and functions.
- Determine the size of other facilities that are not part of the delivery system, such as meeting areas, rest rooms and cafeterias.
- Assess the number, size and position of the entrances, exits, corridors, gangways and walkways required.
- Assess the direction and flow of staff, information and materials through the processes and functions.

The detailed design of these layouts is made more difficult by the large number of different services or products typically handled by the same set of processes or functions. As one of the fundamental tasks in designing these layouts is often to minimize the cost of movement, determining where the different processes or functions are best positioned relative to one another is essential. The common approaches to help resolve this step in the procedure are described below.

Trip, load or movement frequency charts

To help evaluate alternative process or functional layouts, trip, load or movement frequency charts are often used to analyse the number of movements or trips between the processes or functions involved. In the example in Figure 6.10, this is entitled Step 1. So the number of movements or trips from Department 1 to 2 was 12, the number from Department 2 to 1 was 20, and so on.

The next step is to select the dimension that the detailed layout design is aiming to minimize, for example the total distance travelled or the total cost of the movements. In Figure 6.10, it was decided to minimize the distance travelled, and Step 2 provides these data for the existing layout. In most instances, it can be seen that the distance travelled between two departments in one direction was the same as the distance travelled going in the opposite direction. However, in this example, there were three instances where this was not the case due to a one-way system introduced for reasons of safety:

From/To	1 to 4	2 to 5	5 to 6
Distance (m)	28	38	19
From/To	4 to 1	5 to 2	6 to 5
Distance (m)	20	26	29

Figure 6.10 Collecting data using a load, movement or trip frequency chart

Step 1 - Analysis of # trips

From \ To	1	2	3	4	5	6
1		12	26	44	2	18
2	20		10	–	41	20
3	14	6		–	60	15
4	29	–	–		–	3
5	6	40	51	–		68
6	32	25	17	2	72	

Step 2 - Distance travelled (m)

From \ To	1	2	3	4	5	6
1		9	15	28	10	16
2	9		20	16	38	2
3	15	20		12	8	25
4	20	16	12		18	17
5	10	26	8	18		19
6	16	2	25	17	29	

Step 3 - Combine these two to give the total distance travelled (m)

From \ To	1	2	3	4	5	6	Total
1		108	390	1232	20	288	2038
2	180		200	–	1558	40	1978
3	210	120		–	480	375	1185
4	580	–	–		–	51	631
5	60	1040	408	–		1292	2800
6	512	50	425	34	2088		3109
Total	**1542**	**1318**	**1423**	**1266**	**4146**	**2046**	**11741**

The outcome of this analysis is given in Step 3 of Figure 6.10. The 633 trips involved a total distance travelled of 11,741 metres. This figure can then be used as a benchmark against which to measure alternative layouts and the gains that could be made in terms of reducing travel distances. When considering possible changes, this factor, as well as aspects such as the cost of changing an existing layout, would be used to help to evaluate alternatives.

Relationship charts

A second approach to detailed layout design that also uses a matrix format is the relationship chart. This helps to identify the relative closeness between departments. As the example in Figure 6.11 illustrates, this approach makes use of a priority code to show the preferred proximity of two departments (shown as the 'degree of closeness') and a justification code specifying the 'reason' for the desired proximity.

As the complexity of the detailed layout design task increases, these approaches to detailed layout solutions are unable to cope with the number of multiple flow patterns and constraints involved. Several computerized programs are available to overcome these limitations. In a way similar to that used by the manual methods, these use logical rules to list alternatives and then evaluate them against the relevant criteria. The link to a computerized system allows more variables to be included, refinements to alternatives to be assessed and more layout alternatives to be considered.

Figure 6.11 A relationship chart used in the detailed layout design of a hospital

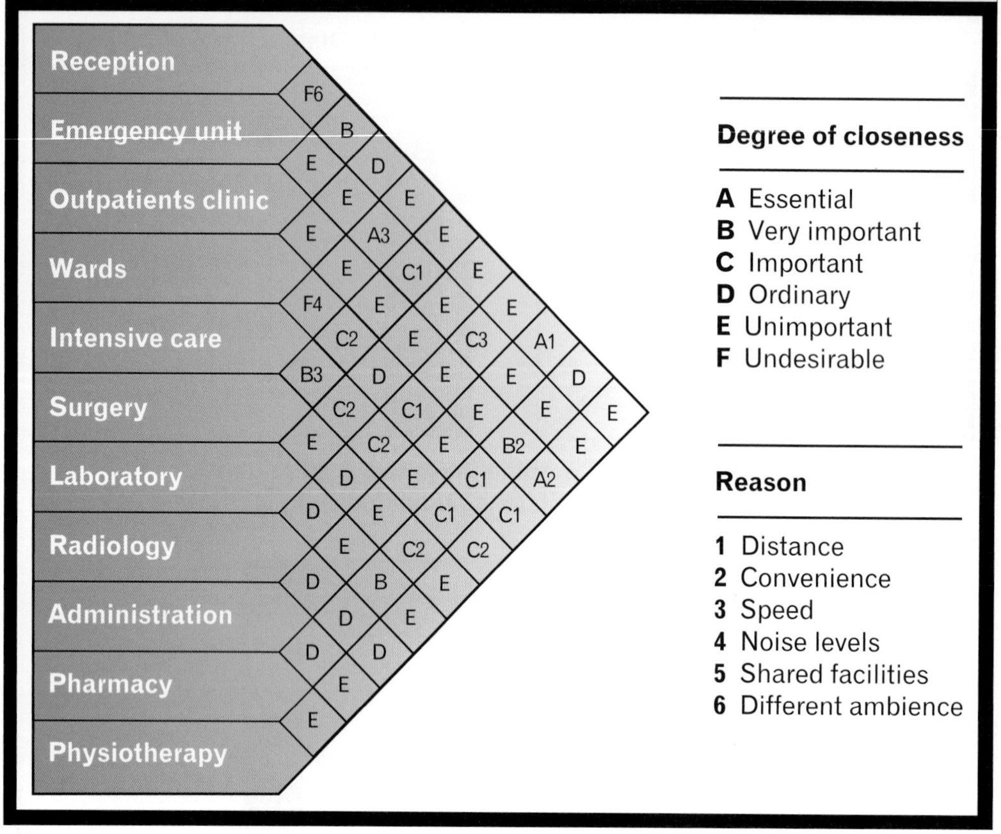

Reception
Emergency unit
Outpatients clinic
Wards
Intensive care
Surgery
Laboratory
Radiology
Administration
Pharmacy
Physiotherapy

Degree of closeness

A Essential
B Very important
C Important
D Ordinary
E Unimportant
F Undesirable

Reason

1 Distance
2 Convenience
3 Speed
4 Noise levels
5 Shared facilities
6 Different ambience

Designing service or product layouts

As explained earlier, this type of layout is based around similar services or products, and its degree of appropriateness reflects the following assumptions:

- The services or products are standardized and involve the same sequence of activities.
- The volumes involved are sufficient to give rise to adequate levels of staff or process utilization to justify a dedicated investment.
- Demand is stable and predictable.

The services or products using this type of layout invariably involve a multi-step process. Two essential layout design outcomes of this are that:

- The layout design will mirror the sequence of steps in the process
- The work content at each step will be similar in length – the concept of 'line balancing'.

Some high-volume, repeat service delivery systems and both line and continuous processes in manufacturing use this type of layout. In assembly lines where parts of products are put together, and in service delivery systems where people provide the services, the work content at one step will be designed to match (in terms of time taken to complete it) the work content at the next step, and so on – which is known as line balancing.[4] If the work content at each step is not similar, delays and waiting will occur. Figures 6.12, 6.13 and 6.14 illustrate this.

The cafeteria staff in this example were concerned about the long queues that formed at lunch times, and also in the early evening when most students took their main meal of the day. On checking, the team found that the work was unevenly divided between the four staff. A flow diagram (see Figure 6.13) clearly illustrates this. A glance at the hourly flow rates for the staff providing Steps 5 to 8 shows the imbalance of these current arrangements. The **bottleneck** is at Step 8. Here, a member staff can only serve a maximum of 65

> **Line balancing** – the assignment of tasks in order to ensure that the work content (the time taken to complete each step) is equal (or closely similar) at each step of the process

> **Bottleneck** – imagine a bottle: the neck is always narrower than the body, and hence it constrains the flow of the liquid when pouring. In business terms, a bottleneck similarly refers to the capacity-constraining stage in a service delivery system or manufacturing process that governs the output of the whole system or set of processes

Figure 6.12 Cafeteria process times

Step	Activity	Served by		Average time in seconds
		Self	Staff	
1	Collect tray/take water	✓		15
2	Select cold drink	✓		15
3	Select salad	✓		10
4	Select dessert	✓		10
5	Serve main course		✓	30
6	Serve vegetables		✓	20
7	Pour hot drink		✓	15
8	Pay cashier		✓	55

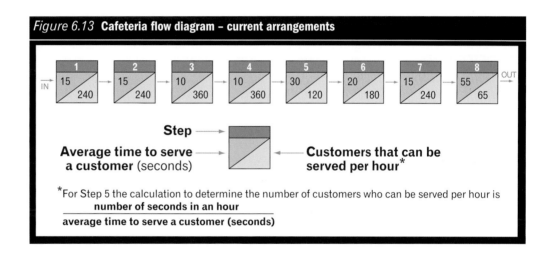

Figure 6.13 Cafeteria flow diagram – current arrangements

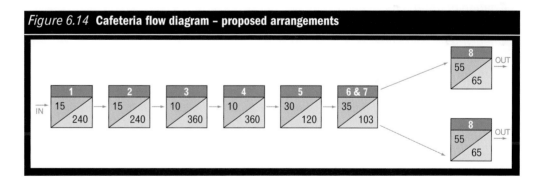

Figure 6.14 Cafeteria flow diagram – proposed arrangements

students per hour, almost half that of the next lowest rate, 120 students/hour at Step 5. Bottlenecks arise because of an imbalance in capacity in relation to the amount of time taken to complete the task at one step or stage in a delivery system or process compared with that at other steps or stages. Here it is staff capacity at Step 8 in relation to the time to complete the 'pay cashier' task, compared with the equivalent ratio at other steps.

The team recognized that an additional cashier would need to be added in order to increase the flow rate. If Steps 6 and 7 were combined and undertaken by one member of staff, this would release someone as an additional cashier. As the flow diagram in Figure 6.14 shows, the flow rates at the four staffed positions were now more in balance, and the hourly flow rate increased from 65 (the bottleneck or limiting factor at Step 8 in the current arrangements) to 103, with the bottleneck or limiting factor now lying at Steps 6 and 7. The two staff now at Step 8 can together handle 130 students per hour.

The above example illustrates, in principle, how line balancing works. As you would imagine, the line balancing requirements of the processes in high-volume manufacturing or chemical plants would be more finely tuned than in this cafeteria example. This would involve small adjustments and readjustments to the process layout until the optimum balance had been achieved, and the line or continuous process would then be designed and built in order to maximize daily output, and hence improve productivity and reduce the unit cost of the product. But the principles involved would be the same.

Queueing and waiting line analysis

Even where line balancing is part of the delivery system design, queues will invariably occur as customers rarely, if ever, arrive at a steady and predictable rate. Consequently, several factors need to be taken into account when designing delivery systems:

- *Arrival rate* As we've just said, customers rarely arrive at a steady and predictable rate. Consequently, arrival rates need to be assessed in terms of probability distributions, which reflect the reality that, at one extreme, there may be no customers to serve, while at the other there may be many arriving at the same time.
- *Variability of service times* The second factor affecting system design is that the length of time to serve a customer may vary, particularly where a wide range of services can be provided by each server.
- *Rejecting customer access to a queue* Where customers are already waiting, the system can be designed to refuse to let further customers enter the queue and thus ensure some control over waiting-to-be-served times. For example, some telephone-based services and websites are designed to prevent additional customers entering the existing queue (that is, access to a system or part of a system) until the queue length has reduced. Customers may feel equally dissatisfied but recognize that the cost benefits of not making a call are a plus factor.
- *Balking* On entering the system, customers may decide not to join the queue but to go elsewhere or, at best, return later.
- *Change of mind* Where queues reduce slowly, customers may decide after a while to leave.
- *Queueing time equality* Queue design should aim to ensure, as far as is feasible, that individual customers' waiting times are similar. A single queue feeding into two or more server positions, as opposed to customers entering the system and joining one of several queues of their choice on an ad hoc basis, is such an example.
- *Psychology of queues* Finally, the design of service delivery systems should take into account customers' perceptions of the waiting itself. Several facts about the psychology of queues can be used to influence customers' responses and attitudes to waiting:
  - Unoccupied time feels longer than occupied time. The system may therefore request customers to complete part of the service process, or it may provide some activity to distract customers, such as a TV news channel or the side shows often provided in theme parks to entertain customers while they wait.
  - Pre-process waits feel longer than in-process waits, so engaging with customers as quickly as possible (such as handing out menus and taking pre-dinner drink orders as soon as customers arrive) ensures customers know that the service provision has started.
  - Queueing time equality – as explained above, seeing noticeably different waiting times can raise anxiety levels, and uncertain and unexplained waiting times drag more than finite waits. Therefore, designing systems that advise customers of the length of the queue they are in and/or the approximate waiting time returns the choice of waiting to the customer and reduces the unknown factor.

Critical reflections

Where best to locate and how best to arrange the people, systems and processes, both within a facility and throughout the delivery system, impact both sales and costs. Consequently, it is essential to reflect both the external, customer/market, and the internal, operational, dimensions in these key decisions. As with many operations investments, their large and fixed nature involves high costs and long timescales where changes are to be made, so getting it right needs care and analysis.

Although convenience often plays a part in location and layout choices, organizations need to be aware of any less than favourable aspects of their decisions and factor these into their expectations and the day-to-day running of the business. Expectations will then be grounded in reality, and performance will be measured against attainable targets. In this way, control will be exercised and developments set in the context of both the short- and long-term objectives of the business.

Summary

- The two tasks of deciding location and layout are distinct yet related. They are distinct in that location concerns where best to site a facility, whereas layout concerns how best to arrange the staff, processes and equipment within that facility. And they are related in that they form two parts of a key decision – how best to position facilities in order to perform the operations task and meet the needs of the business.

- Decisions about where to locate may need to be taken at several levels, from deciding on a continent or region down to the choice of the site itself.

- Within these choices, the factors to be taken in account can be categorized into those of a general nature (broad-based issues that could influence or even override other factors, such as the origin of existing sites and politically based constraints) and those which have economic implications (such as market access).

- A number of specific factors, such as infrastructure and proximity to markets and suppliers, also affect the location decision at each level.

- Weighted factor and centre of gravity methods are two analytical techniques that help companies when making these key decisions.

- Layout decisions are affected by background factors such as the availability of space and meeting the potential need for future flexibility.

- The basic types of layout are fixed position, process or functional, and service or product. The choice of which to use will depend on the type of service delivery system and manufacturing process involved.

- Cells are a hybrid delivery system, developed from a mix of functional and service/product layouts.

- Having decided on the appropriate basic layout, the next step is to design a detailed layout. Frequency charts and relationship charts are used to analyse and design process or functional layouts, while line balancing and waiting line analysis are important aspects of service and product layout design.

Study activities

Discussion questions

1 Select a service outlet and identify the good and bad points of its chosen location.

2 Lord Sieff, when CEO of Marks & Spencer, the UK-based clothing, homeware and food store, is reputed to have said, 'There are three important factors in retailing – location, location and location.' Why would he have made such a comment?

3 Review the layout of a service organization of your choice and identify the good and not so good features of the layout design. Explain your choices.

4 Complete a similar exercise to that given in Figures 6.13 and 6.14 on your cafeteria. How well balanced is the cafeteria's service delivery system? What improvements could you suggest?

Assignments

1 In a team of three, select two supermarkets and individually assess them against the criteria listed in the section 'Factors affecting the choice of site'. Then review your individual ratings against each others', and discuss and list the key areas of agreement and disagreement.

2 In a team of three, individually select one of the following facilities to review – a large retail chemist, a large bookstore and a multiplex cinema, following these steps:

a) Within your team, agree for each location the factors to be used to review each site.

b) As individuals, assess one of the three locations using the agreed factors.

c) Discuss the three sets of findings and then identify the two most important factors that are facility-specific.

3 Complete a similar exercise to the last assignment, but this time analyse the layout of each location with particular reference to customer flows and the type of layout used. Compare and contrast your results. What were the key determinants of layout design for each outlet?

4 A US-based engineering firm has been awarded a contract to build the assembly and fabricating facilities for a new automobile plant in Mexico. It is critical to complete the project on time, given the proposed vehicle launch, and, as with all such assignments, staying within budget is essential. For these reasons, the project manager needs to be continuously kept up to date. The client has assigned its own on-site staff to handle issues as they arise. The desired relationships for the specialist areas involved in completing the project are given in Figure 1. The space allocated to the project team comprises an office for each of the seven sections (see below), together with an office for the client's own staff.

a) Using a relationship chart, complete a suggested layout.

b) Give reasons for your layout proposal.

c) Why do the reasons given earlier in the chapter differ from the reasons used in the example in Figure 6.11?

5 Electronic Controls International (ECI), a US-based technology group, has narrowed its location choices down to four possible sites in Europe. ECI will need to train the relevant staff, and the key factors, their weights and ratings for each location are shown in Figure 2. High scores represent favourable values.

a) Calculate the weighted factor score for each of the four sites.

b) Which site would you choose?

c) Would you reach the same conclusion if the weightings for the operating costs and labour costs were reversed?

Figure 1

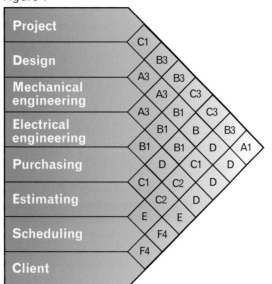

Project
Design
Mechanical engineering
Electrical engineering
Purchasing
Estimating
Scheduling
Client

C1
B3
A3 B3
A3 C3
A3 B1 C3
B1 B B3
B1 B1 D A1
D C1 D
C1 C2 D
C2 D
E E
F4
F4

Degree of closeness

A Essential
B Very important
C Important
D Ordinary
E Unimportant
F Undesirable

Reason

1 Convenience
2 Shared facilities
3 Day-to-day working
4 Potential interference
5 Different ambience

These eight offices are of similar size and comprise four offices on both sides of the same corridor and facing each other

Figure 2

Factor	Weighting	Location			
		A	B	C	D
Staff availability	15	7	8	7	8
Operating costs	25	8	6	8	6
Governing incentives	15	8	8	7	6
Land, construction and other set-up costs	15	7	6	7	7
Labour costs	10	8	8	6	6
Local technical infrastructure	10	4	7	8	7
Transport	10	4	8	8	7

6 The accountancy firm Thomas and Mason is made up of six main sections. Owing to the growth of the business over the last five years, the partnership is planning to move into new premises. These comprise six offices of equal size on each side of a corridor, as shown in Figure 3. The distance between the six offices is also shown in Figure 3, as are the number of trips between each sector. From this information, assign each of the six sections to an office in a way that minimizes the total distance travelled.

7 Review the layout of a high-street branch of three different banks. List the principal similarities and differences between the layouts. Why do you think these similarities and differences exist?

8 One location adage is: 'Manufacturers locate near their resources while retailers locate near their customers.' Discuss.

9 Contrast the location of a food distributor with that of one of the supermarkets to which it delivers products. Which important factors are similar and which are dissimilar in their respective choice of location?

Figure 3

Office layout

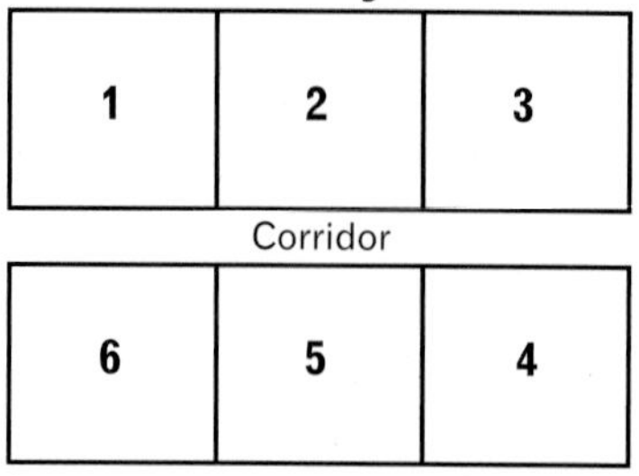

1	2	3

Corridor

6	5	4

Distance between offices (metres)

Office	1	2	3	4	5	6
1	–	8	16	24	16	8
2		–	8	16	8	16
3			–	8	16	24
4				–	8	16
5					–	8
6						–

 # trips between offices

Office	1	2	3	4	5	6
1	–	26	31	82	64	14
2		–	45	29	40	101
3			–	20	39	27
4				–	30	46
5					–	56
6						–

Exploring further

Journal articles

Aron, R. and Singh, J.V. (2005) 'Getting offshoring right'. *Harvard Business Review*, **83**(12), pp. 135–43. In the past five years, a rising number of companies in North America and Europe have experimented with offshoring and outsourcing business processes, hoping to reduce costs and gain strategic advantage. According to several studies, half the organizations that have shifted processes offshore have failed to generate the expected financial benefits. The article discusses a rethink on current offshoring strategies.

Elsbach, K.D. and Bechky, B.A. (2007) 'It's more than a desk: working smarter through leveraged office design'. *California Management Review*, **49**(2), pp. 80–101. Current trends in telecommuting and non-territorial office design (where the desks or work-spaces are used by several staff, thereby increasing the utilization of existing office areas and reducing the need to increase space on the one hand, or being able to reduce the space needed on the other) have changed what it means to work in an on-site office and, subsequently, have increased the number of functions that office design is expected to meet. This article offers a framework for office design that illustrates how managers can make design choices that both capitalize on the newest innovations in office design and serve the emerging needs of workers across a company.

Farrell, D. (2006) 'Smarter offshoring'. *Harvard Business Review*, **84**(6), pp. 84–92. The article looks at new offshoring locations including Morocco, Tunisia and Vietnam as alternatives to the most popular current locations, such as India and Eastern Europe.

Huang, J. (2001) 'Future space: a new blueprint for business architecture'. *Harvard Business Review*, **79**(4), pp. 149–58. The article offers guidelines to help managers and entrepreneurs think creatively about the structures within which their businesses operate in order to reflect the needs of people when designing stores, offices and factories.

West, A.P., Jr., and Wind, Y. (2007) 'Putting the organization on wheels: workplace design at SEI'. *California Management Review*, **49**(2), pp. 138–53. To create an environment that would embody a culture of flexibility, egalitarianism, teamwork and entrepreneurship, SEI Investments built a distinctive headquarters. The article discusses how the offices are open and the desks are on wheels, making it easy for teams to interact and quickly reorganize themselves.

Wieckowski, A. (2010) 'Back to the city'. *Harvard Business Review*, **88**(5), pp. 23–5. Several companies are relocating away from suburban sprawls and back to cities. Many workers prefer to live in cities or revitalized outskirts, where homes, shops, schools, parks and other amenities are close together. The impact for many types of business is discussed.

Books

Hill, T. (2005) *Operations Management: Text and Cases*. Basingstoke: Palgrave Macmillan. This provides a useful supplement to the current book by offering a more comprehensive explanation and further examples (including long case studies) showing how service and manufacturing companies have applied these concepts.

Oshri, I., Kotlarsky, J., Willcocks, L.P. (2008) *Outsourcing Global Services*. Basingstoke: Palgrave Macmillan.

Salvaneschi, L., ed. (2002) *Location, Location, Location: How to Select the Best Site for your Business*. Central Point, OR: Oasis Press. This book analyses how businesses should select the best location for their operation in order to maximize the number of customers they attract and the shopping experience they provide.

Website

NAFTA. http://www.nafta-sec-alena.org/en/view.aspx Visit the NAFTA website for more information on the North American Free Trade Agreement.

Notes and references

1 Kimes, S.E. and Fitzsimmons, J.A. (1990) 'Selecting profitable hotel sites at La Quinta Motor Inns'. *Interfaces*, **20**(2), pp. 12–20.

2 For a comprehensive overview of location models. refer to Brandeau, M.L. and Chiu, S.S. (1984) 'An overview of represented problems in location research'. *Management Science*, **35**(6), pp. 648–74.

3 Hyer, N.L., Brown, K.A. (2003) 'Work cells with staying power: lessons for process-complete operations'. *California Management Review*, **46**(1), pp. 27–52; Bohmer, R.M.J. (2010) 'Fixing health care on the front lines'. *Harvard Business Review*, April, pp. 62–9; Siebdrat, F., Hogel, M. and Ernst, H. (2009) 'How to manage virtual teams'. *MIT Sloan Management Review*, **50**(4), pp. 62–9; Swank, C.K. (2003) 'The lean service machine'. *Harvard Business Review*, October, pp. 123–30.

4 A useful overview of line balancing is provided in Mabs, G.H. (1990) 'Assembly line balancing – let's remove the mystery'. *Journal of Industrial Engineering*, May.

Set back from the main road, the McDonald's in Christchurch, New Zealand is part of a large shopping area with ample parking for people wishing to take a break while they're out and about. From the outside, it has all the usual hallmarks of a traditional McDonald's restaurant, but once you are inside it looks radically different. To improve sales revenue, it recently introduced a McDonald's 'drive-thru' and then separated the inside of the restaurant into a traditional McDonald's 'in-store' area and a 'McCafé' (Figure 1). Although the sales revenue from the McDonald's in-store area has remained constant over the last year, sales within the other two areas have increased significantly, with 'drive-thru' sales up 43 per cent in the last eight months. Of the total restaurant sales, 44 per cent now comes from the 'drive-thru' and 13 per cent from the McCafé.

STAFFING

Reporting to the store manager, two senior managers supervise the three different parts of the restaurant. In addition, the McDonald's in-store and McCafé areas have a dedicated manager and assistant manager working with a team of full-time and part-time staff to prepare food and serve customers. In total, about 75 full-time and part-time staff work within the facility. To help meet the wide daily and hourly fluctuations in demand, all staff are trained across a range of jobs, enabling them to switch from food preparation to serving customers in busy times and to store cleaning and related tasks at quieter times.

McDONALD'S 'IN-STORE' AND 'DRIVE-THRU'

The McDonald's 'drive-thru' facility was created by redesigning part of the rear car park. There are two customer order points and two collection hatches where food and drink orders are collected and paid for. The in-store facility comprises a preparation area (that serves both the in-store and 'drive-thru' areas) and a seating area with small tables and chairs for about 36 customers (Figure 1).

Hourly staffing requirements are based on sales forecasts. The store opens at 6 am each day, and closes at 11 pm Sunday to Thursday and at 1 am on Friday and Saturday. Customers enter the restaurant

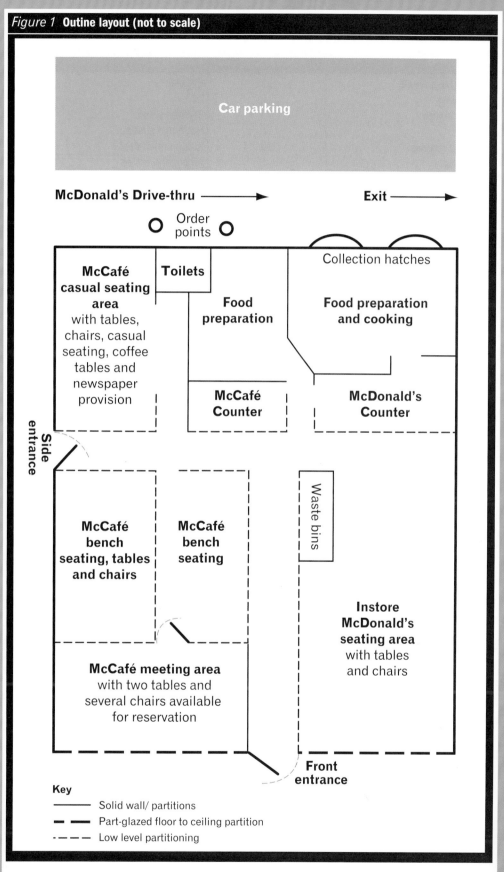

Figure 1 Outine layout (not to scale)

Car parking

McDonald's Drive-thru ⟶   Exit ⟶

O   Order points   O

Collection hatches

McCafé casual seating area
with tables, chairs, casual seating, coffee tables and newspaper provision

Toilets

Food preparation

Food preparation and cooking

McCafé Counter

McDonald's Counter

Side entrance

Waste bins

McCafé bench seating, tables and chairs

McCafé bench seating

Instore McDonald's seating area
with tables and chairs

McCafé meeting area
with two tables and several chairs available for reservation

Front entrance

Key
⎯⎯ Solid wall/ partitions
▬ ▬ Part-glazed floor to ceiling partition
-‐-‐- Low level partitioning

through the front and side entrances and join a queue. When they reach the counter, they place their orders, and the staff assemble the meal(s) from the items kept in the holding bins immediately behind the counter. In times of low demand, some

Figure 2
McDonald's 'in-store' and 'drive-thru' menus

Menu items	Quantity	Example
Beef and fish meals	12	Big Mac
Deli choices	8	BLT
Lighter choices	5	Chicken salad
Desserts	6	Hot fudge sundae
Breakfast options	12	Kiwi big breakfast
Hot drinks	6	Americano coffee
Soft drinks	6	Coca Cola
Shakes	3	Chocolate shake

Figure 3
McCafé menu

Menu items	Quantity	Example
Sandwiches	8	Beef pastrami and salad
Wraps, paninis and melts	11	Mexican wrap
Cakes and muffins	16	Blueberry muffin
Quiche	2	Bacon and brie
Coffees	13	Latte
Other hot drinks	5	Pot of tea
Frappés	4	Mocha
Other cold drinks	16	Organic apple juice

food items are prepared on request, but the food is typically pre-prepared ahead of time to reduce customer waiting time. In recent years, a breakfast menu has been added, as well as a number of deli and 'lighter choices' (Figure 2). Customers then choose to either take the food and drink away or eat in-house.

McCAFÉ

Two staff start at 5.30 am to set up the equipment and receive the daily fresh food deliveries. From 6 am to 8 am, the staff prepare the wraps and other food items while also serving customers. On entering the restaurant, customers queue at the McCafé counter, order their food and drink, pay and then choose where to sit. When the order is ready, a member of staff takes it to the customers at their tables. Although some food items are pre-prepared, the wide choice on offer (Figure 3) means that some have to be made to order, along with the majority of the drinks.

The layout of the McCafé comprises three separate areas (see Figure 1). There is a casual seating area for customers with tables, chairs, casual seating and coffee tables, with in-store local and national newspapers provided free of charge. The second area is a mix of bench seating and small tables and chairs for about 50 customers. The third area is an enclosed space that can be reserved by local businesses, societies and similar organizations for meetings or discussion groups at no cost other than the food and drink purchases being made. When not in use for meetings, this area is used by customers for extra seating.

Questions

1 Provide an overview of the three different restaurants – McDonald's in-store, McDonald's 'drive-thru' and McCafé – in terms of the service delivery system used in each.

2 Explain how the layouts within the restaurants – McDonald's in-house, McDonald's 'drive-thru' and McCafé – differ and why they meet the needs of each set of customers.

Lecturers: visit www.palgrave.com/business/hillessential for additional resources

No. _____

NAME _____

Week Ending _____

YOU ARE YOUR OWN TIMEKEEPER.
WE PAY BY THIS RECORD,
YOUR OWN RECORDING.

102116

	MORNING		AFTERNOON		OVERTIME		TOTAL
	IN	OUT	IN	OUT	IN	OUT	

ORDINARY TIME
OVERTIME
STAT. SICK PAY
TOTAL WAGES
LESS NAT. INSCE
LESS INC. TAX
LESS DEDUCTIONS
AMOUNT PAID

Learning objectives

After completing this chapter, you should be able to:

- Understand the nature of capacity and the mix of resources involved

- Appreciate the purpose of managing capacity and the impact of having too little and too much capacity

- Explain how to define and measure capacity in different organizations

- Appreciate the differences between capacity, utilization and efficiency

- Understand the factors involved in determining the level of capacity required

- Appreciate the demand-related and capacity-related issues of determining capacity levels

- Explain the steps in capacity planning

- Recognize the key factors in managing demand and capacity

Chapter outline

Introduction

An overview of managing capacity

- Defining and measuring capacity

Factors affecting capacity management

- How do the service delivery system and manufacturing process design affect capacity?

- Determining the level of capacity

Planning and managing capacity

- Types of capacity plan

- Managing demand and capacity

Critical reflections

Summary

Capacity – comprises the staff, equipment and processes that make up the value-adding activities to meet a certain level of demand in a given time period

Schedule – a timetable of jobs with start dates to meet customers' delivery requirements

Capacity is made up of the resources needed to serve customers, process information or make products, and is a mix of the people, systems and equipment needed to deliver the services or products involved. The purpose of managing capacity is to match an organization's resources to the demand for its services or products. For example, a bank needs staff to serve customers, IT systems to process transactions and ATMs to enable customers to draw out cash from their accounts, while a manufacturing company needs people and processes to make the products it sells. Having sufficient capacity ensures that customers are served and products are made in line with **schedules** and orders. Too little capacity results in delays and lost sales; too much incurs costs. Effective management of this key element of operations, therefore, underpins the short-term success and long-term growth of an organization.

This chapter will provide an explanation of how capacity is measured and what statements of capacity look like, before addressing how to plan and manage capacity and the systems for doing this. First, we'll take a broad look at the task of managing capacity, and then we'll look at how capacity is measured. After that, we'll consider how service and product delivery systems affect capacity, and the demand- and capacity-related issues that need to be addressed when determining what level of capacity is appropriate. Next, the task and methods for planning capacity will be reviewed, together with the types of capacity plan that can be used. Finally, we'll look at ways of managing demand (for example, through changing demand patterns, using service or product design features and scheduling) and managing capacity (for example, through short-term adjustments and flexible work patterns).

An overview of managing capacity

When organizations develop their short- and long-term business objectives, they need to decide how they will provide the appropriate level of capacity to meet their current and future needs. Decisions relating to capacity (staff skills, processes and systems) will need to take into account the:

- *Delivery system and process capabilities* – to ensure that the technical specification of the services or products can be met
- *Volumes* – how many services are to be processed or products are to be made.

Simple though this seems, it is a challenging task. The types of capability required will vary depending on the nature and range of service and product designs involved. How much capacity is needed will be based on anticipated demand. However, the uncertainty of forecasts and the certainty of reality will continue to result in false starts, underused capacity or an inability to cope with actual demand. Furthermore, capacity considerations in service industries and the perishable nature of service capacity create their own set of difficulties. All in all, these variables and uncertainties create a challenging operations task that needs to be well managed both for its own sake (as it is sizeable and expensive) and to meet the needs of customers.

The costs incurred by investing forward (that is, investing in capacity for the future) when increased sales do not materialize and the lost sales that result from not being able to meet demand support opposing sides of an argument over whether capacity investment should lead or follow demand. Even successful strategies place substantial strain on organizations as they attempt to change direction. Being successful, therefore, requires responses to be coordinated at both the strategic and the tactical levels.

> **KEY IDEA**

A key business strategy decision is whether capacity investment should lead or follow demand

Defining and measuring capacity

There are several ways to define and measure how capacity is provided and used. Recognizing these is a necessary step to avoid confusion and to allow expressions of 'how much of' and 'how well' to be made with understanding and accuracy, as these definitions result in different insights.

Defining capacity

Before we look in more detail at how capacity is measured, it's important to note that two main definitions are used when managing capacity:

- **Planned (or available) capacity** Although operations could theoretically run or be open 24 hours each day throughout the year, in reality this is not normally required, nor does it typically make sense. An exception to this is those companies using continuous processing (such as oil refineries), where the costs of stopping and starting a process are so high that the process is run continuously (see Chapter 5). Planned (or available) capacity is, therefore, a statement of the intended or planned number of hours that are to be made available in a given period.

- **Actual capacity** Although a certain level of capacity is planned (or available), actual capacity refines this by taking into account the **utilization** (the number of hours actually spent working) and the level of **efficiency** achieved (the actual output compared with the expected output while working).

As you can imagine, the variance between these two will differ from one operation to another. Before investing in extra capacity, a firm must first look for ways to increase the utilization and/or efficiency of its existing operation as these improvements are typically less expensive to make and easier to change.

Measuring capacity

There are two common denominators used in businesses to express, calculate and measure activities – time and money. In most parts of a business, money is the dimension used to express and evaluate activity, for example sales revenue and profit. In operations, however, the common denominator is time. Statements and measures of performance regarding capacity and output are calculated using time as the base. So all services and products will need to be measured in terms of the time taken to complete them. Checks can then be made to assess how much capacity is needed and how well it has been used. The second aspect to be clarified concerns whether a firm should use staff or plant/equipment as the basis of these capacity statements, particularly where both are used in providing its services and products. The sections that follow explain the factors affecting the process of measuring capacity but, before addressing the principles involved, it's useful to discuss capacity statements and measurements in general.

To illustrate why time is typically used as the basis for calculating the capacity required and assessing how well available capacity has been used, take a look at Figure 7.1. This shows how many units of two different products are made over two weeks by a manufacturing firm. If it takes 10 minutes to complete product A and 5 minutes to complete product B, the process should produce 6 and 12 items of products A and B, respectively,

Planned (or available) capacity – a statement of the intended or planned number of hours to be made available in a given period

Actual capacity – the measure of planned (or available) capacity, taking into account the number of hours actually worked (utilization) and the actual output compared with the expected output (efficiency) while working

Utilization – the actual capacity used from the planned (or available) capacity

Efficiency (or 'effective performance') – actual output compared with expected output each hour. To assess how many products should be made or how efficient a process was in a given period, the data for products completed need to be converted from the number of units to the equivalent amount of time. For example, if the process was operated for 40 hours in a week and made the following number of products A and B, how would you assess the performance in weeks 1 and 2?

Figure 7.1 Number of products A and B made per week		
Product	**Week (units made)**	
	1	**2**
A	205	50
B	70	375
Total	275	425

Based on the number of products made, week 2 appears the much better week, with over 50 per cent more products made. But when the time taken per unit is introduced into the calculation (Figure 7.2), it shows a different and truer picture of output, with both weeks being almost the same.

Figure 7.2 Time taken to make products A and B						
Weeks	**Product A**		**Product B**		**Total**	
	Units	**Time (mins)**	**Units**	**Time (mins)**	**Units**	**Time (hrs)**
1	205	2,050	70	350	275	40.0
2	50	500	375	1,875	425	39.6

> **KEY IDEA**
> Operations uses time as the common denominator to express and measure its activities. The rest of the business uses money

Overall measurement

Statements and measurements of capacity will often differ within and between the various parts of an organization. Taking a hospital as an example, let us illustrate why this is so:

- *Overall size* A hospital will typically use the number of beds it has as one indicator of overall size as this is a key dimension of its capacity.

- *Emergency unit* Capacity in the emergency unit of the same hospital will reflect the expected levels of demand at different times throughout each day of a week. This will then be translated into the number and mix of staff (the ratio of doctors, nurses and support staff) who need to be on duty for different hours of each day, different days of each week and different weeks throughout the year.

- *Consultant clinics* Based on the average length of appointments, a clinic will be arranged on a number of days each week or each month. The number of clinics will reflect known and anticipated levels of demand (number of appointments), and this will be adjusted to reflect changes that occur in the future. Appointments will then be made in line with the times that the consultants' clinics have been scheduled.

In this way, expressions of capacity will differ, with each emphasizing the dimension that underlines the aspect of capacity that reflects the resource providing the services or

'Should capacity lead or follow demand?'

making the products. However, you will notice from the three examples in the list above that the last two use a time base. Assessing how many emergency staff and how many clinics are required will use time as the means of calculating appropriate numbers.

As these examples demonstrate, statements and measures of capacity will vary because they need to be based on the resource that is most critical for delivering the product or service.

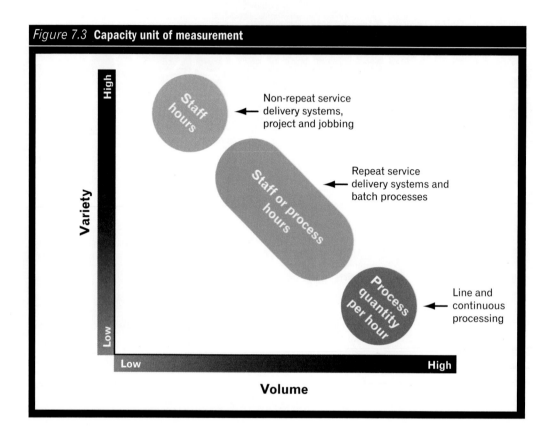

Figure 7.3 **Capacity unit of measurement**

Figure 7.3 shows how staff hours, equipment hours and quantity can all be used as units for measuring capacity, depending on the type of product or service:

- *Non-repeat service delivery system, project and jobbing* In these businesses, skilled staff provide the service or product, with systems and equipment helping them to complete the task. Here, the measure of available capacity will be staff hours.

- *Line and continuous processing* With these processes, the process or equipment makes the product, and people support the process or equipment in this task. Although the speed of a line process can, within certain limits, be adjusted to reflect demand, the statement of capacity in these businesses will typically be based on the number of items the process is able to produce per hour.

- *Repeat service delivery systems* High-volume repeat service delivery systems are often more like line, with the equipment (for example, a cash machine or cheque-processing equipment) providing the service, so levels of capacity are typically expressed in terms of process or equipment hours. However, where staff provide the service, staff hours will be used to calculate capacity.

- *Batch processes* High-volume batch is more like line, so plant/equipment hours are typically the basis used for statements on capacity. Conversely, businesses more towards the low-volume end of batch will use staff hours as the basis of their capacity calcula-tions. This is because people rather than equipment will be the factor governing output.

So the measure of capacity will reflect which input (people or equipment) into the service delivery system or manufacturing process is key to delivering the services and products involved.

Using output to measure capacity

How much operations capacity is needed will be assessed in relation to the size and type of expected demand, which is then translated into time as the way of comparing like with like. To explain this, let's look at a postal service delivering letters. The time taken to deliver letters in a town centre is considerably shorter than that taken for delivery in rural districts. Using the number of letters to be delivered would, therefore, not be a sufficiently accurate statement of demand or capacity. The time taken would need to reflect the number of deliveries, the distances involved and other variables. Using time as the basis for calculating demand and capacity is appropriate for most organizations as the services or products they provide will incur different amounts of staff or process time. But whereas the number of units (for example, letters delivered) is easily known, the time taken has to be calculated.

Although time is the underlying means of assessing capacity in most organizations, in some the number of units will, in fact, suffice. This will occur where the services or products are sufficiently similar to one another – here, units are an appropriate basis for calculating and assessing capacity. For example, the capacity of an oil refinery will be expressed as the number of litres processed per day, the capacity of a car plant by the number of vehicles assembled per day and the capacity of a fast-food restaurant by the number of meals served at given times in a day. These figures will then form the basis for statements of capacity and for calculations of utilization and efficiency.

Measuring capacity in practice

The two worked examples that follow are provided to help you understand the issues to be taken into account when measuring capacity in practice. They are based on real examples, although they have been simplified to help get the key points across.

WORKED EXAMPLE CONFORM

Conform is a small manufacturing business with five machines. One is normally fully used, but the other four machines always have spare capacity. Conform's business is subcontract work for a number of customers. The manufacturing process is simple, with all products being completed as a single operation on one of the five machines. Following machining, the products are packed before being despatched to customers to meet their order dates. Conform employs three machine operators who complete the necessary set-ups on machines and undertake all the machining operations. In addition, there is one full-time and one part-time packer. The former is also responsible for despatch.

Planned machine operator capacity – from Monday to Friday, the three machine operators each work a single shift of seven and a half hours:

Planned capacity = Normal working hours
= 3 operators × 7.5 hours × 5 days = 112.5 hours

MACHINE OPERATOR UTILIZATION – WEEK 1

In week 1, the company arranged overtime of one hour on each of four days for two of the machine operators. The utilization of operators in this week is shown below. As you will see, it compares total hours worked against planned capacity. In this way, it signals to the company that the number of hours required is higher than planned, and allows the company to monitor capacity and adjust if necessary.

$$\text{Machine operator utilization} = \frac{\text{Actual hours worked}}{\text{Planned hours of work}} \times 100$$

$$= \frac{41.5 + 41.5 + 37.5}{112.5} \times 100$$

$$= \frac{120.5}{112.5} \times 100$$

$$= 107 \text{ per cent}$$

MACHINE OPERATOR UTILIZATION – WEEK 2

In week 2, no overtime was worked, and one operator had a period of three hours without any machining work. This operator was (as was normal in these circumstances) reassigned to packing. Machine operator utilization was, therefore:

$$\text{Machine operator utilization} = \frac{\text{Actual hours worked}}{\text{Planned hours of work}}$$

$$= \frac{37.5 + 37.5 + 34.5}{112.5} = \frac{109.5}{112.5}$$

$$= 97 \text{ per cent}$$

MACHINE UTILIZATION – WEEKS 1 AND 2

As we've already said, the company has five machines on which the three operators make a range of products, and the hours worked on each machine vary. The calculations for machine utilization highlight these differences, as shown in Figure 7.4.

Figure 7.4 **Machine utilization at Conform**

Machine	Week 1	Week 2
1	41.5 hours worked / 37.5 hours available = 111 per cent	37.5 hours worked / 37.5 hours available = 100 per cent
2	9.0 hours worked / 37.5 hours available = 24 per cent	8.0 hours worked / 37.5 hours available = 21 per cent
3	22.0 hours worked / 37.5 hours available = 59 per cent	20.0 hours worked / 37.5 hours available = 53 per cent
4	35.0 hours worked / 37.5 hours available = 93 per cent	31.0 hours worked / 37.5 hours available = 83 per cent
5	13.0 hours worked / 37.5 hours available = 35 per cent	13.0 hours worked / 37.5 hours available = 35 per cent
Total hours worked on the five machines	**120.5**	**109.5**

WHAT DO THESE CALCULATIONS REVEAL?

- Higher or lower than 100 per cent utilization figures signal to the company that the number of hours used is higher or lower, respectively, than planned. Monitoring these figures over time will reveal whether or not this is an upward or a downward trend and allow appropriate adjustments to be made .

- Capacity often varies. Different staff skills and types of machine mean that the staff or machines in question can provide different services or products. Therefore, providing an average utilization figure for these five machines for weeks 1 and 2 (in this instance 64 and 58 per cent, respectively) would lack meaning.

> **KEY IDEA**
Utilization compares actual hours worked with planned hours of work

EFFICIENCY – OPERATORS

Standard output – the expected output for the hours worked

Whereas utilization compares the actual number of hours worked with the number of available or planned hours, efficiency (also known as 'effective performance') measures the amount of work produced in the hours worked and compares this figure with the amount expected (known as the **standard**). In a business where all the products made are the same (for example, an automotive company), the calculation would be the number of cars produced in a day compared with the number expected. Where a company makes or provides several different services or products, comparisons are made by converting the services delivered or products made into the equivalent amounts of time. To explain, let's look at a simple example.

Product 1604 is produced by Conform for a customer and has been calculated to take 25 minutes to make. One operator makes the product during the whole of one day and, in all, produces 18 units of the product. The operator's efficiency is calculated as follows:

Output produced = 18 units × 25 minutes = 450 minutes of work

$$\text{Efficiency} = \frac{\text{Output produced (\# units} \times \text{time per unit)}}{\text{Hours worked} \times 60 \text{ mins}} \times 100$$

$$= \frac{450}{75 \times 60} \times 100 = 100 \text{ per cent}$$

To calculate the efficiency for all three operators for (say) week 1, all the products made in week 1 multiplied by the time for each product would be compared with the total number of hours worked in week 1. Such calculations allow an organization to gauge how well staff or a process is working, and also to check that the times used to cost (and thereby price) a service or product are an accurate assessment of how long the process is actually taking.

> **KEY IDEA**
Efficiency compares the actual output with the expected (known as the 'standard') output for the hours worked

WORKED EXAMPLE JOHN MICHAEL

John Michael is a hairdresser in the centre of town. It employs seven part- and full-time staff and has seven hairdressing chairs – one allocated to each member of staff – that are used at different times during a week in line with expected demand, as shown in Figure 7.5. The working pattern illustrated reflects the mix of full-time (chairs 1 to 4) and part-time (chairs 5 to 7) staff, while the opening hours reflect the expected demand levels each day. Figure 7.5 shows that the four full-time staff work five days each week and take a different day off as arranged. The three part-time staff work at pre-arranged times, as shown.

Figure 7.5 Salon opening and hairdressing hours									
Day	**Planned opening hours**	**# Hours available per chair**							**Total hours**
		1	**2**	**3**	**4**	**5**	**6**	**7**	
Monday	8	–	8	8	8	–	–	–	24
Tuesday	8	8	8	8	–	4	–	–	28
Wednesday	8	8	–	8	8	–	4	4	32
Thursday	8	8	8	–	8	4	4	–	32
Friday	10	10	10	10	10	8	8	8	64
Saturday	10	10	10	10	10	10	10	10	70

Note: Utilization on Monday $= \dfrac{\text{Hours used}}{\text{Hours available}} = \dfrac{8 + 8 + 8}{7 \times 8} = \dfrac{24}{56} = 43$ per cent

Hours available = 7 chairs × 8 hours (the opening hours of the salon)

UTILIZATION – FACILITIES

As the facilities (that is, the chairs) are the same, calculating overall utilization is an appropriate statement. However, as capacity needs to match demand levels during each day, the planned capacity will be at different levels to reflect this. The John Michael salon opens for eight hours on Monday to Thursday, but on Friday and Saturday the planned capacity (that is, salon opening times) is 10 hours (see Figure 7.5). During any week, the daily utilization calculations reflect this, as shown in Figure 7.6.

Figure 7.6 Daily facilities utilization levels at John Michael	
Day	**Utilization (%)**
Mon	43
Tue	50
Wed	57
Thu	57
Fri	91
Sat	100

UTILIZATION – HAIRDRESSERS

Similar calculations assessing the utilization of each hairdresser during each day would also be appropriate. In John Michael's case, the schedule for a hairdresser was based on 15-minute booking slots, with longer jobs being allocated more than one 15-minute slot. A simple check on the number of slots not filled during each day gave the owner an adequate statement of the utilization of each hairdresser.

EFFICIENCY – HAIRDRESSERS

The efficiency of the seven hairdressers may be calculated in two ways. The first is based on standard times for each type of service – alternatives such as a trim, restyle, cut and blow dry, highlights and other forms of hair colouring will take different lengths of time. Calculations of efficiency will be similar to those outlined earlier in the Conform illustration under the section 'Efficiency – operators'.

A second method is available for businesses that are not complicated and where the services provided are similar to one another or tend to average out over a given period. This uses a simpler, broadbrush calculation such as the revenue generated by each hairdresser per hour worked. With prices reflecting, in part, the time involved and each hairdresser undertaking a similar mix of work, a 'revenue per hour worked' calculation would give a rule of thumb assessment of efficiency. It would be easy to calculate and yet provide a check on the level of efficiency achieved. In fact, the owner of the John Michael salon used this measure as follows, with net hours equalling staff hours minus the time not booked by clients:

$$\frac{\text{Revenue generated}}{\text{Net hours worked}} = \text{Revenue per hour worked}$$

Using utilization and efficiency data to manage capacity

The last section explained the process used to calculate utilization and efficiency. Before moving on to capacity planning and the task of managing capacity and demand, let's first recap on the insights provided by utilization and efficiency data in helping a business to manage its capacity.

As highlighted at the start of the chapter, the importance of managing capacity concerns meeting customer requirements. Too little capacity means delays and possible lost sales; too much incurs unnecessary costs. Based on known or forecasted sales, companies calculate the staff or process capacity required. But this is often no easy task, especially in the front office of service delivery systems. Different services requiring different levels of skills complicates capacity provision. Add to this the fact that demand varies throughout a period, and capacity calculations need to reflect these hourly, daily, weekly and monthly patterns within the framework of uncertainty that characterizes forecasts.

- *Utilization*

  In the medium and longer term, demand will typically change. To help monitor this, information on utilization levels helps organizations to assess these trends and make any necessary adjustments so that they can maintain service levels while avoiding unnecessary costs. The options available to companies to change their capacity levels include the following:
  - Short-term changes such as:
    - Overtime working, including at the weekend. This option increases the rate of pay per hour by what is known as the overtime premium – for example, the third and the half when the rate for each overtime hour increases to $1\frac{1}{3}$ and $1\frac{1}{2}$ the normal rate, respectively.
    - Employing temporary staff. This option often incurs training costs and using less experienced and less skilled staff.
  - Longer term changes such as:
    - Recruiting additional full- or part-time permanent staff
    - Purchasing additional processes or equipment, together with the staff required
    - Recruiting an additional shift of either full- or part-time staff.

  As you will see from these options, short-term changes are a more flexible alternative and, for this reason, tend to be preferred, especially as a first step.

- *Efficiency*

  Data on how long jobs take are an essential input into cost, price and capacity calculations. What efficiency checks do is to measure how well the service delivery system or manufacturing process is performing against set standards. Differences between actuals and standards alert an organization to changes in the task (for example, if the job is becoming more or less complicated, so the set standards need adjusting) or changes in the delivery system (for example, if additional staff training is required or the manufacturing process needs overhauling). Utilization and efficiency measures help to ensure that adequate levels of capacity are provided and that the service delivery system or manufacturing process is performing to the standards set. In this way, regular checks or 'how much' and 'how well' provide essential insights to help manage this key resource.

Factors affecting capacity management

Now that we know how capacity is measured and defined, let's move on to looking at some background factors that affect the management of capacity. In this section, we'll first look at how aspects of the service delivery system and manufacturing process design affect capacity, including the implications of an organization's chosen delivery system. We will then address how the level of capacity is determined, including the effect of various capacity- and demand-related issues.

How do the service delivery system and manufacturing process design affect capacity?

Aspects of the service delivery system and manufacturing process design – the subjects of Chapters 4 and 5 – affect the provision of capacity within the operations process. Some key issues in relation to this are now discussed.

Customers as a source of capacity

The presence of customers within the front office of a service delivery system becomes a potential source of capacity. The extent to which this is taken advantage of is an important decision in terms of overall capacity, and this unique opportunity needs to form part of the delivery system design. The benefits of customer involvement include:

- It cuts costs.
- It helps to provide capacity at points in the delivery system where all or part of the service is consumed. For example, in a self-service restaurant, the job of the waiter is predominantly, if not totally, provided by the customer.
- Some customers prefer to be able to make their own choices. For example, self-service food shopping is now the norm, and salad bar provision in a restaurant is often preferred by customers.

Customers have proved willing to take part in the service delivery system if it can be shown to be beneficial, supportive of their needs, convenient or an enhancement of the sociable nature of the total process. Examples include self-service facilities of all kinds, direct telephone dialling, purchases via the television, online shopping, investment brokerage services, other financial services (including cash machines) and travel arrangements. The impact of this upon the provision, type and cost of capacity can be considerable.

The perishable nature of service capacity

Service capacity is perishable. It cannot be put into inventory for use or sale in a future time period. In addition to the ways of changing capacity levels described earlier, companies can also seek to adjust demand patterns. The alternative ways available are discussed later in the chapter.

> **KEY IDEA**
>
> Service capacity is perishable in that it cannot be put into inventory for use or sale in the future

Back office versus front office

Within a service business, a distinction needs to be made between the two basic parts of the process – the back office and the front office (see Chapter 4). A fundamental distinction between these two parts of the system concerns the customer interface. In the front office, customers are present, either in person or on the telephone, and the service system has to manage these customers during the delivery of the service. In the back office, customers are not present in the system, so there is no pressure to respond immediately. Consequently, capacity requirements, the opportunity to spread demand and to use technology to process cumulated volumes (thereby reducing costs) will differ between these parts.

Ensuring adequate capacity at each stage of a delivery system

Getting the capacity right significantly affects costs and customer support, which, in turn, affect overall sales revenue and profits, as illustrated by Case 7.1. Where services or products require a single operation to complete them, the task of determining the capacity required is relatively easy. However, several steps and also differing amounts of time at each step are often involved in providing a service or making a product. This makes determining the necessary capacity a more difficult task as there are more stages and more combinations of stages, hence making it more complex.

Flexibility

The different dimensions of flexibility need to be recognized and reflected in capacity calculations. These include the ability to:

A restaurant experiencing high demand increased its capacity in two ways: it added more tables in its existing dining areas, and it increased the speed of service in an attempt to improve throughput. Both provisions had a direct impact on customer' experience. Although the quality of the food and wine remained the same, customers' perception of the service specification on offer changed. Bookings fell, and sales and profit declined.

Questions

1 What were the order-winners and qualifiers for this business?

2 Based on your answer to Question 1, assess the company's decision. What alternative decisions could it have made about its shortage of capacity?

Lecturers: visit www.palgrave.com/business/hillessential for additional resources

- Deliver a wider range of services and products
- Respond to any seasonal demand factors
- Meet shorter lead-times
- Cope with changes in a customer's specification during the process.

Skills and mix

The introduction of technology into parts or all of the operations process will lead to changes in skill requirements and staff mix. This alters the capacity requirements and so needs to be part of the decision process.

The impact of different delivery systems

Operations uses technology as part of its delivery system design, with the technical know-how to install, develop and maintain it being provided by specialists. It is essential, therefore, for operations to understand the business implications of the chosen delivery system or manufacturing process, several of which directly affect the definition, provision and management of capacity, as summarised in Figures 7.7 and 7.8.

Service delivery systems

The factors in service delivery systems that affect the nature of capacity and its management and provision were highlighted earlier. They include the following:

- The nature of the service offering
  - Non-repeat or repeat
  - The level of volume for a repeat service
  - The service/product mix
- What is being processed in the service delivery system – a customer, a customer surrogate (in car maintenance, for example, the car is the surrogate for the customer) or information
- Whether it holds a front- or back-office position in the delivery system
- Whether it is a single- or a multi-step service delivery system.

With these factors in mind, Figure 7.7 provides an overview of how some of the key dimensions of capacity differ in relation to the non-repeat/repeat and low-/high-volume dimensions of services, while the text will provide an explanation and highlights some differences.

Non-repeat services are delivered by skilled staff; consequently, capacity is based on the available working time of this key resource. As the services involved are non-repeat, the ability to define demand in terms of resource requirements will be low (the service has not been provided before), thus making the provision and control of capacity difficult. The flexible nature of the skilled staff, however, will facilitate the use of capacity in meeting the wide range of services on offer, the downside being that losing key staff through absence in the short term or moving to a new company in the longer term will affect capacity.

The transitional nature of these dimensions as the service delivery system shifts to one for a high-volume, repeat service is illustrated by the arrows in Figure 7.7. Calculating capacity in a fast-food restaurant involves a combination of staff and processes, whereas capacity in cash machine services is predominantly to do with the number (and location) of ATMs. Adding capacity is often stepped in nature (for example, adding a new outlet). In either case, the failure of the equipment involved in the system will have a significant impact on a company's ability to deliver services as the equipment is central to provision of the services.

Figure 7.7 **Capacity-related implications of service delivery system choice**

CAPACITY-RELATED IMPLICATIONS		NON-REPEAT SERVICES	REPEAT SERVICES	
			Low volume	High volume
Service	type	Special	⟶	Standard
	range	Wide	⟶	Narrow
Number of customer orders		Few	⟶	Many
Capacity	basis for calculation	Staff	⟶	Staff/process
	size of changes	Incremental	⟶	Stepped
	control	Difficult	⟶	Easy
Demand – level of definition		Low	⟶	High
Delivery system flexibility		Flexible	⟶	Inflexible
Dominant factor in measuring capacity utilization		Staff	⟶	Staff/process
Impact of	staff absence	High	⟶	Low
	equipment failure	Low	⟶	Significant

Figure 7.8 **Capacity-related implications of manufacturing process choice**

CAPACITY-RELATED IMPLICATIONS		TYPICAL CHARACTERISTICS OF MANUFACTURING PROCESS CHOICE				
		Project	Jobbing	Batch	Line	Continuous processing
Product	type	Special/ standard	Special ➡ Standard			Standard
	range	Wide	Wide ➡ Narrow			Narrow
Number of customer orders		Few	Few ➡ Many			Many
Capacity	basis for calculation	Staff	Staff ➡ Process			Process
	scale	Small	Small ➡ Large			Very large
	size of changes	Incre-mental	Incremental ➡ Stepped			New facility
	control	Difficult	Difficult ➡ Easy			Easy
Demand – level of definition		Variable	Low ➡ Established			Established
Process flexibility		Flexible	Flexible ➡ Inflexible			Very inflexible
Set-ups or change-overs	number	Many	Many ➡ Unlikely			Unlikely
	expense per	Variable	Inexpensive ➡ Expensive			Very expensive
Dominant factor in measuring capacity utilization		Staff	Staff ➡ Process			Process
Bottle-necks	number	Few	Few	Often several	None	None
	position & nature	Random & movable	Random & movable	Fixed in the short & medium term	Not relevant	Not relevant
Impact of breakdowns		Variable	Little ➡ Significant			Enormous

Manufacturing processes

The implications for the management and provision of capacity overviewed in Figure 7.8 reflect the nature of the manufacturing process involved:

- *Project and jobbing* In both project and jobbing, the typical firms involved are relatively small in size, skilled staff are central to the process of making the products (equipment having the role of helping the skilled person complete the task), and the firm can offer a flexible response in terms of the range of products that the manufacturing process can handle. Changing from one product to another is an integral part of the manufacturing process and will involve short, inexpensive changes.

- *Line and continuous processing* Moving towards line and continuous processing brings with it a shift to the other end of each of these dimensions. Typically, companies are large in size, with processes rather than people making the products involved. Here, the role of people is to help the process complete the task. Demand is well defined as product knowledge is well established, and it is easy to calculate how much capacity is required. Capacity changes, on the other hand, are large scale in nature. Having been designed to make a given product range, the process is rarely, if ever, changed, except at the end of a product's life cycle. As the process is designed to be balanced, bottlenecks are not a factor. However, the impact of breakdowns is significant as the process itself has stopped, and products cannot be made. In project and jobbing, on the other hand, the skilled staff simply switch to alternative tasks.

- *Batch* As shown in Figure 7.8, batch is a transition between the two extremes of process choice for most factors, as the arrows depict. The exception is bottlenecks, and we will now look at why this is. A bottleneck occurs where the capacity in one stage of a process is less than the capacity in the other parts of the process. To help visualize this, think of a wine bottle and the difference in size between the neck and the body. In multi-step batch processes, there are often differences in demand and capacity ratios at each stage (the neck and body factor). Some of these will invariably show bottleneck capacity characteristics, but it is a factor that will not usually change in the short and medium term.

Determining the level of capacity

Investment in plant and equipment is usually an irreversible decision. Also, staff capacity, once created, is expensive to change. As a result, growth and its associated capacity decisions present a challenging task, especially given the potential impact of these capacity decisions and those of competitors on sales revenue and market share.

The process of deciding on capacity levels is complex. Organizations are faced with a number of important considerations, such as:

- Anticipating the end of growth
- Avoiding overcapacity
- Choosing to plan ahead of growth or to follow growth – the lead or follow demand capacity alternatives
- What action to take in a situation of overcapacity – divest or diversify?

> **KEY IDEA**
> Deciding on the level of capacity involves anticipating the end of growth, avoiding too much, deciding whether to lead or follow demand and deciding what to do with overcapacity – divest or diversify?

Similar dilemmas are also involved in downsizing. When and how much concern not only questions of cost, but also the potential impact on sales and market share, and, as with capacity investment, downsizing decision are costly to reverse.

To help manage capacity, companies consider a range of demand/capacity issues, and these are now discussed.

Demand-related issues

An organization focuses its capacity planning efforts towards meeting its customers' requirements. To do this, it needs to manage demand, which involves identifying the nature and size of the demand and determining how the company is best going to meet it. One characteristic of demand that further complicates this provision and makes managing it more challenging is that it is never the same twice over. Some of these variations are, however, more predictable than others, as explained below.

Predictable variations Although demand levels will vary, there are very often characteristics of sales from which patterns can be identified, enabling such fluctuations to be predicted more easily. For example:

- *Seasonality* The seasonal nature of many services and products is well recognized. Defined as variation that repeats itself at fixed intervals, seasonal patterns are caused by many factors including the weather (for example, holiday bookings and sales of air conditioners and ice-cream) and time of the year (for example, the demand for air travel, types of clothing, gardening equipment, fireworks, training courses and tax processing).

- *Peaks* Whereas seasonality of demand occurs over a year, predictable variations in demand also occur at shorter intervals. To distinguish the two, the latter are normally known as peaks, and, as with seasonality of demand, they are caused by recurring factors that can be identified. For example, working hours affect traffic volumes, and the day of the week can affect demand – the emergency unit in a hospital will be busier than usual late on a Saturday night. Similarly, the time of day will affect the level of demand for sandwiches, and a firm's policies such as billing patterns and the push to meet sales targets will be reflected in the activity levels over a month.

- *One-off demands* Some services and products are subject to a predictable one-off peak in demand. This needs to be successfully managed to ensure that potential sales are maximized. Examples include film premieres, music festivals and book launches. However, there are risks if the certainty of a one-off demand is not guaranteed.

Unpredictable variations Other demand characteristics are less predictable but still need to be managed. For example, airlines overbook on flights to protect against 'no-shows'. The same policy is also adopted by hotel operators, particularly those in locations where the unpredictability of bookings or the frequency of late cancellations brings uncertainty in the pattern of demand and a resulting loss of revenue from having turned business away.

Capacity-related issues

As with demand, there are issues in the provision of capacity that increase the difficulty of this management task. Again, some of these are more predictable than others, as explained below.

> **KEY IDEA**
> Organizations need to separate the predictable from the unpredictable variations in demand and capacity

Predictable aspects of capacity Capacity is typically a mix of different staff skills and process types in order to handle the range of services and products and their associated volumes. Where this range is relatively wide, the demands placed on these different sets of skills and processes will vary and typically result in bottlenecks (the neck of the wine bottle referred to earlier) where the capacity in one phase of the delivery system is less than the demand placed on it. However, bottlenecks are short- to medium-term phenomena so are predictable in terms of their position and extent. Knowing where they are enables a business to manage capacity within this constraint, while directing attention and resources to increasing capacity, reducing demand on the bottleneck by using alternative skill sets or processes to deliver part of the service or product, redesigning the service or product to simplify its delivery or making the delivery system more efficient.

Unpredictable aspects of capacity As with demand, some aspects of capacity are less predictable, and these introduce problems of a more ad hoc nature:

- *Absenteeism* People stay away from work for a number of reasons. Estimates place the direct and indirect costs for UK businesses as high as £16 billion, and absence rates are on average about 3.5 per cent. The short-term impact of this adds to the difficulty of managing capacity effectively. Ways of attempting to cope with this have centred on recognizing absenteeism as a management problem and attempting to reduce it to manageable levels. Lewisham Borough Council in the Greater London area was affected by absentee levels averaging 17 days a year for each employee, but better monitoring over a 24-month period helped bring this down to less than 11 days per year. Others argue that unpaid sick leave encourages employees to believe that no one loses when they are away. Paying for sickness, including the penalty of taking away this benefit for abuse of the system, is part of why Nissan believes it has achieved absenteeism levels of less than 2 per cent at its plant in Washington in the north-east of England.

- *Short-term demand changes* Short-term demand variations can often result in a temporary shortage of capacity, with the difficulties this presents in managing capacity.

Successfully managing these capacity and demand issues is often central to the successful growth of a business and lies at the centre of the operations task.

Planning and managing capacity

The purpose of the chapter so far has been to introduce key definitions, provide an overall review of capacity and illustrate the purpose and outcomes of its provision. The rest of the chapter addresses the task of planning and managing long- and medium-term capacity. It will address the tasks of resource planning and medium-term planning, with short-term operations control and scheduling being covered in Chapter 8.

Capacity management is an essential responsibility of the operations function. The objective is to match the level of capacity to the level of demand, in terms of both quantity (how much) and capability (the skill mix to meet the service or product specifications). Simple though it sounds, meeting this basic requirement is a challenging task and concerns issues of:

- *Uncertainty* – demand is uncertain and can vary by the hour, day, week, month or year
- *Anticipating the future* – although they are much better than nothing, forecasts are, by definition, inaccurate
- *Timescales* – the scope of capacity management spans long-term planning through to day-to-day scheduling
- *Alternatives* – choosing from the different ways of providing capacity to meet demand
- *Execution* – fulfilling the plan.

The optimum approach to planning and managing capacity is to separate the task into its major elements and position these in terms of the time phases in which they need to occur. Figure 7.9 provides an overview of these tasks, showing their position in the overall planning and control system.

Figure 7.9 Operations planning and control systems

TIMESCALES	PHASE		TASK
Years	Planning	Resource planning	Determines the resources to meet the aggregate demand forecasts for all services or products in a future time frame, normally a period of between two and five years
	Planning	Medium-term capacity planning	Partially disaggregated demand forecasts are used to give a 'rough-cut' review of the necessary resources in terms of staff skill and process types. Will be for periods of six months to two years depending on the type of business involved
	Control	Scheduling	Detailed plans to determine the capacity (staff skills and processes) and materials to meet the service or product schedule, together with any contingency plans
Days/hours	Control	Execution	Day-to-day (often hourly) control systems to manage the detailed capacity plans and material requirements to meet the scheduled delivery of services and products to customers

The level of detail involved will reflect the complexity of the services and products provided. As you will no doubt appreciate, managing a sandwich bar will be less complex than managing a large hotel, as would a small assembly shop compared with a large pharmaceutical plant making chemical formulations in a wide range of pack sizes and alternatives. In essence, though, the tasks are the same, as explained below:

- *Planning* Front-end planning provides key communication links between top management and operations. It helps to form the basis for translating strategic objectives and future market needs into operations plans and resources, and is essential in determining what can be achieved, the investments and decisions to be made and the timescales involved. It is during this phase that companies look forward and decide on the 'game plan' for the future. How far forward they look will depend on the investments and timescales involved, and these will be discussed in detail in the next section.

- *Scheduling* The scheduling phase determines capacity several weeks, months and sometimes up to one year ahead. It details how demand will be met from the facilities available and ensures that the capacity and material requirements are, or can be, put into place.

- *Execution* This phase of the system concerns executing day-to-day operations by determining and monitoring capacity and material requirements; this will ensure that customer demand is met and resources are used efficiently.

As Figure 7.9 shows, the planning phase is split into 'resource planning' and 'medium-term capacity planning', and these are now reviewed. Discussion of the scheduling and execution phases of the system is covered in the next chapter.

Resource planning

This strategic business task generally involves looking several years ahead. It aims to meet the long-term capacity requirements and resource allocations that will answer future organizational objectives, and it will do this by planning for capacity changes in line with anticipated increases in market share, the introduction of new services or products and the company's entry into new markets.

> **KEY IDEA**
> Resource planning looks several years ahead to provide future capacity requirements

---

Anticipating future demand in terms of its size (associated volumes) and nature (the service/product mix) involves an essential strategic decision that needs to address three critical dimensions:

- *Amount* – how much is required?
- *Timing* – when is the capacity needed?
- *Location* – where should the capacity be located?

Capacity decisions for several years ahead are difficult to make because of the timescales involved and the fact that the above three dimensions are not stand-alone questions. All three impinge on each other. For example, determining size is not just a question of the total requirement but will need to address issues concerning size (how much capacity per hospital, office, retail outlet, manufacturing plant and so on), the location of this additional capacity and when it needs to be available. Consequently, these elements of operations planning need to be considered as an integrated whole.

Figure 7.9 shows resource planning as the first step in capacity planning. It is the most highly aggregated stage and has the longest planning horizon. It typically involves taking a two- to five-year time frame and converting monthly and annual data from the operations plan into statements of aggregate resources such as total staff hours, office space and support equipment in a service organization, or staff hours, floor space and machine or process hours in a manufacturing firm. This level of planning potentially involves new capital investments such as buildings, warehousing and equipment that often have lead-times of months or years.

As Figure 7.9 explains, the operations planning task takes demand and resource planning information that details what is required and what is available, and then highlights possible constraints in terms of lead-times and levels of investment. These issues are large in size, complex in nature and concern the amount, timing and location, factors that are critical in terms of capacity. Now take a look at Case 7.2, which illustrates some of these issues.

> Medium-term capacity planning (or 'aggregate' or 'rough-cut' planning) – capacity planning developed in broad terms to meet agreed output levels where capacity is considered to be relatively fixed

Medium-term capacity planning

Medium-term capacity planning (also referred to as aggregate or rough-cut planning), for periods up to two years[1] ahead, is used within the overall framework of the long-term plan. It involves medium-term plans to meet agreed output levels where capacity is considered to be relatively fixed. This step in the planning process is designed to look ahead and resolve, in broad terms, the approach that will best provide sufficient capacity to meet the levels of demand that have been forecast. It examines key areas of capacity (for example, skilled staff categories and equipment) to identify any capacity changes that would need to be made, how feasible these would be, the timescales involved and the steps to be taken.

CASE 7.2 WAL-MART USES SCALE TO COMPETE IN THE US FOOD MARKET

Wal-Mart is a US supermarket chain that also owns ASDA in the UK and Bompreço in Brazil, and is one of the largest corporations in the world. Most new Wal-Mart stores have floor space of up to 200,000 square feet, the size of two (American) football fields, and are too big to be built anywhere other than on the edge of towns. But in 2003, Wal-Mart opened its first Neighbourhood Market store in Rogers, Arkansas – with a size of less than 40,000 square feet. The strategy was to limit the store size and thus allow the company to find sites in built-up urban areas, thus allowing it to compete head to head with the traditional supermarkets that dominated the cities. From its small beginnings in food sales in 1983, Wal-Mart had become the biggest seller of food in the US by 2001. Its estimated income of $13.6 billion in 2009 was reportedly almost 50 per cent more than that of its five closest competitors combined.

Wal-Mart's first foray into food was not, however, a success. Inspired by retail giants such as Carrefour and Le Clerc in France, Wal-Mart built large, 260,000 square foot supermarkets. But these proved to be too big for customers to handle, and profits were low. Instead, it decided to move forward with its supercentres by adding groceries to its traditional discount stores and limiting the size to no more than 200,000 square feet. At the end of 2009, it had over 2,700 supercentres, which, with Sam's Club, accounted for 25 per cent of the US grocery market.

Since 1998, Wal-Mart has been tinkering with the smaller store formats. The Neighbourhood Market store offers about a fifth (24,000 against 120,000) of the product items found in a supercentre, including a full assortment of food, health, beauty and household products. It includes a chicken rotisserie and home-made tortilla stand but lacks the extensive salad bars, delicatessens and meat and fish counters that competing supermarkets offer. Meat and fish arrive prepacked, ready for the shelf. There are also convenient extras – a drive-through pharmacy, a half-hour photo processing service and a self-service coffee bar by the entrance. In addition, more than half the checkouts are self-scanning, which reduces queue lengths and staff costs.

Wal-Mart is harnessing the same buying power and supply chain efficiency that enables it to offer food at prices some 10–15 per cent cheaper than its competitors. Its aim appears to be to provide convenience without the premiums that typically go with smaller size.
www.walmart.com

Questions

1 How is Wal-Mart using scale to compete in the US food market?

2 Why is Wal-Mart pursuing its Neighbourhood Market store strategy?

Lecturers: visit www.palgrave.com/business/hillessential for additional resources

> **KEY IDEA**
Medium-term planning looks up to two years ahead to resolve how to provide capacity
to meet forecast demand

Statements of demand (both forecast sales and known orders) are translated into operations requirements, and the medium-term capacity plan takes these and checks them against available capacity. Although small changes to demand forecasts can be accommodated from one period to another, it is necessary to develop medium-term capacity plans in order to know how to cope with an overloading or underloading of capacity in the longer term. In this way, an orderly and systematic adjustment of capacity can be made to meet any significant changes to the level and mix of demand while meeting both deliveries to customers and internal efficiency targets.

Steps in medium-term capacity planning

Figure 7.9 shows the position of the medium-term planning step within the front-end planning phase. This section gives a more detailed explanation of what is involved, with the final section providing details of some of the ways in which the plan is achieved.

1 *Develop operations statements* Sales forecasts and known orders for each service or product within each time period are translated into statements of what operations needs to provide, also known as a master schedule.
2 *Make-or-buy decision* Any changes to the make-or-buy decisions must be measured in capacity terms, initially through the medium-term capacity plans and, where major shifts occur, against resource plans.
3 *Select common measures of aggregate demand* The next step is to aggregate demand for all services and products into statements of similar capacity groups. For single-service or single-product organizations, this is typically not difficult. For the brewer, it could be gallons of beer; for the doctor, patient visits; for a coal mine, tonnes of coal. For multi-service or multi-product organizations, however, great care has to be used when selecting appropriate measures.
4 *Develop medium-term capacity plans* Medium-term capacity plans are then developed primarily to meet demand at the lowest cost while supporting other relevant order-winners and qualifiers.
5 *Select the planning horizon* The next step is to select an appropriate planning horizon for the medium-term capacity plan. Although this will cover several time periods, the plans will typically be considered on a month-by-month basis as decisions made in one time period will often limit the decisions that can be made in the next. Decisions that ignore future consequences will often prove costly.
6 *Achieving the medium-term capacity plan* This step involves choosing between a range of options to best achieve the plan. These include adjusting demand patterns and selecting ways of providing capacity. The next section discusses these in detail.
7 *Select the medium-term capacity plan* The final step is to select the most suitable medium-term capacity plan to meet the agreed corporate objectives.

Achieving the medium-term capacity plan

As the pattern of demand for services and products will vary over time and within a given period, it is not possible to provide services or make products in one time period that exactly match the pattern of demand in the same period. To handle this companies choose between:

1 Making products ahead of demand and holding items in inventory for sale in a future time period. For example, summer clothes will be made several months ahead of time.
2 Holding orders in a queue (known as an order backlog or forward load) waiting to be processed.

In both instances, changes in demand levels will alter the amount of inventory or the length of the queue, with both approaches helping to manage the uncertainty of demand and the relatively fixed nature of capacity that characterize this task.

Types of capacity plan

The second key decision concerns which capacity plan a business decides to adopt. The alternatives are:

- Level capacity
- Chase demand
- Mixed plan

and these are now described.

Level capacity plan – sets operations capacity at the same level throughout the planning period, irrespective of the forecast pattern of demand

Level capacity plans

In a **level capacity plan**, operations capacity is set at the same level throughout the planning period, irrespective of the forecast pattern of demand. In this way, companies uncouple capacity and demand rates. Whether companies choose to make-to-order or make-to-stock, alternative mechanisms are available to adjust demand/capacity imbalances as they occur:

- *In make-to-stock situations* throughput levels can be smoothed by transferring the capacity available in low-demand periods to higher demand periods in the form of inventory. This smoothing can be used by manufacturing companies to create stability in their capacity requirements and has several attendant benefits, especially in terms of continuity of employment. Figure 7.10 provides an illustration of this for a 12-month, medium-term planning period.

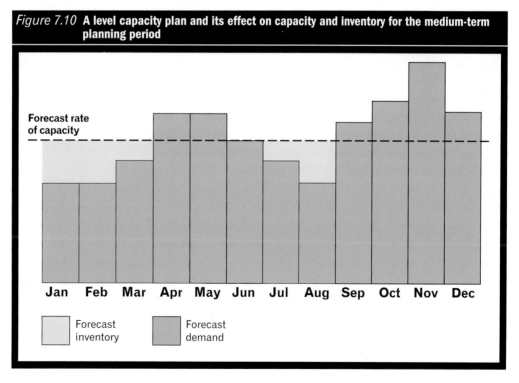

Figure 7.10 A level capacity plan and its effect on capacity and inventory for the medium-term planning period

- *In make-to-order situations* the level of the queue or order backlog becomes the adjusting mechanism used to enable capacity levels to remain level. Figure 7.11 provides an example of this. Here a solicitor's office uses the order backlog/forward load of client jobs to balance the capacity/demand requirements for a 12-month, medium-term planning period.

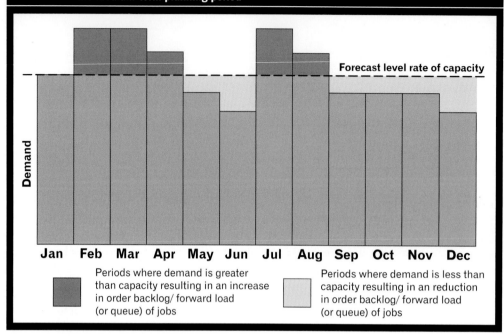

Figure 7.11 A level capacity plan in a solicitor's office using order backlog/forward load during the medium-term planning period

Jan Feb Mar Apr May Jun Jul Aug Sep Oct Nov Dec

Forecast level rate of capacity

Demand

Periods where demand is greater than capacity resulting in an increase in order backlog/ forward load (or queue) of jobs

Periods where demand is less than capacity resulting in an reduction in order backlog/ forward load (or queue) of jobs

Chase demand capacity plans

The opposite of a level capacity plan is one designed to adjust capacity in line with antici-pated changes in demand. Known as a **chase demand capacity plan**, this involves changing capacity levels from one period to another by adjusting some combination of staff numbers, working hours and available equipment. This approach is more difficult to manage than a level capacity plan due to the increased complexity of the task. Factors that make this approach hard to manage include ensuring the availability, training and retention of staff and the potential impact of less experienced staff on quality conformance.

Manufacturing companies making standard products can take advantage of a level or mixed plan by using inventory as part of the means to manage imbalances, whereas service organizations and manufacturing businesses making special products usually cannot. Because most services cannot be stored and special products, by definition, cannot be made ahead of demand, chase demand (Figure 7.12) and order backlog (see Figure 7.11) are the options available to these organizations.

With a chase demand plan, the decisions concern not only by how much to increase capacity, but also demand issues such as:

- Timing – when to increase capacity
- The extent to which a business is prepared to carry excess capacity (and the costs involved) as an alternative to the costs and concerns of repeatedly changing capacity
- The possibility of not being able to meet customer lead-times due to a lengthening backlog of orders/queues.

Mixed capacity plan

The third option to handle capacity/demand differences is to choose a **mixed capacity plan**. Here, some inventory is accumulated to make effective use of existing capacity, and some capacity changes are made to reflect changes in demand. The example in Figure 7.13 shows an increase in capacity during the months of September to December that resulted from introducing a temporary evening shift (18.30–22.00 hrs) to help meet demand in the build-up to peak sales at Christmas.

Chase demand capacity plan – involves changing capacity levels from one period to another by adjusting some combination of staff numbers, working hours and available equipment

Mixed capacity plan – involves some inventory being accumulated to make effective use of existing capacity, and some capacity changes being made to reflect changes in demand

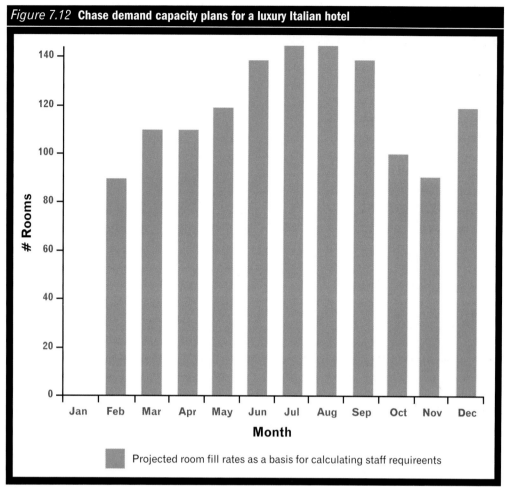

Figure 7.12 **Chase demand capacity plans for a luxury Italian hotel**

Projected room fill rates as a basis for calculating staff requireents

Note: The hotel has a total of 153 rooms.

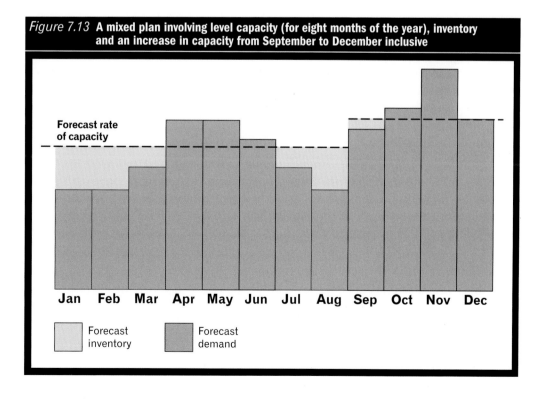

Figure 7.13 **A mixed plan involving level capacity (for eight months of the year), inventory and an increase in capacity from September to December inclusive**

Forecast rate of capacity

Forecast inventory

Forecast demand

Managing demand and capacity

So far, we have discussed the concept and role of medium-term capacity planning and the alternative approaches from which a business may choose. This section discusses the options for adjusting levels of demand and capacity within the overall plan. These will fall within the control of an organization and are designed to help fine-tune capacity plans to better meet the business's objectives as well as the market's needs.

Managing demand

Demand is inherently variable at all times. That is the nature of market demand and the challenging task that operations needs to manage and discharge. Within its overall approach, however, an organization can select from alternatives to help manage demand so that it can better meet the needs of the business and its customers. These alternatives fall within a number of categories, as described below.

Changing the pattern of demand

One way of adjusting demand and capacity differences is to change the pattern of demand. Examples include:

- *Altering price levels* to differentiate, for example, between peak and off-peak periods. In this way, some customers are persuaded to choose periods where demand levels are normally lower in exchange for paying less, for example off-season holidays, matinée cinema and theatre prices, factory discounts for early- or late-season purchases, off-peak rail travel and early-evening menu discounts at restaurants. The purpose of these pricing schemes is to help level out demand through different time periods.

- *Advertising* can be used to stimulate demand. Often working hand in hand with price changes, one purpose of advertising can be to stimulate demand in periods of otherwise low demand and, in that way, change the pattern of demand to help improve the capacity/demand balance for an organization.

- *Complementary services and products* can be developed for counter-cyclical, seasonal trends. In this way, demand for the complementary services and products will occur in the periods of lower sales for the current services and products. Examples include the use of hotels in the winter for conferences, coach tour operators providing school bus services, fast-food restaurants offering breakfast menus, and garden tractor and mower companies developing a range of blowing equipment to handle autumn leaves and winter snow.

Scheduling

A second way is to develop elements of the scheduling procedure that are aimed specifically at modifying demand patterns. These include the following:

- *Reservations and appointments* are an effective way of helping to manage demand. In essence, they are a way to pre-sell capacity within a service delivery system. When preferred slots are already taken, demand can be deflected into other available time slots. Many service delivery systems use this mechanism, including hospitals, dental and other health practices, passenger airlines, hairdressing and beauty salons, hotels and restaurants.

- *Fixed service schedules* are often used by companies to increase the effective use of capacity by forcing customers to adapt their requirements to the capacity schedule available. All forms of public transport use fixed service schedules as one way to help manage capacity.

Managing uncertainty

Demand is uncertain. To reduce this uncertainty, companies use a range of approaches, for example pre-payment coupled to pre-booking, which gets round the problem of late cancellations resulting in lost sales. In other systems, cancellations incur penalties. The passenger airline approach is to offer from a 'no change' deal through to a totally flexible ticket depending upon the level of price discounting the passenger accepts. Those passengers buying a non-discounted ticket have complete freedom to change, while those with a discounted ticket receive no refund if they cancel.

Managing capacity

The other principal way in which companies can take steps to handle the differences in demand and capacity is to consider different ways of managing capacity. These include the following.

Short-term capacity adjustments

These adjustments can be made in two ways – overtime and temporary staff. Although the use of overtime is being reduced in many developed economies, the use of temporary labour is increasing.

Temporary staff have long been used in many businesses as a way to handle marked changes in demand when overtime working is not a sustainable option. As companies continue to restructure to help cope with today's competitive climate, they have slimmed down in an effort to reduce overall costs, and they are often left with a core of permanent staff that represents an insufficient capacity to cope with demand at peak times. Temporary and contract staff are increasingly being used to provide for such capacity shortfalls on a need-to-have basis, and this approach is proving to be a way of providing capacity to meet predictable and random demand patterns while helping companies to better control their costs and respond quickly to fluctuations in demand.

Flexible capacity

The last section dealt with ways of adjusting planned capacity levels. This section considers ways of being able to change capacity within the existing plan:

- *Flexible staff* provide the option of moving existing capacity around within the system or process to reflect changes in demand. Training to increase each person's range of skills is fundamental to this alternative. Switching staff in line with forecast sales and known orders has been an integral part of manufacturing businesses for many years, but is now more important than ever because of the increase in product options on offer and the shorter lead-times often expected by customers.

  This approach is also widely used in service delivery systems. In fast-food restaurants, for example, staff switch from serving to cleaning tasks during periods of low demand and vice versa. Similarly, moving front-office staff to and from back-office tasks is increasingly used by financial service companies to provide better support for customers while managing overall staff capacity within agreed budgets.

- *Arranging different capacity levels* within the same time period is also used to change capacity to reflect different patterns of demand. Part-time staff, temporary staff, shift patterns and staggered working hours (including break times) are some of the more common ways that organizations use.

Changing the form and nature of capacity

To meet the dynamic nature of markets and the varying patterns and fluctuations in demand that follow on from this, companies have been changing the form and nature of their capacity. Some of the more commonly used approaches are now discussed:

- *Annualized hours* entails calculating working time on an annual rather than a weekly or monthly basis, with employees contracted to work, for example, 1,748 hours per year rather than 38 hours per week. (This example comprises 52 weeks less 6 weeks of holidays × 38 hours per week.) The system gives companies more flexibility when scheduling work, allowing for longer hours at some periods and shorter hours at others. Overtime is not ruled out in these arrangements, but being able to match capacity to seasonal patterns of demand leads to marked reductions in overtime and in the attendant costs. Case 7.3 describes BMW's approach.

- *Substituting capacity* can be achieved by increasing the use of technology and/or customers in the delivery system. Both these alternatives reduce the number of employed staff and thereby the overall size of the task of managing capacity, whereas using the customer as part of the delivery system (for example, with ATMs and other self-service arrangements) means that the 'capacity' to serve will always be on hand as customers comprise both the source of demand and the source of capacity.

- *Subcontracting* similarly allows companies to spread the task of handling capacity/demand differences by having suppliers manage part of the capacity implications resulting from changes in demand.

- *Sharing capacity* is a concept designed to spread the cost of expensive equipment or highly skilled staff resources that would normally be underutilized. For example, hospitals may agree to share expensive medical equipment. Similarly, smaller passenger and freight airlines reach agreement on sharing a range of facilities with other airlines, from check-in terminals and staff to baggage handling equipment and ground personnel.

> **KEY IDEA**
Taking actions to change demand patterns and adjust and change the shape of capacity are key tasks when managing these resources

CASE 7.3 FLEXIBLE WORKING AT BMW

One of BMW's key tasks when it took over the Mini car plant in Oxford was to increase productivity and bring the levels of output per worker up to those of its factories in Germany. BMW estimated the gap at some 30 per cent and explained, in discussions with local management and staff, that the options were to close the gap or face significant job cuts. The changes sought concerned working practices that had transformed BMW's shop floor into one of the world's most productive.

Among the important changes that BMW was looking to introduce was flexible working. In its own plants, BMW had dispensed with the standard eight-hour day and five-days-a-week shifts. Instead, BMW staff worked varied shift patterns (including a regular requirement to work on Saturday at no extra pay) that, on average, added up to four days a week. The shift patterns were very varied (about 250 models) to meet different sets of needs. For instance, at one factory in rural Bavaria there is one model for a handful of workers who are also farmers that takes into account their need to leave early to tend their livestock.

The result is that BMW's expensive plants run longer and are not idle at weekends, thereby cutting the actual costs per car by one-quarter compared with traditional work patterns. With machines and processes costing as much as $250 million, the savings are substantial.

Another element of flexible working that BMW has introduced is the time accounting module. This allows the company to increase or decrease a person's hours (up to a maximum at any time of 200 hours) in line with demand, and with workers later taking time off or working longer, again at no extra cost.

www.bmw.com

Questions

1 Explain how these arrangements helped BMW to become more competitive.

2 Give an example of when a company would use flexible working and the time accounting model.

Lecturers: visit www.palgrave.com/business/hillessential for additional resources

Critical reflections

Managing operations capacity is both complex and challenging owing to the size of the task and the need for all facets of capacity to work well both in themselves and together, in an environment where demand is increasingly dynamic and less predictable.

For example, the data in Figure 7.14 provide an illustration of the size and interrelated nature of capacity. This is what it takes an American airline to feed one day's passengers from Atlanta airport and well illustrates the forward-looking as well as the day-to-day nature of capacity management.

Figure 7.14 **What it takes an American airline to feed its passengers from Atlanta airport on one day**

Aspects		Quantity
Number of	passengers	36,800
	flights	274
	trucks	60
	assembly lines	16
Kilograms of	chicken	1,130
	pasta	535
	broccoli	23
	spinach	100
	tomatoes	140
	lettuce	1,120
	butter	235
	coffee	420
Number of	dinner rolls	18,500
	apples	5,800
Litres of	olive oil	86
	wine	6,320

But all this is happening in an environment characterized by high levels of risk. As markets open up, decisions on capacity and location, for instance, will have an impact on future market positions and opportunities. As an example, several major car companies have built assembly plants to help position themselves early in relation to potential market opportunities in China. China and India are two such examples where forecast gross domestic product (GDP) will exceed that of the US in 15 and 35 years, respectively. As a consequence, companies in different sectors have sought to get an early foothold, but all have found it tough going.

Take, for example, pharmaceutical companies that have set up manufacturing facilities in China. Inherent in their decisions to do so are several concerns including moves by the national government to protect the local drug industry, fresh restrictions on a foreign company's ability to sell drugs and serious problems experienced by foreign investors concerning the protection of intellectual property as patents are broken and substitute products are made locally. Although some companies, such as Xian-Janssen and Glaxo-SmithKline, have earned good profits, others are below target. It has been forecast that, by 2018, annual pharmaceutical sales in China will have reached around $133 billion. With predictions that spending on drugs as a percentage of GDP will more than double between 2009 and 2013, companies believe they cannot afford not to be present and are thus planning not only to stay, but to expand. Companies such as Bristol-Myers Squibb, GlaxoSmithKline, Janssen (part of Johnson & Johnson), Novo Nordisk, Pfizer and Pharmacia & Upjohn are prepared to take the risk and gamble on the end game.

For any business, deciding whether to increase or decrease capacity is typically a major question. Capacity comprises not only the level of permanency involved, but also the issue of timing. A loss in market share always goes to a competitor. The competitor who adds capacity first does not necessarily make a profit. But the competitor who trails behind on the growth/capacity path will find great difficulty in regaining its future market share position, whether or not it decides to increase capacity at a later date. On the other hand, adding capacity that is subsequently underused is bound up with unnecessary costs and high exposure. There are few areas of decision-making where the outcomes are under such an intense spotlight. Buying capacity that does not get used or having insufficient capacity to meet demand will always be viewed with a level of incredulity by those outside a company due to the fundamental nature of capacity provision in transacting business.

The example given earlier concerning China reflects the size and nature of the dilemma. Furthermore, the dimensions underpinning these decisions are becoming more difficult to embrace as the timescales become shorter and the risks get bigger. As this chapter has highlighted, the issues impacting demand and capacity have an increasing measure of these characteristics. The dynamic nature of today's markets is matched by developments in technology, the issue of where work needs to be undertaken, and repositioning in terms of the make/buy mix and the impact of all these factors on capacity. The outcome serves only to reinforce the key decisions involved in the choice and management of capacity. A challenging task indeed!

Summary

Managing capacity is central to the basic business task of providing services and products in line with customer demand. As the elements of staff, delivery systems and processes contribute to operations' capacity, its central role is further emphasized by the size and interrelated nature of its provision. Key elements of effectively managing capacity include:

- Determining the way in which capacity is most appropriately measured to reflect the nature of the business involved

- Measuring output needs to distinguish between the dimensions of utilization (a comparison of actual hours worked with planned hours) and efficiency (a comparison of the work produced to the number of hours worked)

- The desired position is to have neither too much nor too little capacity. But corporate decisions concerning make versus buy, service/product range, process design and the perishable nature of capacity (particularly in the service sector) are among the several variables that make this a difficult call.

- Within an environment where definitions of capacity are characterized by uncertainty, operations needs to reduce the planning and managing task in several ways, including:
  - Identifying those parts of total demand that can be predicted (for example, seasonality and peaks) as opposed to those which cannot be predicted, and thereby reducing the truly uncertain aspects when forecasting demand
  - Influencing demand to reduce the peaks and troughs that characterize demand profiles.

The remainder of the chapter addressed the long-term horizons of capacity provision and the ways to help when managing demand and capacity. Key points included:

- The approaches to resource planning (often two to five years ahead) and medium-term planning (typically from six months to two years ahead) – Figure 7.9 provides an overview of these operations planning and control systems.

- The sections on resource and medium-term planning also provided illustrations of alternative approaches that may be used. In resource planning, the amount, timing and location of capacity were central to the discussion. In medium-term planning, the steps used to provide a plan were detailed, together with alternative approaches to achieving the plan – level capacity, chase demand or a mixed plan.

- The final section in the chapter introduced alternative ways of managing demand (including changing demand patterns and scheduling) and managing capacity (for example, short-term adjustments, forms of flexible capacity and changing its basic form).

Study activities

Discussion questions

1 How do the capacity considerations in a hospital, a wine bar and a company making lawnmowers differ?

2 In what circumstances would it be best for a business to adopt a lead and when best a follow capacity provision policy? Give two examples for each alternative to illustrate your arguments.

3 Which approaches to capacity management would you favour using in an Italian ski resort hotel? Explain your choice.

4 In making reservations for services, a common approach where demand is uncertain is to 'overbook' to avoid the cost of no-shows.
   a) Using the examples of a passenger airline and a good-quality restaurant, discuss the pros and cons of this approach.
   b) How ethical is this practice?
   c) How do you think that companies handle those times when more customers show than available capacity can accommodate?

5 Discuss the advantages and disadvantages of the following approaches to meeting demand:
   - The build-up and depletion of the finished goods inventory
   - Subcontact work
   - Using part-time staff.

Assignments

1 A fully integrated oil company is involved in the following major steps in the business process:
   - Searching for new oilfields
   - Drilling for oil
   - Building a new oil refinery or extending an existing one
   - Managing an oil refinery
   - Delivering different fuel grades to petrol stations
   - Managing the sale of non-fuel goods at a petrol station.

What are the likely time horizons in capacity planning for each of the above activities? Fit these into the long-, medium- and short-term time frames introduced in this chapter.

2 Which approaches (order backlog/queues or work-in-progress/finished goods inventory or a mix of the two) would the following organizations use to help handle the medium-term capacity planning issues discussed in the chapter:

- An architect's office?
- A high-quality reproduction furniture manufacturer?
- A management consultancy company?

3 Should an organization always attempt to match its capacity to its forecast and known demand patterns? Give two examples to illustrate your views.

4 Discuss the major differences between a call centre and a soft drinks company producing own-label products for major retailers with respect to:
- Capacity provision
- Facilities location.

Exploring further

Journal articles

Klassen, K.J. and Rohleder, T.R. (2002) 'Demand and capacity management decisions in services: how they impact on one another'. *International Journal of Operations and Production Management*, **22**(5/6), pp. 527–49. The article's findings are based on modelling the impact of automation, customer participation, cross-training employees, informing customers about the operation, and other factors, showing that demand and capacity decisions do indeed impact on each other – sometimes in ways that are not initially obvious.

Books

Chase, C. (2009) *Demand-driven Forecasting: A Structured Approach to Forecasting*. Hoboken, NJ: Wiley/SAS Business Services. This practitioner-focused book is filled with real-life examples and case studies looking at how to improve forecasting within a business.

Hill, T. (2005) *Operations Management: Text and Cases*. Basingstoke: Palgrave Macmillan. This provides a useful supplement to the current book by offering a more comprehensive explanation and further examples (including long case studies) showing how service and manufacturing companies have applied these concepts.

Hill, A. and Hill, T. (2009) *Manufacturing Operations Strategy: Text and Cases*, 3rd edn. Basingstoke: Palgrave Macmillan. The text provides a useful supplement to *Essential Operations Management* by outlining an in-depth approach for developing and implementing operations strategy within manufacturing organizations.

Morlidge, S. and Player, S. (2010) *Future Ready: How to Master Business Forecasting*. Chichester: John Wiley & Sons. This is a thought-provoking and engaging look at how businesses need to rethink the way they forecast in order to navigate through turbulent times. The authors show that a combination of 'good enough' forecasts, wise preparation and timely action is critical within business.

Notes and references

1 As already highlighted, although the timescales for resource and medium-term capacity planning are classically referred to as two to five years and six months to two years ahead, respectively, many organizations do not need to plan that far ahead as the lead-times involved to change capacity are not that lengthy. While capacity that takes a long time to change is a characteristic of some sectors (for example, oil refining and car plants), many organizations may well need to look only one to two years ahead without limiting their options and opportunities.

It's a cold December lunch time and Minkies is buzzing. 'It always brightens up my day,' explained one customer. 'I love popping in for a coffee, something to eat or just to say hello. They're so friendly, and the food is amazing! What more could I ask for? With so much variety, I can eat here seven days a week without getting bored. I love the "minx" on rye, but I'm also always tempted by all the other food they have. The roast chicken I had last week was wonderful, and the salads are truly delicious!'

Doron Atzmon set up Minkies four years ago as a local deli serving a wide range of tasty, nutritious and healthy products. It has been a great success, and he has just opened a butcher across the street from it too. 'People love the food we sell,' he explained. 'We offer a wide range of products, sandwiches, salads and hot dishes. If customers want something that's not on the menu (Figure 1), we'll prepare that too! Some people love this and are happy to wait for what they want. However, I think others customers who have less time would be happy with less choice, if it meant they could get their lunch more quickly.'

PRODUCTS

The deli currently stocks over 400 different items sourced from 30 local suppliers, and Doron constantly travels around the country in search of new and interesting

Figure 1
Deli menu

Breakfast

Minkies Breakfast – organic free-range eggs (scrambled, fried, or omelette), bacon or smoked salmon, toast, freshly squeezed orange juice, coffee, tea or hot chocolate

Kensal Rise Breakfast – muesli or porridge, fresh fruit salad, yoghurt and fresh orange juice

Create your own breakfast – eggs, bacon, smoked salmon, toast, jam, marmalade, honey, marmite, peanut butter, bagel, cream cheese, fresh fruit salad, cereal, porridge, freshly squeezed juice, croissant, almond croissant, pain au chocolate or fruit danish

Sandwiches

Sabich – grilled aubergine, hummus, pickled cucumber, hard-boiled egg & parsley
Clare Bear – grilled aubergine, goats cheese, tahini & baby leaf
Sunday Deluxe – salt beef, pickled cucumber, horse radish & mayonnaise
The Minx – salami, tahini, hummus, grilled vegetables & baby leaf
TLC – organic smoked back bacon, baby leaf & tomato
Italian Job – Parma ham or salami, cheese, tomato & baby leaf
Mozzarella – mozzarella, pesto, tomato & baby leaf
Halloumi – grilled halloumi cheese, pesto, rocket & tomato
Classic – smoked salmon & cream cheese
Too Nice – tuna, avocado & hard boil egg
Avo – brie, avocado, baby leaf & tomato
Omelette – omelette, cream cheese, tomato & green onion
Gorgeous Nicola – bacon, melted mozzarella, mayonnaise, baby leaf, tomato & mustard

Hot dishes

Roasted Chicken – marinated with thyme, olive oil & garlic
Organic Meat Balls – in red sauce
Organic Grilled Chicken
Organic salmon – on a bed of sweet potato, carrot and red sauce
Meat Lasagna
Vegetable Lasagna

Salads	Sweet treats
Feta Goats Cheese	Banana loaf
Baby Leaf	Almond & orange cake
Cooked Carrot	Chocolate cake
Cooked Spinach	Clementine mini-loaf
Moroccan	Triple choc brownies
Green Tahini	Cup cakes
Chopped Mixed	Blueberry muffin
Baba Ganoush	Banana muffin
Homemade Houmous	Banana & raisin mini-loaf
Grilled Vegetables	Butter biscuits
Side orders	Cannoli flapjack
White rice	Pecan pie
Brown rice	Petit fours
Mashed potato	
Hand-cut chips	
Couscous	
Quinoa	

Drinks

Coffee – latte, cappuccino, americano, espresso or macchiato
Tea – English breakfast, Earl grey, chamomile, mint, green or fennel or hot chocolate
Fresh juice – orange, apple, beetroot, ginger or a combination of your choice

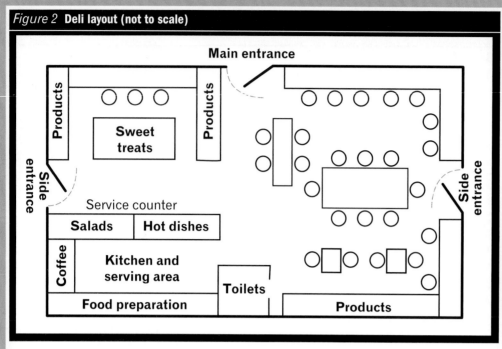

Figure 2 Deli layout (not to scale)

Main entrance

Products

Sweet treats

Products

Side entrance

Service counter

Salads | Hot dishes

Coffee

Kitchen and serving area

Toilets

Food preparation

Products

Side entrance

Notes:
1. The areas marked 'Products' contain pre-packed items that customers can select and then buy at the service counter.
2. The three sides of the building with entrances are predominantly glazed.
3. Customers can select cakes, muffins, and so on from the sweet treats area and pay from them at the service counter.
4. Customers queue in the outlet from the 'service counter' towards the 'main entrance'.

products. 'The products that we sell in the deli are also the ones we use in our sandwiches, salads and hot dishes,' he explains. All our stock is on display, and we simply cook up items that are starting to reach their best before date. For instance, we recently bought some Spanish calasparra brown rice. It's wonderful stuff, but no one bought it! I ended up cooking it up and selling it in the deli instead. Only having a small storage area means that we keep track of everything and only buy what we need.'

KEEPING UP WITH DEMAND

'The original idea was to sell great products and serve fresh food to customers eating in the deli,' Doron continues. 'However, customers also want to take it away to eat either at home or at work. Although we're easily able to cope with the steady flow of customers during the day, lunch time is a challenge! Increasingly, people take food away, and we get at least two large orders each day from local businesses. As well as myself, there is one other person serving customers during the day and two at lunch time. These two work

well together preparing drinks and serving customers. However, I'm struggling to keep up with demand in the kitchen as everything is made to order. Although the large take-away orders are great for business, they don't come in until the last minute and mean that other customers have to wait while I prepare them. I don't really know what to do as we're unable to expand the physical area (Figure 2) and I can't afford to employ any more staff.'

www.minkiesdeli.co.uk

Questions

1. What are order-winners and qualifiers in Minkies' markets?

2. What is the level of demand in these markets? Assess its impact on capacity.

3. How could Minkies manage demand and capacity in its growing business?

Lecturers: visit www.palgrave.com/business/ hillessential for additional resources

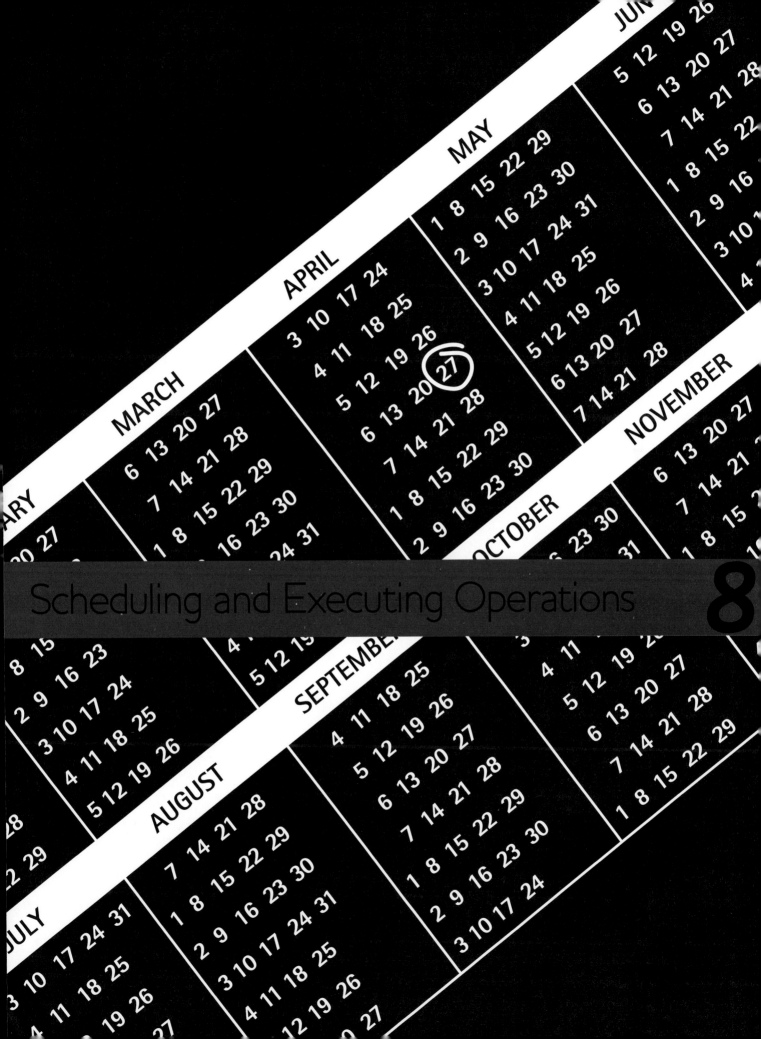

Scheduling and Executing Operations

8

Learning objectives

After completing this chapter, you should be able to:

- Appreciate the key role of operations scheduling within a business

- Recognize the different types of operations scheduling system and for which businesses each is appropriate

- Formulate a simple bar chart and network analysis

- Explain the elements of a material requirements planning system

- Appreciate how manufacturing resource planning and enterprise resource planning have developed and how they supplement a material requirements planning system

- Explain how enterprise resource planning works

- Understand the just-in-time approach both in terms of its role as a scheduling system and as a philosophy of operations management

- Understand how optimized production technology works

Chapter outline

Introduction

What is operations scheduling?

- The role of scheduling in managing operations

Operations scheduling systems

- Project management

- Informal scheduling systems

- Scheduling systems for complex services or products

- Scheduling systems for repeat services or products

Critical reflections

Summary

Introduction

The challenge confronting organizations is how best to meet customers' requirements as well as performance targets such as output, efficiency and costs. The former underpin sales revenue, while the latter underpin profits in a commercial business, or ensure that budgets are well spent in non-profit organizations and the public sector. Scheduling is a vital element of managing operations, as it ensures that both customer requirements and performance targets are met.

This chapter will first define scheduling and discuss its role in the operations process. It will then go on to look at project management and outline the various operations scheduling systems, the processes for introducing them and their relative benefits. To begin with, informal systems (such as bar charts) are described. After that, systems for more complex operations and repeat services and products are explained, including network analysis, material requirements planning (MRPI), manufacturing resources planning (MRPII), enterprise resource planning (ERP), just-in-time (JIT) and optimized production technology (OPT).

What is operations scheduling?

Before examining why scheduling is essential to operations, let's define the term itself and consider the types of tasks involved in it. A schedule is a timetable of jobs with start dates arranged to meet customers' delivery requirements while taking into account the availability of materials and short-term capacity (staff, systems and equipment). The schedule determines the sequence of jobs and then manages and controls these jobs through the service delivery system or manufacturing process. In some businesses, such as rapid-response service operations where customers arrive in an unplanned way, the scheduling of orders is linked to the arrival of customers. Here, the key scheduling tasks concern managing short-term capacity and any materials and services purchased ('bought-out') from suppliers. Detailed scheduling is built around the front-office phase of a service delivery system, where servers and customers interface in a stimulus–response manner. Even so, the task of matching short-term capacity to uncertain patterns of demand is difficult, and companies alleviate this by reshaping demand and varying their capacity, as discussed in Chapter 7.

The role of scheduling in managing operations

Providing the services and products sold to customers is the very essence of the operations task. Scheduling the staff, materials and other resources to meet these requirements lies at the heart of this provision and is essential to the well-being of an organization, as repeat customers are the key to sales revenue growth. This is because:

- Dissatisfied customers don't come back (and they tell others they're unhappy with the service!)
- Satisfied customers return and repeat buy.

Needing to meet both customer requirements and performance targets can make scheduling operations a complex task, because customer requirements and performance targets place differing demands on operations. Whereas markets are inherently unstable, operations needs to maintain a stable delivery system, as changing or disrupting plans and schedules invariably incurs costs, reduces efficiency and results in delays.

Given the nature of markets, organizations need to find ways to handle the unstable nature of demand. As Figure 8.1 illustrates, businesses cushion the delivery systems from the unstable markets into which they sell in a number of ways:

- *Basic mechanisms* As explained in Chapter 7, organizations choose either order backlog (or queues), inventory or a combination of the two as the basic mechanism in this cushioning task.
- *Secondary mechanisms* Again as explained in the previous chapter, organizations can use several additional methods including planned capacity, forecasting and demand management in addition to the basic mechanisms described in the previous point. Furthermore, organizations also use process improvement (the subject of Chapter 12) and scheduling (the subject of this chapter) to help in the cushioning task.
- *Supplementary mechanism* Finally, companies may often use reactive capacity (in the form of overtime working) to supplement demand/capacity imbalances that have slipped through the net.

> **KEY IDEA**
Operations scheduling helps to cushion the delivery system from the instability of the market

As shown in Figure 7.9 in the last chapter, the scheduling and execution phases of operations planning and control systems convert the plans into detailed schedules and then manage these to meet customer requirements. The principal activities of these phases are to create the schedules and instructions to undertake the necessary tasks and ensure that all is available as and when needed.

Not all companies require the same operations scheduling system. The factors that influence the choice they make and the design of the system to be used include:

- *Service/product complexity* The complexity of the service or product directly affects the choice and design of the scheduling system. Service businesses offering a limited and narrow range often deliver a service as a single transaction. Neither the customer nor any information thus needs to be processed at a second stage, and this clearly simplifies the overall scheduling task. At the other extreme, scheduling a range of multi-step services or products completed in different parts of the total delivery system will result in the need for more complex scheduling systems.
- *Special versus standard services and products* In the case of standard services and products, the task is known (as it has been done before), and this provides the opportunity to develop a scheduling system (and, in addition, the repeat volumes involved justify such an investment). Where services and products are specials and hence are not repeated, the steps are less defined and the scheduling system used is less detailed, relying on the skilled staff to undertake the day-to-day scheduling tasks.

Operations scheduling systems

The rest of this chapter describes the scheduling systems used to help manage operations. As we have just explained, services and products differ in factors such as complexity (the number of steps involved to provide a service or make a product), the one-off or repetitive nature of the demand and the range of services or products offered. The simpler the task, the simpler the scheduling system. In businesses with a very simple level of system-based scheduling, capacity and materials will be scheduled against expected levels of demand, but hour-by-hour control will be exercised on an as-needed basis.

Take, for example, a café on a main street that has a limited number of seats inside but space for more on the pavement, while also offering a take-away service. The fresh food requirements will reflect the day of the week and time of the year. Staffing will be scheduled in line with each hour of the day, as will decisions regarding the preparation of some food (for example, salads and sandwich fillings) ahead of time to meet demand in peak periods. Staff training to handle the various tasks (for example, fresh coffee and hot food preparation) will facilitate staff flexibility during busy times. Then, within these dimensions, decisions on who does what will be handled by a combination of allocating the principal tasks to staff that is supplemented by an ad hoc reallocation of work depending upon the level of demand during the day. Attempting to schedule in a more detailed way would be inappropriate.

In other businesses, the level of operations scheduling will be more detailed as the system is more manageable in that customer orders do not have the short duration demand profile described in the example of the café above.

Before we look in more detail at the types of scheduling systems that are used, let's first overview the scheduling task when managing project processes.

Project management

When companies or organizations are engaged in providing services/products or undertaking large, often one-off tasks (such as building bridges or highways), the approach to managing the task falls under the term 'project management'. To schedule such tasks (and as described later in this chapter), companies would typically choose to use scheduling systems such as bar charts and/or networks to help manage the activities involved.

As explained in the next section, informal systems such as bar charts are appropriate where the work involved in delivering a contract is undertaken by individual members of a team who are each responsible for devising and meeting their part of the overall task. Bar charts provide an overview of the timescales involved to ensure that target dates can be met while providing a way to check progress so as to meet deadlines or arrange additional capacity where required, thus avoiding overruns. As we will learn in the next section, there is no need for detailed programming in such situations as the individual team members devise their own plan of work and take on the responsibility for executing the tasks on time or highlighting ahead of time any difficulties in meeting the proposed schedule. Then, as a member of the overall team, they become party to the resolution of any problems.

In contracts that involve many individual but related activities, outside contractors, material supplies, supply chain management and the like, network analysis in one of its forms better meets these more complex requirements.

Informal scheduling systems

> **KEY IDEA**
> Where the demand for services or products is not repeated and the delivery system contains only a relatively few activities, a bar chart or even an informal scheduling system is used

Simpler and more informal scheduling systems are sometimes adequate to meet the control requirements of the operations task. These simpler systems are now outlined and are then followed by an explanation of the more complex ones.

Bar charts

One of the simplest methods of operations scheduling is a bar chart. In essence, this method shows the elements of capacity (for example, staff or process) on the vertical axis with time represented as a bar on the horizontal axis (see Figure 8.2).

Figure 8.1 Cushioning the delivery system – categories and options[1]

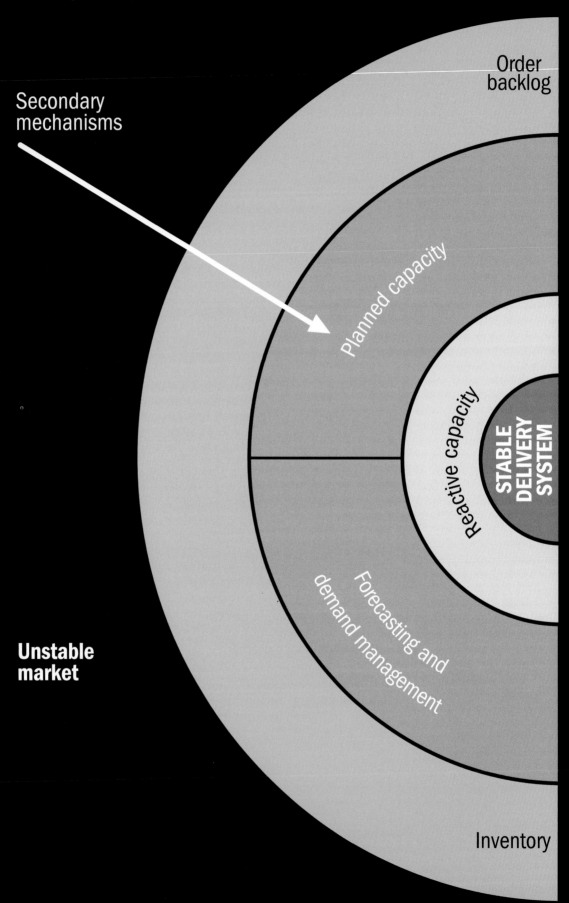

Secondary
mechanisms

Order
backlog

Planned capacity

Reactive capacity

STABLE
DELIVERY
SYSTEM

Forecasting and
demand management

Unstable
market

Inventory

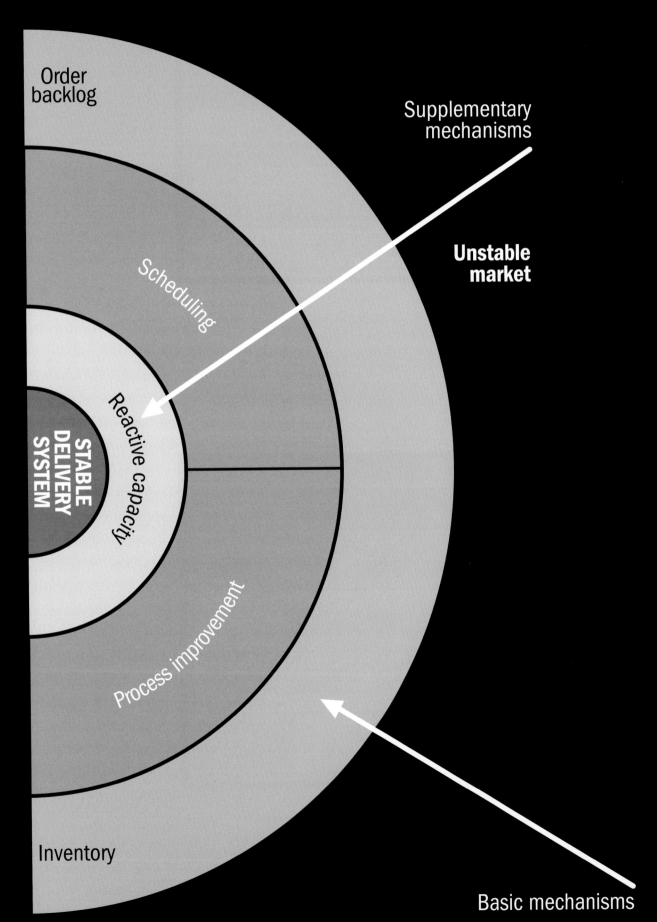

Order
backlog

Supplementary
mechanisms

**Unstable
market**

Scheduling

Reactive capacity

STABLE
DELIVERY
SYSTEM

Process improvement

Inventory

Basic mechanisms

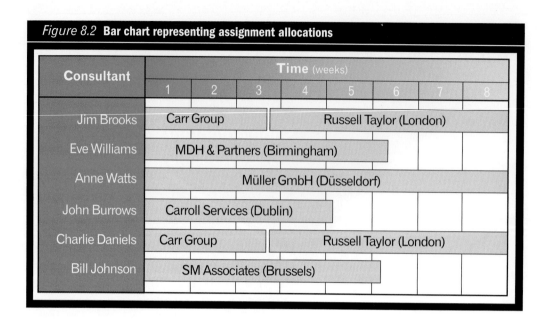

Figure 8.2 Bar chart representing assignment allocations

Consultant	Time (weeks)							
	1	2	3	4	5	6	7	8
Jim Brooks	Carr Group			Russell Taylor (London)				
Eve Williams	MDH & Partners (Birmingham)							
Anne Watts	Müller GmbH (Düsseldorf)							
John Burrows	Carroll Services (Dublin)							
Charlie Daniels	Carr Group			Russell Taylor (London)				
Bill Johnson	SM Associates (Brussels)							

Selecting the appropriate dimension of time (for example, hours, days or weeks) will reflect the nature of the operations system to be scheduled. Figure 8.2 uses weeks as this best suited this company's scheduling needs. In professional companies, there is often an additional aid in the form of a calendar that runs horizontally below the chart to show the schedule against actual dates, in this instance scheduling consultant availability against the start times for new assignments. Finally, a description of the task (the name of the client in Figure 8.2) is added to the chart.

Figure 8.3 Bar chart for scheduling initial tasks

Task	May									
	12	13	14	15	16	19	20	21	22	23
Analyse markets and initial review	Day 1	Max								
	Day 1	Kate							Kate	
Initial analysis of service delivery systems	Day 1	Tom								
Check extent of bought-out materials and identify supplier analysis						Rob				
Supplier analysis								Rob		
								Tom		

Bar charts are also used to schedule and control more complex operations systems, particularly where choices can be made. Figure 8.3 represents an overview of consultant allocations to clients. Within an assignment, the various elements are covered by the team of consultants allocated to that job. The lead consultant typically controls the allocation of tasks to the team to reflect their skills and experience, individual loadings and completion times. Figure 8.3 shows a bar chart to represent this. You will see that it covers the tasks at the start of the assignment. Other tasks will be identified as the assignment continues, and these will then be introduced into the schedule of work, and allocated a team member(s) and a start and finish date. Typically, a weekly review will check the team's progress against the schedule. The bar chart is then updated in terms of the work completed, with any revisions to the schedule being incorporated at the review meeting.

Some services and products comprise several steps, each completed by a different part of the process or delivery system. Again, bar charts can be used to schedule these jobs through the system to meet the required delivery dates.

In this way, a bar chart identifies potential capacity problems, provides short-term control over the progress of the work and allows a business to assess whether or not operations is able to take on additional orders in the light of its existing capacity levels and delivery commitments. Bar charts can be used to manage scheduling tasks of differing complexity in terms of variety and detail, but IT-based systems are typically used to manage more complicated schedules. In many businesses, however, the demands on and requirements of the operations control system lead to other systems being used to meet these more difficult control tasks. The sections that follow describe these.

Scheduling systems for complex services or products

As has already been explained, where the demand for services or products is not repeated and the delivery system contains only a relatively few activities, an informal scheduling approach can be used. More complex, non-repeat services or products involving many interrelated activities, however, require a different scheduling approach. One of these is termed **network analysis**, and the principles underlying are now explained.

> **Network analysis –** a means of scheduling complex operations that involves planning (establishing all the activities or steps to be completed), scheduling (applying limiting factors such as time and cost) and controlling (updating the plan using feedback obtained during the process)

Network analysis
The first task here is to determine the level of detail on which the network will be based. For large projects, an overall network will often be developed to provide a control system to overview the whole task, with more detailed subnetworks to schedule different parts of the task.

In a network, the service or product is broken down into a series of 'activities', all of which have to be completed for the task to be finished. When drawing the network, these activities are shown in the order in which they have to occur. It is, therefore, necessary to establish, for each activity, any other activity or activities that have to be completed before it can begin. This is called 'dependency'. One or more activities will, however, be independent of any other activity being completed before they can start, and these are obviously the ones to be completed at the beginning of the process. When these independent activities have been completed (which in network language is called an 'event'), any activity that can start only when these have been completed can now commence, and so on. In this way, a network is developed. Those activities which follow others are said to be 'sequential', while those that can be completed at the same time as others (that is, they are independent of one another) are said to be 'parallel'. The language and symbols used in constructing networks are explained in Figure 8.4.

When constructing a network, the following steps are used:

1 *Planning* Establish all the activities or steps to be completed, determine the dependency between these activities and draw the network.
2 *Scheduling* Apply to the network any limiting factors such as time, cost and the availability of materials, bought-out services, equipment and staff. These factors will often lead to redrawing some parts of the network to accommodate the constraints they impose.
3 *Controlling* Obtain feedback during a project to ensure that the activities are being completed on time, and to update the plan in the light of any changes.

Figure 8.4 The principal building blocks used to construct networks

Type	Description	Symbol
Activity	Activities are tasks that have a time duration At the start and finish of each activity, there will be, in network language, an event	—————▶
Event	Events occur instantaneously and state that the preceding activity (or activities) is (are) now complete, and that other activities that depend on its (their) completion can now start As this is instantaneous, it has no time duration	◯
Dummy activity	Dummy activities are used in two ways • As an aid to drawing the network • As a way of extending the dependency of one or more activities to other activities	– – – ▶

Planning

The first step is to list the activities necessary to complete a project and determine their dependency on each other. Then draw the network using the following guidelines:

- All activities start and end with an event.
- An activity is a time-consuming task.
- An event is instantaneous; its occurrence means that all activities entering that event have now been completed and, therefore, all activities leaving that event can now be started.
- Any number of activities can go into and out of an event.
- Activities, wherever possible, should go from left to right when drawing up the network.
- Activities occurring on the same path are sequential and, therefore, directly dependent on each other.
- Activities on different paths are parallel activities; they are independent of other sets of parallel activities and can, therefore, take place at the same time.
- Dummy activities are not time-consuming (as the time involved has already been registered with the original activity), hence their name. They are used in two ways:
  - As an aid to drawing a network – as such, they form part of the set of conventions to be followed. One of these conventions is that two or more activities cannot leave one event sign and enter the next event sign. In order to accommodate such situations, dummy activities are used (Figures 8.5 and 8.7).
  - To extend the dependency of one or more activities to other activities (Figures 8.5, 8.6 and 8.7).

To explain using a practical example, Figure 8.6 lists the activities to be undertaken to complete a task and indicates those activities on which an activity is dependent. Therefore, Activity B cannot start until Activity A has been completed, and so on. The resulting network is shown as Figure 8.7. It starts with Activity A as this is the only activity that does not depend upon any other activity before it can start. The rest of the activities are then built into the network to represent the statement of the task.

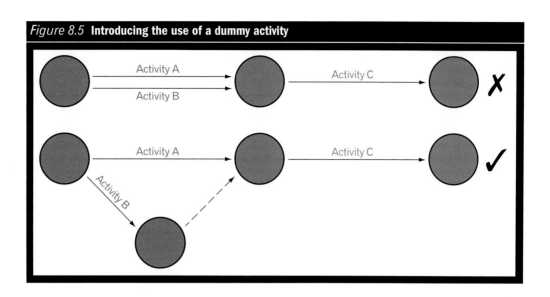

Figure 8.5 Introducing the use of a dummy activity

Figure 8.6 Activities undertaken to complete a task

Activity	Activities on which it is dependent
A	--
B	A
C	B
D	B
E	A
F	C and D
G	E
H	F and G

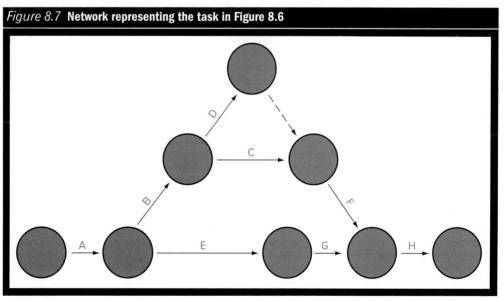

Figure 8.7 Network representing the task in Figure 8.6

Notes: Activities A, E, G and H are examples of sequential activities.
Activities B, C, D and F are parallel to activities E and G.

Scheduling

The next step is to schedule the network. This involves applying to it limiting factors such as time and cost. In the example given in Figures 8.8 and 8.9, the activities for putting up a sign are listed. Staffordshire County Council asked Claymore Construction to tender to erect 1,275 signs throughout the county. To maximize the use of vehicles to travel to these different locations, the company decided to use a team of three, and developed the network diagram shown in Figure 8.9 to establish the shortest time for doing the job.

Figure 8.8 Activities to erect a road sign

Activity	# People	Duration (minutes)
Dig hole	1	35
Hold sign and backfill hole	3	15
Add water to concrete and mix	1	10
Assemble sign onto post	1	30
Unload sign, equipment and materials	3	15
Mix concrete	1	25
Position sign into hole	1	10
Clear site and reload vehicle	3	10

Figure 8.9 Network diagram for activities listed in Figure 8.8

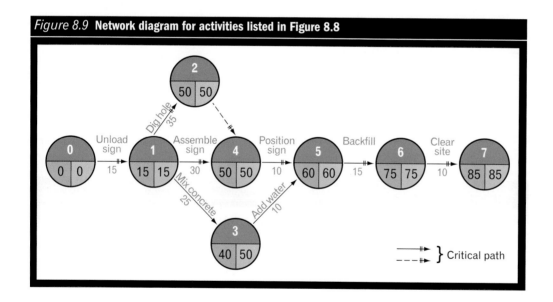

There are three additional points to note from Figure 8.9:

- Activity descriptions, often abbreviated, are written above the arrows. It is important where possible to avoid using, for example, numbers that then need to be checked to understand what activity is taking place because it makes reading the network laboured and may lead to errors.
- The time duration for an activity is written below the relevant arrow.
- The event signs (often known as 'nodes') have been used to provide additional information. This is explained in Figure 8.10.

The earliest start time for a particular event is calculated from the beginning of a network by adding together the times taken for all the sequential activities before it. It expresses the earliest time by which any activity leaving a particular event can start. Where two or more activities enter an event, the activity to finish last will establish the earliest start time

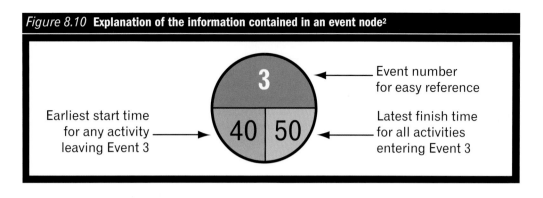

Figure 8.10 **Explanation of the information contained in an event node[2]**

Event number for easy reference

Earliest start time for any activity leaving Event 3

Latest finish time for all activities entering Event 3

for any subsequent activities. Thus, in Figure 8.9, two activities enter Event 5. Activity 'Add water' between Events 3 and 5 will result in an earliest start time for activities leaving Event 5 of 40 + 10 = 50 minutes. However, activity 'Position sign' between Events 4 and 5 results in an earliest start time of 50 + 10 = 60 minutes. Consequently, activity 'Backfill' can only start after 60 minutes, so '60' is recorded as the 'earliest start time' for activities leaving Event 5.

The planned finish time for a project is recorded in the final event sign for a project. In Figure 8.9, this is 85 minutes, and this recorded in Event 7.

The latest finish time is calculated from the end of a network. The same cumulative time as that entered in the earliest start time segment of the final event node is also entered in the latest finish time segment of that node – for example, 85 in Figure 8.9. Then the duration of activities is successively subtracted from this finish date and entered into the appropriate event sign. Where two or more activities back into one event, the earliest of the cumulative times will determine the latest finish time for all previous activities.

For example, look at Event 1 in Figure 8.9. Activities from Events 2, 3 and 4 back into this event. While the calculation for Event 3 would be 50 – 25 = 25, and that for Event 4 would be 50 – 30 = 20, that for Event 2 would be 50 – 35 = 15. Thus, the 'latest finish time' for Event 1 is recorded as 15. The reason is that unless the 'latest finish time' requirement of 15 minutes is met at this point in the network, more time than originally planned will need to be added into the sequence of activities, and this, in turn, will result in the overall time for the job being increased.

> **Critical path** – the longest sequence of activities through a network, so any delay in these activities is deemed 'critical'

The minimum length of time to complete a project is an essential aspect of scheduling. This is determined by finding the longest path through a network, which represents the **critical path**. Each task on this path is known as a 'critical activity' because delays to any of these activities will increase the overall length of the project. The critical nature of these tasks is shown by the fact that the earliest start and latest finish times recorded in the series of events on the critical path are the same. There is no flexibility for these activities; if the start of any of them is delayed, the whole project will be delayed. The critical path is then marked in one of several ways (see Figure 8.9, for example).

> **Slack (also known as total float)** – the extent of the delay before the overall time taken to complete a project is affected

However, a delay in activities that do not fall on the critical path will not immediately affect the project's completion time. The extent of the delay before the overall time is affected is the difference between the earliest start time and the latest finish time minus the activity duration. This is known as **slack** (or total float) and is usually entered on the network diagram as part of the information necessary for the control phase of a project.

Controlling

A network is a control mechanism. Information on the tasks completed and delays anticipated or incurred needs to be fed back so that the network can be updated. Knowledge of these changes and the impact they have on a project as a whole are essential for three important reasons:

- This is a prerequisite for effective control.
- Throughout the life of a project, decisions need to be made on the best course of action to take in the light of changing circumstances, and networks readily help managers to appreciate the impact of delays. In turn, this allows them to consider in advance the action to take as they have knowledge of the impact on aspects such as cost and completion dates and so will not have to take decisions in a crisis situation with insufficient time to evaluate alternative courses of action.
- Out-of-date networks soon fall into disrepute and managers stop using them.

Scheduling systems for repeat services and products

Where a business provides repeat services or products, it needs a scheduling system that can handle the control requirements involved. The purpose of this short section is to introduce these systems before explaining them more fully later.

As we mentioned earlier in the chapter, operations scheduling systems start with a statement of demand. Where several products are standard (that is, they repeat), a key dimension to take into account is the principle of independent and dependent demand:

> **KEY IDEA**
> Requirements for services or products with an independent pattern of demand have to be forecast or based on known orders

Independent demand – describes services and products for which the pattern of demand has to be forecast or based on known orders

- Requirements for services or products with an **independent pattern of demand** have to be forecast or based on known orders. Examples include finished goods and services, such as automobiles, or pre-prepared sandwiches sold in a coffee bar.
- **Dependent demand** describes services and products for which the pattern of demand is directly linked to the use of other items, for example tyres that go onto automobiles, and the bread and fillings that make up sandwiches. Such items do not have to be forecast as they can be calculated.

Dependent demand – describes services and products for which the pattern of demand is directly linked to the use of other items

> **KEY IDEA**
> Requirements for items with a dependent demand pattern can be calculated

In a fast-food restaurant, the daily demand for each type of main item, fries and other items on the menu is classed as being independent. The demand for burgers, buns, other ingredients and packaging is classed as dependent. Similarly, the oil and packaging for fries would have a dependent pattern of demand and, as with all such items, would not need to be forecast as they could be calculated.

With these principles now in place, let us turn our attention to the various scheduling systems to help manage these requirements.

Material requirements planning

The role of a scheduling system is to translate demand into statements of requirements for capacity (staff and/or process), materials and bought-out services in terms of how much is needed and when. The starting point is to establish the statement of demand for all the services and products that have an independent pattern of demand. In make-to-order businesses, the requirements for services and products (that is, customer orders) will have been received beforehand. In make-to-stock businesses, the statement of demand may comprise both known orders and forecast requirements, or solely the latter.

Material requirements planning (MRPI) is a system that determines the services and products with an independent pattern of demand (in terms of which ones and how many) that a company will provide during a future period and then specifies the inputs that are needed to meet that demand. For example, the demand for engines, wheels, body panels and other parts that go into vehicle assemblies is linked to the demand for those vehicles. To determine the number of engines, wheels, body panels and other parts, we have first to determine the number of vehicles to be built in different time periods and then calculate the requirements for all such dependent items.

The advent of low-cost computing has allowed widespread use of MRPI systems in the planning and control of different processes and requirements. The systems that went before were typically characterized by confusion and disorder supported by **expediting** and involving constantly changing priorities. By comparison, MRPI offers a well-ordered system that reduces the need for frequent rescheduling.

With MRPI, the first task, as always, is to determine the future demand for all independent items. For each final service or product, an MRPI system contains a recipe (or **bill of materials** in systems language) of the inputs necessary to make one unit. The system then simply multiplies the number of finished services or products required by the values in the recipe. This results in a statement of the requirements to meet known and/or forecast orders. Any existing inventory of dependent items will then reduce the final requirement to give a net requirement figure.

> **KEY IDEA**
> MRPI determines the future demand for independent items and then calculates the requirements for dependent items

What makes MRPI attractive is that it is straightforward, makes sense and is practical to use. Reality, of course, brings issues of uncertainty (for example, suppliers meeting agreed delivery dates and whether the actual internal capacity matches the plan), but the fundamental logic of MRPI offers many advantages over past approaches. Having set the context in which it was developed, let's now look at MRPI in more detail.

The master schedule

As described above, MRPI starts with a statement of demand for independent items, determined from known and/or forecast orders and modified by any existing inventories of the independent items. This forms what is known as the **master schedule** and normally spans one or more time periods. It is then used as the input into MRPI which, by means of a **parts explosion**, calculates the requirements for all dependent items by generating statements of the materials, services, components and subassemblies necessary to complete the master schedule.

This is known as a 'push' system (as opposed to a 'pull' system, such as JIT, which is described in a later section), in that statements of requirements are made in line with agreed delivery dates, and the necessary materials, components and subassemblies are 'pushed' into the process. In order to keep inventory as low as possible and the associated inventory control task as simple as possible, the dates on which orders are due (referred to as 'due dates') are checked to ensure that materials are available. Materials are then 'pushed' through the process to meet these due dates. As explained earlier, MRPI is based on the independent and dependent demand principles, and, as such, only one forecast is necessary. Requirements for all dependent items are, as highlighted earlier, then calculated based on the known and/or forecast demand for the independent services and products in which they are used.

'**Actions** speak louder than words'

For organizations with a range of services and products, MRPI is practical only with some form of data-processing. Without this, it would normally be too difficult to recalculate requirements with each change in schedule.

The development of a master schedule needs to be completed no matter what type of control system is chosen to manage the operations scheduling task. Without a master schedule, operations cannot function. But how a business then schedules and executes the operations control task will depend upon which system it chooses, a decision that should reflect its own business needs and characteristics.

A master schedule (or operations statement) is completed for each service or product, and is a management commitment to provide or produce certain quantities of services or products in particular time periods. To do this, the system takes the statements of demand (both forecast sales and known orders) and tests them against statements of capacity and resources (medium-term capacity plans and short-term elements of capacity) for the same period(s). As such, this is a statement of operations output and not of market demand. However, by taking into account capacity limitations as well as the desire to utilize capacity fully, the master schedule will optimize the position by resetting levels of production to match capacity, and this forms an important communication link between sales and operations. The schedule states requirements in terms of service or product specifications (for example, part numbers or service/product descriptions) for which bills of materials (the 'recipes') exist. The detailed schedule that is produced then drives the MRPI system that, in turn, drives the operations and purchasing records and procedures.

The master schedule (or operations statement) thereby leads to an agreement between marketing and operations on what to provide or produce, and the financial implications that result from these decisions. Accurate information is essential if this task is to be performed well. Information requirements include inventory records, the quantity and timing of current operations schedules, outstanding purchase orders, up-to-date bills of materials ('recipes') and clear information about existing customer requirements, current orders and sales forecasts. It is likely that the schedule will contain a major proportion of firm customer orders in the more immediate time periods and will be based mostly on forecasts in the later periods of the planning horizon, as shown in Figure 8.11.

The length of the planning horizon is determined by calculating the operations lead-time for an item (materials lead-time plus process lead-time) and adding a period of time to allow the purchasing function a window of visibility over what might happen in the future so that price and delivery advantages can be secured (Figure 8.12).

Service/product structure records

Service/product structure records provide information on materials and components (the bill of materials) and how each service or product is made. The bill of materials is a file or set of files that contains the 'recipe' or 'formula' for each finished service or product (Figures 8.13 and 8.14).

Depending upon the complexity of the structure for the particular service or product, there will be a number of levels within a bill of materials. The end-item itself is termed level 0. The components (subassemblies, parts and materials) that together make the end-item will be listed in the parts explosion and designated level 1. Any level 1 components that themselves have a components list will, in turn, be exploded as level 2 and so on (Figure 8.14). This calculation will be completed for all components across all services and products.

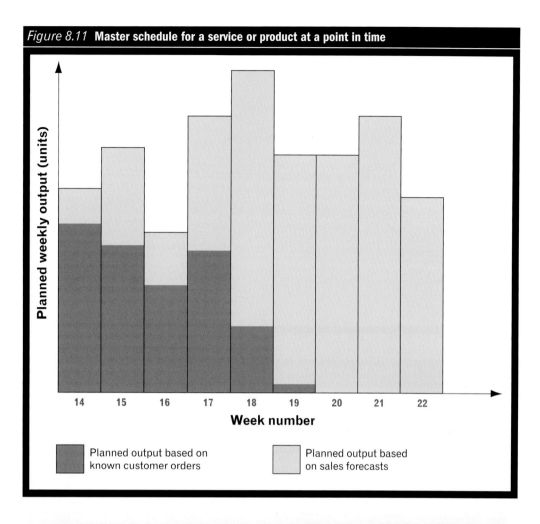

Figure 8.11 **Master schedule for a service or product at a point in time**

Planned weekly output (units)

Week number

14 15 16 17 18 19 20 21 22

▨ Planned output based on
known customer orders

▢ Planned output based
on sales forecasts

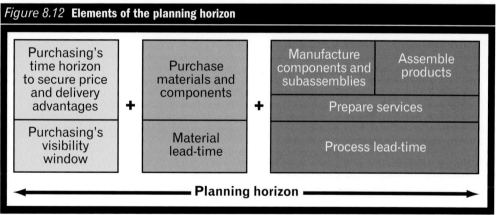

Figure 8.12 **Elements of the planning horizon**

Purchasing's time horizon to secure price and delivery advantages	+	Purchase materials and components	+	Manufacture components and subassemblies	Assemble products
Purchasing's visibility window		Material lead-time		Prepare services	
				Process lead-time	

◄────────── **Planning horizon** ──────────►

Inventory status records

The inventory status file records all transactions (receipts and issues) and inventory balances. Adjustments to recorded balances will also be made as a result of inspection reports identifying rejects and physical inventory checks revealing balances different from those recorded on file.

The main requirements of inventory information are accuracy and timeliness. These are critical to the running of an MRPI system and form the basis of the operations and purchasing plans.

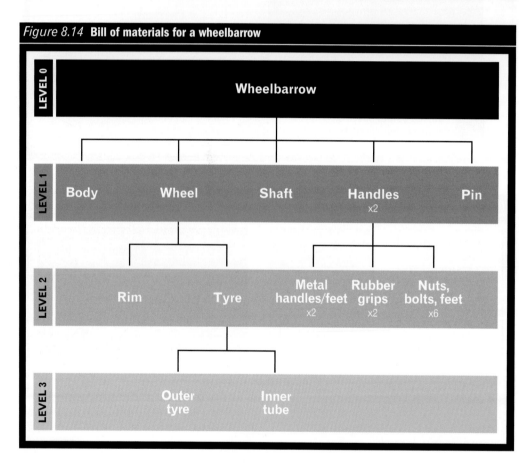

Figure 8.13 Hand sketch of a wheelbarrow as detailed in Figure 8.14

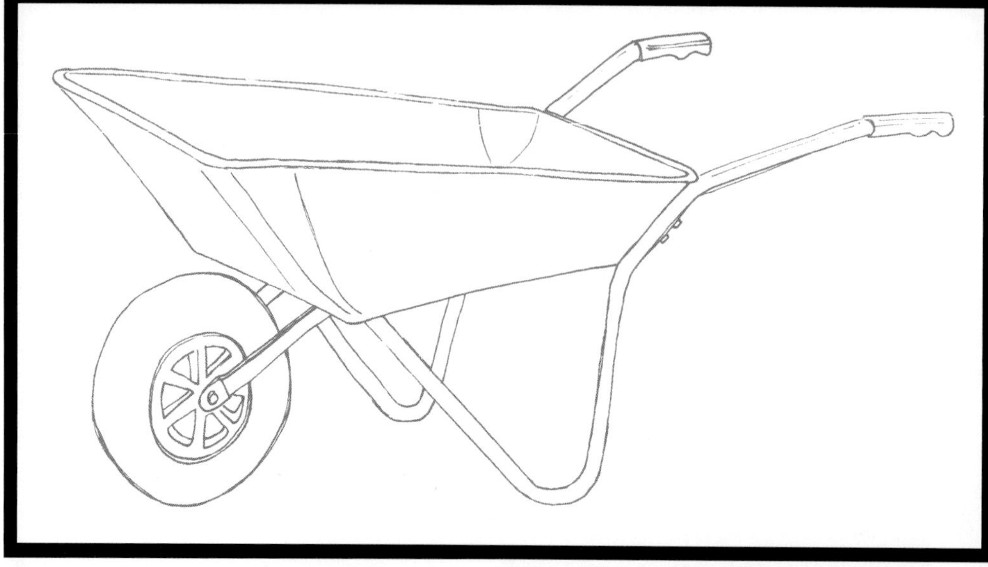

Figure 8.14 Bill of materials for a wheelbarrow

LEVEL 0

Wheelbarrow

LEVEL 1

Body   **Wheel**   **Shaft**   **Handles**   **Pin**
x2

LEVEL 2

Rim   **Tyre**   **Metal handles/feet** x2   **Rubber grips** x2   **Nuts, bolts, feet** x6

LEVEL 3

Outer tyre   **Inner tube**

Manufacturing resource planning

> KEY IDEA

When the scheduling activities in MRPI are tied in with the activities of other relevant functions, the result is MRPII.

When the scheduling activities of material requirements planning are tied in with purchasing, sales, engineering, accounting and other relevant functions of the business, the result is known as **manufacturing resource planning**. As both systems have the same initials, they are abbreviated to MRPI and MRPII, respectively.

Increasingly powerful desktop computing and the advent of local area networks that link personal computers, servers and the like provided both markedly higher levels of processing power and the opportunity to increase communications within a business. With these available, MRPII was in a position to be developed.

The organizational needs that stimulated MRPII developments include the following:

- *The need for integration* In today's dynamic business environment, integrating different parts of a business brings major gains as it ensures that all aspects of a business are taken into account when reaching an effective corporate decision. One principal facet of MRPII is an integrated system with one database used by the whole business according to individual functional requirements. This allows the aspects of a business managed by individual functions (for example, inventory and capacity in operations, and cash flow controlled by accounting and finance) to form part of the corporate decision-making process. A single database reduces inconsistencies, facilitates updating and allows multifunctional perspectives to be taken into account when making decisions.
- *Time-based competition* Key order-winners in many markets increasingly include delivery speed and the need for shorter operations lead-times. More sophisticated IT systems provide managers with timely and essential data to help support customers' changing demands and to respond more quickly to decisions and enquiries in a more informed manner.
- *National and international communications* Many companies currently support their markets using a national and international provision. Information embracing the whole supply chain enables operations executives to better coordinate worldwide operations and purchasing activities. Satellite-based communications displaying real-time information from around the world enable operations to respond to changes and react quickly even with widely dispersed systems and operations locations.

Powerful computer-based systems with large storage capacities enable expanded MRPII systems to support companies' wide-ranging needs for real-time data and comprehensive reviews. Information on corporate activities and resources is continuously updated, and this leads to decisions being made on the basis of the business as a whole, with real-time information providing an up-to-date picture.

Enterprise resource planning

With the complexities of modern business, the global nature of today's commercial activities and the increasingly competitive and dynamic nature of current markets, companies continue to seek better ways of integrating the planning and execution of their activities so that the efforts of the whole organization can be coordinated. To help address these issues, **enterprise resource planning** (ERP) systems evolved out of MRPII and are designed to provide the information backbone to cope with these requirements. These systems provide a seamless integration of all the information that was previously dispersed throughout a company, and turn it into a tool that managers can use. This includes information from the supply chain, customers, human resources, finance and accounting and management reporting.

> **KEY IDEA**
ERP evolved out of MRPII and is designed to embrace the whole organization

As shown in Figure 8.15, ERP is designed to embrace the whole organization and shows a common database, allowing integration between the different parts of the company without duplicate information systems running in parallel.

Figure 8.15 **ERP system**

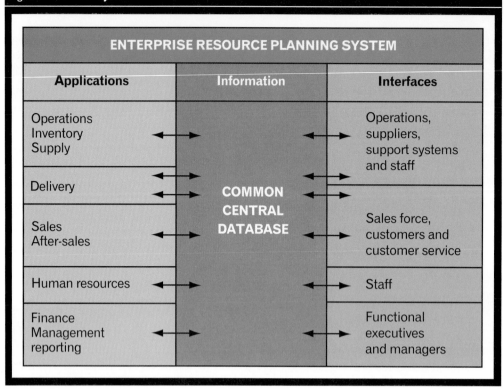

As the software communicates across all functions, everyone can see what is happening in different parts of a business, along with the capability to link customers and suppliers into a complete supply chain.

In the late 1970s, the Germany company SAP (Systeme, Anwendungen und Produkte in Datenverarbeitung, or Systems, Applications and Products in Data Processing) released an early version of ERP software referred to as R/2. However, businesses did not begin investing in ERP systems until the mid-1990s, when SAP released R/3, the next generation of software, which marked a shift in the technology platform from the mainframe to the increasingly popular UNIX-based client–server architecture. Since then, sales by providers such as SAP (with over one-third of world sales), Oracle, Infor Global Solutions, PeopleSoft and JD Edwards have grown significantly.

Software characteristics Each provider has a unique approach to packaging ERP software. To ensure that these packages provide the system with its intended gains, they need to have the following characteristics:

- The software should be multifunctional in scope, thereby meeting the day-to-day needs of system users. In this way, the information on which to base decisions and the outcomes of the decisions made is expressed in terms that reflect each function's requirements. So, for example, the software should be able to track financial results in monetary terms, sales in units and value, operations in time and cost, and so on.
- The software should have a modular structure, enabling the parts to be combined into a single system on the one hand, while allowing it to be easily expanded on the other.
- The software needs to be integrated so that if a transaction or change is made by one part of the business, the data are automatically amended in related functions.
- The software must encompass the essential operations planning and control activities, including forecasting, operations planning, operations scheduling and inventory management, in order to provide a business-wide set of tools to help manage demand and capacity in line with customers' requirements and corporate performance objectives.

There are several benefits for companies implementing ERP, four of which are discussed here:

A common systems platform ERP can trace its origins back to the MRPI systems that provided control over operations processes. MRPI became MRPII with the addition of more supply chain activities, such as distribution and other related activities in a business. These developments then broadened into ERP to take in financial control, human resource management and the international and diverse activities and locations that characterize today's companies.

Companies collect, generate and store vast quantities of data, but in many instances this is undertaken by separate computer systems that cannot talk to one another – each of these so-called 'legacy' systems provides invaluable support for the individual functions, business units, regions, factories or offices for which they were developed. The source of this disconnection is simple – IT developments have been undertaken in businesses over many years. The initial choice would have reflected specific sets of needs and, while the decision was sound in itself, it was taken, understandably, to meet a set of specific requirements. This piecemeal growth of IT accepted the inherent lack of system interfacing, and the need to start again with a common system would have been postponed until some later, often unspecified, time. The growing internationalization of business and the flurry of takeovers and mergers in the past 25 years has heightened the size of this incompatibility problem. ERP, however, meets today's needs and in particular:

- Avoids future duplication of systems, thereby reducing costs and avoiding misunderstandings
- Integrates the business with the external phases of the supply chain including Tier 2 and Tier 3 customers and suppliers
- Improves the speed of responding to customer queries and requirements.

Process improvements Having multiple systems in place made a firm's underlying information platforms highly inefficient, expensive to maintain and update, and unreliable. An integral part of introducing an ERP system has been the opportunity to improve processes such as logistics and scheduling by standardizing and re-engineering the business activities in these areas, both to take out costs and to enable them to respond to market challenges. In this way, an ERP system leads to best practice being agreed, implemented and maintained as it becomes integrated into management routines and used throughout the organization.

Data visibility The highly integrated nature of ERP systems increases data visibility and provides an end-to-end view of the supply chain. As common databases are continuously updated, accurate and consistent information is shared across the business, leading to more informed decision-making. Furthermore, the online, real-time transactions that characterize ERP systems provide current as opposed to historical data, thereby improving a firm's response to customers' needs and making better use of its internal resources.

Web-integrated ERP ERP provides the opportunity for a business to link up with the outside world through e-commerce. Although a company may currently be restricted in terms of such developments due to the practical problems of integrating different systems, the potential for this next move is built into the system and can be developed as and when the opportunity arises. The expansion of Internet-based trading in the future is a given, and ERP systems provide the basis for taking these developments forwards.

So how would an ERP-based system work? Let's say that a Milan-based sales team of a US-based software house is preparing a quotation for a customer. With an ERP system, basic information about the customer's requirements will be entered and a formal contract, in Italian, will be produced, specifying the product and service configuration, the range of applications and locations involved, the lead-times concerning the pre-application review, development phase and installation, post-development support, training and price. After contract discussions, any modifications will be made on the system and quotations updated as required. When the customer accepts the quotation, the order is recorded in the system, credit checks are made, and all functions within the business are brought into the loop. Relevant functions check proposed lead-times, capacity allocations are verified and recorded, schedules are revised, materials are ordered, and the whole operations system is brought up to date and into line. The benefits that user companies enjoy are wide-ranging:

> **Computer aided design** – the use of computer technology in the product or service design process

- Autodesk, a leading US maker of **computer-aided design** (CAD) software, reduced its delivery lead-times from a two-week average to 24 hours for 98 per cent of orders.
- The storage systems function at IBM reduced the time to re-price all its products from 5 days to 5 minutes, the time to deliver a replacement part from 22 to 3 days, and the time to complete a credit check from 20 minutes to 3 seconds.
- Fujitsu Microelectronics reduced its order fill time from 18 to 1.5 days and halved the time to close its financial records to 4 days.
- Owens Corning replaced its grand total of 211 existing systems with an ERP system that has coordinated order management, financial reporting and the company's diverse, worldwide supply chain. It is now able to track its finished goods inventory daily in all parts of its delivery systems and has cut its spare parts inventory by some 50 per cent.

However, as with all applications, success is bound up with fitting the system to a business's needs, including its strategic positioning. Two areas of concern, which reflect the size of ERP undertakings, are noted by companies:

- *Failed or out-of-control applications* The cost of ERP projects in larger organizations can run from $50 million to over $500 million. The issue, however, is not just the investment costs but the fundamental nature of such sizeable developments. FoxMeyer Drug, a US pharmaceutical company, alleges that its ERP system installation helped drive it into bankruptcy. Mobil Europe spent hundreds of millions of dollars on its ERP system only to abandon it when it merged with Esso/Exxon. Dow Chemicals spent seven years and $0.5 billion implementing a mainframe ERP system before deciding to start all over again on a client–server application. In 2010, Waste Management took SAP to court claiming $500 million compensation for a failed ERP implementation. Case 8.1 outlines Dell's experience.

- *ERP systems: standard versus customized offering* Clearly, ERP systems offer substantial benefits. However, with past IT systems, organizations would first decide on what the business needed and then choose a software package that would support those needs. They often rewrote large portions of the software to provide a better fit. With the size (investment and timescale) of ERP systems, the sequence is reversed, and the business often needs to be modified to fit the system.

Just having good data does not mean that a business will improve. To gain the most from ERP systems, companies need to recognize the full business implications. Organizations may have good reasons to change: they may have struggled for years with incompatible information systems and may see ERP as a quick fix. However, before moving forwards, organizations need to address some key questions, including:

- How might an ERP system strengthen our competitive position?
- How will the system affect our organizational structure?
- Do we need to extend the system across all functions, or across all regions, or only to implement certain modules and reflect differences in need by differences in approach?

CASE 8.1 IT SYSTEMS CHANGES AT DELL

Dell spent two years implementing SAP's R/3 to run its manufacturing operations and then found that its ERP system did not fit its new decentralized management structure. SAP was found to be 'too monolithic' to be altered for its changing organizational needs when its business model changed from a worldwide focus to a regional focus.

Some time later, Dell chose an i2 Technologies system to manage raw materials, an Oracle system for order management and a Glovia system for manufacturing. Putting in a piece at a time has worked for Dell.

www.dell.co.uk

Questions

1 What appeared to be principal reasons why the SAP R/3 application failed at Dell?

2 Why is the IT systems approach that Dell later installed working?

Lecturers: visit www.palgrave.com/business/ hillessential for additional resources

Because of the profound implications for a business, any ERP developments must be assessed in terms of meeting the needs of a business and the way an organization works. There is no one right answer. For instance, take Monsanto and Hewlett-Packard. After studying the data requirements of each business unit, Monsanto's managers placed a high priority on achieving the greatest possible degree of commonality across the whole company even though they knew it would be difficult to achieve and that it would not be possible to standardize fully on more than 85 per cent of the data used. At Hewlett-Packard, a company with a strong tradition of business unit autonomy, applications specific to each part of the business were developed. With little sharing of resources, the estimated investment was over $1 billion, but autonomy, a recognized corporate strength, was preserved.

Just-in-time control system

> **KEY IDEA**

Whereas MRPI is plan–push, JIT is a demand–pull system

An alternative approach to the operations control task that originated in the Japanese automobile industry and has since gained much support in other industrial countries and types of business is the JIT system. Whereas MRPI is a plan–push system, JIT is a demand–pull system (Figure 8.16).

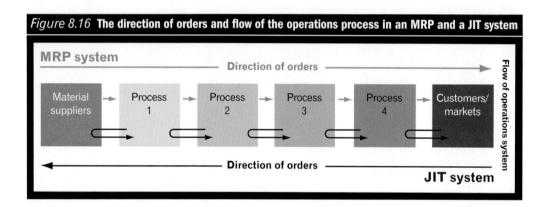

Figure 8.16 **The direction of orders and flow of the operations process in an MRP and a JIT system**

The JIT operations system is relatively simple, requires little use of computers and, in some sectors, can offer far tighter levels of control than computer-based alternatives. The idea is to produce and deliver goods and services just-in-time to be sold, subassemblies just-in-time to be assembled into finished goods, parts just-in-time to go into subassemblies, and purchased materials just-in-time to be transformed into parts.[3] The aim is for all materials to be in active use within the total process. In this way, materials are always a productive element within the operations system, which avoids incurring costs without any corresponding benefits. Thus, the JIT system is based upon the concept of producing small quantities just-in-time, as opposed to many alternative philosophies that are based on making inventory to optimize process capacity utilization or 'just-in-case' it is required.

JIT control systems are based on the principle that each part of the total operation (including suppliers as well as a company's internal processes) delivers to the next stage the exact quantity needed for the following period's requirements. The period involved varies. In some instances, the quantities equate to one or more days' requirements, whereas in others there may be several deliveries a day. The outcome is that each stage in the process receives sufficient from the previous stage just-in-time to enable it to complete a given quantity. The more deliveries during a day, the less inventory is held in the operations process. The number of deliveries is, however, typically not the same between all stages. Factors such as length of the process set-up time for a part, the physical size of the part and, in the case of suppliers, the travelling distance will affect this decision. However, the procedure used to call for an order quantity is similar:

- Parts, components or materials are delivered from one stage in a process to the next in agreed quantities and in a designated container, together with a card or document relating to that part or material.
- When a container of parts, components or materials is taken by the next stage in the process, the card (the most well-known system being *kanban*, which means visible record or sign board in Japanese) or similar signal is sent to the previous stage in the operations system. This signal now authorizes that part of the system to make an agreed order quantity.
- In turn, this stage uses materials, components and subassemblies, and this triggers its own signal(s) to the previous part(s) of the process, and so on. In this way, all parts of operations supply the next stage just-in-time.

For suppliers, the frequency of deliveries is bound up with the distance between the locations and the (monetary) value of the parts involved. Normally, the longer the distance and the lower the (monetary) value of a part, the less frequent the deliveries. To help to increase the number of deliveries and hence reduce inventory, suppliers are encouraged to build smaller facilities close to a plant. For example, Johnson Controls, the Milwaukee-based international manufacturer with automobile sector sales alone of $12 billion in 2009, has 260 car-seat plants mainly in North America and Europe serving all the major car companies including Fiat, Ford, GM, Honda, Mazda, Mitsubishi, Nissan, Peugeot Renault, Toyota and Volkswagen. Although the seat plant is off site, it is typically connected to the car plant by an overhead conveyor system that transports the seats directly onto the assembly line to exactly match the build programme.

Similarly, several suppliers to the Nissan car plant in Washington, UK, are located just a few minutes away. To keep inventory as low as possible, deliveries are made every two hours throughout the day. To ensure that delivery times are met, Nissan has agreed three different routes for suppliers' vehicles. These need to be used in a preferred order, thus providing alternatives in case of difficulty. Case 8.2 provides more detail.

For a JIT system to work, end users need to fix their own output programme that cannot then be altered. Only with this certainty of requirements can a JIT control system be introduced and maintained with the result that inventory is kept to a minimum at all stages of a supply chain.

The main features of JIT systems and some prerequisites for their introduction are now summarised:

- JIT systems reverse the flow of information concerning parts and materials so that each stage calls up requirements from the previous stage as needed.
- Work-in-progress (WIP) inventory is kept to a minimum.
- Bottlenecks need to be eliminated. As WIP is now minimized, there is no longer a cushion of inventory between the stages. Process uncertainty, therefore, has to be kept to a minimum.
- Changeover or set-up times need to be reduced so that smaller order sizes become practical. For example, the set-up time for a hood and fender stamping operation in other automobile plants was estimated by Toyota as follows: USA 6 hours, Sweden and Germany 4 hours, while Toyota's time was 0.2 hours.

The concept of JIT is very appealing, but there are several prerequisites if it is to be achieved. These include:

Nissan's JIT system developments include synchronizing supplier deliveries with its own car assembly programme. One such link is between Nissan and Sommer-Allibert, a French-owned carpet and trim manufacturer that has a satellite plant 3 km away from the car factory. As each car starts its journey through Nissan's manufacturing system, a special coding tag triggers a message to Sommer-Allibert that specifies which of the 120 variations of carpet and trim is needed for that particular vehicle, a factor that reflects colour, right- or left-hand drive, engine size and option selection. At Sommer-Allibert, the correct set of requirements (including carpets, parcel shelves and boot linings) is selected, trimmed and finished before being stacked in sequence and loaded onto a vehicle in reusable carriers. On arrival (which can be as many as 120 times a day), the driver takes the sets straight to the assembly line.

www.nissan-global.com

Questions

1 Why is a car assembly plant particularly well suited to JIT scheduling systems?

2 What developments in this example have been important in making the system work?

3 What advantages and disadvantages are inherent in these arrangements?

- It is most suited to situations with high-volume, low-variety and repetitive operations.
- It must be end-user driven. The business making the final services and products must take responsibility for instigating this development and liaise with its suppliers accordingly.
- Operations schedules must be fixed. The desired state in JIT is for no excess material in the system. Consequently, scheduled quantities cannot be increased (as there is no material) or decreased (as unnecessary inventory would be the by-product).
- Suppliers must be geographically close to customers, thereby enabling regular deliveries to be made. Where the geographical distance is long, frequent deliveries of small quantities are not feasible. Larger amounts at longer intervals will be the alternative and inventory will result.

Key factors for this system to work effectively are stable schedules (which are fixed and cannot be changed inside the agreed material lead-times of a supplier's supplier) and developing close relationships with suppliers. In many companies, however, control systems more typically have to handle the impact of inherent market instability and a lack of close liaison with suppliers. Customers desiring the benefits of JIT sometimes introduce or demand a JIT materials or parts provision, yet are unable to keep suppliers' schedules stable. The outcome is that suppliers hold inventory, with all its attendant costs, as a practical way of meeting the resulting short lead-time demands of their customers.

Physical changes
Several physical changes need to become an inherent part of the JIT process:

- *High-volume, low-variety demand* needs to underpin operations. This justifies the investment and allows the creation of a series of processes that are as near to the coupled nature of a line process as possible. In was not just chance that JIT was first developed in the automobile industry – the conditions there provided many of the prerequisites (especially the high volume) necessary for JIT control systems. Ways to increase volumes include simplifying products in terms of width of range, and using standard parts in as many products as possible.
- *Set-up reduction* will, in turn, allow order quantities to be reduced. There are no set-ups in a line process. If processes need to be reset when a different product is to be made, reducing the time this takes will allow smaller order quantities to be made.[4] This is necessary to enable quantities of components, subassemblies and final assemblies to be made in line with demand rather than in terms of the length of time it takes to reset the process.
- *Layouts* are changed so that the flow of products consistently follows the preferred routing (Figure 8.17).
- *Operations arrangements* are often based on autonomous cells, each responsible for its own tasks and for the supply to and from adjacent cells.
- *Balanced flow of materials* occurs throughout the processes.
- *Standard containers* that hold predetermined quantities are used to fix material levels, and also as partial substitutes for a control system and paper-based procedures.
- *Improved levels of quality conformance* are achieved throughout the process. This is based on the use of statistical process control techniques and is explained more fully in Chapter 10.

Staff involvement
The role of staff in the process is also radically changed, in the following ways:

- *A broader, day-to-day role in terms of job content* This includes cross-training with a range of tasks often now involving indirect work such as improving operations and scheduling. This not only improves job interest, but also means that when there are no products to make (remember that in JIT the authority to make an order quantity must be received before work can commence), staff can undertake indirect tasks that add value.

Figure 8.17 **Simplified operations unit controlled by a JIT system**

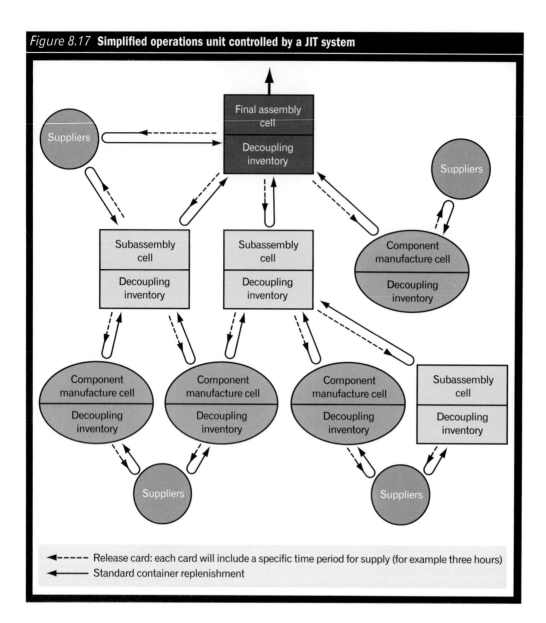

- _Responsibility for quality conformance_ As part of the last point, staff assume responsibility for the quality conformance checks completed during the process (see Chapter 10). This typically includes the authority to stop the process if a product defect is discovered.
- _Continuous improvement_ The increased involvement of staff is also designed to use their knowledge to improve the system as part of the drive for continuous improvement (covered in detail in Chapter 12).

Lean – a philosophy of operations management

The introduction and development of JIT within businesses involves a set of approaches that are integral to its success as an operations scheduling system. This overall approach has, over the years, been extended into many aspects of operations management, to the point that it is now appropriately referred to as **lean management**, signalling a fundamental change of approach to managing operations.

Many of the techniques that underpin JIT are now in general use as stand-alone approaches while also forming part of several other areas of operations management, such as continuous improvement. These approaches, which emanate directly from lean management itself, are now briefly reviewed, with a fuller coverage provided in Chapter 12.

Lean management – has developed from JIT to become a philosophy of operations management that focuses on eliminating waste and reducing inventory in all parts of the supply chain

Asset emphasis: inventory versus process

In the past, one driving force for many businesses was the high utilization of fixed assets. Prior to the mid-1960s, when, in most sectors, world capacity was less than world demand, a high utilization of fixed assets (such as manufacturing processes) was the way for a business to maximize its output and profit. This view continued to be held even in sectors where the imbalance between capacity and demand had been reversed. Lean management, however, challenged this approach by trading off the objective of high utilization of processes for lower levels of inventory and the elimination of waste, as shown in Figure 8.18.

Figure 8.18 **The different orientation of traditional and lean approaches**			
Aspects		**Traditional approach**	**Lean approach**
Focus		Make so as to keep processes and staff working – the objective is high utilization	Make only when needed – the objective is low inventory
Uses of inventory[a]	cycle	Large order quantities to reduce the impact of set-ups on the net available capacity	Make as little as possible – reduce set-ups or leave processes pre-set until the next order arrives
	decoupling	Allow processes to make to and draw from WIP inventory, so decoupling the dependency between processes and thus allowing them to operate independently of one another	Minimize inventory between processes. This increases their mutual dependency and the need for cooperation and coordination throughout the delivery system
	overall	Make inventory just in case it is needed	Make inventory just at the time it is required
Operations emphasis		Process throughput speeds. Inventory facilitates high process utilization and supports a high level of efficiency objectives	Reduce set-ups or hold excess capacity to allow small order quantities to be scheduled and low inventory levels to be maintained

Note: [a] These types of inventory are explained in Chapter 11.

The advantages of scheduling material using a lean approach are not restricted to those associated with the investment and cash benefits inherent in having lower levels of inventory. There are additional and sizeable gains concerning an easier scheduling task, simpler and less expensive systems and controls, and lower overhead costs to manage the material system. The downside is that, as products are made only on an as-required JIT basis, spare process capacity typically exists throughout the system.

Improvement through exposing problems

The lean approach is designed to deliberately expose problems and use this as a vehicle for improvement. Figure 8.19 provides a classic example.

This shows how excessive inventory (in the form of water depth) allows the delivery system (in the form of a ship) to operate with a whole range of problems going undetected. It creates a situation where management is unaware of the type and size of the inefficiencies that exist in the operations system and the improvements that need to take place. By reducing inventory (water) levels, the problems (depicted in Figure 8.19 as rocks) are exposed, the ship will now founder (management is alerted to issues), and the areas for improvement are highlighted. In more traditional approaches, problems are viewed as being a sign of inefficient management, are not deliberately sought and often are covered

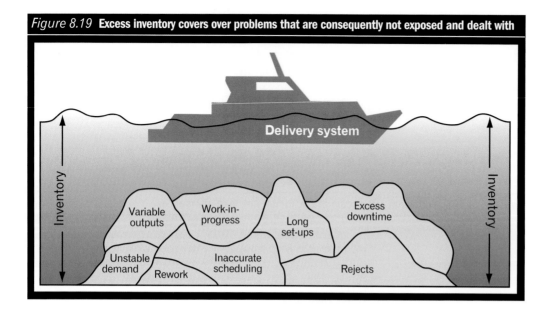

Figure 8.19 Excess inventory covers over problems that are consequently not exposed and dealt with

over (for example, with excess inventory as depicted in Figure 8.19). The opportunity to identify areas for improvement is thereby lost.

Incorporating indirect activities into the remit of direct staff

In traditional organizational approaches, direct staff are employed to undertake direct work. Thus, direct staff only provide services or make products. There are several consequences that result from this traditional approach:

- In circumstances where there is no demand for a service or product, operations managers either have to make inventory or record direct staff as an excess cost (that is, they are not working). Most corporate performance measures make the latter less preferable than the former.

- The experience and capability of direct staff is limited to providing services or making products. Indirect activities such as scheduling, quantity conformance and improvement are not an integral part of the role of direct staff and, consequently, are neither provided for as part of their job nor seen as part of the direct staff's contribution to a business.

One element of the lean approach is to increase the involvement of direct staff (supported by appropriate training) in indirect areas of work such as day-to-day scheduling, quality conformance and the drive for continuous improvement. By incorporating indirect tasks into the role of direct staff, the new mix of work will then be reflected in the time allocations and expectations related to the performance and output of those involved. This approach not only secures the contribution of all staff in areas such as continuous improvement, but also eliminates the 'make inventory' or 'no work' scenario. If there is no direct work on hand, staff now have 'legitimate' indirect tasks to undertake.

Eliminating waste

Waste is any activity that does not add value. One of the cornerstones of the lean approach is to identify and reduce or, where possible, eliminate waste that occurs throughout the operations system. Examples of waste include the following:

- *Inventory* The drive to reduce inventory has already been highlighted. The benefits of lower investment, the release of cash to be used elsewhere in a business, the simplification of systems and the reduction in the overhead costs associated with the level of material control needed result in significant gains for a business.

- *Movement* The unnecessary movement of materials and people results in unproductive activity and introduces uncertainty into a system. While the waste element of unnecessary movement is easy to visualize, it is not often appreciated how common it is in operations systems, or indeed the size and extent to which it occurs. Changing layouts to reduce movement and improving systems and procedures to eliminate the need to check, ask questions or fetch necessary materials that should have been on hand are common improvements that result in significant gains.

- *Lead-times* One by-product of waste is that operations lead-times are extended. Unnecessary movement has already been highlighted. Other causes include waiting time (as having material in the operations system that is not being worked on results in delay and additional lead-time), set-ups (lengthy changeover times increase lead-times) and process failures (equipment breakdowns introduce delays and lengthen lead-times).

Set-up reduction

Making products as required and using JIT implies making smaller quantities on a more frequent basis. Reducing set-up times allows this to happen while keeping the ratio between set-up times and the length of a production run to complete an order quantity at an acceptable level. For example, a one-hour changeover to make an order quantity equivalent to six hours of processing time offers the same ratio as a 10-minute changeover and an order quantity taking one hour.

Optimized production technology

Over the last two decades, much attention has been focused on a proprietary system called **optimized production technology** (OPT). In essence, OPT addresses the following issue.

> **KEY IDEA**
> Capacity constraints govern the rate of flow in operations

With multi-step delivery systems, there will typically be some parts of the total system that have less capacity to handle the work required than other parts of the same delivery system. These are known as bottlenecks. What OPT recognizes is that these capacity constraints or bottlenecks will limit how much work can flow through the total system, and that consequently it is necessary to schedule the amount of work into operations in line with these constraints. The level of throughput that bottleneck processes can handle will determine the amount of product that can be completed and made available to sell. Companies, particularly in the past, have often followed a policy of maximizing the utilization of all available resources. Where this policy is adopted, a business will generate part-completed work at some stages in the process that cannot be worked on at other stages (that is, the bottleneck processes) because of a lack of capacity. The result is WIP inventory.

Loading in line with the available capacity at bottleneck (or scarce resource) processes enables companies to manage the flow of work so as to achieve maximum saleable output. Leading on from this, OPT prioritizes attention on increasing capacity at these bottlenecks by improvements such as reducing set-ups and improving process yields. Thus, any improvements will result in increasing saleable output and with it greater profits.

In line with these central features, the OPT literature highlights other points to reinforce the logic and provide direction on which actions to follow when adopting an OPT system:

- The aim is to balance flow rather than capacity. Reducing bottlenecks will increase the total flow through the system, thus releasing the potential capacity of non-bottleneck processes.

- As a consequence of the above, an hour lost at a bottleneck is an hour lost for ever, but an hour saved at a non-bottleneck is of no consequence. Thus, reducing set-ups at a bottleneck increases capacity and throughput of the whole process, while additional set-ups at a non-bottleneck process do not affect output but do minimize WIP inventory.

Theory of constraints

The principles underlying the OPT philosophy have universal applicability. Consequently, they can be used to enhance many existing control systems as well as provide useful insights into the more effective management of operations in both service and manufacturing companies. To this end, the general use of the concepts introduced in the last section on OPT is encapsulated in the term 'theory of constraints', where a constraint is anything that limits an organization's ability to provide services or products. Constraints can be physical (for example, process capacity or resource availability) or non-physical (for example, procedures or systems) in nature. It is the effective management of these constraints that makes the OPT approach such a useful tool in managing a range of functions. The six-step process below can help managers to get the most out of an organization's resources:

1 Identify a system's constraints, whether physical or non-physical.
2 Ascertain those which affect the overall throughput of that part of the organization (the idea of bottlenecks and non-bottleneck processes described earlier).
3 Decide how to get the best possible throughput within the limits imposed by the current constraint(s).
4 Avoid keeping non-constraint resources busy as this produces unneeded work that sits in the form of WIP inventory or part-completed tasks.
5 Evaluate a system's constraints and take actions to reduce the effects of these constraints, such as reducing existing capacity losses, increasing available capacity and offloading demand or parts of demand to another part of the system. It is important here to make everyone aware of these constraints and their effects in order to focus attention on the problem and its solutions.
6 Where constraints are relaxed in Step 5, go back to Step 1.

Critical reflections

Operations strategy has been highlighted throughout the book in terms of its role of supporting a company's markets by meeting the requirements of relevant order-winners and qualifiers. One key part of this support is provided by the operations control system and its essential role in the effective and efficient provision of services and products.

Operations control links market demands with the necessary capacity and materials requirement, and contributes to the flow and control of services and products through the system. This part of operations will affect the competitive dimensions of many markets, such as delivery speed and delivery reliability. Selecting how best to provide this function is, therefore, a key operations management task. The alternative approaches, explained earlier in the chapter, to fulfilling this essential task are, however, characterized by a number of challenges.

Need for integration

It is essential that the services and products, the delivery systems and processes for providing them and the system(s) to control them are developed as integrated parts of the one task. Controls must be integrated into the other functions of operations that affect key issues, such as delivery reliability and delivery speed.

One scheduling system to support diverse needs

Many organizations implement a single scheduling system to meet the diverse needs of their various markets. A preference for single solutions, a desire to keep investment and running costs as low as possible and a failure to recognize that different delivery systems, processes and business needs require different scheduling systems are some of the reasons why this frequently happens.

Where the operations' activities of a business are common in terms of the tasks and order-winners and qualifiers to be supported, a single scheduling system will suffice, as Cases 8.1 and 8.2 illustrate. Many businesses, however, compete in a number of different markets, resulting in different operations tasks and different sets of order-winners and qualifiers that need to be supported. Here, different scheduling systems are required to meet these different sets of needs. The arguments relating to the attraction of economies of scale are well recognized but need to be countered by an acknowledgement that as scheduling forms an integral part of the operations function it needs to reflect the different needs of the markets it supports.

Beware of suboptimal applications

Attracted by the benefits that will accrue from changing the existing system, companies sometimes try to introduce a new system without ensuring that it fits their needs or that the prerequisites for its introduction are in place. JIT scheduling systems provide a classic example of this. Whereas, in Japan, companies only apply JIT to control operations processes with certain characteristics, the allure of the benefits of JIT has led to suboptimal applications by Western companies:

- *Japanese view* The term 'just-in-time' is used very strictly in Japanese companies and reflects the fact that its use is ideally related to supporting markets characterized by stable volumes and a product mix that is known well in advance. Delivering JIT means planning in plenty of time. Furthermore, when Japanese managers refer to the approach embodied by the term 'just-in-time', they prefer to speak of the JIT philosophy embodied by the Toyota production system that originally spawned the development of the JIT system (see the earlier section on 'Lean management').

- *Western view* Although displaying the appropriate characteristics of a high volume and a stable product mix, Western companies have introduced JIT control systems without creating the environment for JIT to be developed in its optimum form. Two of the more critical dimensions essential to the introduction of a JIT system that Western companies often fail to provide are:

- Not fixing forward schedules. As a consequence, the end-user, while requiring a JIT response from its suppliers, still retains the 'right' to change call-offs within material lead-times. The only option for a supplier wanting to meet such schedule changes in terms of quantity and/or delivery date is to hold inventory, thus undermining the underlying principle of minimizing inventory throughout a supply chain.

- Overlooking the technical and staffing changes described earlier that are necessary to bring about reductions in WIP inventory. This is often because of the greater corporate influence exerted by accountants relative to that exerted by operations.

The central role of scheduling within a business rightly attracts attention and discussion. Furthermore, it is an aspect of the field of operations management that has undergone regular development over the years in keeping with the importance of the scheduling task and the increasing demands placed on operations in facing up to more complex business requirements, more competitive markets and more demanding customers. The developments leading from MRPI to ERP, which we covered earlier, are a testament to this. Add into this the tendency to evaluate existing systems by what they do not provide while evaluating alternatives by the gains they bring, and companies may too often look to an all-in-one, quick-fix type of change without sufficient analysis of what the current system does well and less well, the alternatives for improvement (both fixing the old and investing in the new), the prerequisites for the successful introduction of the new approach and the costs and timescales involved. Operations needs to be at the forefront of these reviews and evaluations of alternative approaches as the role of scheduling in the selling process is a key factor in retaining and growing market share.

Summary

- In many markets, meeting customers' on-time delivery needs is a prerequisite for getting and staying on a customer's shortlist, and providing this qualifier is a key operations management task.

- Businesses use a number of ways to cushion the delivery system from the instability of their markets. These ways are classed as basic, secondary and supplementary mechanisms.

- Although the need is the same in all organizations, the way of scheduling operations to meet this requirement differs from business to business and needs to reflect those dimensions which alter the control task and the control design system. These include the complexity of the service or the product, and whether the services and products are specials or standards.

- The main section of the chapter introduced the alternative scheduling systems that are available, explained these in detail and illustrated their use with examples. These were:

  - Bar charts – recording capacity (for example, processes or staff) against a timescale. Figures 8.2 and 8.3 illustrated some of the applications.

  - Network analysis – organizations often use this method to plan, schedule and control complex, one-off tasks. The simple example in Figure 8.6 is then followed by a slightly more complex, real-life example in Figure 8.8.

  - MRPI and JIT – two of the most widely used systems to schedule standard products and services. Referred to as a push and a pull system, respectively, these two systems, and how they differ, are explained in detail.

- All operations control systems start with a statement of demand, produced from data on known and/or forecast sales. One other key reminder at this time is the principle of independent and dependent demand. Whereas assessing demand levels by known and/or forecast orders is a fundamental task for independent demand items, requirements for dependent items can be calculated as they are directly related to the pattern of demand of the independent items to which they relate.

- Once the master schedule for a service or product has been established, the scheduling task of determining material requirements and process/staff capacities can be completed. These, in turn, provide the inputs for the day-to-day execution of the plan. Detailing the MRPI and JIT systems then completed this section of the text.

- Next came sections on MRPII and ERP. Where scheduling activities in MRPI are tied in with the tasks of other relevant functions, the result is known as MRPII. ERP evolved out of MRPII and is designed to embrace the whole organization using a common database, thus allowing integration between the different parts without the use of duplicate information systems. The section on ERP outlined the benefits and concerns relating to it while highlighting the key dimensions to ensure its successful application.

- Finally, OPT and its finite scheduling role in refining existing control systems were explained. The final section addresses the developments in ERP systems, outlining the benefits and concerns and highlighting the key dimensions to ensure their successful application.

Study activities

Discussion questions

1 Give an example of a business that would use a push and one that would use a pull operations control system. Explain your choice and briefly describe how the system would work.

2 What is the difference between independent and dependent demand? Give two manufacturing and two service examples to illustrate your answer.

3 Under what conditions should a company refuse a customer order that it is technically able to provide?

4 Your local dry cleaner always specifies a two-day lead-time, no matter what items of clothing you take in to be cleaned. Suggest reasons why the outlet is able to do this and how it works.

5 Describe a service application where the principles of the theory of constraints can apply.

6 In operations, priorities manifest themselves in a conflict between meeting customers' lead-times and due dates, and the productivity and efficiency goals of the operations system staff. Discuss and provide examples to illustrate your points.

Assignments

1 A small business consultancy company has three specialists in one area of its work. Furthermore, each of these three is further specialized to undertake certain phases of an assignment. Jim Brown handles phase 1, Anne Dewar phase two, and Jean Holden undertakes phase 3. Details of the work to complete each of these assignments, together with agreed completion dates, are given below. In all cases, the phases need to be completed in the order 1, 2 and 3. The three consultants can also complete other fee-paying work during the period.

Client	Phase			Agreed completion # Days[a]
	1	2	3	
McCanley	10	16	8	49
Williams	3	9	16	46
Beattie	12	10	10	45

Note: [a] Calculated from day 1 as start date.

Using day 1 as the start date, draw a bar chart to schedule the above tasks in order to meet the agreed completion dates and release each consultant as early as possible to take on other fee-paying work when their part of these three jobs has been completed.

2 A piece of equipment requires the times shown in the table for its manufacture.

Activity	# Days	Activity	# Days
1 Purchasing	15	5 Assembly	7
2 Fabrication	5	6 Controls	6
3 Hydraulics	5	7 Test	3
4 Electronics	18	8 Packaging	1

Each of the activities must be completed sequentially (that is, Activity 2 follows Activity 1 and so on), except that fabrication can be started 10 days after purchasing begins, and the hydraulics and electronics steps can be completed in parallel. Draw a bar chart for this job.

If the hydraulics and electronics steps could also be started 10 days after purchasing begins, what would the network look like for this job? Also, calculate the critical path.

Exploring further

Journal articles

Davenport, T.H. and Glaser, J. (2002) 'Just-in-time-delivery comes to knowledge management'. *Harvard Business Review*, **80**(7), pp. 107–11. Knowledge workers could benefit from a just-in-time knowledge management system tailored to delivering the right supporting information for the job at hand. An analysis of the knowledge management initiative at Partners HealthCare System is provided to illustrate the potential gains.

Shapiro, B.P., Kasturi Rangan, V. and Sviokla, J.J. (2004) 'Staple yourself to an order'. HBR Classic. *Harvard Business Review*, **82**(7) pp. 162–71. The article is based on a detailed analysis of how an order was processed in 18 companies and highlights the findings.

Books

Dennis, P. (2007) *Lean Production Simplified*, 2nd edn. New York: Productivity Press. This book provides a simple introduction to the application and benefits of lean production.

Heerkens, G.R. (2007) *Project Management: 24 Steps in Helping you Master a Project*. McGraw Hill. This provides a short (128 pages) practical overview of project management.

Hill, A. and Hill, T. (2009) *Manufacturing Operations Strategy: Text and Cases*, 3rd edn. Basingstoke: Palgrave Macmillan. The text provides a useful supplement to *Essential*

Operations Management by outlining an in-depth approach for developing and implementing operations strategy within manufacturing organizations.

Hill, T. (2005) *Operations Management: Text and Cases*. Basingstoke: Palgrave Macmillan. This provides a useful supplement to the current book by offering a more comprehensive explanation and further examples (including long case studies) showing how service and manufacturing companies have applied these concepts.

Jacobs, F.R., Berry W.L., Whybark D.C. and Vollman T.E. (2011) *Manufacturing Planning and Control Systems for Supply Chain Management*, 6th edn. McGraw-Hill. This provides a detailed review of the MRPI, MRPII, ERP and JIT systems.

Liker, J.K. (2004) *The Toyota Way: 14 Management Principles from the World's Greatest Manufacturer*. McGraw Hill. This book lists the key principles that underpin Toyota's approach to managing operations.

Phillips J (2010) *IT Project Management*, 3rd edn. McGraw Hill. This addresses the practical issues when managing and implementing IT projects, emphasizing the key aspect of final completion.

Notes and references

1 This figure is developed from Exhibit 10.11, p. 319, in *Managing Operations Strategy: Text and Cases* (see 'Exploring further').

2 In more complex networks, the event node often contains more information.

3 One of the earliest statements providing this definition comes from Schonenberger, R.J. (1982) *Japanese Manufacturing Techniques: Nine Hidden Lessons in Simplicity*. New York: Free Press, p. 16.

4 If a 30-minute set-up time is reduced to 10 minutes, the order quantities to be loaded can be reduced to one-third while maintaining the ratio between the length of set-up and the length of the run time.

Ash Electrics (AE) makes doorbells, door chimes, switches, industrial alarms and a range of small transformers. Producing over five million units per year (from a 38 cm diameter bell to a replacement bulb in a light switch), the company sells to electrical wholesalers throughout its domestic and export markets.

The range of manufacturing activities includes coil winding, simple cropping and punching, and other operations such as bending, forming and crimping simple components for later assembly. The principal activity, however, is the assembly, testing and packing of products made from the bought-out and made-in-house components, mouldings and parts (Figure 1). To reduce material costs and inventory levels, the company has standardized many product components, from fixing screws through to clips, bobbins, coils, lamps and multilingual instruction leaflets. Apart from the metal bars or domes that produce the sound of the bell, the principal material used is plastic. Plastic bases, front pieces and components are bought in from outside suppliers to meet demand forecasts for each final product.

The company schedules production based on 13 four-week periods (starting in January each year) and forecasts for each product both sales and end-of-period finished goods inventory levels for several periods ahead. When setting the production schedule, any anticipated differences between actual and forecast sales and any known large orders for delivery in the next or subsequent periods will be taken into account so that the actual end-of-period finished goods inventory is as close as possible to the forecast level. These adjustments are made at the start of each period when firm production outputs are agreed.

The sales revenue of the company has grown year on year, particularly in its export markets, which now account for 58 per cent of total sales. The company recognizes that its order-winners are product design and delivery speed. To maintain its position as market leader, it frequently

Figure 1
Outline of the operations process

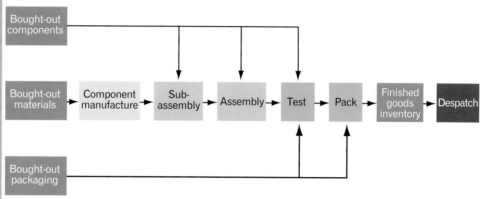

Figure 2
High Tone data

Period	10	11	12	13
Forecast sales	8,500	9,500	10,000	8,500
Forecast end of period inventory	2,100	2,000	2,000	2,350
End of Period 9 inventory	1,960			

Figure 3
Zig-Zag data

Period	10	11	12	13
Forecast sales	10,500	12,000	14,000	9,000
Forecast end of period inventory	2,800	2,100	2,100	3,700
End of Period 9 inventory	2,390			

Notes: 1 The 13 four-week periods start in January.
2 Order from Australia for 3,400 Zig-Zag units to be delivered in Week 2 of Period 10.
3 Order from Germany for 2,800 Zig-Zag units to be delivered in Week 1 of Period 11.
4 Period 9 has just been completed.

introduces new designs, some to add to its range, others to replace existing products. Delivery speed is provided by holding finished goods inventory. This enables AE to send out products for home orders on the same day the order is received, while for export orders it sends out products to catch the next available container ship or container train (using EuroTunnel) or in line with a customer's delivery date. The result is that AE's customers can, in turn, hold only a limited amount of inventory themselves, knowing that their order will be met quickly.

The qualifiers in AE's markets are quality conformance (products are made to specification every time), delivery reliability (AE always delivers to the promised date) and price. Given the design and delivery speed advantages it has created, AE is able to price its products at the top end of the market, resulting in high profit margins that fund its design investment and the costs of holding inventory.

As an illustration of how operations scheduling is completed, Figures 2 and 3 provide data for two representative products. The High Tone is a long-established product

that enjoys steady demand and has fairly accurate forecast sales. The Zig-Zag, on the other hand, is a new product whose demand has so far been greater than AE's initial forecasts. The export market for Zig-Zag is also taking off and, as shown in the notes to Figure 3, two large orders need to be delivered in the next period (note that Period 9 has just finished). Meeting the 'end of period inventory forecasts' is obviously a key performance target for operations as it underpins the company's ability to always meet the short lead-time promises that it has set itself to support its customers and win more business.

Questions

1 What are the critical features of operations scheduling in Ash Electric?

2 What is the key operations scheduling task?

3 Develop a schedule for Period 10 for both the High Tone and the Zig-Zag. Explain your decisions.

Lecturers: visit www.palgrave.com/business/hillessential for additional resources

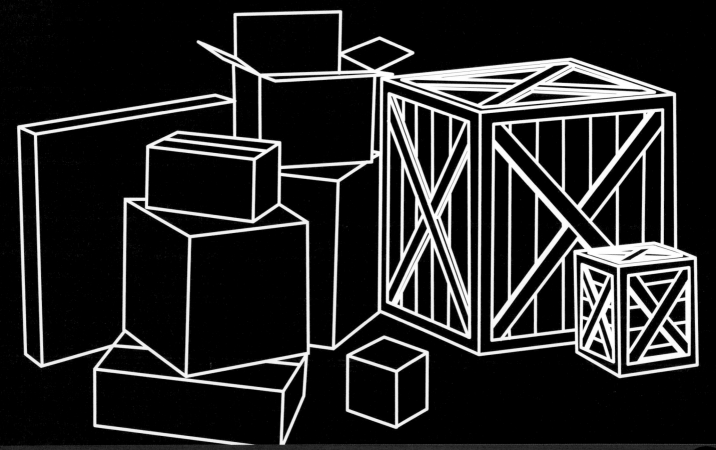

Managing Inventory

9

Learning objectives

After completing this chapter, you should be able to:

- Explain the different types of inventory and their roles

- Show the presence of the different types of operations inventory in manufacturing processes and service delivery systems

- Review the approaches to address the key inventory questions relating to:

  - What items to hold in stock?

  - How much to hold, and how much and when to order

- Examine the different inventory systems and identify which should be used for different types of business

- Understand how to analyse inventory in order to keep levels to a minimum

Chapter outline

Introduction

What is inventory?

- Functions of inventory

Models and approaches for managing inventory

- Background issues and approaches

- Key inventory decisions – what to stock and when to order

Inventory systems and analysis

- Inventory control systems

- Inventory analysis

Critical reflections

Summary

Inventory – also known as stock, comprises the inputs (materials) into the delivery system or manufacturing process, part-finished items (services or products) within the service delivery system or manufacturing process and outputs (finished items) to be sold or supplied to customers

Introduction

In Chapter 7, we dealt with managing capacity (the capability to provide services and make products). This chapter will cover issues surrounding the management of the materials that go into the services and products at different points in the conversion process from input to output, otherwise known as **inventory**. Inventory management is a key operations task because it is typically a large financial investment, helps operations to run smoothly and efficiently and also affects the supply of services and goods to customers.

This chapter will discuss why inventory is kept, the level of inventory involved and its management and control. First, the forms and functions of inventory are explained and the division between corporate and operations inventory is defined as part of the way to effectively manage this important asset. Second, background issues relating to the management and control of inventory are discussed. These include the independent/dependent demand principle, the Pareto principle, the use of economic order quantities (EOQs), and how reorder levels are calculated and used. Third, the key questions of what and how much to hold and to order are discussed, including the approaches to follow and the concepts to use when resolving these key questions. Finally, the different systems to manage inventory are explained. This section then goes on to give a detailed review of analysing inventory by cause and using this as the basis for reducing its levels.

What is inventory?

Fixed assets – assets that are held in the long term and that are not intended to be sold or transformed into products and/or services

What are the roles of and why do organizations hold inventory? Before answering these questions, let's first discuss what we mean by inventory. In the context of this chapter, it comprises the inputs (services or materials) used, any part-finished items (services or products) in a process (called work-in-progress inventory) and the outputs (finished items) to be sold or supplied to customers. On the other hand, it does not comprise the equipment or fixtures and fittings (for example, the tables, chairs, tablecloths, napkins, cutlery, plates, dishes and glasses in a restaurant) needed to provide services or make products. These are classed as the **fixed assets** of a business as they do not form a direct part of what it sells.

Perhaps the easiest way to explain and illustrate these differences is to ask you to reflect on the inventory you keep and why you keep it. You hold stocks of food and other items that you use as part of day-to-day living. In addition, you have other assets such as cooking utensils, a mobile telephone, IT equipment and clothes that are used and reused as part of everyday living. The former set of items are used and replenished, while the latter items are purchased and consumed (that is, the functions they provide are used) over a much longer period. This chapter concerns the management and control of a company's equivalent of the stocks of food and other consumables you keep. And, just like you, the company needs to make decisions about which items to hold, how much of each item (that is, inventory) to carry, when to replenish stocks and how much to buy at any one time.

However, before addressing the management and control of inventory, let's first consider its roles, the types of inventory and the functions they provide.

The role of inventory

> **KEY IDEA**
  The underlying purpose of inventory is to uncouple the various steps of the service delivery systems/manufacturing processes in order to allow each to work independently of the other parts

The underlying purpose of inventory is to uncouple the various phases of a service delivery system or manufacturing process and thereby allow each phase to work independently of the other parts. Hence, keeping food in the kitchen allows you to prepare a meal without first having to shop. In reality, however, there are many other issues and dimensions involved. For example, you may need fresh milk only for your breakfast coffee, but you have to buy milk in larger quantities as prescribed by the retail store from which you buy it. Similarly, you may buy a larger box of food or more than the one item that you need for a meal in order to reduce costs as the direct result of a price deal offered by the food store or to avoid the inconvenience and time taken to purchase a particular food item each time you need it.

In the context of operations, Figure 9.1 shows the forms in which inventory is present throughout the three phases of operations – inputs, operations process and outputs – in two different types of organization.

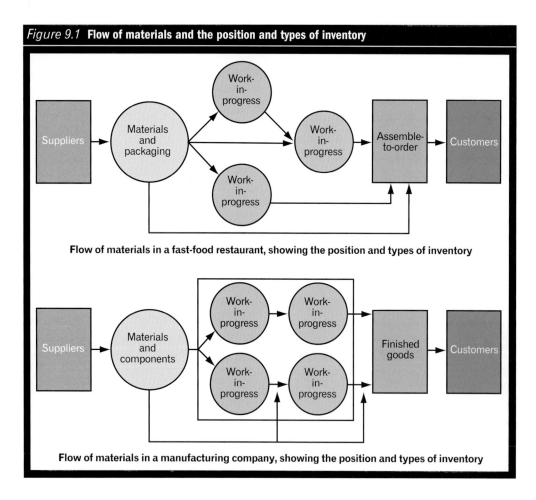

Figure 9.1 Flow of materials and the position and types of inventory

Flow of materials in a fast-food restaurant, showing the position and types of inventory

Flow of materials in a manufacturing company, showing the position and types of inventory

As the flow of materials into and through a process invariably differs from the pattern and rate of customer demand, inventory will be held to help cushion the operations delivery system from these changes. How much inventory there is will depend upon the relative rates of demand and supply, as illustrated in Figure 9.2. This depicts the relationship between the rate of supply, the rate of demand and the level of inventory, using the analogy of a water tank. In this example, the rate of inflow and outflow of water will directly affect the level of inventory (stored water) in the tank (which represents the conversion process).

These dimensions of inventory management will be addressed later, but they need to be recognized early on.

Types of inventory

There are two principal categories of inventory: process and support:

Process inventory – items directly used in providing the services and making the products sold by a business

- **Process inventory** comprises items directly used in providing the services and making the products sold by a business. Thus, the ingredients to bake bread and pastries form part of the process-related inventory for a bakery, as will the foodstuffs used to prepare meals in a restaurant. The wheels, subassemblies, windscreens, engines and other parts that go into a motor vehicle are, similarly, examples of process-related inventory. All items going into the services or products, from raw materials through to packaging, fall within this category.

Support inventory – items that are not an integral part of the service or product but are essential to the overall running of any organization (for example, office supplies and spare parts for equipment)

- **Support inventory** comprises items that are not an integral part of the service or product but are essential to the overall running of any organization. Maintenance and office supplies (such as spare parts for equipment and stationery) are examples for the bakery and car assembly illustrations earlier. Cleaning materials for kitchen utensils, ovens and the like are examples for the restaurant.

Generally, businesses with activities centred on products and manufacturing processes have more inventory and need to develop more controls and systems than organizations where the service/product mix is oriented more to the service end of the service/product continuum described earlier in Figure 1.8. This is principally because the fewer operations materials that are involved, the less inventory there will be in the system to control. For example, in a bank, most services are consumed as they are generated, and the material content is negligible. In fact, the forms and other paperwork used in a bank's delivery system are examples of support inventory. The control of support inventories is an important task for all organizations, but more emphasis will be given to process inventories because these are an integral part of the service and product provided and also involve a much higher investment.

> KEY IDEA

There are three categories of process inventory – raw materials/components, work-in-progress and finished goods

Finally, within process inventory, there are three categories – raw materials and components, work-in-progress and finished goods. Figure 9.3 shows how these link to the stages in the process and provides a brief explanation of each. These categories provide an essential insight into the management and control of inventory and will feature throughout the rest of the chapter.

Functions of inventory

Why, then, does an organization invest so much in inventory? Why does it exist, and what are the benefits? Earlier, the underlying purpose of inventory was identified as one of uncoupling the various phases of the service delivery system or manufacturing process. This is a common, overall function, but there are also important advantages that relate more to one type of inventory than to another, as outlined in Figure 9.4 (p. 297).

Figure 9.2 **Rate of supply and demand and level of inventory**

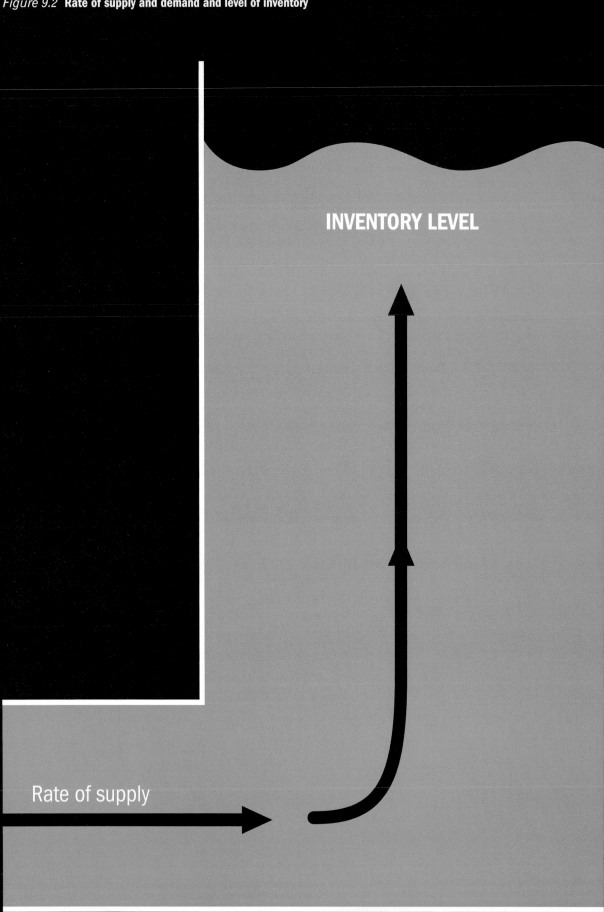

INVENTORY LEVEL

Rate of supply

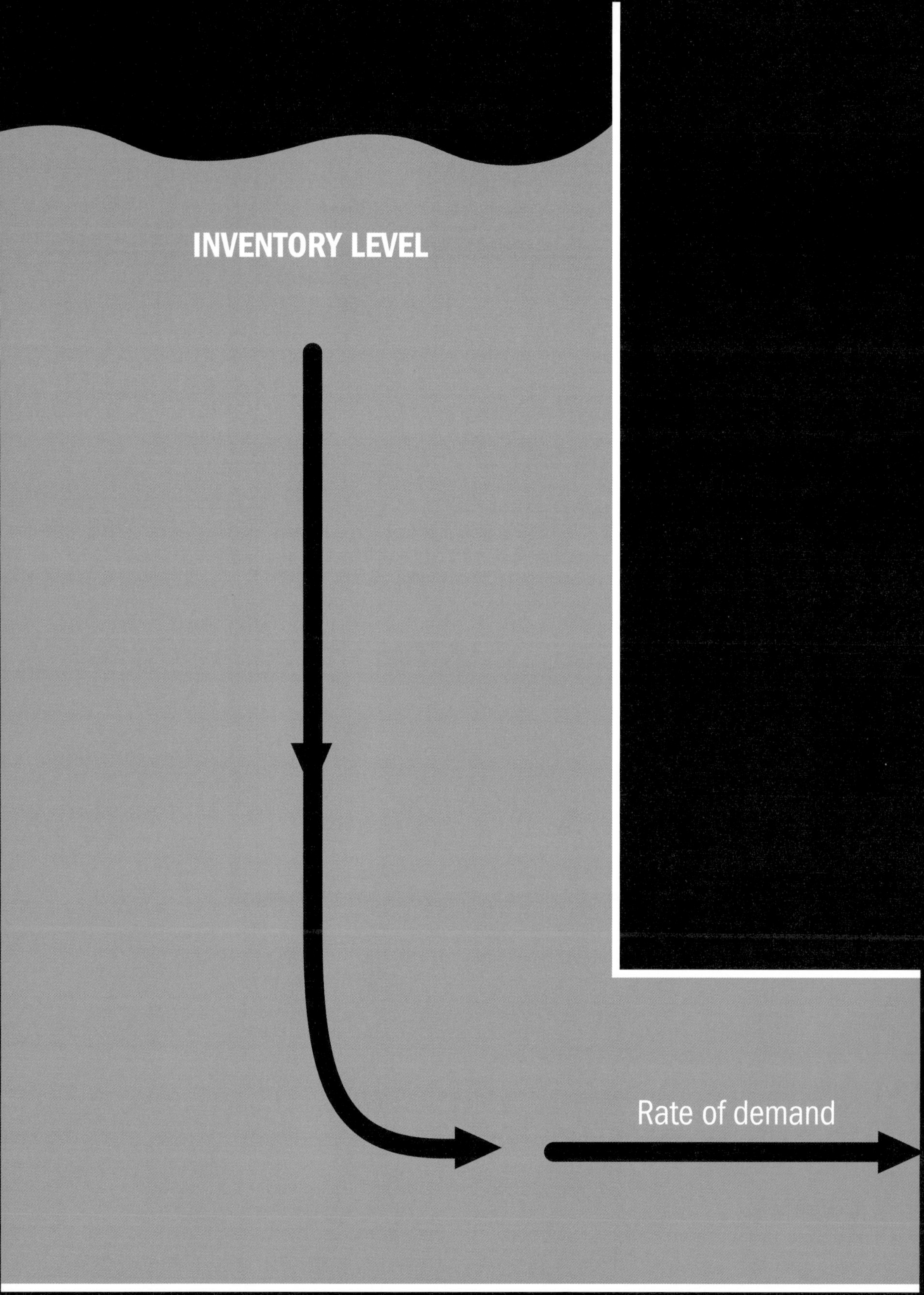

INVENTORY LEVEL

Rate of demand

Figure 9.3 Process stage, types of inventory and examples

PROCESS STAGE	TYPES OF INVENTORY	PROCESS		SUPPORT
Inputs	Raw materials	Sandwich bar	Sandwich fillings – e.g. a range of meats and cheeses, green salad and tomatoes Beverage ingredients – e.g. coffee, tea and milk Other foodstuffs – e.g. bread, cakes, pies, pasties and bought-out salads	Supplies that are not central to the services or products provided
		Toy manufacturer	Plastic granules and other materials Bought-out components Packaging Instruction leaflets	
Operations process	Work-in-progress	Sandwich bar	Prepared fillings – e.g. chicken, egg and tuna mayonnaise Soup Range of salad dishes – e.g. mixed and green	These include maintenance and office supplies and consumables such as cleaning materials
		Toy manufacturer	Components made in-house Subassemblies – e.g. wheels attached to axles Assembled toys awaiting packing	
Outputs	Finished goods	Sandwich bar	Range of completed and packaged sandwiches Pastries, pies and pasties Packaged snacks – e.g. crisps and nuts Bottled drinks	
		Toy manufacturer	Packaged toys Packaged spare parts	

As you read the detail in Figure 9.4, you will notice that some advantages relate to operations issues, while others relate to the business as a whole. To help identify these different functions, it is helpful to categorize them into two broad types of inventory, each of which comprises a number of subfunctions. These two types are known as **corporate inventory** and **operations inventory**. Whereas the latter directly helps operations to undertake its basic tasks, the former comprises inventory that is held to provide advantages for other parts of an organization. These two categories and their assorted subcategories form a useful way to help manage and control inventory, and will be used in some of the sections later in the chapter.

**Corporate inventory – **
inventory that does not provide an operations function, but is held to provide advantages for other parts of an organization

**Operations inventory – ** inventory held to undertake the basic tasks of operations

Corporate inventory

Corporate inventory is inventory that does *not* provide an operations function. The types of corporate inventory are numerous and reflect the nature of the organization involved.

Figure 9.4 **Role of different types of inventory**
Raw materials and bought-out parts inventory allow an organization to: • Cater for the variability of supply • Reduce costs by taking advantage of quantity discounts or market prices • Provide holdings of parts that could in future be in short supply due, for instance, to an anticipated increase in world demand • Form an investment when price increases are anticipated • Reduce operations lead-times
Work-in-progress inventory helps to maintain the independence of stages in the process by uncoupling the steps involved. This leads to: • Orders being easier to schedule • Stabilizing the different output rates at each part of a process • Reducing the total delivery lead-time to supply customer demands • Facilitating a higher utilization of plant, processes and staff
Finished goods inventory enables an organization to: • Provide fast, off-the-shelf delivery • Achieve a steady delivery of goods to customers in the face of intermittent production or supply • Cope with fluctuations in demand, particularly in the case of seasonal products • Provide an insurance against equipment or process breakdowns and, in some instances, against suppliers' strikes

One dimension of corporate inventory is, however, a common feature – typically it accounts for 20–25 per cent of the total. Examples include:

• Sales inventory to support customer agreements
• Sales inventory owing to actual sales being lower than forecast sales, and where operations has produced to agreed schedules
• Corporate safety inventory due to the uncertainty of supply (for example, in anticipation of national or international strikes)
• Purchasing inventory incurred to take advantage of quantity discounts
• Marketing inventory to support a service or product launch.

Note that when categorizing the types of corporate inventory, the function or business-based decision is specified. So, 'sales inventory to support customer agreement' refers to the fact that the sales function negotiated the holding of this inventory as part of a customer's contract.

> **KEY IDEA**

Corporate inventory typically accounts for 20–25 per cent of the total inventory held

Operations inventory in manufacturing processes

Regardless of whether the operations inventory under review is at the raw material, work-in-progress or finished goods stage, it may be further described as one or more of decoupling, cycle, pipeline, capacity-related or buffer inventory, with each fulfilling a specific function. Figures 9.5 and 9.6 illustrate these, and below is an explanation of how they relate to both the category of inventory and the particular choice of manufacturing process.

> **KEY IDEA**

The five functions in operations inventory are decoupling, cycle, pipeline, capacity-related and buffer

Decoupling inventory

Decoupling inventory – this inventory is used to 'decouple', or detach, one process from another

Decoupling inventory allows processes to work independently of one another, with materials waiting for the next step rather than processes waiting for materials. The outcome is a higher utilization of processes.

Figure 9.5 Inventory functions related to categories of inventory in manufacturing

Inventory function	Inventory category		
	Raw materials	**Work-in-progress**	**Finished goods**
Decoupling		✓✓✓[a]	
Cycle		✓✓✓	
Pipeline		✓✓✓	✓
Capacity-related		✓✓	✓✓✓
Buffer[b]	✓✓	✓✓	✓✓✓

Notes: [a] ✓, Degree of function typically provided.
[b] Concerns variation in supply or demand around the average, essentially to cover instances when supply delays or actual levels of demand are above average. However, where inventory is held for reasons such as uncertainty of supply, it should be identified under a relevant category within corporate inventory.

Figure 9.6 Inventory functions related to the type of manufacturing process

Inventory function		Type of manufacturing process				
		Project	**Jobbing**	**Batch**	**Line**	**Continuous processing**
Decoupling		✓		✓✓✓		
Cycle		✓✓		✓✓✓		
Pipeline			✓✓	✓✓		
Capacity-related	Work-in-progress	✓✓		✓		
	Finished goods	✓		✓✓	✓✓✓	✓✓✓
Buffer	Raw materials	✓		✓	✓✓	✓
	Finished goods			✓✓	✓✓✓	✓

In project processes, the use of decoupling inventory varies. When the task involves a single product (for example, a bridge or tunnel), the use of decoupling inventory is either restricted or unwarranted. However, where a number of houses are being built at the same time, work on one stage may be scheduled ahead of time so that other skilled tradesmen are not kept waiting.

In jobbing, there is no decoupling inventory as the skilled person will always be progressing the job. Similarly, in line and continuous processing, there is no decoupling inventory as they are both sets of coupled processes.

It is in batch processes that the function of decoupling inventory is best illustrated. As a batch process is designed to be used and reused by different products, having inventory to decouple processes from one another facilitates scheduling and ensures that processes (specifically those with high utilization levels) are fully used. Having part-finished (work-in-progress) inventory waiting means that processes always have materials on which to work.

Cycle inventory

The rationale behind using **cycle inventory** in the operations system is to reduce the number of set-ups (the time taken to stop work on one item and make ready the delivery system or process or get everything together to start the next task). This increases the amount of capacity that can be used to make saleable output, while also spreading the

> Cycle inventory – relates to the decision to make a given quantity of products (referred to as an order quantity or 'batch size') at the same time in order to reduce losses in processing time when a set-up occurs

costs of a set-up over the number of products made (the order quantity), which thereby reduces the set-up costs per unit.

Cycle inventory is a feature of batch processes where set-ups are an inherent feature of this process. The principle here is to make more than one item at the same time, thus reducing the loss of processing time when a set-up occurs and also spreading the cost of a set-up over all the products made in the order quantity. How many are to be made at one time will take into account the length of the set-up time, the value and physical size of the products and the time needed to make a product.

In a project process, where a number of houses (say) are being built at the same time then, for similar reasons to those explained above, a stage in the build (for example, putting in the foundations, laying down the concrete floor, plastering the walls or installing the plumbing and electrics) will often be completed on several houses one after the other. In this way, costs such as the hire of special equipment and contractors' time (for example, travelling to the site) is reduced in overall terms.

In jobbing, there is little need for this inventory function as the skilled person will set up for each job individually and is often making an order quantity of one. Similarly, cycle inventory has no function in line or continuous processing as these are set up to manufacture an agreed range of products and are not reset – see Figures 9.5 and 9.6.

Pipeline inventory

The decision to subcontract that results in **pipeline inventory** can be made part way through the operations process or at the distribution stage. Examples during the process include a manufacturer having the finishing processes (for example, plating and painting) completed by a subcontractor.

In both jobbing and batch processes, companies may decide to subcontract a particular step part way through the manufacturing process and, in so doing, create pipeline inventory in support of that decision. Subcontracting one operation in project process, line process or continuous process is typically infeasible, so pipeline inventory is not a feature of these processes.

Capacity-related inventory

Capacity-related inventory transfers work from one time period to the next in the form of inventory and provides one way of stabilizing operations capacity in an environment of fluctuating sales levels. For example, the seasonal demand for fireworks to celebrate national festivals and the high demand for toys and gifts at peak periods such as Christmas are accommodated, in part, by capacity-related inventory.

In jobbing, products are made to order, and hence capacity-related inventory is not typically used. The same is true for make-to-order (MTO) products using a project process. However, where building firms construct several houses at the same time, they may well use capacity-related inventory in the form of both work-in-progress and finished goods to help balance out changing patterns of demand and the efficient use of their skilled workforce. For similar reasons, capacity-related inventory is used in batch, line and continuous processing.

Buffer inventory

Buffer inventory relates to the fact that average demand, by definition, varies around the average. In order to cope with situations where demand exceeds the average, businesses hold buffer inventory. The function of this inventory holding is to help cushion the manufacturing process against unpredictable variations in demand levels or supply availability. The higher the delivery on-time performance level set by a business or the lower the level of **stockout** risk it is willing to endure, the higher the size of buffer inventory it must carry.

However, note that inventory exceeding buffer levels falls into the category of corporate inventory known as 'safety stock'.

You will see by looking back at Figure 9.6 that all process types other than jobbing will typically use buffer inventory for these reasons. On the other hand, jobbing, with its MTO position, will order materials as required and linked to the start date of a job.

Operations inventory in service delivery systems

Now let's review the use of inventory in service delivery systems. As the roles and rationale are the same in service delivery systems as in manufacturing processes, this part of the discussion will not be repeated. So first let's clarify what constitutes inventory in a service company. A delivery system can involve the processing of:

- Customers
- Customer surrogates (a car being serviced is a surrogate for the customer)
- Information
- Materials that go into the product element of the service/product offering.

Although inventory in the form of customers, customer surrogates or information does not have a direct cost or investment dimension, it will impact the ability of operations to meet certain order-winners or qualifiers, such as delivery speed and delivery reliability. The sections that follow illustrate how the five functions of operations inventory form part of the service delivery systems of different organizations – see Figure 9.7.

Figure 9.7 **Inventory functions in relation to different service delivery systems**

Inventory function	Type of service delivery system		
	Non-repeat	Single-step repeat	Multi-step repeat
Decoupling			✓✓✓
Cycle		✓✓	✓✓✓
Pipeline	✓✓		✓✓
Capacity-related		✓✓	✓✓
Buffer	✓	✓	✓✓

Decoupling inventory

Decoupling inventory in a service delivery system allows steps in the system to work independently of one another and thereby facilitates the efficient use of resources (staff or equipment). For these reasons, decoupling inventory is typically found in multi-step delivery systems where information or customers wait for the next step in the system to be available. Thus, a patient in a hospital typically waits at each step in the delivery system (for example, for a hospital consultant or X-ray facility) before being processed at that step. Similarly, in a garage handling bodywork repairs, cars will often have to wait for the next stage (for example, one of the spray booths) to become available.

Cycle inventory

Cycle inventory relates to a decision to hold back information or customers and then process a large quantity or number at the one time. In most delivery systems, information and customers are processed singly, but there are examples where an organization clusters two or more together before starting the next step. Examples of cycle inventory being used include back-office processing such as cheque clearance and the preparation of personal or business bank statements, and customer clustering during a conducted tour of a museum or art gallery, where some customers wait until the group is sufficiently large for that stage in the system to begin.

Pipeline inventory

Pipeline inventory within services is used to provide the same role as in manufacturing. Examples of pipeline inventory in service delivery systems include a dentist subcontracting the manufacture of a crown for a patient's tooth and a doctor having blood samples analysed off site. In both instances, the completion of the service for a customer is put on hold while the subcontracted dimension of the total service is finished.

Capacity-related inventory

An example of capacity-related inventory is where a city centre sandwich bar prepares the fillings and garnish for its products (or the finished items themselves) in the hours before its peak demand periods (say) around lunch time. Fast-food outlets and restaurants do the same, using work-in-process (part-finished) and finished goods inventory to transfer staff capacity in low demand periods to be sold in high demand periods. In addition, by changing a service delivery system from one based on **make-to-order** (MTO) to one based on **assemble-to-order** (ATO) or **make-to-stock** (MTS), service delivery system lead-times are reduced.

Buffer inventory

Where products are involved and demand is uncertain, companies may decide to use buffer inventory by increasing the inventory levels of some items to avoid being out of stock should demand substantially exceed forecasts.

Models and approaches for managing inventory

This section first covers some of the broader approaches to managing inventory. Once these have been explained, the key decisions relating to inventory (what to order, how much, and when to order it) are then discussed in detail.

Background issues and approaches

The independent/dependent demand principle

The starting point for the management and control of inventory is customer demand. Companies translate their forecasts of demand or actual orders received into statements of operations requirements, such as the capacity and materials needed. In completing this task, companies use the principle of dependent/independent demand.

> **KEY IDEA**
> Dependent demand items are the components or materials used to provide a service or make a product. They are, therefore, dependent on the number of services or products provided. Consequently, the quantity required can be calculated

- *Dependent demand items* These are the components or materials used in a process to provide a service or make a product. They are, therefore, dependent on the number of final services or final products sold. Hence, an automobile company will need four wheel rims and five tyres for each vehicle it makes, and the total quantity of these and other parts directly relates to the number of automobiles made. The wheel rims, tyres and other components and materials can be calculated based on the number of vehicles to be made and are said to be dependent demand items. Similarly, a fast-food restaurant will calculate the number of fillings, buns, frozen French fries and other items based on its sales forecast for each type of meal on the menu.

- *Independent demand items* These are, on the other hand, the final services provided or products made. They are independent because they are not linked to the demand pattern of other items. Thus, the demand for automobiles and meals is classed as having an independent pattern of demand. The choice of inventory management

'Many profitable companies go **bankrupt** because they run out of **cash**'

system reflects whether an item has a dependent or independent pattern of demand, as will be explained later. The key difference here is that with independent demand items, the number of services or products is either known (that is, orders have already been received) or has to be forecast. With dependent demand items, the number can be calculated.

> **KEY IDEA**

Final services or products sold have an independent pattern of demand in that they are not linked to any other service or product. Here the number of items required is either known (they have already been ordered) or has to be forecast

Pareto analysis[1]

The size and importance of items will vary, and the relationship between the relative value or importance of a range of items will typically reflect what is known as the **80/20 rule** or the Pareto principle. A review of inventory will typically show support for this principle. The 80/20 rule states that 80 per cent of the inventory value will be accounted for by 20 per cent of the items in stock.[2] Given this relationship, most of the effort in managing inventory should be concentrated in the areas of high value. In that way, the number of items to manage is reduced, but most of the inventory value is under control.

> **KEY IDEA**

The Pareto principle (or 80/20 rule) highlights the fact that 20 per cent of items typically account for 80 per cent of the total value of inventory. Concentrating time and resources on these items is a key factor in managing inventory

Where to direct effort is derived from a Pareto analysis based on the **annual requirement value** (ARV) of each item. To calculate this for each item of inventory, two facts are needed: unit value and annual usage. The product of these two figures is known as the ARV.

The inventory items are now placed in order, that with the largest ARV first, then the next largest, and so on. Figure 9.8 so lists a representative sample of 30 items. Such a list is typical of many organizations. Because of the wide range of ARVs, it does not make sense to spread the inventory control effort equally over each part. Pareto's 'vital few' and 'trivial many' idea, or the 80/20 rule, applies here, as illustrated by Figure 9.9. The summary in Figure 9.9 shows that 74 per cent of the total ARV is accounted for by as little as 23 per cent of the total items held in inventory.

This approach to inventory control can then be further extended into an ABC analysis. Here, the high-ARV items are classed as A items, the middle range as B items and the low-ARVs as C items (Figure 9.10). Once this has been determined (bearing in mind that the ARV for an item may change over time and so, therefore, will its classification), the approach used to control items in each of these categories will differ to reflect the varying levels of inventory value.

It stands to reason that A items should be checked and controlled, and requirements calculated, in order to keep inventory levels in line with forecast usage. It is worth the administrative and management costs involved. C items, on the other hand, will be managed with less control and effort, as explained later in the chapter. B items fall in the middle ground, and the level of control and attention to be assigned needs to be considered individually for each item in this category.

Economic order quantity and economic batch quantity/economic lot size

One of the fundamental decisions in inventory management concerns how much to order in terms of securing the lowest total cost. The order quantity decision, therefore,

Figure 9.8 A representative sample of inventory items in order of decreasing annual requirement value

Part number	Unit value (£)	Annual usage (units)	Annual requirement value (£) Actual	Annual requirement value (£) Cumulative
303-07	58.50	6,000	351,000	351,000
650-27	2.46	80,000	196,800	547,800
541-21	210.00	500	105,000	652,800
260-81	164.11	450	73,850	726,650
712-22	2.39	25,000	59,750	786,400
054-09	5.86	10,000	58,600	845,000
097-54	136.36	300	40,908	885,908
440-18	17.30	2,000	34,600	920,508
440-01	337.35	100	33,735	954,243
308-31	136.20	200	27,240	981,483
016-01	12.89	2,000	25,780	1,007,263
305-04	45.30	475	21,518	1,028,781
155-29	38.02	500	19,010	1,047,791
542-93	62.91	300	18,873	1,066,664
582-34	32.08	500	16,040	1,082,704
323-34	71.30	200	14,260	1,096,964
412-27	23.01	600	13,806	1,110,770
540-80	24.76	500	12,380	1,123,150
137-29	12.31	1,000	12,310	1,135,460
401-53	30.64	400	12,256	1,147,716
418-51	168.86	65	10,976	1,158,692
418-50	168.80	65	10,972	1,169,664
390-02	17.47	500	8,735	1,178,399
037-41	24.05	200	4,810	1,183,209
402-50	22.00	600	4,400	1,187,609
900-01	41.64	100	4,164	1,191,773
543-61	15.10	200	3,020	1,194,793
900-11	46.80	50	2,340	1,197,133
003-54	11.41	200	2,282	1,199,415
691-30	0.41	5,000	2,050	1,201,465

Figure 9.9 Summary of items in Figure 9.8

	Percentage of total items	Percentage of total ARV
	23	74
	44[a]	21
	33	5[a]
Total	100	100

Note: [a] Figures have been rounded up.

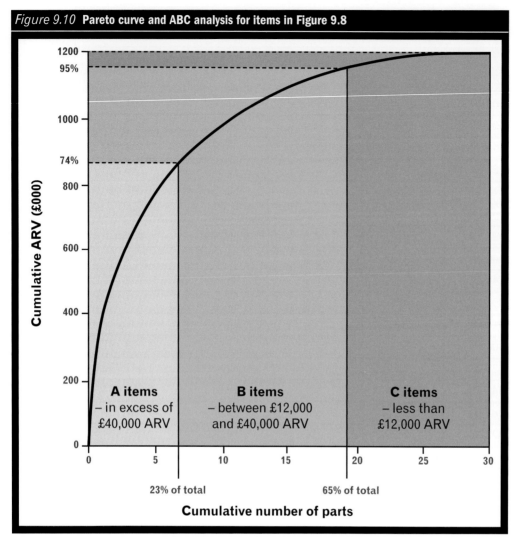

Figure 9.10 Pareto curve and ABC analysis for items in Figure 9.8

Note: ARV, annual requirement value.

needs to relate the various costs of placing an order and carrying the inventory to the value of the quantity ordered. The economic order quantity (EOQ) and economic batch quantity (EBQ)/economic lot size (ELS) models address the question of how much to order in order to minimize the total cost of holding inventory. The formula for each of these is given below:

$$EOQ = \sqrt{\frac{2zC_s}{cC}} \quad \text{for instantaneous replenishment}$$

and

$$EBQ/ELS = \sqrt{\frac{2zC_s}{cC}} \times \frac{p}{p-d} \quad \text{for replenishment at rate } p$$

where z = total annual usage, C_s = cost of placing an order, c = unit cost of the item, C = carrying cost rate per year, p = production provisioning rate (units) per day and d = demand rate (units) per day.

However, it is important to note that these models make the following simplifying assumptions:

- The rate of demand is constant.
- Costs remain fixed.
- Operations capacity and inventory holdings are unlimited.

Yet despite these assumptions, the models provide a useful guideline for ordering decisions in most operating conditions.

Determining the reorder level

A key question in any inventory system concerns when and how much to order (something we'll look at in more detail in the next section). In some situations, these decisions are made in response to another event. For example, ordering dependent items is typically linked to the decision of when and how many independent items are to be provided. The same goes for companies working on an MTO basis as explained earlier. Here, customers' orders trigger the subsequent decisions about when and how much to order.

In other situations, companies need to deal with the question, when should an order to replenish inventory be placed? Assuming that a company does not wish to run out of inventory, the level at which it must reorder is calculated by multiplying the time it takes to get an order into the company from an outside supplier (the material lead-time) by the number of units of this particular item used during the same period. So, if the material lead-time for an item is one week and the weekly usage is 100 units, the **reorder level** is $1 \times 100 = 100$ units.

But the rate of usage will vary with demand, often considerably. Furthermore, it is only where demand/usage rates are higher than average that stockouts will occur. To avoid this, it will be necessary to carry inventory to cater for the above-average demand during a lead-time. This extra quantity is called buffer inventory, as explained earlier. Hence, the reorder level calculation can now be modified as follows:

Reorder level = average usage in a material lead-time + buffer inventory

So far, we have discussed inventory levels without stating what they mean. As the example below illustrates, physical inventory levels need to be adjusted for both allocations and material on order.

Item 746B		
Actual physical inventory	152	= the actual number of items in inventory
Less allocated inventory	38	= items needed to fulfil any existing sales orders
Available inventory	114	= physical less allocated inventory
Plus material on order	100	= the quantity on any outstanding purchase orders
Total	214	= available inventory plus outstanding purchase orders

Reorder level decisions are normally based on 'available inventory' figures (114 items for 746B above), any 'material on order' quantities and their expected delivery dates, as well as the anticipated pattern of future demand for the item.

Key inventory decisions – what to stock and when to order

Once the models for managing inventory on a broader scale have been applied, key decisions can be made relating to inventory, including:

- What items to hold in stock
- How much to hold, and how much and when to order.

The answer to these questions will relate to the background issues that we've just covered, as well as other agreements with customers and suppliers and any internal decisions made within a business. One of the fundamental factors affecting the decisions to be made, systems to use and approaches to follow is the independent/dependent demand principle, which was explained earlier.

Call-off – an agreed future delivery to a customer.

Deciding which items to hold in stock

Companies will decide to complete services or make products ahead of time for a number of reasons. The known orders or scheduled **call-offs** (agreed future deliveries) required to fulfil customer contracts will often be produced or provided in advance to ensure that due dates are met. Similarly, inventory to meet future demand peaks or known seasonality patterns, and to level out operations capacity requirements over a period of time, are practical inventory responses used by companies to manage these different circumstances. The factors affecting the decision of which items to hold in stock are now discussed.

Make-to-order, assemble-to-order or make-to-stock

A major factor influencing the decision of what to hold in stock is whether a company selects an MTO, ATO or MTS response to meeting customer needs:

- *MTO* businesses are usually involved in the provision of special (that is, not to be repeated)[3] services and products. In addition, some companies decide to meet demand for standard (that is, repeat) items only on an MTO basis. Either way, an MTO response means that inventory will not be held as either part-finished or finished items. What may be held in stock, however, are the materials and components that form all or part of an item.

- *ATO* businesses are those that part-finish an item beforehand and then complete it on receipt of an order. The stage to which an item is part-completed reflects the associated value of inventory and process lead-time reduction that results. Fast-food restaurants prepare beforehand the individual items in the range (for example, French fries and different types of burger) and then assemble these to customers' requirements. Similarly, top restaurants part-prepare some food (for example, desserts and vegetables) ahead of time.

- *MTS* businesses are those that complete or purchase items ahead of demand and then meet orders from finished goods inventory. Examples include all retail outlets and manufacturers making finished goods. Others such as newspaper shops can only sell this way – if a newspaper is not available on the day, the sale is simply lost.

80/20 rule

Based on the 'vital few' and 'trivial many' phenomenon, companies typically decide as follows:

- For high-ARV items – maintain a low inventory holding (high total value) and purchase in line with demand
- For low-ARV items – maintain a high inventory holding (low total value) and purchase in bulk (lower purchasing costs but with a relatively small increase in inventory value).

Independent/dependent demand items

Decisions to hold items in stock are affected by whether or not they fall within the independent or dependent demand categories. As explained earlier, the former are end-items and are open to the choice of whether or not to hold them in stock. However, as the usage for dependent items is linked directly to the demand for independent items, there is no requirement to hold inventory for these until a decision is made to provide relevant independent items. Exceptions to this are holding inventory for dependent items for reasons such as safety (to guard against uncertainty of supply) and buffer (to reflect the variance within suppliers' delivery times), as well as EOQ benefits, purchasing discounts, reduced transaction costs, and so on. Holding dependent demand item inventory to gain lower costs or improve a company's ability to support its markets and customers makes for sound management practice.

Corporate inventory

Companies often hold inventory for non-operations reasons. Classic categories include customer agreement and corporate safety stock:

- *Customer agreement inventory* – where a company agrees with a customer to hold a given level of inventory at all times in anticipation of an order. This may also be provided as **consignment inventory** held on a customer's own premises.
- *Corporate safety stock* is held due to the uncertainty of supply, for example to guard against national or international strikes or in anticipation of a general national, regional or world shortage.

Illustrations of corporate decisions on inventory that reflect the nature of a company's business or to meet market needs are now provided. First, though, take a look at Case 9.1 and reflect on what has been covered so far.

Deciding how much inventory to hold, and how much and when to order materials

The three issues of how much inventory to hold and how much and when to order materials make up an integral set of decisions and so the factors that affect these questions are addressed here together.

Make-to-order – special services and products

Companies providing special services and products will use customer orders already received (known as order backlog or forward load) together with forecast sales profiles to estimate capacity and determine material requirements. Decisions regarding how much and when to order the necessary materials will be made depending on the size and start dates of the orders on hand. In some instances, particularly where expensive materials are involved, customers will, as part of the contract, provide materials on a 'free issue' basis (that is, a customer buys the materials and has them delivered to the supplier). Companies will often hold inventory for some non-specific materials that are in general use and replenish these as necessary, while for materials that are specific to an order, companies will typically purchase as required.

> **KEY IDEA**
> In MTO conditions, materials are purchased solely for a given order and in line with customers' delivery dates

Make-to-order or make-to-stock – standard services and products

Companies providing standard services and products can do so using either an MTO or MTS approach. Using MTO as the basis for scheduling means that companies provide services and products only in line with actual customer orders or contract call-offs. This means that the timing and quantity of materials required are known and built into the scheduling procedure.

Companies choosing to provide services and products on an MTS basis convert sales forecasts of demand into statements of operations requirements. These are then, in turn, converted into schedules and material call-offs.

> **KEY IDEA**
> In MTS conditions, items are made in line with sales forecasts

CASE 9.1 APPROACHES TO MANAGING INVENTORY

HOLDING INVENTORY IN RETAIL OUTLETS

Retail outlets need to hold inventory in order to sell products and display the extent and nature of a range of goods. Where the purchase price is low or a lack of inventory will lead to a lost sale (for example, a newsagent or food store), the policy will be to hold inventory in line with forecast sales and to reflect demand fluctuations. Where the items are of high value (for example, a suite of furniture or a range of china dinner services or cut-glass wine glasses), examples of the range (typically those which sell the most), supported by fabric choices in the case of furniture, or catalogues and the like in terms of dinner services and wine glasses, will be the basis for which items are held in inventory.

BALANCING INVENTORY APPROACHES

A company selling a range of household items used two approaches to holding inventory of its products. Products classed as Category 1 were made in anticipation of sales and on a make-to-stock basis. Orders for products classed as Category 2 were allowed to go into arrears, and then a quantity of a product was made that covered:

(a) Outstanding sales orders
(b) Sales orders received during the process time to make the order quantity
(c) Inventory to cover a given number of weeks of future sales.

When that quantity had been made, outstanding orders in (a) and (b) were met. Future sales were then met from the finished goods inventory that remained. Eventually, the company would again go into an outstanding order position for its Category 2 products, and the procedure outlined above would be repeated.

Question

What is the role of inventory in these two illustrations?

Make-to-order versus make-to-stock

In MTO conditions, items to fulfil an order will be purchased either:

- Solely for the given order (typically high value and/or not often used)
- To meet the requirements of several orders and consequently kept in stock (typically low value and frequently used)

In MTS conditions, items are made ahead of demand in line with sales forecasts.

Approaches to managing inventory

To help manage decisions on how much inventory to hold and how much and when to order materials, companies use a number of approaches, as follows.

1 *Reorder point* Companies use the principle of reorder levels as the basis for deciding how much inventory to hold and when to reorder. This system can be used for finished items as well as for raw material and component inventory. The logic of an order point system is to trigger the reorder of a part or item every time the inventory level of that part or item falls to a predetermined level. The item illustrated in Figure 9.11 is for material sourced from an outside supplier. It shows how the timing and quantity of the reorder level need to take into account the average usage in the delivery lead-time plus the agreed buffer inventory as follows:

Delivery lead-time for an item	=	1 week
Average weekly usage delivery	=	100 units
Average usage in the delivery lead-time	=	1 × 100 = 100 units
Agreed buffer inventory	=	25 units
Reorder level	=	125 units

Note: For finished items, lead-time is the time taken to make a product (known as process lead-time). For raw materials and components, lead-time is the time taken for a supplier to deliver (known as material lead-time), while the next section explains how to calculate the level of buffer inventory.

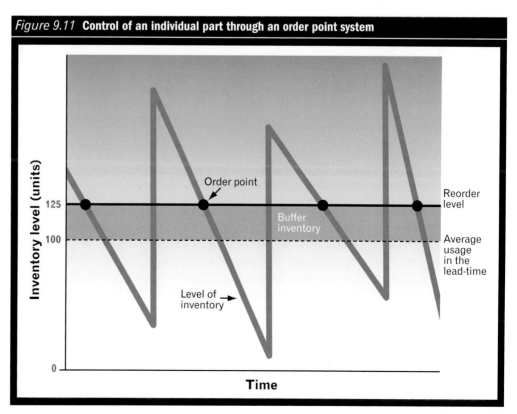

Figure 9.11 Control of an individual part through an order point system

Figure 9.11 shows the importance of recognizing that only usage patterns after the reorder level has been reached are of consequence in terms of stockouts, so the period following an order point is known as 'being at risk'. Let's explain this important point more fully. Demand patterns above a reorder point will only result in inventory falling to this level either more quickly or more slowly than average, depending upon whether actual demand is higher or lower, respectively. As far as potential stockouts are concerned, demand patterns above the reorder point are not a factor.

However, above-average demand patterns experienced after a reorder point has been reached influence whether or not stockouts occur. Above-average demand will result in a stockout if the amount of buffer inventory is insufficient to cover the level of actual demand experienced. Hence the term 'being at risk', as illustrated in Figures 9.12 and 9.13. In Figure 9.12 above-average demand is followed by a period of below-average demand, whereas in Figure 9.13 the reverse demand patterns are shown and their impact on inventory levels and stockouts is illustrated.

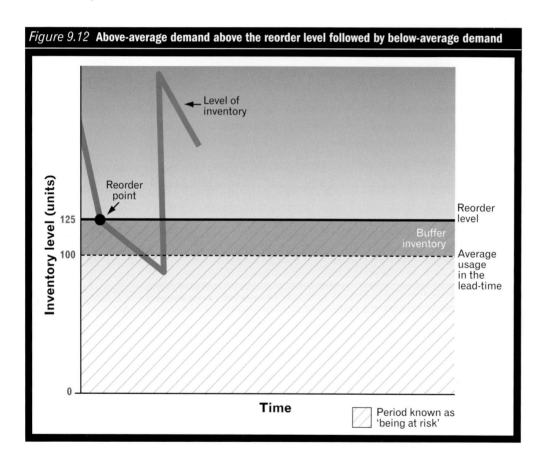

Figure 9.12 **Above-average demand above the reorder level followed by below-average demand**

2 *Buffer inventory* The function of buffer inventory is to provide a safeguard against periods of above-average demand and thereby avoid or reduce the number of stockouts. Where there is sufficient information, buffer inventories can be calculated using basic statistics. The first step is to calculate the average usage for an item and the standard deviation of usage around that average. For example, assume that an item has an average weekly usage of 100 units and that this is normally distributed with a standard deviation of 12 units. By applying normal distribution curve theory (Figure 9.14), the individual weekly usage would be within two standard deviations either side of the average for 95 per cent of the time (the mathematical explanation is not given here, but for those interested it will normally be available in any textbook on inventory control). Of the 5 per cent of the time that usage does not fall within two standard deviations, half can be expected to be less than average and half to be more than average. Now, an organization is concerned only

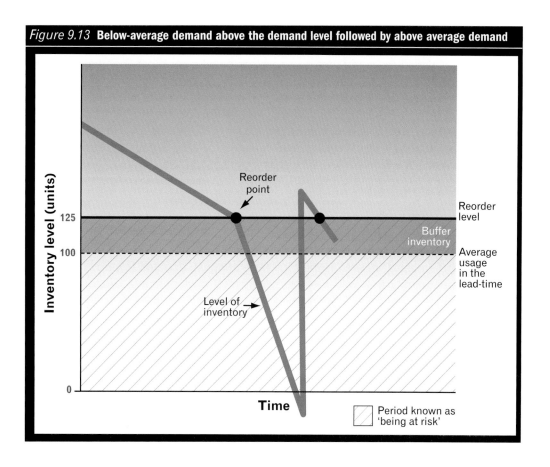

Figure 9.13 Below-average demand above the demand level followed by above average demand

with instances where usage is above average, and therefore it can expect that only for 2.5 per cent of the time will usage exceed the average plus two standard deviations, that is, 100 + 2(12) = 124. In this situation, if the reorder level were set at 124, a stockout would not be expected more than 2.5 per cent of the time, or once in 40 occasions.

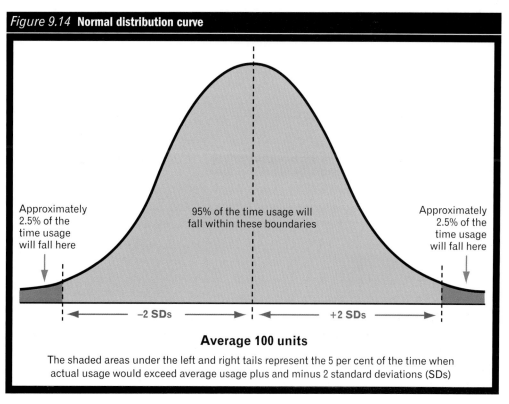

Figure 9.14 Normal distribution curve

Approximately 2.5% of the time usage will fall here

95% of the time usage will fall within these boundaries

Approximately 2.5% of the time usage will fall here

–2 SDs   +2 SDs

Average 100 units

The shaded areas under the left and right tails represent the 5 per cent of the time when actual usage would exceed average usage plus and minus 2 standard deviations (SDs)

Calculating buffer inventory in this way, however, normally applies only to A and possibly some B items (see Figure 9.10). In these instances, the high ARV and resulting impact on inventory levels would make the time and cost worthwhile. For other B and all C items, buffer inventory levels will be determined using much cruder methods.

3 *Service levels* A further measure that may be used to gauge the level of customer support are service levels. The level of service that an organization wishes to maintain can be established, and the level of buffer inventory needed to yield acceptable service levels can be calculated. One commonly used way of expressing service levels is given below:

$$\text{Service level (percentage)} = \frac{\text{\# Customers served without delay}}{\text{Total orders received}} \times 100$$

4 *Economic order and economic batch quantities* The EOQ and EBQ or ELS models were explained earlier. They are, as their full titles suggest, directed towards helping to determine the quantity that will give the lowest total cost outcome. Although these models are built on a number of simplified assumptions, they are useful in providing guidelines on how much to order or provide.

Some companies use different criteria for arriving at the order quantity to be processed. For example, a company making high-specification reproduction furniture restricted its order quantity to that equating to no more than two days of work for their staff. For this company, limiting the amount of time spent working on the same piece of furniture helped to ensure that conformance to the very high specification demands of its product range would best be met by varying the task and maintaining job interest for its skilled staff.

5 *Consignment stock* As explained earlier, consignment stock describes inventory held at a customer's premises that is not paid for until it is used. Suppliers typically retain the responsibility for checking inventory levels and replenishing stock as needed. In these instances, how much to hold on a customer's site and when to replenish are based on actual usage and agreed minimum stock levels.

6 *Corporate inventory* The level of inventory for items can also be directly influenced by corporate decisions on a range of issues. As mentioned earlier, these are classified as corporate inventory that comprises many categories such as 'customer agreement' and 'safety' inventory that have already been explained. Other illustrations of corporate inventory include purchase-discount inventory (that held at above-normal levels to acquire the price discounts on offer) and marketing inventory (that held at above-normal levels to support a marketing initiative, for example, promotions).

Inventory control systems and analysis

The models and approaches described so far to help control inventory have simplified the size of the problem. Coping with thousands of stock items, supplied by many different suppliers and supporting the needs of numerous customers, results in a complex and dynamic operations task. To cope with this level of complexity, operations managers need to engage in several basic tasks:

- Recognize that the level of control to be provided reflects the ARV of an item
- Select and develop an inventory control system in line with other existing systems (for example, operations scheduling) and the nature of the item itself (for example, dependent versus independent items)
- Undertake checks on current inventory levels to verify the system, test how well it is working and identify changes in working practices, customer demands and other busi-

ness issues, and how they affect inventory. Regular stocktaking is an integral part of managing inventory and helps to check on the current position.

Inventory control systems

Companies use a variety of systems to help manage and control inventory. Which to use will reflect the nature of their business and take into account several background issues, as discussed earlier and listed below:

- *Operations scheduling systems* are linked to the control of inventory. The task of inventory control is an integral element of the material schedules that form part of the operations control system. High-volume, MTS or MTO businesses (for example, motor vehicles) typically use just-in-time systems that dictate material call-offs and help to control and maintain low levels of inventory. Where companies adopt an MTO policy for scheduling standard services and products, actual customer orders and call-offs will trigger the operations schedule that, in turn, activates the demand for materials.

- *Dependent demand items* are, by and large, calculated in line with requirements for independent demand items, as described earlier. In addition, for low value ARV items simple systems would be used and managed on the principle of ensuring no stockouts.

- *The 80/20 rule* should determine the level of control that companies provide. The selection of appropriate systems for low-ARV items is concerned with keeping the management and control costs low while ensuring that stockouts are avoided (as highlighted in the last point). Calculating and ordering small quantities of these items would not make sense. For high-ARV items, the reverse is true.

Corporate inventory control

In most companies, some 20–25 per cent of inventory is held for corporate rather than operations reasons. Several categories of these have been given earlier. Companies will need to assess the investment in terms of its (monetary) value and return (what advantages and functions the inventory provides). Each category will need to be assessed item by item (see the later section on 'Causal analysis').

Operations inventory control

> **Continuous review system (Q system)** – when inventory is monitored after each transaction and a predetermined quantity is reordered when inventory falls to a given level

Operations inventory typically accounts for 75–80 per cent of the total. This inventory exists for operations reasons and provides a number of the functions described earlier. The systems used to control operations inventory are now discussed. Several of the aspects and issues introduced earlier in the chapter are included, which enables us to refer to them without going into detail.

Continuous review systems

In a **continuous review system** (or Q system for short), the inventory level is monitored after each transaction (that is, continuously). When the inventory drops to a predetermined level (or reorder point), a fixed quantity is placed on order. Since the order quantity is fixed, the time between orders will vary in line with the pattern of demand. Figure 9.11 earlier provided an example of this principle and showed the following characteristics:

- A fixed quantity (that incorporates the EOQ principle) is purchased.
- The material lead-time (the time between an order being placed and its delivery) is deemed to be the same.
- The gap between purchase orders will vary in line with the different patterns of demand.

Expensive items are best managed using this approach as it helps to keep the value of inventory to a minimum. The increase in costs associated with these systems and the management of higher ARV items is justified by the greater control provided and the associated lower inventory levels that result.

Periodic review systems

While the virtue of the continuous review system is that it can make use of EOQs, monitoring and checking inventory levels continuously (even when using computer-based systems) is time-consuming and expensive. An alternative and similar approach is the **periodic review system**, also known as the 'fixed order period system' (or P system for short). In a periodic review system, the stock position is reviewed at fixed intervals and a reorder quantity is then placed that constitutes the difference between the actual level and the target level of the inventory. The target level is set to cover demand until the next periodic review plus the delivery lead-time. As usage varies, so the amount ordered will vary, and hence one disadvantage of this system is that the EOQ principle cannot always be used.

Inexpensive items not maintained on inventory records should use a P system. Low-value items such as fasteners (for example, nuts, washers and bolts) could be stocked in bins and periodically checked and replenished to a given target quantity. No records of use or receipts of inventory would be made, in keeping with the low-cost management needs of such items.

> **Periodic review system**, also known as 'fixed order period system' (or P system) – here the inventory position is reviewed at fixed intervals and the reorder quantity that is then placed constitutes the difference between the actual level and the target level of inventory

Supplementary systems and approaches

In addition to the systems described above, companies use a number of supplementary systems and approaches to manage different inventory requirements. Two of the more common requirements are now explained:

1 *Managing low-ARV items* The costs involved in managing and controlling inventory can be high. For low-ARV independent and dependent items, we need systems that ensure there are no stockouts but are not costly to maintain. Two of the more commonly used systems that provided this low-cost requirement are now described:
   - *Single-bin systems* involve periodically filling up a shelf, bin or tank. Examples are shelves in retail outlets, and bins holding commonly used nuts and washers in repair shops. These are examples of P systems. Individual records of receipts and usage are normally not made. Control is provided by checking expected usage levels over a period compared with the level of purchases made during this time.
   - *Two-bin systems* comprise inventory held in two bins. The one in current use is open and the second is sealed. When the first container is empty, the second is opened and this act triggers a replacement order. This is a Q system, with the quantity in the second container being equal to the reorder level. As with single-bin systems, records of individual transactions are not kept, with control provided by periodic checks similar to those described for single-bin systems.

2 *Seasonal demand* Demand patterns for many businesses have a seasonal element. Some companies alter capacity to meet these changing requirements, as explained in Chapter 7. Where companies can make products in one period to sell in the next, meeting seasonal demand by using capacity-related inventory is an alternative to changing capacity levels. While the downside of using inventory is the investment and cost involved, advantages include maintaining a stable and experienced workforce, reducing the costs of training and avoiding the lower productivity levels associated with temporary staff.

Inventory analysis

Inventory is an integral part of business activity. It is an asset that helps companies in the provision and sale of services and goods. Recognizing that an organization needs inventory and that this investment is costly, the more pertinent question concerns 'Is the amount of inventory that the company is currently holding of inventory necessary?'

To evaluate how well their control systems are working, companies need also to analyse inventory as part of this review process. In most businesses, the recording and valuation of inventory leads to statements that separate the total inventory into the categories of raw materials and components, work-in-progress and finished goods. Typically, this is done once or twice a year, in line with the need for the accounting function to prepare a profit and loss account and balance sheet. But although this analysis meets these requirements, it does not provide enough useful information to help in the task of managing inventory. The insights on inventory provided by categorizing it as raw materials/components, work-in-progress and finished goods relate to the state and position of material within the system. In other words, material has not been processed (raw materials and components), the processing of material is now complete (finished goods) or the material is somewhere between these two positions (work-in-progress). While this is adequate as a basis for assessing the value of inventory, it fails to provide the key insight to help manage and assess inventory levels, that is, why is it there in the first place? To provide this key insight, a review of inventory is necessary to determine why it is there, or what caused the inventory.

> **KEY IDEA**

Causal analysis asks the question, why is the inventory there? These insights allow any necessary changes to be made so stopping inventory at source

Causal analysis

It is not necessary to undertake this task at the same time for all the inventory held as parts can be reviewed at different times. The first step is to select a portion of the inventory holding for review and then ask the question, why is it there? The answers are then categorized into:

- One of the many categories of corporate inventory that exist
- One of the five functions of operations inventory explained earlier.

At the same time, the position and value of the inventory in the operations process is recorded. 'Position' here identifies the stage through which the inventory was last processed and the stage it is waiting to enter. Where inventory is recognized as providing more than one category or function, the value of the holding is split equally between the categories or functions provided and recorded as separate entries.

In this way, a picture of inventory is developed that shows clusters of inventory by category or function and stage in the operations process. Large clusters are then checked to see why they exist. This allows the rules and procedures involved to be reviewed and modified where it is considered that such changes would still meet the relevant corporate or operations needs but would reduce the amount of inventory involved. This approach is based on a recognition that changing the rules that allow inventory to be made will reduce the level of inventory entering the system, thereby lowering inventory holdings.

Let us consider the examples in Case 9.2, one involving corporate and the other operations inventory.

REDUCING THE LEVEL OF CUSTOMER SUPPORT INVENTORY

Corporate inventory – support inventory for a customer was agreed and to be held at the equivalent of three weeks-worth of sales. On reviewing the current position, it was found that weekly sales of this item to the customer had reduced but the inventory holding had not been recalculated to reflect this lower sales position. As a result, the inventory holding at the time of the analysis was much higher than the equivalent of three weeks of sales. Discussions with the customer also included revising the agreement. The overall result was that the level of customer support inventory was reduced to one week of sales at current levels.

REDUCING THE LEVEL OF OPERATIONS INVENTORY

Operations inventory – a review of inventory highlighted a large cluster of work-in-progress inventory waiting to enter a given process. The resulting analysis led to the purchase of additional equipment, as it was found that there was currently insufficient capacity at this stage. The alternatives to handling this bottleneck were considered, but as the process investment costs were low, it was decided that purchasing additional equipment was the most effective solution. Once the additional capacity was in place, associated inventory levels were systematically reduced.

Question

How did causal analysis help the companies in these two examples?

Lecturers: visit www.palgrave.com/business/ hillessential for additional resources

Critical reflections

Inventory is a significant asset in most organizations, and its effective management is a key task within operations. But controlling inventory is far from easy and represents a challenging task. It involves a complex set of decisions due to the many forms that inventory takes and the many functions it provides. In addition, inventories are the result of functional policies within an organization as well as the short- and long-term decisions taken by the purchasing, operations and sales functions. There is, therefore, a need for the decisions on how much inventory to hold to be taken at the highest level, as well as the appropriate control systems and procedures to be used lower down in an organization. The all-embracing and interrelated nature of this investment necessitates that all concerned share its provision and control.

The challenging task facing operations is to ensure that the amount of inventory held is sufficient to provide the many benefits and functions that come with holding inventory while ensuring that no more than necessary is held in order to minimize the level of investment involved. Accomplishing this needs sound and appropriate systems supplemented by analysis. While businesses typically have inventory systems in place, the information necessary to help control and keep inventory to a minimum is often limited. Evaluating inventory as raw materials/components, work-in-progress and finished goods, although necessary to prepare profit and loss accounts and balance sheets, is of little help in checking and controlling inventory levels for the following reasons:

- They are a record (reflecting a stage in the process) and not a control.
- The information fails to address the questions of why the inventory is there and how much is necessary.

Causal analysis supplements inventory systems as it provides answers to these questions and so enables a business to keep inventory low while retaining the benefits and functions that inventory provides and that are so essential to the business overall. Finally, inventory is an integral part of a business. As such, it reflects the dynamics that characterize the organization. It facilitates meeting customers' needs, oils the wheels of the organization, is the outcome of corporate and functional decisions, is sizeable and is subject to change over short time frames. As a result, managing inventory is a complex but key task. The maxim that prevention is better than cure fits well here but relates as much to meeting market requirements as to keeping levels in check. As such, it needs to be well managed throughout an organization.

Summary

- Inventory is not only sizeable in asset terms, but is also complex to manage and control.

- Companies wish to keep the investment in inventory as low as possible. Nevertheless, inventory is an integral part of a company's activities and central to the workings of its processes and delivery systems, so it must be efficiently managed and controlled within the context of the overall business and market requirements.

- One overriding principle is that of distinguishing between independent and dependent demand items. As usage rates of the latter are linked to the levels of demand of the former, requirements for dependent demand items can be calculated and scheduled in line with demand for the independent items to which they relate.

- The principle of calculating requirements for dependent demand items is central to managing and controlling this type of inventory. However, it may make more sense for a company to hold inventory of some of these dependent demand items at a level that is not tied to a calculated rate of requirement. Reasons for severing this link are to do with issues of overall cost. For items that have a low unit cost (for example, C items), buying in quantities that exceed demand patterns may lower the total unit cost (price per unit plus related inventory costs). Buying or making in large quantities will almost always lower the actual cost per unit, and such items lend themselves to the use of systems such as two-bin type controls that are simple to operate and inexpensive to manage.

- The approaches to managing and controlling independent items need to reflect the several issues and dimensions that were introduced and discussed throughout the chapter. Foremost will be the choice of whether to provide services or make products on an MTO, ATO or MTS basis.

- In MTO businesses, material and work-in-progress inventory will reflect the delivery dates of customer orders for the services and products provided. When they are finished, items will go straight to customers.

- Where items are part-made and then assembled or finished in line with customer orders and where items are MTS, what and how much is made and when and how much to order need to take into account issues such as the 80/20 rule, corporate inventory commitments, the reorder point, buffer inventory requirements and EOQs.

- The key throughout is fitting the decisions to the characteristics and requirements of an organization. Knowing the alternatives that can be used and incorporating relevant dimensions into the decision-making process should always form the basis of the management and control outcomes.

Study activities

Discussion questions

1 What types of material inventory would you find in the following businesses? Give an example of each:

- A retail pharmacist

- A petrol station

- A coffee bar

- A stone and gravel extraction company.

2 Illustrate the difference between independent and dependent demand with two examples from a pizza restaurant.

3 List the 10 most valuable items you own, with an estimated unit value for each (if you own more than one of an item, multiply the unit value by the total number of items you own and use the total for this exercise). Now undertake a Pareto analysis.

Assignments

1 What difficulties are, in general, forced on service organizations as a result of their inability to inventory their capacity? How do organizations attempt to manage these difficulties? Illustrate your answer using the following businesses:

- A sandwich bar

- A passenger airline

- A bank

- A call centre.

Following your analysis, compare and contrast the approaches you identified.

2 Textet Computing sells software via the Internet. With each purchase, the company includes a computer manual, and it is currently rethinking whether it should outsource the preparation of these manuals or continue to make them in-house. Below are the cost estimates for the options:

Outsourced   – total cost of £0.50 per manual
Make in-house   – variable cost per manual £0.30
                    – annual fixed costs of £7,500.00

(a) Which alternative has the lower total cost if annual demand is 30,000 copies?

(b) At what annual volume do these alternatives have the same cost?

(c) Textet Computing estimates that its sales of software next year will increase to 55,000 units. The outside supplier will drop the price per manual to £0.43 for these volumes. At what quantity of manuals are the cost of making in-house and the cost of outsourcing equal at £0.43?

Exploring further

Journal articles

Abernathy, F.H., Dunlop, J.T., Hammond, J.H. and Weil, D. (2000) 'Control your inventory in a world of lean retailing'. *Harvard Business Review*, **78**(6), pp. 169–76. Despite ever more demanding retailers and rampant product proliferation, manufacturers have stayed with dangerously indiscriminate production schedules and sourcing strategies. Manufacturers tend to treat every stock-keeping unit (SKU) within a product line in the same way. The article argues that, by differentiating SKUs according to their actual demand patterns, inventories on some can be reduced and on others increased, thereby improving overall profitability. An SKU-level analysis shows the true risks and returns associated with each item, and helps manage them accordingly.

Arnold, D. (2000) 'Seven rules of international distribution'. *Harvard Business Review*, **78**(6), pp. 131–37. Companies entering markets in developing countries quickly learn that they need to work with local distributors. Some guidelines are provided to help multi-nationals anticipate and correct potential problems in these arrangements.

Chopra, S. and Lariviere, M.A. (2005) 'Managing service inventory to improve performance'. *MIT Sloan Management Review*, **47**(1), pp. 56–63. This article shows how service inventories allow firms to buffer their resources from the variability of demand and reap benefits from economies of scale while benefiting customers. Using examples from the travel, hospitality and insurance industries, the authors discuss how service firms can use inventory as a strategic lever in designing and managing service offerings.

Books

Donath, R., Mazel, J. and Dublin, C. (2002) *The Ioma Handbook of Logistics and Inventory*. Chichester: John Wiley & Sons. This book provides practical insight when planning logistics strategies (from selecting carriers to streamlining shipping) as ways to reduce inventories and logistics costs.

Hill, A. and Hill, T. (2009) *Manufacturing Operations Strategy: Text and Cases*, 3rd edn. Basingstoke: Palgrave Macmillan. The text provides a useful supplement to the current book by outlining an in-depth approach for developing and implementing operations strategy within manufacturing organizations.

Hill, T. (2005) *Operations Management: Text and Cases*. Basingstoke: Palgrave Macmillan. This provides a useful supplement to this book by offering a more comprehensive explanation and further examples (including long case studies) showing how service and manufacturing companies have applied these concepts.

Wild, T. (2002) *Best Practices in Inventory Management,* 2nd edn. Oxford: Elsevier Science. This text offers a useful overview of the basis and reasons for inventory and practical approaches to successfully reducing inventory while meeting customer requirements.

Notes and references

1 In 1906, Vilfredo Pareto observed that a few items in any group contribute the significant proportion of the entire group. At the time, he was concerned that a few people in a country earned most of the income. The law of the significant few can be applied in many areas, including inventory. See Pareto, V. (1969) *Manual of Political Economy*. Fairfield, NJ: Augustus M. Kelley.

2 The 80/20 relationship implied in the rule is only intended as an indication of the size of the actual figures involved, as shown in Figures 9.8 and 9.9.

3 Special services and products are ones that will not be repeated or ones for which the time gap between one order and the next is so long that investments (including inventory holding) will not be made.

In January 2007, Michael Dell was reinstated as CEO of Dell. The company he had lovingly built was in trouble, and its shareholders were getting nervous. Market share had fallen, particularly to Hewlett-Packard (HP), now the world's largest PC manufacturer. Some analysts felt that Dell's 'direct' business model no longer gave it a competitive edge, and that its lack of focus on product innovation and customer experience was causing it to lose sales. Demand for desktop PCs was falling as notebooks and mobile devices became more popular. As product innovation grew, life cycles shortened and choice widened. As a result customers increasingly wanted to talk to someone about a product's features before buying it, and many critics argued that Dell's current business model did not allow for that.

THE EVOLUTION OF DELL

In 1983, Michael Dell was studying at the University of Texas and selling cost-effective computers by buying components, assembling them and selling them directly to customers. Three years later, he was running a company with $34 million annual sales, 100 employees and a 3,000 square foot facility. To meet the growing demand, he established retail agreements with CompUSA, Staples, BestBuy, Costco, Business Depot and PC World to serve small businesses and individual consumers. This was working well, but in 1994 inaccurate sales forecasts left the business with high inventories and it lost $36 million. To avoid such a situation reoccuring, Dell exited the retail market and went back to selling products direct to customers.

Eliminating middlemen and distributors allowed Dell to better understand customer needs and then it passed this understanding onto its suppliers. As a result, it reduced component inventory from 70 to 20 days and average delivery lead-time from 45 to 10 days. Finished goods inventory was eliminated as products were now assembled to order within five days after receipt of an order. The cash released by the inventory reduction was invested in higher specification products to compete with Compaq and IBM. To help to sell products directly to customers, Dell launched its website (www.dell.com) in 1998, and by 2000 over half its sales were now made via the Internet. A year later, it became the largest PC manufacturer in the world, with annual sales of more than $32 billion (Figure 1). In 2004, Michael Dell stepped down as CEO to become Chairman of the Board of Directors.

DELL'S DIRECT BUSINESS MODEL

Using the 'direct' business model summarised in Figure 2, Dell continually looks for ways to reduce inventory and delivery lead-time. In 2004, its inventory turned over 107 times, compared with 8.5 times at HP and 17.5 times at IBM. This means that it does not have to discount products when they become obsolete, and that new products are introduced almost two months before those of competitors because Dell does not have existing component inventory to sell before new products can be introduced. Its direct client interface has helped link product and service innovation to customer needs, reduced distribution costs and allowed its sales force to focus on end-users rather than distributors.

Dell collaborates closely with suppliers, sharing information about inventory levels, demand expectations and long-term plans. All suppliers are required to have a warehouse called a supplier logistics centre (SLC) located within a few miles of each Dell factory. In fact, some small component suppliers actually have premises within the Dell factory next to the production line. Dell schedules its production lines every two hours, and then the SLCs supply components to meet these requirements. Suppliers have to maintain 8–10 days of inventory for each component within their SLC, and most suppliers replenish this inventory three times a week. Daily performance figures in terms of price, quality conformance, delivery speed and delivery reliability are posted on https://valuechain.dell.com to show a comparison across its different suppliers. And, based on their performance, suppliers are awarded a percentage of Dell's purchases for the next quarter.

Dell's marketing department generates 75 per cent accurate sales forecasts based on new product developments, purchasing patterns, budget cycles and seasonality trends, such as the end of a government

Figure 1
Dell business performance (1996–2009)

Business performance	1996	1998	2000	2002	2004	2006	2007	2008	2009
Size									
Market share (% units sold)	4	8	10	15	17	18	15	15	12
Sales revenues ($million)	7,759	18,243	31,888	35,262	49,121	57,420	61,133	61,101	52,902
Profitability									
Gross profit ($million)	1,666	4,106	6,443	6,438	9,018	9,516	11,671	10,957	9,261
Gross profit (% sales)	21	23	20	18	18	17	19	18	18
Inventory management									
Inventory ($million)	251	273	400	306	459	660	1,180	867	1,051
Inventory turns (sales/inventory)	31	67	80	115	107	87	52	70	50

Source: Dell, *Annual reports* (1996–2009), Dell Corporation.

Figure 2
Dell's product and service delivery system

Aspect	Description

Product selection	• The website caters for different market segments: individuals, home office computers, small businesses, medium businesses, large businesses and public sector companies
	• Customers customize their order on the website by selecting:
	  • **Features** – such as processors, display screen, memory, hard drive, video card and audio card
	  • **Accessories** – such as printers, power options, TV tuners, batteries and carrying cases
	  • **Software** – such as Microsoft Office
	  • **Services** – such as warranty, installation and Internet
	• At every step, customers are warned if shipping could be delayed due to the unavailability of components

Sales order processing	• Orders are received by telephone or by e-mail, or are downloaded from the Internet, every 15 minutes (50 per cent on average being received via the Internet) • Customer credit and order configuration is checked • Orders are then sent to the order management system, which reviews component inventory, generates material requests and sends these to the relevant suppliers
Production planning	• All products are assembled to order • Once all the components for an order are available, a bar code is printed and attached to the necessary components • Production lines in all factories around the world are rescheduled every two hours • Dell only assumes ownership of the components when they reach the assembly line • Once the production plan has been established, a message is sent to the relevant supplier logistics centre(s) telling it which components it should deliver and to which 'delivery dock' they should go • Suppliers are given 90 minutes to deliver components to the 'delivery dock', and Dell has 30 minutes to move them from there to the assembly line before the next production cycle starts • Production is planned on a first-in-first-out basis • All orders are planned to be fulfilled within five days after receiving the customer's order • All factories have flexible assembly lines that can be used for desktop PCs, notebooks or servers • Activities within a factory are rescheduled if defective units need to be replaced or if there is a large corporate order

Assembly	• Once all the components for an order are received at the delivery dock, the bar code is scanned and parts are sent on a conveyor belt to the assembly line
	• The assembly process consists of a number of steps:
	  1 The computer system is assembled by a single worker in a single location
	  2 Software is loaded onto it
	  3 Authenticity labels such as Intel and Microsoft are added
	  4 The system is cleaned and placed into a box
	  5 Inspection is completed on a random selection of 10 per cent of the systems
	  6 A separate box containing the keyboard, documentation and mouse (all supplied by one subcontractor) is added to the existing box
	  7 The order is packaged and sent to distribution

Distribution	• Using the bar code on the box, orders are sorted depending on their final destination • Products are then shipped to the relevant distribution hub before travelling on to the final customer
After-sales service	• All subsequent technical and after-sales services is handled by Dell through its call centres

Source: www.dell.com

department's financial year, the beginning of the academic year or the Christmas holiday period. Weekly meetings are held, involving sales, marketing and supply chain executives, to interpret demand trends. resolve supply issues and manage delivery lead-times to customers. For instance, if component lead-times increase, orders are expedited, additional suppliers are brought in or customers are encouraged to buy substitute products. On the other hand, within hours of a weekly meeting, the marketing team creates advertisements for computers for which abundant components are available. These adverts are then posted on the Dell and other popular websites. Similarly, if component inventory accumulates, customers are provided with incentives to buy the products using these. Pricing is changed from week to week to reflect the balance between demand and supply, and lead-times are updated on a daily basis.

COMPETITIVE PRESSURES

By 2006, Dell had been successful for a number of years and could not seem to put a foot wrong. Suddenly, however, competitive pressures then caused its market share to drop, and many analysts started to question Dell's strategy. Potential customers could be dissuaded by the fact that they cannot touch and feel products before purchasing them, and Dell's wide product range means that it does not benefit from economies of scale like its competitors do. The lack of after-sales service centres may also mean that customers decide to buy elsewhere.

NEW DIRECTION

Shortly after being reappointed as CEO in 2007, Michael Dell put in a new management team who started to consolidate the company's operations and move away from its direct-only model by opening retail stores in the US and by launching a 'PartnerDirect' programme with a number of 'value-added resellers' in the US, Europe and Asia. In these stores, customers can see products, touch them and place orders, but they still cannot take them away as no inventory is actually held there. Dell's new strategy has received a mixed response. Some analysts have expressed concerns that Dell's supply chain is not geared up for this significant change. Inventories need to be managed differently, and the company's cost advantage might be weakened. The shift from a direct to a channel-based model will inevitably not be easy, and the question is, will its new model meet the same fate as the one it used in the 1990s?

Questions

1 How does Dell manage inventory within its supply chain?

2 How has it used inventory management to drive the performance of its business?

3 How well is Dell positioned for the future?

Lecturers: visit www.palgrave.com/business/hillessential for additional resources

Managing Quality **10**

Learning objectives

After completing this chapter, you should be able to:

- Explain what quality is and why it is important

- Understand the stages involved in managing quality conformance

- Apply alternative tools and techniques to improve quality conformance

- Critically evaluate the quality conformance levels within an organization and suggest improvements

- Understand the alternative approaches to managing quality

- Propose and substantiate quality improvements within a given operational context

Chapter outline

Introduction

Defining quality and its role

Quality philosophies: the work of Deming, Juran and Crosby

The steps to effectively managing quality

- Tools and techniques

Approaches to managing quality

- Total quality management

- Quality management frameworks: ISO 9000, Baldrige Award and EFQM Excellence Award

Critical reflections

Summary

Introduction

A range of quality philosophies, approaches, tools, techniques and frameworks have been developed to help companies measure, control, manage and improve quality. This chapter examines how to do this by looking at the following aspects:

- What is quality and what is its role?
- What are the stages a business must go through to manage quality?
- What tools and techniques are available to help improve quality?
- How should businesses manage quality?
  - What management philosophy should they use?
  - What systems and procedures need to be in place?
  - Which frameworks should be used?

Defining quality and its role

Quality gaps – these occur when customers' expectations of the level of service or product quality to be delivered are not met by their perceptions of the service or product quality delivered

Quality conformance is either an order-winner or a qualifier for most customers. However, before 'quality' can be measured and improved, it first must be defined. Within operations, 'quality conformance' means consistently delivering services and products in line with their design specifications, which (as we learned in Chapter 3), in turn, reflects customer needs and expectations. Figure 10.1 shows how these different aspects interact. As indicated by the arrows in the diagram, **quality gaps** can exist between what customers want and expect, what a company sells, how services and products have been designed and what operations delivers. These gaps need to be constantly managed, a task we'll look at in more detail later in the chapter.

> **KEY IDEA**
> Quality conformance means consistently delivering services and products in line with their design specifications, which, in turn, need to reflect customer needs

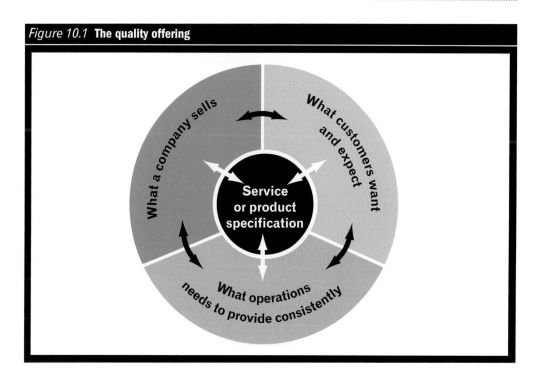

Figure 10.1 **The quality offering**

So how does quality management help organizations to attract and retain customers? One example is provided in Case 10.1, which shows the results of effective quality management in practice.

By modifying the service or product specification, companies can not only win (and secure returning) customers, but also reduce delivery costs and increase customer and staff loyalty. Case 10.2 shows two examples of how changing the quality specification of the service or product can both improve sales and help meet customer expectations, while also reducing staff turnover and eliminating costs.

As you can see from the examples in Case 10.2, effectively managing the quality of services and products, and changing the specification when necessary, is essential to maintaining customer satisfaction and securing repeat sales. But how does an organization go about selecting which characteristics make up a specification, and how are standards for quality set and met? The next sections will look at these questions in more detail, but first let's review the work of some key pioneers in the field.

Quality philosophies: the work of Deming, Juran and Crosby

The drive to improve quality in European and North American organizations stemmed from the superior levels of quality conformance achieved by Japanese and South East Asian companies from the 1960s onwards that had changed the competitive dimension of quality conformance from a qualifier into an order-winner. The figureheads of this response were provided by three principal contributors whose work is now briefly reviewed.

W Edwards Deming

Deming is widely credited with leading the Japanese quality revolution. He exposed Japanese managers to the fundamental tools and techniques they needed for this (and which are dealt with later in this chapter), such as statistical process control, with the Japanese government recognizing his contribution by creating, in 1951, the Deming Prize.

Deming summarised his views for quality management using 14 points:

1 Managers need to improve services and products by promoting a clear vision for the firm, its customers and the role of quality in that provision.
2 A philosophy should be introduced in which mistakes, inadequate training and ineffective supervision and management are unacceptable, and in which putting systems and procedures right is essential.
3 A dependence on mass inspection should be replaced with a drive to eliminate errors and defects.
4 The practice of awarding purchasing contracts on the basis of lowest price should be ended, with a move to building long-term relationships with fewer suppliers.
5 Waste should be reduced throughout a company's delivery systems and processes by never-ending quality improvements.
6 Training needs to be centred on the concept of acceptable work.
7 The job of management is not supervision but leadership.
8 People must be encouraged to ask questions, report failures and come up with solutions.
9 The barriers between functions should be broken down by developing a team-based approach throughout the organization.
10 Instead of slogans and posters exhorting improvements, management should ensure that people have the right tools and training to do the job and improve the process.
11 Quotas and targets should focus on the quality and not the quantity of output.
12 Barriers that hinder pride in one's work should be removed.

ANSTRUTHER FISH BAR

How was Ian Whyte able to sell his small fish and chip shop, housed in a modest building overlooking the harbour in Fife – a quiet Scottish fishing town – for £1.6 million? Because it attracts over 2,000 customers a day, with daily takings exceeding £10,000 and queues of up to 1.5 hours at busy times.

The Anstruther Fish Bar has managed to win customers and keep them coming back by consistently giving them what they want. The secret to perfect fish and chips is the consistency of the batter and the quality of the fish. This may seem obvious, but it's not always easy to get right. Whyte noticed that the quality of haddock varied considerably throughout the year. For example, fish caught in early spring, the spawning season, are much thinner, and haddock caught in early summer are more oily as they feed on herring and land eels at that time of year.

Ian discovered that quality could be managed by altering the batter recipe to suit the changing specification of the haddock caught throughout the year to ensure that it always only lightly coats the fish fillet and literally drops off when it is broken. Then, it must be fried consistently to create fish and chips to die for!

www.anstrutherfishbar.co.uk

Questions

1. How do the changes in the specification of the fish batter affect customer sales?

2. What do you think are the order-winners and qualifiers in this example? Give reasons for your choice.

Lecturers: visit www.palgrave.com/business/hillessential for additional resources

CASE 10.2 CHANGING THE QUALITY OFFERING

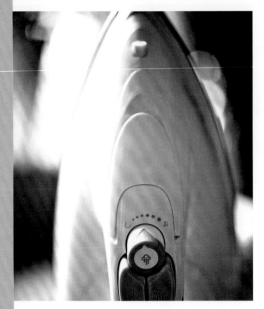

HAMPTON INNS

The US-based chain decided to offer guaranteed refunds to customers who were in any way dissatisfied with their stay. Subsequent research showed that implementing this policy persuaded people to stay and brought in additional sales revenue at a level almost 11 times that of the refunds paid out. By also empowering all staff to grant refunds, staff in the front office found that job satisfaction increased, with staff turnover falling from 117 to 50 per cent over the following three years. The refund programme also helped to identify aspects that most annoyed guests. One of the biggest issues was the lack of irons and ironing boards in their premium 'Embassy Suite' rooms. As a result, the company spent $0.5 million putting an iron and ironing board in each room and found that it saved more than this in the first year by reducing staff costs as they no longer had to move equipment between rooms.
www.hamptoninn.com

UNITED PARCEL SERVICES

United Parcel Services (UPS) had always assumed that on-time delivery was critical for its customers, and it defined 'quality' as meeting its delivery promise. For example, all 'next-day packages' had to be delivered by 10.30 am the following day. The company's operations were prioritized and measured accordingly, with elevator times and delays in customers answering their door-

bells being measured and included in schedules. Drivers even shaved the corners off their van seats to help reduce the time getting in and out of their vans! Frequent customer surveys showed they were happy with UPS's delivery performance, but UPS didn't ask customers what they actually wanted. When the company finally looked at customers' wants and expectations, it was surprised to find they wanted more contact with drivers to discuss aspects such as how best to ship their products. As a result, UPS drivers are now given 30 minutes each day to spend with customers to build relationships and bring in new sales. The programme costs UPS over $4 million in drivers' time, but the value of additional sales is many times higher. Furthermore, drivers are now also encouraged to visit customers with UPS sales staff to undertake regular customer reviews.

www.ups.com

Questions

1 Review these two cases and identify the elements of the quality offering that the companies changed or improved.

2 What benefits did these companies gain and their customers receive, and what disadvantages or costs were involved?

© Alex Hill and Terry Hill 2011

13 Continuous training will keep people up to date with new developments, design and process improvements, new tools and innovative techniques.
14 To accomplish these steps, management needs to work continuously on the other 13 points.

Deming used his 14 points to highlight the central role of managers in bringing about essential changes. He saw managers as the real obstacle to improvement, pointing out that 85 per cent of quality problems could be traced to management actions and failures. To help managers change, he advocated that they needed to address five 'deadly sins':

1 A lack of constancy of purpose
2 An emphasis on short-term results
3 The use of performance evaluation and annual reviews that reinforce short-term actions and goals
4 The practice of moving managers every two or three years, thus promoting short-term approaches to improvement and change
5 The practice of measuring corporate performance using visible, financial numbers, thus again promoting short-term actions.

Joseph M Juran

Juran defines quality as 'fitness for use'. His work on quality spanned 30 years and his approach to quality management is based on an analytical approach centring on the cost of quality where all costs needed to be allocated to one of the following four categories:

1 Internal cost of failure, including defects, rework, yield losses, reinspection and disposal
2 External costs of failure such as detection after despatch to a customer, complaints, returns, field service support and repairs
3 Appraisal costs associated with assessing services and products, including inspection, checks, quality assurance and control and the cost of test equipment
4 Prevention costs including quality planning, new service and product reviews, process control and data collection, analysis and reporting.

Of these categories, Juran highlighted the first two as they typically account for 50–80 per cent of the total costs. Juran's goal for a quality programme was to bring about a fundamental shift in which quality management became a 'quality habit'. To this end, he advocated a four-stage approach:

1 Goals – establish specific goals for an organization
2 Plans – detail ways to achieve these goals
3 Responsibilities – assign tasks for executing the plans
4 Rewards – base rewards on results.

Philip B Crosby

Crosby addresses his message to top management proposing that quality management offers a viable strategy for company survival and growth. He further stresses that the returns for investing in quality are such that, in fact, 'quality is free', so highlighting the high return on investment involved.

Crosby points to the fact that the cost of quality is as high as 15–20 per cent of sales, and puts forward a 14-point plan for improving quality:

1 Management must be clearly committed to the importance of quality.
2 Quality improvement programmes need to be supported by a multifunctional team.
3 Quality measures need to be in place.
4 The cost of quality needs to include the price of non-conformance as well as the price of conformance so as to help prioritize action.
5 Quality awareness needs to be promoted throughout the organization.

6 Improvements and ideas need to be actioned at the appropriate level of an organization.

7 The goal is to achieve a position of zero defects.

8 Education and training should form the basis of any quality programme.

9 A specific future date should be established as zero-defects day.

10 Management need to set goals.

11 Everyone is to be responsible for identifying the source of defects and errors.

12 A quality programme should receive public, non-financial recognition.

13 A quality council should be formed to help share experiences, problems and ideas.

14 To highlight the never-ending process of quality programmes, companies then need to return again to Step 1.

The steps to effectively managing quality

To manage quality, firms must first control it through a number of steps:

1 *Determining quality characteristics* The first step is to determine the characteristics that make up the service or product to be provided. These must cover all aspects of the **service package** and need to be defined in such a way that enables them to be measured and controlled, as shown in Figure 10.2 for a restaurant:

- **Explicit services** – such as the design and specification of the food and how it is served in the restaurant
- **Implicit services** – for example, the level of attention and recognition given to regular customers by restaurant staff
- Supporting structural facilities – including the quality of the table linen, plates, glasses and cutlery in a restaurant.

Figure 10.2 **Defining quality characteristics for a restaurant**

Dimension	Example quality characteristics
Explicit service	• Minimizing delays at different stages in the delivery system – for example, greeting guests, taking pre-dinner drinks orders, offering menus and taking orders for dinner in a timely manner • Food ingredients – for example, freshness by food type, and size of portions • Food preparation – including taste and texture • Food presentation such as layout on a plate, spacing and colour combinations
Implicit service	Regular guests: • Identified by name • Staff advised ahead of time • Table preferences noted and allocated
Supporting structural facilities	• Table spacings • Table layout • Glassware and cutlery checked and polished with a dry cloth

2 *Measuring quality characteristics* The characteristics that describe quality fall into the following two groups, with an example in Figure 10.3 to illustrate the varying characteristics of a teapot:

- **Variables** can be measured on a numerical scale, for example, the length of a product or the time taken to serve a customer.
- **Attributes** are measured by using the qualitative conditions of a process. These can be based on judgements or checks without detailed measurement, with a service or product simply passing or failing its requirement. For example, a **go/no-go gauge** is

Service package – the collection of individual services and products provided by an organization, including both explicit and implicit services and products

Explicit services – the primary services delivered to customers, such as the food and level of service in a restaurant

Implicit services – the secondary services delivered to customers, such as the atmosphere within a restaurant and customer attention throughout

Variables – quantitative service or product characteristics that can be measured on a numerical scale, such as the length of a product or the time taken to serve a customer

Attributes – qualitative characteristics of a service or product that are measured by judging a service or product against the level required

Go/no-go gauge – a device that can be used to judge whether a service or product characteristic meets or does not meet its qualitative requirement

an inspection tool that indicates whether the specification has been met without taking an exact measurement.

Figure 10.3 **Teapot quality characteristics**		
Characteristics	**Variables**	**Attributes**
Dimensions Shape Durability	● ● ●	
Surface appearance Design/styling Performance as a teapot Ease of use Value for money Packaging		● ● ● ● ● ●

3 *Setting quality levels* – defining the level of quality for each characteristic that sets the boundary between acceptable and unacceptable. For example, a retail outlet might decide that customer queues should for 95 per cent of the time be no longer than three minutes, which would then become the quality standard for this service package.

4 *Deciding how to monitor quality levels* – once quality levels have been set, a company must decide how to measure conformance across the service system or process in order to ensure consistency in delivering quality. To monitor quality conformance effectively, two decisions must be made:
  • Where in the process to check that services or products meet the agreed level of quality – checks can be made at various points within the delivery system, as shown in Figure 10.4
  • How many services or products should be checked to guarantee that the quality level is met – this is a key decision as checking everything is expensive and increases operations lead-times.

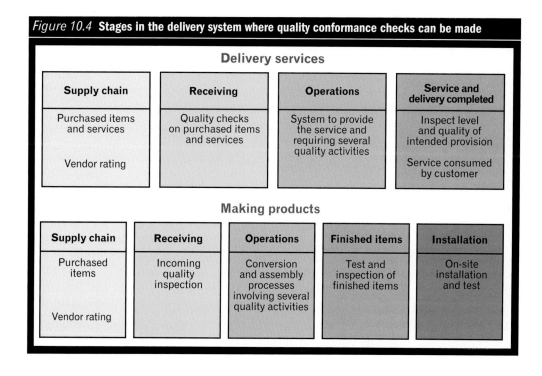

Figure 10.4 **Stages in the delivery system where quality conformance checks can be made**

Once the level of quality conformance is consistent and under control, it can then be improved in the following ways:

5 *Correcting and improving quality* By recording instances of below-standard quality conformance and identifying their causes, the more common reasons for **quality failure** can be identified and corrected. Once quality problems have been identified, companies need to react quickly so as to maintain market share and consumer confidence. Case 10.3 provides details of two such responses by companies to the contamination of their products.

6 *Continue to make improvements* Once an organization has eliminated the quality problems within its operation, it can then start to take a more **proactive approach** to improving quality by preventing errors from occurring in the first place. This involves identifying what could go wrong before it does, and having in place appropriate **preventive action** and back-up plans. This will, in turn, mean that customer requirements are more consistently met in the long run. Case 10.4 shows how the US Department of Transport monitors the on-time performance of US airlines to improve quality conformance by identifying the percentage of flights that are late due to the air carrier, the weather, the national aviation system, security or the aircraft. Publishing these figures helps to identify areas for improvement by **benchmarking** performance between airlines and identifying common issues within the industry.

Tools and techniques

A number of **tools and techniques** have been developed to help organizations improve the level of quality conformance within their businesses by improving how their services and products are designed or delivered:

- *Designing services or products* Design tools help staff to develop services and products that better meet customers' needs and expectations.
- *Delivering services or products* Process tools help staff to assess the conditions and capabilities of existing delivery systems by drawing pictures of the process, monitoring existing quality conformance levels and identifying areas for improvement

Some of the principal tools and techniques available to companies are now discussed and show how they can be applied and the insights they give. As Case 10.5 illustrates, it is important to motivate and support employees to improve quality conformance, but they must have the right tools for the job and be able to use them properly.

Checklists

A **checklist** is a simple, widely used tool to collect information in a form that records the size and other dimensions of quality (and other) problems. Figure 10.5 is an example of a checklist at a retail outlet recording the frequency of quality conformance problems that have occurred in a month. This shows that two of the five problems account for 71 per cent of the total problems that occurred. Therefore, the company now needs to focus on

---

Quality failures – occur when the service or product delivered does not meet its design specification

Proactive approach – involves anticipating quality problems that may occur and taking action to prevent them from occurring

Preventive action – involves improving how a service or product is designed or delivered before a quality failure has occurred

Benchmarking – comparing methods and performance between companies, parts of an organization or processes. It can be used to help start or maintain an improvement process by identifying, setting and measuring improvement targets

Quality tools and techniques – ways to visually display quantitative or qualitative information in order to help identify the number of times a quality problem occurs and the reasons for these occurrences

Checklists – these collect real-time data at the location where the data are generated to show how frequently a quality problem is occurring

COCA-COLA

In 1999, Coca-Cola finally admitted that products going into some European markets (particularly Belgium) had been tainted by the accidental injection of 'defective' carbon dioxide gas into some of its products. However, the admission only came after several days of Coca-Cola assuring consumers that its products were safe, during which time dozens of children were hospitalized following complaints of stomach cramps, dizziness and vomiting. Coca-Cola planned to only partially withdraw its products, but the governments of Belgium and Luxembourg and some major supermarkets (for example, Carrefour in France) banned the sale of all its products to avoid confusion. The media also attacked Coca-Cola, with one newspaper showing its trademark polar bear doubled up in pain and another renaming it 'Coca-Colic'.

www.cocacola.com

PERRIER

In 1990, Perrier, the French sparkling water producer, reacted slowly and begrudgingly to traces of benzene found in its products. After tarnishing its reputation and losing market share, it was eventually forced to recall every bottle of its water at a cost of $200 million.

www.perrier.com

Sources: Abelson, R. 'In a crisis, Coke tries to be reassuring'. *New York Times*, June 16, 1999. Available from http://www.nytimes.com/1999/06/16/business/in-a-crisis-coke-tries-to-be-reassuring.html (retrieved September 8, 2010).

BBC News. 'The company file European warning over Coca-Cola'. Available from http://news.bbc.co.uk/1/hi/business/the_company_file/369684.stm. (retrieved September 8, 2010).

James, G. 'Perrier recalls its water in U.S. after benzene is found in bottles'. *New York Times*, February 10, 1990. Available from http://www.nytimes.com/1990/02/10/us/perrier-recalls-its-water-in-us-after-benzene-is-found-in-bottles.html?sec=health&&pagewanted=1 (retrieved September 19, 2007).

Skapinker, M. 'Bottled water and the madness of crowds'. *Financial Times*, September 25, 2007. Available at www.ft.com/cms/s/0/68f82cc0-6aff-11dc-9410-0000779fd2ac.html (retrieved September 8, 2010).

Questions

1 Describe the reaction of these two companies to the quality conformance problems they faced.

2 Was quality conformance an order-winner or a qualifier for these companies, and how did it affect their markets?

3 What role would operations have in each situation? Give details to explain your points.

Lecturers: visit www.palgrave.com/business/hillessential for additional resources

CASE 10.4 ON-TIME PASSENGER FLIGHTS: IMPROVING QUALITY

Airline	Flights	Percentage of flights							
		On time	Air carrier delay	Weather delay	National aviation system delay	Security delay	Aircraft delay	Cancelled	Diverted
Alaska Airlines	147,854	83.1	4.1	0.4	6.5	0.1	4.5	0.9	0.4
American Airlines	598,168	77.4	6.6	1.1	7.	0.0	5.7	1.7	0.3
American Eagle	473,751	76.9	5.3	1.0	6.3	0.0	7.5	2.6	0.3
Continental Airlines	314,278	79.0	4.8	0.7	10.5	0.2	4.0	0.5	0.3
Delta Airlines	485,005	78.9	4.5	0.5	9.7	0.0	4.9	1.2	0.2
Hawaiian Airlines	78,654	91.7	6.0	0.0	0.1	0.0	1.9	0.2	0.1
JetBlue Airlines	210,586	77.2	5.5	0.2	9.0	0.0	6.4	1.4	0.3
Northwest Airlines	293,133	79.2	6.1	1.0	8.8	0.0	4.1	0.7	0.2
Southwest Airlines	1,222,381	82.8	4.6	0.5	2.8	0.1	8.3	0.9	0.2
United Airlines	404,793	81.2	4.0	0.4	6.2	0.0	6.4	1.7	0.2
US Airways	447,656	80.8	4.1	0.3	8.9	0.1	4.3	1.4	0.2
Total	6,972,094	79.4	5.0	0.7	7.0	0.0	6.2	1.5	0.2

Source: Bureau of Transportation Statistics (US Department of Transport), Airline On-Time Data, 2009.

Customers want their flights to arrive on time. To ensure that their needs are met, relevant overseeing organizations (such as the Association of European Airlines and the US Department of Transport) monitor the on-time performance of airlines as shown above for 11 US companies.
www.transtats.bts.gov

Questions

1 Why is this level of detail collected by the Bureau of Transportation Statistics?

2 What reasons can you suggest for the different levels of on-time flights for the 11 carriers?

Lecturers: visit www.palgrave.com/business/hillessential for additional resources

The Nashua CEO, Bill Conway, when addressing some top management visitors from Ford, started the meeting with a challenge:

Suppose I ask two of you successful vice-presidents at Ford to enter a contest. The winner will win a trip around the world for his whole family. I know that both of you are totally motivated and dedicated by virtue of your exalted positions at Ford. The contest is to see who can drive a nail into this wall. One of you will get a hammer, the other nothing but management encouragement. Who do you think will win?'

The answer was obvious. Motivation and management support are important, but employees must have the right tools to do the job.

www.nashua.com

Questions

1 What point is Bill Conway, the Nashua CEO, trying to make?

2 Why it is important for people to realize this when they are trying to manage quality within their business?

Students: www.palgrave.com/business/hillessential provides learning resources for this case

reducing the number of times that the 'length of the checkout queue exceeds the target' (42 per cent) and the number of occasions when there are 'no goods are on the shelf' (29 per cent).

Figure 10.5 **Checklist showing frequency of quality conformance problems at a retail outlet**			
Problem	**Frequency**	**Total**	**Percentage of total**
Shelf display differs from bar code record	1̶1̶1̶1̶ 1̶1̶1̶1̶ 1̶1̶1̶1̶ 1	16	14
No goods on shelf	1̶1̶1̶1̶ 1̶1̶1̶1̶ 1̶1̶1̶1̶ 1̶1̶1̶1̶ 1̶1̶1̶1̶ 1̶1̶1̶1̶ 1111	34	29
Goods out of stock	1̶1̶1̶1̶ 1̶1̶1̶1̶	10	8
Length of checkout queue exceeds target	1̶1̶1̶1̶ 1̶1̶1̶1̶ 1̶1̶1̶1̶ 1̶1̶1̶1̶ 1̶1̶1̶1̶ 1̶1̶1̶1̶ 1̶1̶1̶1̶ 1̶1̶1̶1̶ 1̶1̶1̶1̶ 1111	49	42
Items returned faulty	1̶1̶1̶1̶ 111	8	7
Total		**117**	**100**

Pareto analysis

As shown in Figure 10.6, we often find that 80 per cent of quality conformance problems result from 20 per cent of causes. This is referred to as the 80/20 rule or Pareto principle (a general rule that we learned, in Chapter 9, and its application to inventory), and consequently companies must focus on improving the causes that result in the highest number of problems. To help identify these, companies can use a **Pareto analysis** (like that used to manage inventory) listing the quality problems identified, how often they have occurred and the costs (for example, of rectification or rejection) associated with each problem. Placing the highest number of occurrences or the total costs, depending on which dimension was perceived to be the more relevant, at the top of the list, the second highest next and so on gives a Pareto analysis, as shown in Figure 10.6.

The principle here is to direct time and resources towards the top 20 per cent (or so) that typically account for 80 per cent (or so) of the problems. In the example shown in Figure 10.6, this involves not 'accepting late passengers', which accounts for 39 per cent of flight departure delays. Once this problem has been solved, the airline then needs to reduce the number of times a plane is 'waiting for a tug pushback', and so on. As you would expect when each problem is eliminated, the percentage of incidences caused by the remaining problems increases as the total number of problems decreases.

Cause and effect diagrams

Also known as fishbone diagrams (due to their shape) or Ishikawa charts (after the person who developed them), **cause and effect diagrams** identify potential causes and help to direct improvement efforts to the most likely causes of quality conformance problems. These diagrams are built through the following steps:

Pareto analysis – shows the frequency and cost associated with a quality problem. Problems are listed in descending order to highlight those that are causing the greatest cost to a business

Cause and effect diagrams – these identify the potential causes of quality failures in order to help identify the root causes of a problem, identify relationships between causes and determine which ones to address first

Figure 10.6 Pareto analysis of the reasons for flight departure delays

Problem	Percentage of incidents	Cumulative percentage
Accepting late passengers	39	39
Waiting for tug pushback	24	63
Waiting for refuelling	14	77
Late weight and balance sheet	9	86
Cabin cleaners take longer than scheduled	8	94
Waiting for food services	4	98
Other	2	100

1 *Identify the problem to be addressed* This becomes the label for the root effect arrow. For example, Figure 10.7 looks at the potential reasons why a flight departure is delayed.

2 *Identify the major categories of causes* The second step is to identify major categories of causes for the problem identified in Step 1. These are then drawn at an angle to the root effect arrow. For example, in Figure 10.7, flight delays could be caused by problems with the aircraft, airport, personnel, procedures or other factors such as weather, outbound traffic and air traffic control.

3 *List all the detailed causes* The next step is to list all the detailed causes within each of the major categories. For example, personnel problems can result from delays at check-in, late cabin cleaners, cabin crews and cockpit crews (Figure 10.7).

4 *Identify the principal causes* The final step is to identify the principal causes within the detailed list based on frequency data that might have been gathered using a checklist or Pareto analysis. For example, in Figure 10.7 the major causes of flight departure delays are incoming flight delays, engine faults, too few agents at check-in, agreeing to accept late passengers too close to the departure time and baggage arriving late to the aircraft, as marked with an asterisk in Figure 10.7.

This process helps to identify the root cause of problems, and any relationships between causes, and to determine which to address first. So, based on the information in Figure 10.7, airlines need to focus on those it can directly address – increasing the reliability of their aircraft engines, having more agents at check-in, stopping late passengers being accepted onto the flight and ensuring that the baggage arrives to the aircraft on time.

> **KEY IDEA**
> Cause and effect diagrams help to identify the root cause of a problem

Gap analysis

The gap model, initially developed by Parasuraman, Zeithaml and Berry,[1] can be used to help understand why **customers' perceptions** of a service or product do not match their **expectations**. As Figure 10.8 shows, the overall gap between customers' expectations and perceptions of a service or product (Gap 5) is an accumulation of the following other gaps that may exist:

1 *Knowledge gap* Gap 1 occurs when there is a difference between customers' expectations and management's perceptions of customer expectations. For example, this would occur if a hotel manager did not know what customers expected from their room or any additional services that they might require. Aspects that can cause this are poor communication feedback between customers and the business, too many management layers within the organization and inadequate customer research.

Customer perceptions – these come from customers' actual experience of the quality of a service or product delivered to them

Customer expectations of the quality of a service or product come from what they have been promised by communication from the company (such as advertising) or from other customers who have previously purchased or experienced the service or product

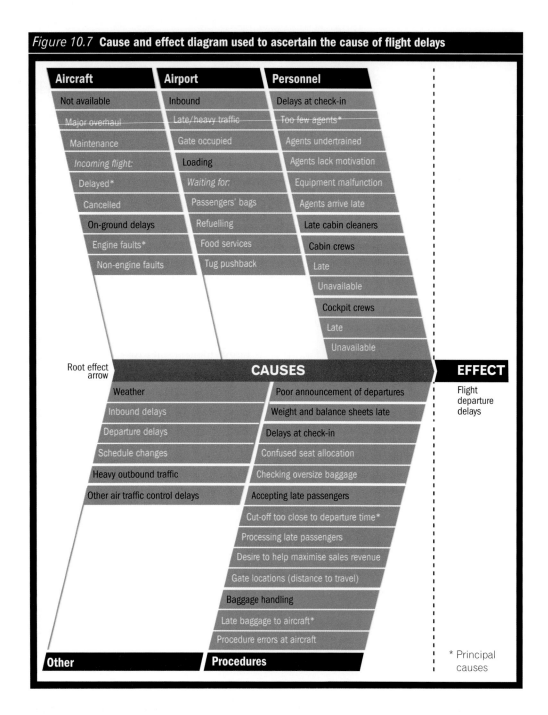

Figure 10.7 **Cause and effect diagram used to ascertain the cause of flight delays**

2 *Design gap* Gap 2 occurs when a service or product design does not match manage-ment's perceptions of customer expectations. For example, a restaurant manager may realize that customers expect to be served within 20 minutes of ordering, but may not have a delivery system designed to do this. This gap can result from aspects such as an inadequate service delivery system design or delivery.

3 *Performance gap* Gap 3 occurs when the service provided or product produced does not match the design specification – an issue of quality conformance. Factors that can cause this include inadequate employee skills, insufficient training, lack of employee responsibility and poorly defined roles.

4 *Communication gap* Gap 4 occurs when the service or product delivery does not match what customers have been promised. For example, a hotel may show beautiful rooms, swimming pools and lobbies in its advertisements that are different from those

actually used by its customers. This gap can result from factors such as over-promising and poor communication with the advertising agency that a company uses.

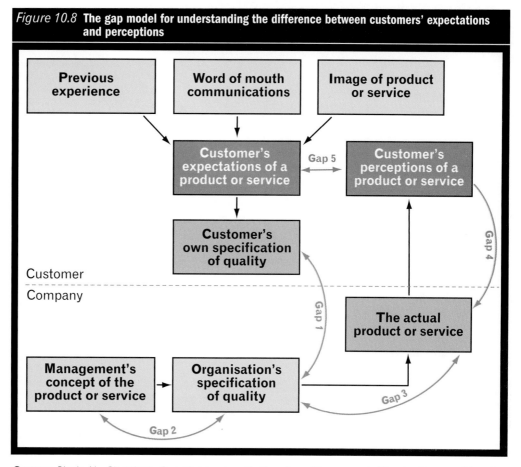

Figure 10.8 The gap model for understanding the difference between customers' expectations and perceptions

Source: Slack, N., Chambers, S. and Johnston, R. *Operations Management*, 6th edn. Pearson Education Limited. Adapted from Parasuraman, A., et al. (1985) 'A conceptual model of service quality and implications for future research'. Reproduced with permission from *The Journal of Marketing*, published by the American Marketing Association, Vol. 49 (Fall 1985), pp. 41–50.

As with the cause and effect diagram, this technique can be used to identify the root cause of a problem by looking at the relationships between the different causes and determining which ones to address first.

> Control charts – can be used to monitor a process and ensure that it performs consistently over a period of time

> **KEY IDEA**
> Gap analysis helps to identify why customers' perceptions of the quality of a service or product are less than their expectations

Control charts

Control charts can be used to monitor a process and ensure that it performs consistently over a period of time. This is done by asking the following questions:

- *What?* – determine which aspect of performance needs to be controlled, such as the output of the process, its delivery performance or the characteristics of the services or products it delivers

- *Where?* – at which points within the delivery system will performance be measured

- *How?* – which control charts will be used to measure performance, how frequently performance will be measured and what sample size will be taken

'**Organizations** must **identify** what could go **wrong** and then **prevent** it from happening'

- *By whom?* – who will measure performance and be responsible for taking corrective action for improving performance when it moves either above the **upper control limit** or below the **lower control limit** (Figure 10.9). It is usually best if the person delivering the service or product is also responsible for measuring and improving its quality.

Using this approach, control charts can be used to ensure that a process performs within specified limits against both its variable and attribute characteristics:

- *Control charts for variables* The original design of a service or product usually specifies the mean (average) and acceptable levels of deviation for each of its characteristics. For example, a retailer may specify that customers should be served within three minutes on average, but that between two and four minutes is acceptable. In this case, three minutes is the mean performance for this process, two minutes is the lower control limit and four minutes the upper control limit. The level of time to serve a customer should then be monitored selecting an agreed sample of customers (for example, 20 per cent) at agreed intervals (such as every half an hour). The level of time to serve a customer could then be measured over the day and plotted on chart similar to that shown in Figure 10.9. If a customer was served within less than two minutes or more than four minutes, the cause of this would need to be identified and, if necessary, corrective action taken (here it could be to reduce or increase the number of staff in certain time periods) to stop this from reoccurring.

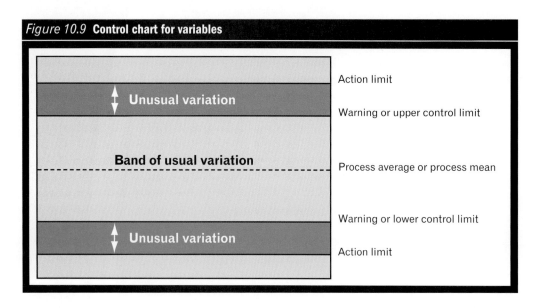

Figure 10.9 **Control chart for variables**

- *Control charts for attributes* Similarly, performance against attribute characteristics can also be measured and plotted on a control chart, as shown in Figure 10.10. For example, a restaurant may measure whether customers are satisfied with the level of service they have received by simply using a 'yes' or a 'no' tick box on a compliment slip. The level of customer satisfaction could then be measured for an agreed sample of customers (such as 80 per cent or possibly even all customers) at agreed intervals (for example, every half an hour) and plotted on a chart similar to that shown in Figure 10.10. If a customer was not satisfied, the cause of this would need to be identified and, where necessary, corrective action taken to stop this from reoccurring.

Statistical process control

Statistical process control involves methodically using control charts across a business similar to those shown in Figures 10.9, 10.10 and 10.11 to help employees identify areas of underperformance and take corrective action. It is important to recognize that the purpose of this is not simply to achieve a situation where all sample points are within the upper and lower control limits. Once this happens, the control limits then need to be

Figure 10.10 Control chart for attributes

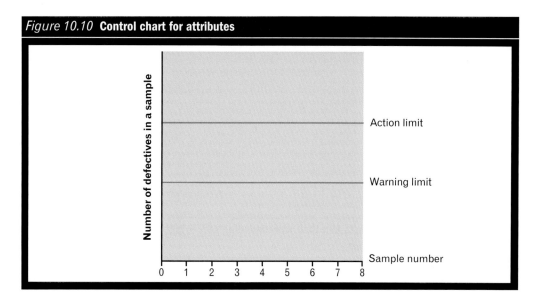

reviewed and brought closer to the average value, so setting new targets to further improve performance. Typically, a business should aim to have two-thirds of the points within the limits as this means it is continuously looking for ways to reduce variability and improve the overall performance of its processes.

Figure 10.11 Control charts in a call centre

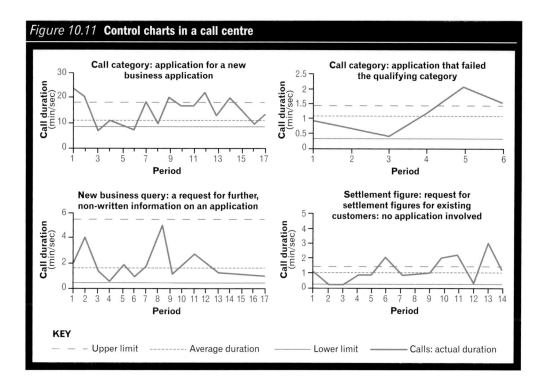

Six-sigma quality

Some companies have chosen to take statistical process control one step further and set a 'six-sigma' quality target for their organization. For example, in the late 1980s Motorola's

Semiconductor Products Division challenged itself to only make 3.4 defective products within every million it made (the target by setting a goal of six-sigma quality), and then set a similar target for its product design, sales and service functions. Most companies currently fall well short of such a target, typically generating about 35,000 defects per million, which sounds (and is) a lot and constitutes, in statistical terms, three and a half sigma quality (Figure 10.12). As such, pursuing this sort of initiative will help a company to gain a competitive advantage that can be used to drive a market in a new direction. Examples of companies who have managed to do this are General Electric (Case 10.6), 3M, which makes a wide range of products from dental fillings to Scotchguard tape, Sun Microsystems, a manufacturer of servers and software, Carlson Companies, whose businesses include the Radisson hotel chain, and Home Depot, the US retailer.

Figure 10.12 **Specification limits and their corresponding percentage of good quality and defects per million**		
Specification limit	# Defects per million	Percentage good quality
±one sigma	691,000	31.00
±two sigma	308,700	39.13
±three sigma	66,810	93.32
±three and a half sigma	35,900	96.41
±four sigma	6,210	99.37
±five sigma	233	99.98
±six sigma	3.4	99.99

Approaches to managing quality

A number of approaches can be used to manage and direct the improvement tools and techniques outlined earlier. This section looks at the management philosophies (such as total quality management [TQM]) and systems, procedures and frameworks (such as ISO 9000, the Baldrige Award and the European Foundation for Quality Management [EFQM] Excellence Award) that can be used to manage quality within an organization.

> **TQM** – a philosophy and set of guiding principles for managing quality within an organization

Total quality management

TQM is a approach to and set of guiding principles for managing quality within an organization. It draws on a number of management theories (including those outlined in earlier sections), approaches, tools and practices that can help a business improve its performance as a result of increasing the level of service and product quality conformance and decreasing its costs. It does this by focusing on seven key elements:

- *Understand and work out how to meet customer needs and expectations* Understand the key order-winners and qualifiers and how these should be met.

- *Cover all functions* All functions must be involved in improving quality.

- *Involve all levels* Everyone in the organization must be involved.

- *Examine the current cost of quality* This is done in order to determine the impact of the existing level of quality conformance and the key areas to improve first, by looking at the following sources of cost (see the earlier section on Juran):
  - External failure – loss of sales, warranty costs and customer complaints
  - Internal failure – scrap, reworking and lost productive time
  - Appraisal – inspection, quality control and customer surveys
  - Prevention – quality systems, design costs and quality training.

Jack Welch, when CEO of General Electric (GE), set the organization the goal of becoming a six-sigma quality company within five years, which means one that produces virtually defect-free services, products and transactions. Three-sigma to four-sigma quality typically means that 10–15 per cent of an organization's sales revenues is lost due to poor quality. As GE, at the time, had sales of over $80 billion, poor quality would have cost it then between $8 and $12 billion each year through scrap, rework and rectifying mistakes that had occurred. It is not difficult to understand why the company wanted to reduce this!

But beyond the purely financial reasons, there were even more important rewards that would come with dramatically improved levels of quality conformance. Among them was the potentially unlimited growth from selling services and products universally recognized by customers as being at a completely different level of quality from those of its competitors. Welch recognized that the pursuit of 'six-sigma' would be an exciting journey, and the most difficult and invigorating goal the company had ever undertaken. The magni-

tude of the challenge of going from 35,000 defects to fewer than four defects per million was huge. It required the company to reduce defect rates 10,000-fold – about 84 per cent for five consecutive years. But GE wanted to make its quality so special and valuable to its customers that they would never even consider going elsewhere for their services or products. The company continues to use the six-sigma method with successful results, and quality has proved vital to customers, even during periods of economic downturn – for example in 2009, when GE achieved sales of $157 billion and profits of $11.2 billion despite the poor financial climate.

www.ge.com

Questions

1 What were the key tasks for GE to reach its goal?

2 How did this change the competitive factors in GE's markets, and what strategic advantages resulted?

Lecturers: visit www.palgrave.com/business/hillessential for additional resources

- *Work out how to deliver services and products right first time* This will help reduce the quality costs identified above.

- *Develop a quality management approach* Doing this will allow a company to manage quality conformance, as discussed in more detail in the following section.

- *Continuously look for ways to improve the business* The organization must continuously assess its capabilities, looking for improvements through all its activities.

TQM requires a broadening of outlooks and skills, an innovative approach to improvement, a more sophisticated application of quality management tools and approaches, and an increased emphasis on people and their involvement. A number of aspects are required to make these changes, including the following:

- *Develop a quality strategy* that will integrate into the overall business strategy and cover all functions and levels within an organization. Quality conformance needs to be built into all aspects of service and product design and delivery, and to form part of the way a company's performance is measured.

- *Get top-management support* – as with many approaches, the belief and commitment of those at the top of an organization is critical to its success. TQM will not succeed unless it is given a high-priority standing and allocated the appropriate time and resources within an organization.

- *Use a TQM steering group* to guide the implementation, prioritize areas for improvement and allocate the necessary time and resources to improving quality.

- *Use improvement teams* – managers need to release and empower people to form teams that will identify and make improvements. This will help to gain the commitment and participation of employees that is essential to the successful implementation of this initiative.

- *Recognize success* – improvements must be recognized and encouraged through regular communication, feedback and support, for example communicating performance against targets, and benchmarking them against other parts of the business.

- *Use quality tools and approaches* to identify problems, facilitate improvements, implement solutions and sustain the new ways of working.

- *Train staff in the aims and tools of TQM* – everyone needs to have a general awareness of quality management aims, tools and techniques. A formal education programme is required to help people identify and make improvements.

For many organizations, a TQM approach requires significantly different attitudes, behaviours and working practices for it to be adopted throughout the organization. Case 10.7 illustrates that although James McNerney launched a corporate-wide quality initiative when he arrived at 3M, he knew that it would take 10–15 years to change the DNA of the organization. In fact, it took Japanese companies more than 30 years to change their reputation for producing poor quality products! However, to start this journey, companies need to make:

- Everyone responsible for their own quality
- Improvement a part of everyone's job
- Everyone focus on meeting customers' needs
- Suppliers and customers part of the improvement process
- Mistakes to be seen as opportunities for improvement rather than reasons for criticism.

> **KEY IDEA**

To implement TQM, companies must broaden their skills and be more innovative. This requires changes in attitude, behaviour and working practices

TQM steering group – a cross-functional group or committee that guides the implementation of a TQM initiative within an organization by prioritizing areas for improvement and allocating time and resources to improvement projects

The **DNA** of an organization can be described as its values, philosophy, personality and behaviours

In 2001, James McNerney became CEO at 3M (the multi-national conglomerate corporation behind a wide range of brands in the fields of technology, stationery and health care). He immediately launched a corporate-wide quality initiative by introducing a one-week training programme for all 28,000 employees and selecting 500 up-and-coming managers to work full time on quality programmes over the first two years. However, he knew that things were not going to change overnight and saw this as the first step in a 10–15-year journey to change the DNA of the 3M organization.

Joseph M Juran was a management consultant (see also the earlier section outlining his contribution) who was well known for his many books on quality management. He believed that it takes at least six, and more usually 10, years for companies to become quality leaders within their industries. Because of this, companies must not use top management-led programmes that aim to change the whole

company at once. The Harvard professor Mike Beer has argued that it is a mistake to think that a large company can be changed all at once, something he terms 'the fallacy of programmatic change'. To make improvements, organizations must bring about change unit by unit in order to get real buy-in from the organization as a whole.

www.3m.com

Sources: Beer, M., Eisenstat, R.A., and Spector, B. (1990) 'Why change programs don't produce change'. *Harvard Business Review*, **68**(6), pp. 158–66.

Juran, J.M. (1989) *Juran on Leadership for Quality: An Executive Handbook*. New York: Free Press.

Questions

1 What do these examples say about how firms should introduce TQM?

2 What do you think of James McNerney's approach to introducing TQM at 3M?

Lecturers: visit www.palgrave.com/business/hillessential for additional resources

Quality management frameworks: ISO 9000, Baldrige Award and EFQM Excellence Award

Although most companies have developed their own approaches to managing quality, a number of formal national and international frameworks are also available to help organizations consistently design and deliver services and products in line with their specifications. The three most widely used programmes – ISO 9000, the Baldrige Award and the EFQM Excellence Award – are now discussed in more detail.

> **KEY IDEA**
>
> A number of frameworks are available to help organizations consistently design and deliver services and products

ISO 9000

Established in 1947, the International Organization for Standardization (ISO) is a non-government body that secures international agreements on key topics and publishes these as international standards in over 100 countries. In 1987, it published the ISO 9000 series as a set of internationally accepted standards for business quality, and certifications have now been awarded to over 400,000 firms in 158 countries. Most countries have their own equivalent, if not identical, standards, but they accept ISO 9000 as the internationally recognized and accepted certification. The standards provide a framework that governs the activities and procedures that help companies to control their processes within a variety of aspects of their business such as:

- Designing and developing new services and products
- Controlling materials and keeping **traceability records**
- Controlling systems and processes for delivering services and making products
- Inspecting, measuring and testing services and products
- Handling, storing and packing products
- Servicing products after they have been installed
- Maintaining and auditing quality records for all of the above aspects.

Traceability records – show the complete history of a service or product by recording the person, material or information used in each step of its design and/or delivery

Baldrige Award

In response to the competitive challenges it faced in the early 1980s, the US government developed the Baldrige Award to recognize and encourage quality and productivity improvements by:

- Stimulating companies to attain excellence in quality
- Recognizing outstanding companies and helping to disseminate experience and **best practice** across companies
- Establishing guidelines for organizations on how to assess and manage quality
- Gathering information on how to change **corporate cultures** and practices to help develop best practice.

Best practice – the most effective way of designing or delivering a service or product

Corporate culture – comprises the values, beliefs, behaviours and paradigm (or taken-for-granted assumptions) within a business

The award is administered annually by the National Institute of Standards and Technology, with companies being reviewed by independent outsiders, on-site visits and judges. The award examines a business using the seven categories outlined in Figure 10.13, with the emphasis being placed on business results, which account for 450 of the total of 1,000 points awarded. Companies can apply for the award in the service, manufacturing or small business (fewer than 500 staff) categories. Up to two companies in each category are given the award each year, and past winners include Motorola, Xerox, Federal Express, Ritz-Carlton Hotels, AT&T, Cadillac and Texas Instruments.

> **KEY IDEA**
>
> The Baldrige Award aims to improve the performance of US businesses

Figure 10.13 **Baldrige Award criteria for performance excellence**		
Categories and items	**Points**	
1 Leadership · Organizational leadership · Social responsibility	70 50	**120**
2 Strategic planning · Strategy development · Strategy deployment	40 45	**85**
3 Customer and market focus · Customer and market knowledge · Customer relationships and satisfaction	40 45	**85**
4 Measurement, analysis and knowledge management · Measurement and analysis of organizational performance · Information and knowledge management	45 45	**90**
5 Human resource focus · Work systems · Employee learning and motivation · Employee well-being and satisfaction	35 25 25	**85**
6 Process management · Value creation processes · Support processes	50 35	**85**
7 Business results · Customer-focused results · Product and service results · Financial and market results · Human resource results · Organizational effectiveness results · Governance and social responsibility results	75 75 75 75 75 75	**450**
Total		**1,000**

Source: Baldrige National Quality Programme, 2009–2010. www.baldrige.nist.gov.

EFQM Excellence Award

The EFQM was founded in 1988, and had 850 members in 2010. In 1991, it launched its Excellence Award (initially called the European Quality Award) to recognize quality achievement, with companies applying each year for a national award, and the top firms from each country competing for a European award. Figure 10.14 shows how 1,000 points are awarded across the following nine aspects:

• *Leadership* – how its leaders inspire, support and promote a quality culture

• *Policy and strategy* – how it formulates, deploys, reviews and implements its quality policy and strategy

• *People* – how it realizes the potential of its people

• *Partnerships and resources* – how effectively and efficiently it manages resources

• *Processes* – how it identifies, manages, reviews and improves its processes

• *Customer results* – how satisfied its external customers are

• *People results* – how satisfied its employees are

- *Society results* – how satisfied the local, national and international communities are within which it operates

- *Key performance results* – whether it is meeting its planned objectives and satisfying the needs and expectations of everyone with a financial interest or stake in the organization.

> **KEY IDEA**
The EFQM Excellence Award aims to improve the performance of European organizations

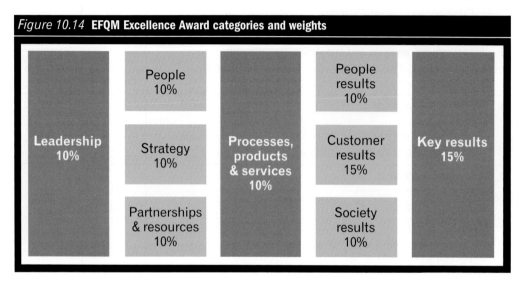

Figure 10.14 **EFQM Excellence Award categories and weights**

Source: www.efqm.org, © EFQM 2009.

The evolution of quality management

The evolution of quality management has, to some extent, come full circle. In times before the Industrial Revolution, skilled craftsmen were responsible for both delivery (making services and products) and quality (ensuring that they met their design specifications). After the Industrial Revolution, production volumes increased, and firms decided to make different individuals and departments responsible for delivery and quality. However, as Figure 10.15 shows, the systems for monitoring and managing quality have evolved rapidly since the 1970s, with simple inspection activities first being replaced by quality control and then enhanced by quality assurance, with many organizations now working towards a TQM approach in which everyone in an organization is again responsible for the quality of the work they produce.

Applying quality approaches to other aspects of business performance

The need for quality improvement to be applied at all levels and all aspects of a business has recently been highlighted by the scandals at WorldCom, Enron, Tyco and Parmalat and the banking activities that led to the recent world recession. As a result, the Baldrige Award now includes 'Governance and social responsibility results' (Figure 10.13) and the EFQM Excellence Model also includes 'Society results' (Figure 10.14). Quality tools, techniques and approaches could easily be used to improve executive board performance by looking at factors such as how they use independent directors, govern the business, comply with accounting regulations and compensate their executives. Companies that apply quality approaches to other aspects of their business may well be the ones that succeed and prosper or, at least, will not be the ones that stumble and fall.

Summary

- Quality conformance is either an order-winner or a qualifier in most markets. However, the word 'quality' needs to be defined before it can be measured. For operations, quality conformance means consistently delivering services and products in line with their design specifications, which, in turn, reflects customer needs.

- To manage quality, firms must first control it by determining which quality characteristics need to be delivered, deciding how to measure each of these quality characteristics, setting the required level of quality for each characteristic, and monitoring quality levels to ensure that these standards are met.

- Once the level of quality conformance is consistent and under control, it can then be maintained by correcting quality if it falls below the required standard, and continually improving the management of quality levels.

- A number of tools and techniques have been developed to help organizations improve their level of quality conformance for designing or delivering services and products. Some of the main tools used to improve quality are checklists (for collecting information recording the size and other dimensions of quality [and other] problems), Pareto analysis (for identifying the frequency of causes of quality conformance problems), cause and effect diagrams (for identifying the root cause of a problem, identifying the relationships between causes and determining which ones to address first) and gap analysis (for understanding why there is a gap between customers' expectations and perceptions by identifying whether there is a gap in knowledge, design, performance or communication).

- TQM is an approach and set of guiding principles for managing quality within an organization by focusing on seven key elements:

  1 Meeting customers' needs and expectations

INSPECTION

- Checking work after the event
- Identifying sources of non-conformance
- Taking corrective action

QUALITY CONTROL

- Self-inspection
- Quality planning and procedures
- Use of basic statistics
- Quality manual
- Use of process performance data

- Compliance to specification
- Blame culture
- Internally focused
- Process-driven

Changing characteristics

QUALITY ASSURANCE	TQM
· Develop quality systems	· Teamwork
· Use of quality cost data	· Employee involvement
· Quality planning	· Process management
· Use of statistical process control	· Performance measurement
· Involve non-operations functions	· Involves: – all operations – suppliers and customers
and switch in orientation	· Continuous improvement · Involvement · Ownership of issues · Empowerment of people · Externally focused · Customer-driven

2 Covering all parts of the organization

3 Involving everyone in the organization

4 Examining all quality costs

5 Getting things right first time

6 Developing quality systems and procedures

7 Continuously making improvements.

- TQM can be implemented by:

  - Developing a quality strategy and getting top-management support

  - Using a steering group

  - Using improvement teams

  - Recognizing success

  - Using quality tools and approaches

  - Training staff in the aims and tools of TQM.

- The successful implementation of TQM often requires a culture change. It is necessary for employees to be responsible for their own quality and for the task of making improvements to become part of everyone's job. Employees must focus on meeting customers' needs, and suppliers and customers should be involved in the improvement process. A working culture needs to be developed where mistakes are seen as opportunities for improvement rather than reasons for criticism.

- Although most companies have developed their own approaches to managing quality, a number of formal national and international frameworks are also available to help organizations consistently design and deliver services and products in line with their specifications. The three most widely used programmes are ISO 9000, the Baldrige Award and the EFQM Excellence Award.

Study activities

Discussion questions

1 The table below lists data concerning the errors in an account management function in the financial services sector.

Error type	Frequency in last period	Estimated costs involved (£s)
A	40	12,500
B	4	2,800
C	33	36,000
D	56	15,500
E	22	7,500
F	12	5,750
G	16	23,000
H	28	116,000

Prepare two Pareto lists – the first based on frequency and the second on estimated costs.

Comment on these rankings.

2 Discuss the advantages and disavantages of staff recording their own performance data in the form of a control chart and analysing the outcomes for the delivery system for which they are responsible.

3 The evolution in how best to manage quality has been described as follows:

Product reliability ⟶ Process reliability ⟶ People reliability ⟶ Total quality management

Comment on these rankings.

Assignments

1 Draw a fishbone diagram to represent why your car might be two hours later than the promised completion time at an auto service centre.

2 To access part of its service delivery system, a fast-food chain undertakes regular checks on certain elements of the system. One such check at an outlet revealed the control data below.

Aspects	Product freshness (minutes)	Queue length (# customers)	Time to serve (# minutes)	Cleanliness	
				Floor (# items)	# Tables not cleaned
Upper control limit	7.0	8.0	3.0	10	6
Average	3.0	4.0	2.0	5	4
Lower control limit	1.0	2.0	0.5	0	0
Sample #					
1	6.5	3.0	1.5	8	3
2	4.5	7.0	3.0	6	5
3	5.0	6.0	3.0	2	1
4	3.5	2.0	1.5	4	5
5	2.0	8.0	1.5	3	4
6	6.0	5.0	2.0	7	6
7	3.0	6.0	3.5	9	3
8	2.5	10.0	1.5	12	8
9	6.0	4.0	1.0	2	1
10	6.5	3.0	2.5	4	0
11	5.5	2.0	2.5	6	2
12	1.5	9.0	3.5	8	4

Notes: Product freshness – length of time (to the nearest half-minute) since any of the next-to-be-used main item products were made. Any product made eight or more minutes before is discarded.

Queue length – number of customers waiting: assessment above was made on all customer queue lengths in the service delivery system.

Time to serve – worst and best times in a 10-minute period for a selected server to serve a customer (to the nearest half-minute).

Cleanliness – floor: number of items (for example food, packaging and cutlery) on the floor; tables: number of free tables that have not been wiped down since the last customers left.

3 An operations manager records the daily output and number of rejects on a bag-making line that runs for a single eight-hour shift with occasional overtime on a Saturday. The data for the last 40 days are given below.

(a) Construct a control chart for these data

(b) What does the data analysis tell you?

(c) What management action should be taken?

Day #	Day	Output Rejects (# Bags)		Day #	Day	Output Rejects (# Bags)	
1	Mon	2,040	24	21	Wed	2,440	36
2	Tue	2,210	28	22	Thu	2,290	30
3	Wed	2,090	34	23	Fri	2,180	26
4	Thu	2,235	20	24	Sat	2,260	31
5	Fri	2,050	14	25	Mon	2,095	37
6	Sat	2,240	32	26	Tue	2,080	19
7	Mon	2,080	39	27	Wed	2,290	22
8	Tue	2,280	34	28	Thu	2,260	38
9	Wed	2,260	30	29	Fri	2,125	41
10	Thu	2,260	41	30	Sat	–	–
11	Fri	2,150	38	31	Mon	2,235	37
12	Sat	2,290	18	32	Tue	2,140	38
13	Mon	1,970	29	33	Wed	1,985	24
14	Tue	2,285	41	34	Thu	2,195	31
15	Wed	2,265	26	35	Fri	2,180	37
16	Thu	2,160	32	36	Sat	–	–
17	Fri	2,165	37	37	Mon	2,165	41
18	Sat	2,365	20	38	Tue	2,265	37
19	Mon	2,100	26	39	Wed	2,280	44
20	Tue	2,190	24	40	Thu	2,165	39

4 Casual Elegance is a mail order business in clothes for the younger businessperson. From time to time, customers complained about errors in their orders – wrong style, wrong size, and so on. The company wishes to keep order errors to less than 2 per cent. To check how well the system was working, a sample of 50 orders was taken several times over a representative period. The results are shown below.

(a) What type of control chart is appropriate for checking the process capability of the ordering operation?

(b) Construct a control chart using these data. What observations can you make about the process?

# Orders					
#	OK	Problem	#	OK	Problem
1	50	0	11	47	3
2	47	3	12	50	0
3	49	1	13	45	5
4	48	2	14	48	2
5	48	2	15	47	3
6	46	4	16	46	4
7	50	0	17	48	2
8	50	0	18	50	0
9	49	1	19	50	0
10	48	2	20	49	1

Exploring further

Journal articles

Hall, J.M., and Johnson, M.E. (2009) 'When should a process be art, not science?' *Harvard Business Review*, **87**(3), pp. 58–65. The purpose of this article is to help executives understand which processes should not be standardized and how to manage 'artistic' and 'scientific' processes in the same organization.

Markey, R., Reichheld, F., and Dullweber, A. (2009) 'Closing the customer feedback loop'. *Harvard Business Review*, **87**(12), pp. 43–7. Many companies devote a lot of energy to listening to the voice of the customer, but few are very happy with the outcome of their effort. This article suggests an approach that should work well across a range of industries. The Net Promoter Score categorizes customers into promoters, passives and detractors, and thus allows employees throughout a company to see right away whether a customer experience was a success or a failure, and why.

Books

Evans, J.R. and Lindsay, W.M. (2007) *The Management and Control of Quality*, 7th edn. Cincinnati, OH: South-Western. This provides a comprehensive review of quality issues that is well supplemented by a range of business illustrations.

Heskett, J.L., Sasser, W.E. Jr and Schleringer, L.A. (2003) *The Value Profit Chain: Treat Employees Like Customers and Customers Like Employees.* New York: Free Press. Building on research in more than 200 large corporations, the authors show how the loyalty, trust and satisfaction of customers, employees, partners and investors leads, in turn, to increased profit and growth within an organization.

Hill, T. (2005) *Operations Management: Text and Cases*. Basingstoke: Palgrave Macmillan. This provides a useful supplement to the current book by offering a more comprehensive explanation and further examples (including long case studies) showing how service and manufacturing companies have applied these concepts.

Zeithaml, V.A. (2009) *Delivering Quality Service: Balancing Customer Perceptions and Expectations.* New York: Free Press. This looks at how the SEVQUAL measurement tool can be applied to identify and then reduce the gap between customers' expectations and perceptions of service quality.

Websites

The Baldrige Award: www.baldrige.nist.gov

The European Foundation for Quality Management: www.efqm.org

Terry Tate, Office Linebacker: www.returnofterrytate.com

Notes and references

1 Parasuraman, A., Zeithaml, V.A., and Berry, L.L. (1985) 'A conceptual model of service quality and its implications for further research'. *Journal of Marketing*, **49**, pp. 41–50.

'We were running the final workshop of our Horizons Management Development Programme at the Crown Hotel in Paris,' explained Julie Coen, the Federal Talent Development Director. 'This was the final day of the two-year programme we run for "high-potential" employees working in our European businesses. We run similar programmes in Asia and in the US. It is a high-profile corporate programme, and that evening at the final dinner, we had not only the participants on the programme, but also their managers, mentors and some senior leaders from the business. In total, there were just over 80 of us. We'd been working there during the day and everything had gone well, but when we came down for dinner, things started to go wrong.

'The drinks we had ordered before dinner didn't all arrive in the reception area, and the snacks that had been split on the floor were not cleared up. Not a great start! But things got worse. Dinner was almost an hour late, and, when we finally sat down, I noticed the flowers looked past their best and were only on some of the tables. We had to wait another half hour for our food, and then not everyone's arrived. We'd ordered from a set menu and sent through our options the week before, but we didn't all get what we'd chosen. I ended up having salmon even though I'd ordered lamb! And most of my table had finished eating by the time our CEO Keith Grant's food finally arrived. Then when we went to show a video of the programme highlights from the last two years, the equipment didn't work. It was all very embarrassing and cast a bad light on the programme as a whole! We've used this hotel before and everything has been fine, but after this experience we won't be back!'

'Horizons are an important customer to us,' explained Alex Robson, the Crown Hotel Manager. 'They run conferences with us at least six times a year, each with slightly different requirements. Usually we're really good at meeting their needs, but not last night! I've spoken to Mika, the Conference Manager, and it seems we didn't receive the checklist back from the client. Therefore, we just set up the dinner in the same way as last time. We didn't realize they wanted video equipment or microphones on the tables until they told us that afternoon. The equipment has been playing up recently and is going to be serviced later this week. If we'd known it was required, we could have hired in another one just to be on the safe side. We'd already set up the tables when we realized that they needed to have microphones on them. This meant having to strip them back, wire up the microphones

and then relay the tables with the table cloth, glasses, cutlery and flowers. Unfortunately, the technicians moved the flowers off the tables and put them near the heater when they were setting up the microphones. By the time we'd realized this, the flowers had started to wilt and we had to throw some of them away. All this confusion and delays meant the room wasn't ready until an hour later than we had planned.'

'We always ask a group of this size to pre-order their food from a set menu,' explained Colin James, the Head Chef. 'This usually works well and means we can just focus on preparing and serving the food, but something went wrong last night. I'm not really sure what happened – either our customers had forgotten what they had ordered or we'd counted them up incorrectly. Fifteen of the starters we'd originally made were sent back so we had to prepare some new ones. This wasn't too bad as they're relatively simple to prepare, but it meant we had to throw a lot of food away. However, you're always playing catch-up when something like this happens at the beginning of service. We decided to delay cooking the main courses until all of the starters had been served, but when the main courses went out 18 were sent back and had to be remade. This caused a major problem as it took us a long time to make them and they had to be sent out after the original ones. At this point, everything started to spiral out of control. Evenings like that are a nightmare! Everyone was stressed and I'm not sure if we even made a profit that night!'

Questions

1 What problems occurred at the dinner, and what caused them to happen?

2 What key measures would you take to prevent them from occurring again in the future?

3 What lessons can be learnt from these problems?

Lecturers: visit www.palgrave.com/business/hillessential for additional resources

After completing this chapter, you should be able to:

- Define what a supply chain is and outline the steps that make up the chain

- Explain the factors that affect the design of a supply chain, including the decision to make or buy, the alternatives to making or buying and the issues surrounding outsourcing, both domestically and offshore

- Understand the processes of managing and developing supply chains, and the techniques used in these approaches

- Outline the benefits of effectively managing supply chains

Chapter outline

What is a supply chain?

Designing the supply chain

- Deciding whether to make or buy

Managing supply chains

- Types of supplier relationship

- Digital supply

Developing supply chains

- Stages of development

- Tools and techniques for developing supply chains

- The benefits of improving supply chains

Critical reflections

Introduction

Companies rarely, if ever, own the resources and activities they need to provide a service or make a product from start to finish, including delivery to their customers. Consequently, they need to decide what to provide or make internally and what to buy in. Furthermore, whether a company makes or buys an element of the eventual service or product it sells, it needs to manage effectively the internal and external phases of the supply chain, both in terms of its parts and as an integrated whole.

Businesses need to recognize that they are at the centre of networks of **material flows** and **information flows**. These flows extend from the customer interface through operations to the building of relationships with suppliers. The operations role, however, is not just the integration and management of the parts of the supply chain, but also the constant reviewing and alignment of these closely linked networks. In this way, operations can better meet the changing needs of an organization's markets and help to achieve its sales revenue and profit goals. This chapter first defines the supply chain, and explains how the types and locations of the suppliers used affect the design of the overall network. The advantages and disadvantages of making in-house and sourcing externally are then outlined. After this, the process of managing suppliers is described, including the tools and techniques that can be used, and how factors such as **corporate social responsibility** and the growth of digital supply chains affect the task of supply chain management. Finally, we'll look at the importance of continuing to improve the supply chain, and the benefits that this can bring to organizations.

> **KEY IDEA**

> Businesses have to manage flows of material and information across supply chain networks

What is a supply chain?

The supply of any service or product involves a number of steps that are known as a supply chain. These steps start with the original request from a customer for a service or product and finish with the delivery of the order to that customer. Organizations undertake some of the steps in the chain themselves and buy in the other steps in the form of materials and/or services from other businesses. Figure 11.1 shows a supply chain for a sandwich bar and a consumer products manufacturer. As you can see from these examples, all the steps necessary to provide a service or product will have to be completed. What is done externally (the decision of what to buy from an external supplier) and what is done internally (the decision of what to make or provide in-house) will not alter the total number of tasks to deliver the service or product, but will alter the internal/external mix and the size of the task of managing suppliers. The decision on the external/internal split will be based on many factors, and these, together with the task of managing suppliers, are dealt with in later sections.

> **KEY IDEA**

> A supply chain comprises all the steps required to supply a service or product to a customer

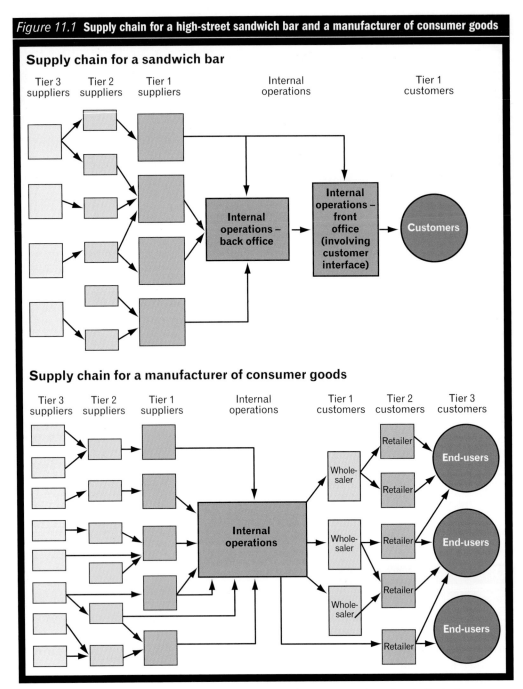

Figure 11.1 Supply chain for a high-street sandwich bar and a manufacturer of consumer goods

Note: The above diagrams are not to scale, and the number of customers and suppliers is illustrative.

As you can imagine, the number of tiers of suppliers and customers varies depending on the complexity of the service or product being supplied and how many steps in the chain are bought in from outside. Managing a supply chain effectively is a considerable challenge, and requires a shift away from traditional functional thinking to managing a set of integrated processes across multiple functions, as shown in Figure 11.2.

Designing the supply chain

The developments and improvements made to the supply chain need to be based on a vision of the entire supply chain that reflects a company's market and business requirements. As we'll learn in the following section, the decision about what to make and what to buy affects how much of the supply chain is internal and how much is external to an

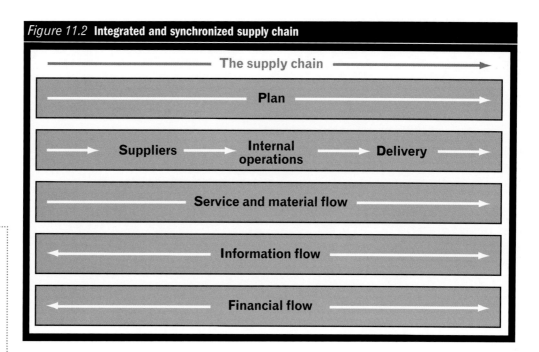

Figure 11.2 **Integrated and synchronized supply chain**

The supply chain

Plan

Suppliers → **Internal operations** → **Delivery**

Service and material flow

Information flow

Financial flow

organization, the task then being to integrate these internal and external parts so that they work as one. As Figure 11.2 illustrates, achieving this requires material, information and financial details all to flow across the whole supply chain, enabling all the activities to be synchronized with each other. They therefore work, in effect, as a single entity using the same data and time frames. **Integrated** and **synchronized supply chains** thereby allow companies to better respond to market opportunities and competitive pressures by:

- Collaborating throughout the supply chain
- Exchanging information to ensure that customer needs are met
- Working to the same time frames
- Operating as a **demand chain** rather than a supply chain by using customer requirements as the basis on which to provide services or make products.

In this way, companies compete as a supply chain rather than as a number of individual organizations.

Deciding whether to make or buy

The first step in the design and management of supply chains is to decide what to make and what to buy. This key decision will be based on the following business-related factors:

- The market order-winners and qualifiers the company needs to support
- How the company could create **barriers to entry** for new competitors
- Whether the company needs to maintain a supply of key materials
- How best to understand customer requirements
- Which core capabilities need to be retained in-house
- Which external capabilities need to be accessed from elsewhere
- How a company wishes to take advantage of the trend for countries to reduce the level of import duty on goods and services.

> **KEY IDEA**

The first step in designing a supply chain is to decide what to make and what to buy

Although, in theory, every service or product can be either provided internally or bought from outside, in reality the choice is far more restricted. In many instances, organizations have no alternative other than to outsource materials, components, products or services

‘Supply chains
should be **aligned**
and **synchronized**’

because they lack the in-house technical capability, or the high levels of investment required cannot be justified. However, companies should consider a number of aspects when deciding whether to make or buy, as outlined below.

Supporting market order-winners and qualifiers

Make-or-buy decisions need to be made within the strategic context of a business, in particular how these decisions will affect the company's ability to support its market order-winners and qualifiers (such as price, delivery reliability, delivery speed and quality conformance). For example:

- Dell developed the capability to assemble personal computers quickly in response to customers' orders, but found that this was constrained by the long lead-times of component suppliers.
- Lego, the privately owned Danish toy manufacturer, concentrates its production in Europe and the US, arguing that this best satisfies its customer requirements in terms of design and quality conformance.
- Benetton, the Italian clothes manufacturer, decided to source garments locally rather than in a low-cost region such as South East Asia or Eastern Europe, in order to meet the fast response needs of its fashion-conscious customers.

Creating barriers to entry

Keeping processes in-house and developing them over time can create strong barriers to entry due to factors such as the high levels of investment or technical capabilities necessary to compete effectively in a given market.

Maintaining the supply of key resources

Companies may choose to make, rather than buy, to ensure their supplies of key components or materials. As with all forms of **backward integration**, this decision brings its own set of advantages and disadvantages that need to be considered.

> **Backward integration** – with regard to activities that take place earlier in the supply chain, the decision to change an existing decision to buy into a decision to make, thereby moving the internal part of a supply chain more towards the source of supply

Understanding customer requirements

As well as integrating backwards, companies can also **integrate forwards**. As this happens, they start to better understand customers' requirements as a result of greater contact, knowledge and feedback from them. For example, Apple's decision to set up its retail stores in 2007 has increased its understanding of how customers use its products and what they might want from future product developments.

> **Forward integration** – with regard to activities that take place after those currently completed in-house, the decision to change an existing decision to buy into a decision to make, thereby moving the internal phase of the supply chain more towards the market

> **KEY IDEA**
> Companies should keep in-house the services, products or processes that help them to understand customer requirements and build customer relationships

Retaining core capabilities

Companies need to keep their core capabilities in-house so that they maintain control of those processes that create value for customers. These are the key processes to support the critical order-winners and qualifiers within their markets. In manufacturing firms, they are often the production processes from assembly onwards, whereas in service businesses they are usually the final link with customers. For example, in the late 1990s NatWest Bank considered subcontracting the back-office cheque processing and account management activities for its retail and corporate customers. In the past, these activities were an integral part of its in-house operation, but now options to subcontract were available. In the end, NatWest decided to keep these activities in-house as they provided an essential link with its customers. Similarly, Fidelity, one of the world's largest investment fund managers, considers administrative systems to be a core part of its business and has, therefore, kept them in-house through significant systems technology investment over several decades. Some of the issues are discussed in Case 11.1.

Accessing external capabilities

As well as wishing to retain **core capabilities**, companies may also find that they need to access capabilities from elsewhere that they do not have in-house. As a result, they buy in the capability in the form of materials, components, products or services from external suppliers. For example, in 2005 a US fund manager had to reduce the time it took to settle trades from 3 days to 1 day. This could only be done through a large IT investment and upgrades. Instead of developing this capability in-house, the company chose to buy it in from outside. Similarly, an upmarket ladies' clothes outlet makes minor garment alterations in-house, but outsources more complex modifications for which it does not have the in-house capability.

Taking advantage of reduced trade barriers

Trade barriers across much of the world have declined sharply over recent years. For example, in 1998 average import **tariffs** were 94 per cent less than in 1960. This has made **global manufacturing** more commercially feasible. In turn, this has reduced the need for local manufacturing plants as companies can now easily import goods from overseas. For example, in Australia the tariff on imported cars dropped from 57.5 per cent in 1987 to 10 per cent in 2005. As a result, the proportion of imported cars rose from 15 to 70 per cent of the market in that period, and domestic car plants started to close.

Advantages and disadvantages of make or buy

The decision to make or buy brings with it a number of advantages and disadvantages, which are summarised in Figure 11.3 and discussed in more detail below.

Figure 11.3 **Advantages and disadvantages of make or buy**

Option	Advantages		Disadvantages	
Make in-house	Increased control over	• Processes and capabilities • Supply of materials • Market and service/product know-how	More difficult to manage costs	• More difficult to control cost • Increased overhead costs
	Increased opportunity to	• Differentiate and customise services or products • Reduce costs	Less focus	• More complex task • Less focus on core issues • Investment spread over a wider set of tasks
			Reduced access to	• External capabilities • Up-to-date technologies
Buy/ outsource	Easier to manage costs	• Easier to control as the unit price is known • Lower overhead costs	Increased risk	• More vulnerable to supply problems • Expose intellectual property to others • Less control of processes, capabilities and developments
	Increased focus	• Frees up resources to focus on core issues	Difficult to reverse	• Inherent skills lost • Stepped investment to buy in capabilities in the future
	Increased access to	• Capacity • Up-to-date technology • World-class capabilities	New skills required	• To manage supply chain
			Less flexible	• No longer own the skills or capabilities

When an organization decides to serve its customers over the telephone rather than face to face, it first needs to consider whether this function should occur in-house or be outsourced. Should the company hand over something as important as customer relations to an external provider? And, if so, where should the facility be located?

It's cheaper to outsource call centre services as specialist organizations have greater call volumes and lower costs, incur lower staff salaries and can more easily manage alternating staff capacity requirements. However, some companies still prefer to set up and run their own call centres. For example, the US credit card company Capital One outsources only a few specialized parts of its service, such as debt collection from customers who are very late in making payments, as it believes that effective customer management is key in its market. Equally, the US airline Delta sited its European customer reservation centre in London, where wage costs are high and competition for staff is fierce, as it believes that the access to staff speaking a wide range of languages makes this worthwhile. **www.capitalone.com; www.delta.com**

Questions

1 Why are most companies subcontracting call centre facilities?

2 What reasons would make a company elect to set up and manage its own call centre?

Advantages of making in-house

Making in-house brings with it several advantages, including:

- *Increased control over:*
  - Processes and capabilities that support the key market order-winners and qualifiers
  - Supply of materials as backward integration reduces dependency on suppliers
  - Knowledge of the market and services or products as forward integration allows better business forecasts (ranging from demand patterns to identifying technology and cost changes) to be made that will help strengthen a firm's competitive position
  - Service/product know-how and specialist staff are exposed to developments and resolving technical problems.

- *Increased opportunity to:*
  - Differentiate services or products, including customization, by using alternative materials and designs to meet varying market requirements
  - Reduce costs by increasing internal demand. For example, Japanese semiconductor manufacturers such as Fujitsu, Hitachi, Mitsubishi, NEC and Toshiba are able to make their products at increasingly lower costs than their competitors due to the high-volume base created by demand for semiconductors from all their diverse businesses making everything from robots to cars and satellites. As a result, Japanese companies currently hold over 50 per cent of the world semiconductor market.

> KEY IDEA

Making in-house provides increased control over processes, material supply and service/product knowledge, and a greater opportunity for differentiation and cost reduction

---

Disadvantages of making in-house

Making in-house, however, also brings with it several disadvantages, including:

- *Costs are more difficult to manage:*
  - Costs are more difficult to manage and control as the costs of all the resources (including staff, materials and overheads) used to produce a service or product have to be estimated, measured and controlled
  - Increased overhead costs as making in-house requires staff and resources to undertake the additional tasks that come with making in-house, and these costs are difficult to assess and evaluate.

- *Less focus:*
  - Making in-house leads to more tasks and more complexity, and consequently management time is spread more thinly, resulting in less focus on core issues
  - Having more tasks in-house spreads available investment across more tasks and similarly dilutes the focus on core issues.

- *Reduced access to:*
  - External capabilities and up-to-date technologies where specialist suppliers invest in and develop the services or products in their own specific area of expertise. Making in-house reduces access to these external sites of capabilities and up-to-date technologies.

> **Outsourcing –**
> one of the terms to describe the process of hiring out or subcontracting some of the work that a company needs to do

Advantages of deciding to buy/outsource

Deciding to buy, or **outsourcing**, brings with it several advantages including:

- *Costs are easier to manage:*
  - Costs are easier to control as only a supplier's quoted price for a service or product needs to be checked and controlled, instead of all the different costs associated with making in-house
  - Lower overheads as the associated support costs are reduced.

- *Increased focus:*
  - Not making in-house simplifies the operations task and frees up resources that can then focus on core issues.

- *Increased access to:*
  - Capacity as outsourcing allows access to suppliers' capabilities and capacity across the supply chain that can also be used to help absorb fluctuations in demand
  - Up-to-date technology as outsourcing enables a company to access the technology investments made by suppliers in their own specialist areas
  - **World-class capabilities** as all companies strive to develop world-class capabilities to remain competitive in their markets. Outsourcing allows a firm to access the capabilities of their suppliers and the benefits they bring. As shown in Case 11.2, guitar manufacturer Fender International used outside expertise to enhance the delivery of products to its customers.

> **World-class capabilities** – having staff, processes and equipment that rank among the best in the world

> **KEY IDEA**
Deciding to buy makes it easier to manage costs, provides an increased focus on critical tasks and increases access to external sets of capabilities

Disadvantages of deciding to buy
Outsourcing, however, also brings with it several disadvantages, including:

> **Intellectual property** – knowledge, strategies, creative ideas or other intangible assets that have commercial (monetary) value

- *Increased risks in terms of:*
  - Sales are more vulnerable to supply problems as a company becomes more dependent on its suppliers
  - Exposure of a company's own **intellectual property** to others as the more suppliers that are used to provide a service or product, the greater the exposure of the company's own intellectual property and the greater the potential loss of a technical advantage over its competitors
  - Less control of processes, capabilities and developments as these as now provided by suppliers.

- *Difficult to reverse:*
  - Once a product or service has been outsourced, it is rarely brought back in-house due to a reluctance to change direction by reversing a previous decision, and because of the amount of time and investment necessary to re-create the required level of in-house capability.

- *New skills are required:*
  - Managing supply chains is different from, and often more demanding than, managing in-house processes.

- *The process is less flexible:*
  - When market requirements change, it may be more difficult for a company to modify its processes and capabilities as it no longer owns them.

Furthermore, and as shown in Case 11.3, there are clearly potential risks inherent in single sourcing (only having a single supplier) as opposed to multisourcing (having more than one supplier).

Similarly, a review of the data in Figures 11.4, 11.5 and 11.6 illustrates the mix of advantages and disadvantages when sourcing from domestic as opposed to overseas suppliers. However, the advantage of lower costs when outsourcing to suppliers in Central America, Asia and similar low-cost regions has to be set against the disadvantage that such suppliers are less willing to respond to changes in quantities and order mix once an order has been placed.

CASE 11.2 FENDER INTERNATIONAL: CREATING A POSITIVE RETAIL EXPERIENCE

Fender International, the US manufacturer of world-famous electric guitars such as the Stratocaster, Telecaster and Precision Bass, set an objective to double its market share in Europe, the Middle East and Africa. Part of its strategy to achieve this was to create a 'positive retail experience' that meant a guitar must be playable when taken out of its box. It was able to achieve this in the US, but was struggling in Europe, the Middle East and Africa until it set up a partnership with United Parcel Services (UPS).

The UPS European Distribution Centre at Roermond in The Netherlands now receives guitars from Fender manufacturing sites around the world and then uses local professional and amateur musicians to tune them prior to final distribution. All guitars, from standard models to some of the most expensive and elite guitars in the world, are now inspected by players before being sent to customers. UPS also han-

dles the return of damaged guitars for repair, and the central facility manages inventory for the whole region. This has led to lower inventories in the supply chain and shorter distribution lead-times, and has enabled Fender to get closer to distributors, retailers and customers. One unexpected outcome is that many distributors are ordering products that they never ordered before.

www.fender.com

Questions

1 What is the significance for Fender International of the guitar tuning service offered by UPS?

2 Why do you think distributors are now ordering products that they never ordered before?

UPF-Thompson, the sole supplier of chassis frames for Land Rover's Discovery model, went bankrupt in 2001. Critics said that Land Rover should never have single-sourced such a crucial component for this range of vehicles that accounts for 35 per cent of its sales revenue. KPMG, the receivers brought in to run UPF, poured fat on the fire by demanding that Land Rover should pay off UPF's debt of £50 million in order to guarantee chassis supply for the next year. Land Rover took UPF to court and won a High Court injunction guaranteeing supply for the following year.

Single sourcing is now the norm for most automobile companies as it reduces investment in terms of tooling and equipment, which was £12 million for the Land Rover chassis frame. Land Rover and KPMG came to a compromise, but this incident demonstrates how vulnerable Land Rover had become, with over 90 per cent of their components being single-sourced from 900 suppliers.

www.landrover.com, www.kpmg.com

Questions

1 Comment on KPMG's role in this dispute with Land Rover.

2 What would you advise Land Rover to do in general about its single sourcing policy?

Figure 11.4 Percentage discount by supplier location agreed with North American and UK retailers

Retailer	% Discount by supplier location					
	Asia	Africa	Central America	Europe	North America	UK
North America	20–30	10–15	20–25	5–10	0	–
UK	25–35	15–20	–	10–15	1-5	0

Source Based on Lowson, R.H. (2001) Offshore sourcing: an optimal operational strategy? *Business Horizons*, Nov–Dec, pp. 61–6.

Figure 11.5 Percentage of suppliers not allowing any change to order volume once orders have been placed before and after the season has started

Relative to start of season	% Suppliers not allowing any change to order volume once orders have been placed					
	Asia	Africa	Central America	Europe	North America	UK
Before	66	58	41	29	16	9
After	70	66	52	35	39	19

Source Based on Lowson, R.H. (2001) Offshore sourcing: an optimal operational strategy? *Business Horizons*, Nov–Dec, pp. 61–6.

Figure 11.6 Percentage of suppliers not allowing any change to an order mix once orders have been placed before and after the season has started

Able to change products ordered	% Suppliers not allowing any change to order mix once orders have been placed					
	Asia	Africa	Central America	Europe	North America	UK
Before	70	62	46	37	21	21
After	86	73	63	41	47	28

Source Based on Lowson, R.H. (2001) Offshore sourcing: an optimal operational strategy? *Business Horizons*, Nov–Dec, pp. 61–6.

Case 11.3 and Figures 11.4–11.6 help to illustrate the fact that the decision of where to outsource greatly affects an organization's ability to support its own customers' needs.

Alternatives to outsourcing

The discussion so far has implied that companies must either make or buy. However, other alternatives are also available such as:

Joint ventures – where two or more companies set up a separate organization to provide a range of capabilities for those companies involved

- **Joint ventures** are a useful alternative when two or more organizations wish to exploit similar opportunities, particularly in areas such as applied technology and research. These companies can set up a separate entity that draws on the strengths of their owners, taps into the synergy of such a relationship and improves the competitive capability of all the organizations involved. Since the late 1970s, the number of joint ventures has increased substantially, particularly in the communication, IT and service industries.

Co-sourcing – when two or more competitors collectively source a service or product

- **Co-sourcing** occurs when a company works with one or more of its competitors to collectively source a service or product. For example, in 2003 Barclays and Lloyds

Banking Group, the UK's third and fourth largest banks respectively, both decided to outsource their cheque processing service and set up a new company to be managed by the US consultancy firm Unisys. The new company, in which each bank has a 24.5 per cent stake, expects to generate £500 million of sales revenues during the next 10 years and now competes for business from other banks. This solution has meant Barclays and Lloyds could take advantage of outsourcing without losing complete control of these operations.

> **KEY IDEA**
To reduce the potential disadvantages of deciding to buy, business can instead use joint ventures or co-sourcing

Managing supply chains

The balance of internal and external parts that make up an organization's supply chain is determined by the decision of whether to make or buy. Once the balance between making in-house and buying from suppliers has been decided, it is necessary to manage these external and internal parts as an integrated and synchronized whole that is able to support customer requirements, as emphasized earlier (see Figure 11.2 and its accompanying text). This is especially important in a business environment where companies increasingly compete as supply chains rather than individual organizations. To successfully integrate supply chains, organizations need to rethink the relationship they have with suppliers and realize that they must be proactive in encouraging improvement and change when it is required.

First and foremost, organizations have to recognize that their suppliers are an integral part of the total supply chain and are, in many ways, their partners in the task of competing effectively. For the best results, suppliers have to be involved early on (for example, when introducing new services or products, and for design changes), and essential information (including sales trends and financial data) has to be shared in a timely fashion. Only then can the benefits of a totally integrated supply chain be effectively used to compete in today's markets.

> **KEY IDEA**
Businesses must see suppliers as an integral part of the total supply chain and realize that the whole chain is only as strong as its weakest link

As Case 11.4 shows, an integrative supply chain, and the need for collaboration between organizations and their suppliers, can lead to a fundamental rethink of its corporate objectives and the structure and style used within an organization, as well as affecting its position on broader issues such as corporate social responsibility.

In the 1980s, companies focused on fixing problems within their internal operations. However, by the early 1990s many companies were starting to look across the whole of their supply chains as part of the way of meeting shorter service and product life cycles, wider customer choice, reducing lead-times and growing world competition. The challenge of managing supply chains effectively continues to grow as more companies outsource operations. A key factor in managing supply chains is the type of supplier relationship that an organization decides to adopt. The alternatives and how they differ are now explained.

Types of supplier relationship

The relationship between customers and suppliers is influenced by the level of dependency they have on each other, as shown in Figure 11.7. Companies can manage these relationships in a number of ways, as now explained:

CASE 11.4 CHIQUITA RELOCATES FROM CINCINNATI TO COSTA RICA

Chiquita, the global food company, moved its main purchasing team from the US to Costa Rica to forge closer links with its fruit-growing producers. Chiquita Fresh (one of the world's largest banana producers) transferred its 20-strong procurement team from Ohio, along with several staff from the US Head Office in Cincinnati, to San José, one of its seven Latin American export locations. As well as having procurement skills, buyers must also speak Spanish and understand local cultures.

This move was part of a wider initiative to integrate procurement, which had previously been seen as a support function, within the wider supply chain operation. The relocation provided the opportunity for procurement specialists to provide direct, on-the-spot support to those who were buying fresh fruit for the company's world

markets – more than half of Chiquita's products are sold in Europe.

The company is also stepping up its corporate social responsibility policy by getting its materials and services suppliers to adhere to its own code of conduct in all future contracts.

www.chiquita.com

Questions

1 Why did Chiquita move its main purchasing team to Costa Rica?

2 What opportunities did the relocation offer?

Students: www.palgrave.com/business/hillessential provides learning resources for this case

Figure 11.7 Customer and supplier dependence

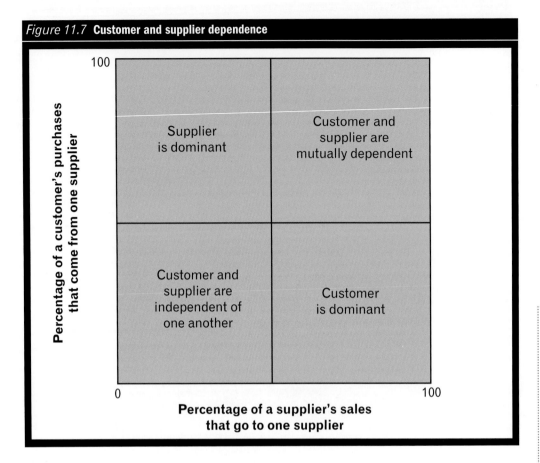

Prequalified vendors – the practice of requiring suppliers to demonstrate their ability to meet selected criteria (qualifiers) that entitles them to be placed on a supplier's shortlist

Commodities – typically, high-volume items that can be sourced from a wide range of suppliers

Non-value adding – services and products that do not directly provide value to customers

- *Trawling the market* Here suppliers are kept at arm's length, and transactions often completed over the Internet. For example, General Electric (GE) in the US increasingly purchases components over the Internet by posting the contract details and then asking **prequalified vendors** to quote for it. These Internet auctions have little face-to-face interaction, and products are bought on price alone (the order-winner) with on-time delivery and quality conformance as qualifiers for becoming a potential supplier. GE estimates that it has also reduced order processing costs by 90 per cent using this method. However, this approach is only appropriate for **commodities** and **non value-adding** services and products.

- *Ongoing relationships* involving medium-term contracts that are established with suppliers to help develop relationships and share information.

- *Partnerships* where long-term contracts are established with suppliers to further develop relationships, share information and build trust. For example, US automotive manufacturers have doubled the average length of supplier contracts over the last 20 years.

- *Strategic alliances* are established to further increase the depth and breadth of the supplier relationships. Such alliances usually have long timescales and require extensive information sharing, increased trust and joint service, product and process development. For example, the aircraft manufacturer Boeing has strategic alliances with GE, Rolls-Royce and Pratt & Whitney to help reduce the financial risk of new aeroplane programmes and to better manage new product developments. A prerequisite for establishing strategic alliances is to dramatically reduce the number of suppliers used. For example, Xerox, the office equipment and document management systems provider, has reduced its suppliers from over 5,000 to about 400. However, if managed correctly, strategic alliances can bring significant benefits. For example, automobile maker Chrysler has saved more than $0.5 billion from supplier-generated ideas.

- *Backward integration* The final step is to change from a relationship to ownership by acquiring a supplier. This leads to full information and, if managed correctly, creates consistent objectives and cultures.

Corporate and social responsibility

The need to rethink corporate norms in the context of outsourcing does not stop with the sharing of information. Other corporate values will also come under scrutiny when selecting which supplier to use. High on this agenda is corporate and social responsibility.

Digital supply

Developments in IT have changed the format of some services and products together with the supply chain used to deliver them. One recent change is in the form of digital supply. Digital supply chains initially evolved from the delivery of digital media (such as music or video) by electronic means from the point of origin (the content provider) to a destination where the media are then consumed (such as a computer, mobile phone or television). One outcome has been to simplify the provision of services and products and, with it, the task of managing the associated supply chain. The growth in digital supply was triggered by a couple of significant IT developments (Figure 11.8), and these developments below provided the opportunity for companies to restructure their service and product provision:

- *An increase in electronic and mobile devices* such as mobile phones and portable electronic devices (for example, iPods and iPhones)
- *Faster and more mobile Internet access* through faster broadband speeds and more Wi-Fi hotspots and 3G mobile networks.

Figure 11.8 **Factors affecting growth in global digital media markets**

Key indicators (millions)	2003	2004	2005	2006	2007	2008
Broadband lines	104	151	209	280	350	411
Mobile phone subscriptions	1,185	1,350	1,817	2,017	2,500	3,087
3G mobile phone subscriptions	–	25	90	137	614	895
Portable music player sales	2	12	84	120	140	160

Source: PWC Global Entertainment and Media Report (2009).

By moving from physical to digital products, companies can deliver their products through digital supply chains. This has led to a number of benefits for both the supplier and the customer, including:

- *Customer benefits:*
  - Increased delivery speed as products can be consumed within seconds of being ordered
  - Wider availability as products can be downloaded from any location
  - Ease of use, as products are simpler to find and purchase than through traditional retail channels
  - A lower price as products bought through traditional retail channels are more expensive.

- *Supplier benefits:*
  - Reduced cash holdings as companies do not have to hold product inventory. Instead, they can put one digital version of the product into a data centre and sell this one product many times over
  - Lower costs as there is no excess or obsolete inventory and no physical supply chain costs
  - The supply chain is easier to manage as there is no physical inventory, no inventory management systems, no quality issues and no purchase order paperwork.

> **KEY IDEA**

Digital supply chains give customers access to a wider range of less expensive products that can be ordered and delivered more quickly. Such chains are also easier to manage, enabling suppliers to reduce cash holdings and supply costs

Such developments are well illustrated by the digital recorded music industry, the growth of which is shown in Figures 11.9 and 11.10. Apple's iPod and iTunes retail stores are driving the revolution as they offer an increasingly diverse range of products and services (Case 11.5). In fact, PriceWaterhouseCoopers forecasts that revenues from the global media industry will rise by 6.6 per cent per year to $2.2 trillion in 2012. However, these ideas are also starting to affect other industries and consultancy firms, such as Hewlett-Packard and Capgemini, which now offer digital supply chain services.

Figure 11.9 **Growth of the global digital recorded music market**

Digital recorded music	2003	2004	2005	2006	2007	2008
Revenues ($M)	20	380	1,125	2,174	2,900	3,712
% total industry	–	2	5	11	15	20

Source: PWC Global Entertainment and Media Report (2009).

Figure 11.10 **Examples of the growth in global digital media markets**

Media category	Global digital revenues (% total)					
	2003	2004	2005	2006	2007	2008
Recorded music	–	2	5	11	15	20
Newspapers	–	–	–	–	2	4
Films	–	–	–	–	3	4
Books	–	–	–	–	2	4

Source: PWC Global Entertainment and Media Report (2009).

Developing supply chains

The goal of supply chain management is to more efficiently and effectively align customers, distribution channels, operations and suppliers so that market needs can be better

iTunes software was created in 2001 to let customers manage the music on their iPods. Two years later, the iTunes music store was launched selling 200,000 songs that could each be downloaded for $0.99. It took three years for them to sell 1 billion songs, but then things started to take off. By February 2008, iTunes had sold more than 4 billion songs, owned 70 per cent of the worldwide digital music market and was the third-largest US music retailer after Wal-Mart and Best Buy. Profits on sales are low (about 9 per cent), but Apple's iPod sales have grown sevenfold since iTunes was first introduced in 2003, and the buying process also keeps customers locked in to using its iPods.

By June 2010, 300 million iPods had been sold. The company has 70 per cent of the MP3 player market, where competitors are becoming fewer and fewer as rivals have decided to leave the market. Estimates show that each iPod customer also spends another 30 per cent of their iPod value on accessories. In June 2007, Apple launched the iPhone, combining its iPod Touch with a mobile smartphone, and by January 2010 it had sold 45 million iPhones and had 16 per cent of the smartphone market. Building on this success, Apple launched the iPad in April 2010 as a tablet computer running a similar operating system to the iPod Touch and iPhone. By June 2010, just 60 days after its launch, 2 million iPads had been sold, averaging one sale every three seconds.

www.apple.com/iTunes

Questions

1 What is Apple's business model?

2 How has its digital supply chain contributed to its recent success?

supported. As outlined earlier, many companies in the 1980s focused on fixing their own operations problems, but few looked across the whole supply chain. However, in the 1990s this changed, as a European-based survey in 1996 showed.[1] Of the companies reviewed, 88 per cent had significantly overhauled their supply chains and saw this as key to improving their overall performance. However, this is not radically different from Ralph Borsodi's observation in 1929 that the cost of distributing necessities and luxuries had nearly trebled between 1870 and 1920, while production costs had come down by one fifth[2]... and what was being saved in production was being lost in distribution. Companies need to look both upstream towards suppliers and downstream towards customers if they are to improve overall supply chain performance and market support. Supply chain activities thus require integrating, coordinating and synchronizing across the whole chain.

> **KEY IDEA**

Supply chains can be developed to more efficiently and effectively support market needs by integrating, coordinating and synchronizing activities across the chain

Stages of development

This section reviews the origins and evolution of supply chains and examines the steps typically involved in their development.

Origin and evolution of supply chains

The functional management and control used to manage organizations in the past resulted in fragmented supply chains by focusing on managing **vertical processes** rather than **horizontal processes**, as illustrated in Figure 11.11. This figure shows how functions within an organization have their own self-contained reporting structures and systems. This results in artificial barriers being created between the different steps of the supply chain, which causes fragmentation, delay or unnecessary inventory to be locked in the system.

> Vertical processes – processes resulting from hierarchical reporting structures
>
> Horizontal processes – managing across the processes within and between businesses

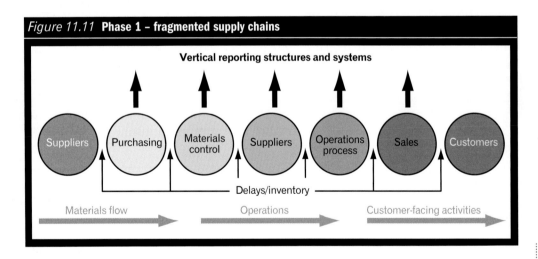

Figure 11.11 **Phase 1 – fragmented supply chains**

Integrating activities

The first step in developing a supply chain is to integrate activities within the internal supply chain, as illustrated in Figure 11.12. To do this, companies must align all the activities involved from initial customer contact to final service or product delivery. Forging cooperation across all these steps will create an integrated **internal supply chain** and identify opportunities to reduce costs and improve customer support.

> Internal supply chain – the part of a supply chain that is managed within a business

Coordinating activities

Once the internal supply chain has been integrated, companies can start coordinating activities between the different businesses within the **external supply chain**. As shown in

> External supply chain – the part of the supply chain managed by suppliers

Tier 1 supplier – one
that supplies directly
to an organization,
while a Tier 2
supplier supplies
materials to a Tier 1
supplier, and so on

Tier 1 customer –
one that is supplied
directly by an
organization, while
a Tier 2 customer is
supplied by a Tier 1
customer, and so on

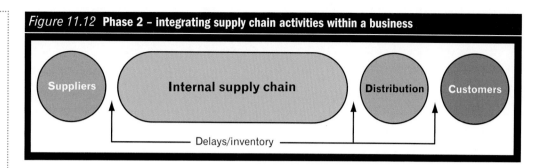

Figure 11.12 **Phase 2 – integrating supply chain activities within a business**

Figure 11.13, this coordination across all parts of the chain, such as Tier 2 suppliers, **Tier 1 suppliers, Tier 1 customers** (such as wholesalers/retailers or distributors/dealers) and Tier 2 customers (such as end-users), is needed to ensure that there is collaboration across the whole of the chain.

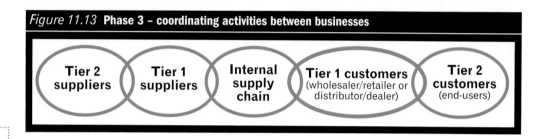

Figure 11.13 **Phase 3 – coordinating activities between businesses**

Synchronizing activities

Real-time
information –
information that
represents the
current position

The final phase is to synchronize all the activities across the supply chain, as shown in Figure 11.14. This requires partnership and strategic alliances to help create **real-time information** flows across the chain in terms of aspects such as customer management, order placement, service or product design, payment and final delivery. This necessitates dramatic changes in roles and responsibilities across the chain, with suppliers, distributors and customers often being involved in service or product design and deciding how much and when to despatch. This is significantly different from the original supply chain design shown in Figure 11.11. However, to bring this about, companies must address a number of issues, including:

- *Overcome the barriers to integration* Functions within organizations, as well as organizations themselves, create barriers to integration. Businesses must view the supply chain as a whole before thinking about how best to use it to make greater improvements in performance and market support.

- *Respond to short lead-times* Delivery speed is an order-winner or qualifier for many customers. Reliably supporting this requires the development of lean logistics and management of the supply chain as an integrated whole. A study completed by Ernst & Young and the University of Tennessee in the late 1990s showed that average order cycle times fell from 6.3 to 3.5 days when parts of a supply chain were outsourced.[3]

- *Eliminate costs* Integrating and synchronizing the supply chain lowers costs by reducing inventory, simplifying procedures, eliminating duplication and removing other non-value-added activities together with their associated overheads. In the same Ernst & Young and University of Tennessee study, outsourcing in participating businesses led to a fall in average logistics costs and average logistic assets of 8 and 22 per cent, respectively.

Real-time needs –
customers' immediate
requirements

- *Move information, not inventory* Focusing on moving information rather than materials enables companies to reduce delays and deliver against **real-time needs** rather than using inventory to cushion themselves against uncertain demand.

SYNCHRONIZED AND REAL-

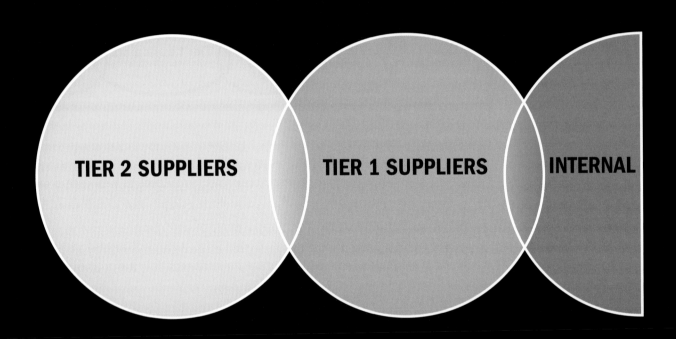

TIER 2 SUPPLIERS   TIER 1 SUPPLIERS   INTERNAL

TIME INFORMATION FLOWS

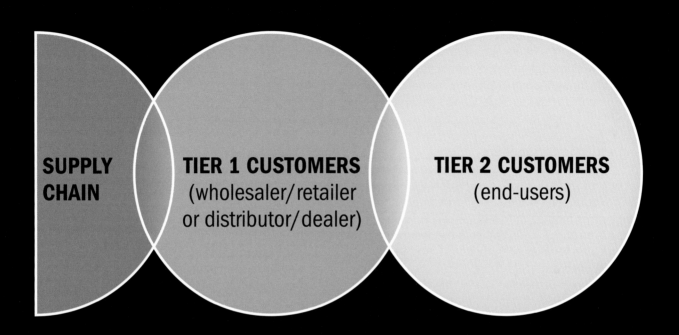

SUPPLY CHAIN

TIER 1 CUSTOMERS
(wholesaler/retailer
or distributor/dealer)

TIER 2 CUSTOMERS
(end-users)

> KEY IDEA

To develop a supply chain, companies must first integrate activities across the chain, and then look for ways to coordinate them, before finally working out how to synchronize them

An example of **lean supply chain management** involves the revolutionary changes brought to high peak climbing by Reinhold Messner, as described in Case 11.6.

Tools and techniques for developing supply chains

Making the changes outlined in the last section involves addressing a number of critical issues within the business, and the key ones are now discussed.

> KEY IDEA

Businesses can develop their supply chains by improving customer support, changing attitudes towards suppliers, using IT, developing strategic partnerships and working with customers to better understand their needs

Lean supply chain management – extending just-in-time principles to the whole supply chain in order to eliminate waste and reduce inventory throughout. It is typically based on close, long-term relationships with a small number of suppliers

Improving consumer support

There is more to supply chain management than hard-nosed procurement and tight inventory control. Although effective management aims to eliminate delays and reduce resources along the way, such improvements need also to create more effective support. To do this, companies need to understand market requirements and how best to support them, rather than simply aiming to reduce price.

Changing attitude to suppliers

Traditionally, companies have not cooperated with suppliers with the aim of building long-term relationships. Instead, they have ruled through threat and fear by maintaining control over product or service design and order scheduling, and then pitting suppliers against each other to meet their requirements. To change this attitude, companies must bring suppliers on board much earlier in the design process, and even invite them to help in identifying future services and products. Companies need to understand how to reward and collaborate with suppliers if they are to build integrated and synchronized supply chains, and to recognize that this is a lengthy development process that goes through the series of phases shown in Figure 11.15. An illustration of the type of change required is described in Case 11.7.

Increasing use of IT

Since the early 1960s, four major IT developments have transformed the way in which companies conduct business and the opportunity to better manage their supply chains from suppliers through to end-users:

- *Mainframes* In the early 1960s, companies began using mainframe computers to manage their businesses. Business applications included material requirements planning and manufacturing resource planning (see Chapter 8), which enabled companies to standardize and systemize their day-to-day tasks. However, these emphasized the functional divisions within organizations as people became systems experts within their own business area.

- *Personal computers* In the 1970s, personal computers started to be used within companies to run applications such as word processing, spreadsheets and presentation software. This development started to put the power of computing back into the hands of users and helped break down functional barriers by creating cross-functional processes.

Reinhold Messner, the Italian climber, is one of the great sports heroes of Europe. His claim to fame is not so much that he has climbed all 14 of the world's highest peaks, but that he introduced a totally new way of climbing – the direct alpine approach – which uses little equipment and no oxygen support to reach the top.

The conventional mountaineering approach is based on massive support, including extra oxygen, which was thought to be essential for ascents of over 25,000 feet. Men such as Sir Edmund Hillary and Chris Bonington relied on hundreds of guides who carried food, oxygen and supplies – a 1963 American expedition to climb Everest included over 900 porters carrying 27 tonnes of equipment! Messner argues that with this approach, the slowest man sets the pace. His goal, however, is speed of execution. Although assisted by guides up to

the base of a mountain, Messner makes the final assault by himself, or with one other person, in a single day. When Hillary and Tenzing first climbed Mount Everest in 1953, they took 7 weeks. On 21 May 2004, Pemba Dorji Sherpa took 8 hours 10 minutes using the direct alpine approach!
www.reinhold-messner.de

Questions

1 Review the stages in the supply chain represented in Figure 11.11 with that of the conventional mountaineering approach described above. What similarities can you draw?

2 Repeat the analysis for Figure 11.14 and Messner's approach to mountaineering.

Reproduced with the permission of Canon (UK)

Viewed in the past merely as purchasing, supply chain management is now recognized as a strategic part of operations that stretches from suppliers to end-customers. Suppliers are no longer transient providers selected solely on the basis of lowest price, but partners contributing to the continuous improvement of the supply chain that delivers value to customers. While Japanese buyer–supplier relationships vary from firm to firm and sector to sector, companies as diverse as Nintendo, Canon and Toyota display certain common aspects in their different approaches to suppliers.

Once selected, suppliers are retained during the life cycle of the specific model. Staff from the buyer will typically train the supplier's staff on their operations and quality procedures and on other aspects of the organization. Finally, the buyer firm will evaluate the supplier organization to test the viability of a long-term relationship by assessing the robustness of the whole organization.

www.nintendo.com, www.canon.com, www.toyota.com

Questions

1 Review the common aspects of the Japanese companies' approach to suppliers.

2 How do these illustrate the 'Changing attitude to suppliers' section described in the text?

Figure 11.15 **Phases in changing attitudes to suppliers**

Threat and fear	**Traditional stance. Perceptions based upon:** · Customer dominates the relationship with suppliers · Suppliers respond to demands · Suppliers pitted against each other · Constant threat of purchases being given to other suppliers · Supplier's ongoing fear of losing a contract
Reward	**First step towards cooperation and moving from a reactive to a proactive stance. Characterized by elements such as:** · Fewer suppliers · Long-term contracts · Customer is proactive in building a relationship with suppliers
Collaborate	**Progressive move towards fuller and more cooperative relationships, the pace of which is set predominantly by the customer. Evolution through a series of steps such as:** · Customer identifies improvements that a supplier can make · Customer provides support and resources (for example, technical capability) to undertake improvements within a supplier's delivery systems · Customer gives actual help to improve a supplier's capabilities, including training a supplier's staff · Customer takes into account the processes of its suppliers when designing services and products to help them improve their support · Customer focuses attention on Tier 2 suppliers as a source of improving Tier 1 suppliers' support (see Figure 11.13)
Integrate and synchronize	**The final step is to integrate activities achieving benefits typically associated with ownership – the concept of virtual ownership. Based upon mutual respect and trust, these include suppliers' access to real time information, with customers harmonizing their suppliers' work and synchronizing their support. These changes range from:** · Access to design-related information and responsibility for service/product design · Suppliers' responsibility for deciding when and how much to despatch

Electronic data interchange – a system using remote computer networks to exchange business data between companies within a supply chain without going through any intermediaries

Electronic point-of-sale – a system that records sales and payment transactions at cash terminals in retail stores as and when they happen. This is typically used to track sales trends, which are then used as the basis for purchase orders and to replenish goods in stores

E-commerce – the use of the Internet to transfer information across the supply chain, or to buy or sell services and products

- *Network computing* In the mid-1980s, computer networks were introduced with customer/supplier applications, **electronic data interchange**, **electronic point-of-sale** (EPOS) and electronic mail (e-mail). This significantly reduced the costs of handling information and increased its speed of exchange, allowing companies to develop real-time systems and responses, as illustrated by Case 11.8.

- E-commerce In the early 1990s, the Internet was developed, providing a universal infrastructure that facilitates the interchange of information between businesses. This further helped cooperation across the supply chain, enabling priorities and performance to be managed across the chain through better communication and a better interchange of information between companies. The earlier section on digital supply highlights the continued use of IT developments in the management of supply chains.

Over the last 30 years, these IT developments have continually broken down the barriers between individuals, functions, business and corporations within supply chains, as

Caterpillar, the giant US manufacturer of earth-moving equipment, has developed electronically based systems that identify ahead of time when equipment needs servicing. An electronic message is relayed to the Caterpillar Centre. The local dealer is then alerted, and the necessary parts to complete the servicing requirement are sent. Dealers agree appropriate dates with customers, and the specified work is then completed.

www.caterpillar.com

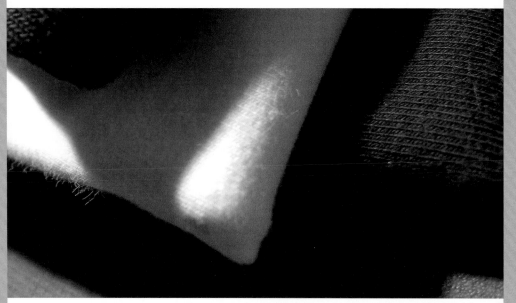

GAP, the US-based apparel company, is currently achieving 14 **inventory turns** a year while also being able to change the stockholding in all its outlets 13 times per year and on the same day. The information requirements and real-time systems that underpin these arrangements include accurate inventory data, EPOS facilities and synchronized logistics.

www.gap.com

Inventory turn – relates the level of inventory (£s) to sales revenue (£s) by dividing sales revenue by the average inventory holding in the period; the answer represents the number of time inventory turns over in one year

Question

Explain how IT developments have enabled Caterpillar and GAP to change their business models.

Lecturers: visit www.palgrave.com/business/hillessential for additional resources

shown in Figure 11.16. E-commerce presents some businesses with new opportunities and poses a significant threat to those who ignore it. Many sectors have already seen the increasing and competitive impact of the Internet. For those who have adapted to the new technology, it represents an opportunity to rethink all aspects of **order fulfilment**, from order entry to distribution, as shown in Case 11.9.

Figure 11.16 **The evolving role of IT in managing supply chains**	
Phase	**Aspects of change**
1 Cross-individuals	Broke down barriers between functional experts themselves and between these and the executives responsible for managing core parts of a business, particularly operations
2 Cross-functional	Facilitated links between functions by requiring and helping the interchange between different parts of the same business
3 Cross-businesses	Impacted on the way companies conduct business by removing barriers within an organization and between parts of the immediate supply chain
4 Cross-corporate	Continued the cross-corporate changes by facilitating cooperation of business within a supply chain including Tier 2 suppliers

Strategic partnering

The ultimate aim is for companies to move to the level of strategic partnering. This embodies a conscious decision to **virtually integrate** the supply chain by working with other companies in the chain. However, this requires a major change in customer–supplier relations in order to synchronize activities across a chain so that it becomes virtually integrated (see Figure 11.15). How far customers' attitudes to suppliers can be changed depends on not only the companies involved, but also the evolution of the industry within which the company operates. For example, in the early days of the computing industry, the major players had no option but to make all their components in-house. However, as the sector grew, companies emerged that produced specific components, giving new industry entrants the opportunity to buy rather than make. As Michael Dell (founder of Dell) explained:

> As a new start-up, Dell couldn't afford to create every piece of the value chain. But more to the point, why should we want to? We concluded we'd be better off leveraging the investments others have made and focusing on delivering solutions and systems to customers ... It's a pretty simple strategy, but at the time it went against the dominant 'engineering-centric' view of the industry. The IBMs, Compaqs and HPs subscribed to a 'we-have-to-develop-everything' view of the world. If you weren't doing component assembly you weren't a real computer company.[4]

Delivering to customers

On the delivery end of the chain, companies can work with their customers to better understand their needs. For example, some retail stores share EPOS data with their suppliers to help them meet market trends and changes. At the sourcing end of the chain, suppliers can deliver more frequently, keep consignment inventory in a customer's warehouse (and only invoices it when it is used) and manage inventory replenishment. This frees up customer resources while providing the supplier with a longer term commitment, increased barriers to entry that reduce a suppliers' sales and marketing expenses, and firm information that a supplier can use to plan and schedule its own operations and supply chain. One illustration of increased partnering is provided by Case 11.10.

One company that is building on its current history of excellent supply chain management is Dell Computer Corporation. Dell uses supply chain management to continuously improve its direct business model by sound supply chain integration as follows:

- Dell only makes-to-order – no resources are committed until a customer order is received.
- Dell purchases components on a JIT basis, thus benefiting from the latest (that is, lowest) component prices.
- By holding little inventory, Dell is able to respond to component developments quickly and without incurring inventory losses through obsolescence.
- Short component lead-times also allow Dell to meet the delivery speed characteristics of its market with minimum investment in inventory.

Dell continues to develop and improve the capabilities of its supply chain in several ways. In 2009, the Dell website was generating daily revenues of more than $25 million. The website makes online ordering quick and convenient by allowing customers to specify the product features they want and instantly receiving a quoted price.

In the corporate sales market, Dell has also created 'Premier Pages'. These are websites dedicated to corporate clients that can be accessed by a client's authorized employees to research, configure and price personal computers before purchase. Each website page holds client-specific data such as preferred configurations, specifications and prices. This development increases the accuracy of orders and simplifies Dell's customer ordering process resulting in the overall cost of buying PCs being greatly reduced. For example, the Ford Motor Company estimates that using Premier Pages saves it up to $2 million annually.

www.dell.com

Questions

1 Explain how Dell integrates its supply chain.

2 How does the Dell website feature in these integrative developments?

3 How is the Ford Motor Company able to save up to $2 million annually by using Dell's Premier Pages?

Lecturers: visit www.palgrave.com/business/ hillessential for additional resources

© Alex Hill and Terry Hill 2011

© Alex Hill and Terry Hill 2011

Calyx & Corolla, a US-based company, pioneered the delivery of fresh-cut flowers directly to their customers from the growers. Using the delivery firm Federal Express (FedEx), customers' orders are relayed to one of 25 suppliers (the flower growers), who assemble the chosen bouquet from one of 150 products.

Within the supply chain, FedEx visits all the suppliers to train their staff on the best ways to pack the flower arrangements, and to ensure that the delivery phase of the chain synchronizes with the work schedules and product availability of individual growers. Direct supply results in the flowers lasting nine or ten days longer than competitors' offerings.

For Calyx & Corolla, this not only results in an arrangement in which no inventory needs to be held, but the delivery speed and quality conformance advantages also allow the company to price its products at a 60 per cent premium. Sales revenues in the period 1992–98 grew from $10 million to $25 million when the company was acquired by the Vermont Teddy Bear Company.

www.calyxandcorolla.com

Questions

1 How has Calyx & Corolla synchronized its supply chain?

2 What advantages has the company gained from these developments?

Lecturers: visit www.palgrave.com/business/hillessential for additional resources

The benefits of improving supply chains

Applying the principles of lean operations to managing the supply chain (the external phase of the operations process) is part of the operations management task. Improving supply chains (using the approaches outlined in Chapter 12) will improve the performance of the whole chain and yield a range of benefits, particularly lower costs, shorter lead-times and reduced inventories, as explained below, while supply chains also bring the benefits of increased technical expertise.

> **KEY IDEA**
   Businesses can develop their supply chains to lower costs, shorten lead-times, reduce cash holdings and give greater access to technical expertise

Lean supply chains

Reduced costs

As supply chains develop, the overall cost of supplying services or products through that chain reduces. A.T. Kearney Inc., a Chicago-based consulting firm, estimates that the cost of purchased parts and services can be reduced by up to 30 per cent by incorporating suppliers into a company's service or product development process. Large savings can also be made by encouraging suppliers to suggest cost-cutting ideas and design innovations for existing services and products.

Shorter lead-times

Improving supply chains can greatly reduce the overall lead-time of the chain by getting suppliers to become more than just parts providers. Involving suppliers and using their expertise provides several different ways to shorten the time it takes to supply a customer, as the following examples illustrate:

- *AW Chesterton Co.*, a US family-owned seal, pump and packing manufacturer, found that customers now wanted its products in days or even hours, compared with 12–16 weeks a decade previously. To meet this requirement, it installed computer systems allowing customers to transmit drawings and engineering specifications directly to its manufacturing plant, which was geared up for a fast response. However, this only reduced the company's in-house lead-time. To ensure customer needs were met, it then also reduced the number of suppliers it worked with from 1,300 to 125, and gave delivery reliability, delivery lead-times and quality conformance twice as much importance as price when evaluating with which suppliers it should go into partnership.

- *IKEA*, the Swedish home furnishings retailer, has also worked with its suppliers and made a number of in-house developments to meet the delivery speed requirements of the fashion market it serves. This has been achieved through long-term relationships with 1,800 suppliers and a sophisticated in-house logistics and warehouse system. EPOS information from its 100 retail stores in over 50 countries provides online sales data to the nearest warehouse and the operational head office in Älmhult in Sweden, where information systems analyse sales patterns worldwide. In turn, the warehouses work with retail stores to anticipate demand and eliminate shortages while keeping inventory and floor space low.

- *Acer*, the Taiwanese personal computer maker, meets the short product life cycles of its market by working on a 10-month rolling product life cycle: three months for product development, six months for sales of the product, and one-month to sell old inventory before the next cycle begins.

- *Dana Corporation*, a major supplier of truck axles, has an entire 60-engineer laboratory near Toledo, Ohio in the US, dedicated to making U-joints. Using a computer-aided design system, Dana can design new products cheaply and build prototypes for customers in just a few hours.

Lower inventories

Managing supply chains as a whole means moving to a 'one-firm concept' in which external providers are treated like partners and as if they were inside the company, as illustrated in Figure 11.17. For example:

- *Eastman Chemicals* uses 1,500 different raw materials provided by 850 suppliers. To make sure there is as little idle inventory as possible, Eastman uses a 'stream inventory management' system in which the whole supply chain is treated as a single pipeline. When an order comes in from the customer, one pound of product is taken out of the tail end, with the raw material function working with the supplier to put another pound in on the other end. The desired aim is to achieve continuous flow. Eastman monitors inventory at its suppliers and uses accurate forecasts to reduce excess inventory across the whole supply chain. As a result:
  - Total inventories halved in the last decade and are now 9 per cent of sales, with raw materials and supplies accounting for less than 2 per cent
  - The supply of wood pulp stock has been reduced from three months to nine days, with the next target set at four days
  - The inventory of paraxylene, a material used for polyethylene terephthalate (plastic soda bottles), has reduced from 18 million pounds held 20 years ago to 14 million pounds today even though production volumes are three times higher.

- *Dell*, the US personal computer manufacturer, significantly reduced its costs and inventories by selling directly to customers rather than through a third-party retailer. To do this, it has used technologies and information to 'virtually integrate' the chain and

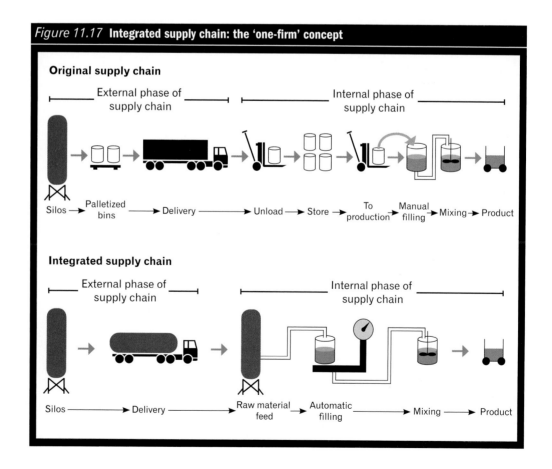

Figure 11.17 Integrated supply chain: the 'one-firm' concept

Original supply chain

External phase of supply chain   Internal phase of supply chain

Silos → Palletized bins → Delivery → Unload → Store → To production → Manual filling → Mixing → Product

Integrated supply chain

External phase of supply chain   Internal phase of supply chain

Silos → Delivery → Raw material feed → Automatic filling → Mixing → Product blur the traditional boundaries in the supply chain between suppliers and customers. This has enabled it to tap into the benefits of a coordinated supply chain that were traditionally only available through vertical integration, while also tapping into the benefits of **specialization**, where each company within the chain (Dell and its suppliers) focuses on what it is good at. Keeping inventories low is critical in the fast-changing technology business to protect the business from falling material prices and to reduce the time taken to launch new products. For these reasons, Dell works closely with its suppliers to keep inventories low. For example, Airborne Express and UPS collect computers from Dell and then match them with the same quantity of monitors from Sony's plant in Mexico before delivering them directly to Dell's customers. To do this, Dell has developed real-time information on its own demand profile and linked this into its suppliers, sometimes every few hours. 'The greatest challenge in working with suppliers is getting them in sync with the fast pace we have to maintain. The key to making it work is information,' explained Michael Dell.[5] As a result, Dell's total inventory is less than 10 per cent of sales.

> Specialization – concentrating on a limited area of expertise

Increased access to technical expertise

In addition to the benefits of having leaner supply chains, suppliers can also be a great source of technical expertise, as the following examples illustrate:

- Japanese automobile manufacturers Honda and Toyota do not source much from low-wage countries as the technical capability of their suppliers is seen as being more important than low labour costs.

- US PC manufacturer Dell recently increased the value of purchase orders placed with Taiwanese suppliers from US$8 billion to US$12.5 billion on the agreement that they deliver the 'newest, greatest technology'.

Critical reflections

Increasingly, businesses must recognize that they are at the centre of material networks and information flows. These flows extend from the customer interface through operations to the building of relationships with suppliers. The operations role, however, is not just the integration and management of the parts of the supply chain. It is also the constant reviewing and alignment of these closely linked networks to better meet the changing needs of the company's markets and to help achieve the sales revenue and profit goals of the organization.

Increased outsourcing is creating more complex supply networks

Since the mid 1980s, companies have chosen to outsource more services and products from an outside provider. As a result, supply chains are becoming more complex and have evolved into supply networks. For example:

- Dell, Cisco (a US-based networks solution company) and Wal-Mart have all outsourced their logistics functions.

- Amazon relies on publishers for product development, Visa and Mastercard for revenue collection and UPS for logistics.

- Xerox uses GE Capital for customer financing, revenue collection and billing.

- Cable & Wireless (a leading telecommunications company) has outsourced its human resource processes to e-Peopleserve, a joint venture between Accenture (a global consultancy and technology services company) and British Telecom.

- BP (an international petroleum products company) and Bank of America have outsourced their human resource administration processes to Exult (a California-based provider of business services related to human resources).

- The Royal National Institute for the Blind uses Arval PHH (an international contract hire and fleet management business) to manage its vehicle fleet.

Supplier relationships

- The benefits from developing supplier relationships are two-way, as the following illustrations show. Where companies develop the long-term supplier relationships that go hand in hand with developments of supply chain management, one test of the new depths of these joint working arrangements is their response in times of reduced sales. For example, Toyota's commitment to its suppliers is underlined by the fact that none of its suppliers has closed down in the last decade even though Toyota's total production has dropped 25 per cent since the early 1990s. Western companies, as part of developing more effective and more responsive supply chains, are moving into closer collaborative relationships and agreements with suppliers than in the past.

- With global gross domestic product estimated to be in the order of $30 trillion, and the cost of loading, unloading, sorting, reloading and transporting goods to be some 12 per cent (or about $3.5 trillion) of this total, the opportunities for savings provide an overwhelming case for supply chain development. But the spirit and practice of customer–supplier relations need to fundamentally change for this to happen. While the potential benefits are considerable, the necessary time and investment need to be recognized by top management as a corporate priority, and this must be demonstrated by commitment throughout the organization.

Summary

- When designing their supply chains, companies need first to decide what to make and what to buy based on:

- The market order-winners and qualifiers they have to support

- How they could create barriers to entry

- Whether they need to maintain a supply of key materials

- How best to understand customer requirements

- Which core capabilities need to be retained in-house

- Which external capabilities need to be accessed from elsewhere

- How the company wishes to take advantage of the trend to reduce barriers on import duties imposed by countries.

- In reality, however, these decisions are governed by other factors such as continuing previous decisions, meeting cost targets, shedding difficult tasks and fulfilling political requirements. Choosing whether to make or buy brings with it a number of advantages and disadvantages, but some of these can be altered by choosing from other alternatives to outsourcing such as joint ventures and co-sourcing.

- Making in-house offers firms greater control over their processes, capabilities and business environment. It also increases market knowledge, product knowledge and technological innovation, while providing a greater opportunity to reduce product cost. However, it can also dilute a company's focus on its core tasks and reduce its access to external sources of capacity, up-to-date technologies and world-class capabilities. On the other hand, it can increase operating costs and make them more difficult to control.

- To some extent, the advantages and disadvantages of outsourcing are the inverse of those of making in-house. If used appropriately and managed well, outsourcing can free up resources and increase the focus on the core tasks that add value for the customer. Outsourcing can reduce operating costs and make them easier to control, while improving the design and market perception of services and products by giving a company an increased access to external sources of capacity, up-to-date technologies and world-class capabilities. However, it can also result in a loss of control of key processes and capabilities, and can make a business more vulnerable by potentially exposing its intellectual property to outside organizations. Equally, once a process has been outsourced, it is then difficult to move it back in-house as the knowledge is no longer to be found within the organization and the investment involved can be prohibitive.

- Increasingly, companies compete as supply chains rather than individual organizations. Totally integrating a supply chain from material producer through to end-customer greatly improves how a business operates and supports its customers. However, effective collaboration and fuller relationships across the supply chain are required to achieve this.

- To develop supply chains, companies must focus on improving consumer support, changing their attitude to suppliers, investing in IT and creating strategic partnerships with companies upstream towards suppliers and downstream towards customers within the chain. The first step is to integrate activities within the internal supply chain by aligning all the activities from initial customer contact to final service or product delivery. Once the internal supply chain has been integrated, companies can start coordinating activities between the different businesses within the chain.

- Finally, the supply chain can be synchronized using partnerships and strategic alliances to help create real-time information flows across the chain in aspects such as customer management, order placement, service or product design, payment and final delivery. This requires dramatic changes in the roles and responsibilities across the chain, with suppliers, distributors and customers often being involved in key decisions from service or product design through to delivery schedules. To achieve this, companies must overcome barriers to integration and focus on moving information rather than inventory across the chain.

- Integrated and synchronized supply chains allow companies to respond better to market opportunities and competitive pressures by competing as a supply chain rather than as a number of individual organizations, and by collaborating with other parts of the chain to improve its efficiency and effectiveness. Such supply chains also allow information to be exchanged, ensuring that end-user needs are met.

- Operating as a demand chain rather than a supply chain allows organizations to reduce inventory levels across the chain while making them more responsive to changing customer requirements.

Study activities

Discussion questions

1 What factors should be taken into account when making make-or-buy decisions? Illustrate your answer with examples from a service and a manufacturing organization.

2 Given the increasing importance of environmental concerns, how would a company incorporate these issues into the make-or-buy process? Give two examples to illustrate your views.

3 How will e-commerce continue to impact the supply chain?

4 What benefits do suppliers receive from developing closer ties with major customers?

5 A major company decides to move to a more collaborative stance with a supplier. What would be the first key changes it would need to make? What possible initial responses might be made by the supplier?

6 Give two examples (with reasons) for both a service and manufacturing company where outsourcing a service:

- Makes sense

- Does not make sense

7 What type of call centre service providers lend themselves and do not lend themselves to overseas provision?

8 What benefits would a company derive from introducing e-procurement? What are the obstacles you would expect to hinder this development?

Assignments

1 What criteria do you think the owner of each of the following independent outlets would use to evaluate and select key suppliers?

- A restaurant

- A stationer

- A coffee shop.

Now visit an independent outlet for each of these types of company and ask the owners how they evaluate and select key suppliers. Compare the results and explain any significant differences.

2 In what circumstances would you consider that each of the following would be advantageous to a company:

- Single sourcing

- Multisourcing

Use a service and a manufacturing organization to illustrate your views.

Exploring further

Journal articles

Aron, R. and Singh, J.V. (2005) 'Getting offshoring right'. *Harvard Business Review*, **83**(12), pp. 135–43. In the past decade, many companies in North America and Europe have experimented with offshoring and outsourcing business processes, hoping to reduce their costs and gain a strategic advantage. According to several studies, however, many have failed to generate the expected financial benefits. The article presents a three-part methodology that can help improve the current success rate.

Lee, H.L. (2004) 'The triple-A supply chain'. *Harvard Business Review*, **82**(10), pp.102–12. This article puts forward the view that supply chains that focus on speed and costs tend to deteriorate over time. It argues that only companies building supply chains that are agile, adaptable and aligned get ahead of their rivals. All three components are essential; without any one of them, supply chains break down.

Lewin, A.Y. and Peeters, C. (2006) 'The top-line allure of offshoring'. *Harvard Business Review*, **84**(3), pp. 22–4. The article reports a study of offshore arrangements and concludes that not only are there gains of lower costs, but also that 73 per cent of offshore arrangements support companies' growth strategies, with 32 per cent of those initiatives involving product innovation and design, research and development, or engineering.

Narayanan, V.G. and Raman, A. (2004) 'Aligning incentives in supply chains'. *Harvard Business Review*, **82**(11), pp. 94–102. An analysis of more than 50 supply networks demonstrates that companies often look after their own interests while giving far less attention to those of their suppliers. The result is that supply chains typically perform poorly. The article argues that a supply chain will work well only if the risks, costs and rewards of doing business are distributed fairly across the network.

Slone, R.E., Mentzer, J.T. and Dittmann, J.P. (2007) 'Are you the weakest link in your company's supply chain?' *Harvard Business Review*, **85**(9), pp.116–27. This article identifies the key areas in which CEOs can influence their supply chains and shows them how to assess the influence they currently exert.

Books

Christopher, M. (2010) *Logistics and Supply Chain Management*. London: Financial Times. This looks at how to develop and manage supply chain networks in order to gain sustainable advantage in today's turbulent global markets.

Cordon, C. and Vollmann, T.E. (2008) *The Power of Two*. Basingstoke: Palgrave Macmillan. This text provides a practical approach to collaborating with, developing and harnessing suppliers.

Cousins, P., Lamming, R., Lawson, B. and Squire, B. (2007) *Strategic Supply Management: Principles, Theories and Practice*. Prentice Hall. This book traces the development of purchasing and supply management from its origins as a tactical commercial function into a key strategic business process.

Hill, A. and Hill, T. (2009) *Manufacturing Operations Strategy: Text and Cases*, 3rd edn. Basingstoke: Palgrave Macmillan. The text provides a useful supplement to the current book by outlining an in-depth approach for developing and implementing operations strategy within manufacturing organizations.

Hill, T. (2005) *Operations Management: Text and Cases.* Basingstoke: Palgrave Macmillan. This provides a useful supplement to the current book by offering a more comprehensive explanation and further examples (including long case studies) showing how service and manufacturing companies have applied these concepts.

Nassimveni, G. and Sartor, M. (2006) *Sourcing in China*. Basingstoke: Palgrave Macmillan. Nassimveni and Sartor's book provides comments on the types of strategy and critical issues when outsourcing in China.

Patel, A.V. and Aran, H. (2005) *Outsourcing Success: The Management Imperative*. Basingstoke: Palgrave Macmillan. This addresses the practical issues in developing a sourcing strategy, the risks involved and the guidelines for choosing outsourcing partners.

Willcocks, L.P. and Lacity, M. (2006) *Global Sourcing of Business and IT Services*. Basingstoke: Palgrave Macmillan. This book contains 11 contributions by a number of authors on a range of topics including managing the sourcing of services and products through their life cycles and how to assess suppliers' capabilities.

Notes and references

1 Economist Intelligence Unit and KPMG Management Consultants Report, *Supply Chain Management: Europe's New Competitive Battle Ground*, 1996.

2 Borsodi, R. (1929) *This Ugly Civilization*. New York: Simon & Schuster.

3 As reported in Allen, E. (1999) 'One-stop shop is no cure-all'. *Financial Times*, June 17, p. 16.

4 Margretta, J. (1998) 'The power of virtual integration: an interview with Dell Computer's Michael Dell'. *Harvard Business Review*, March–April, pp. 78–84.

5 Margretta, J. (1998) 'The power of virtual integration: an interview with Dell Computer's Michael Dell'. *Harvard Business Review*, March–April, pp. 78–84.

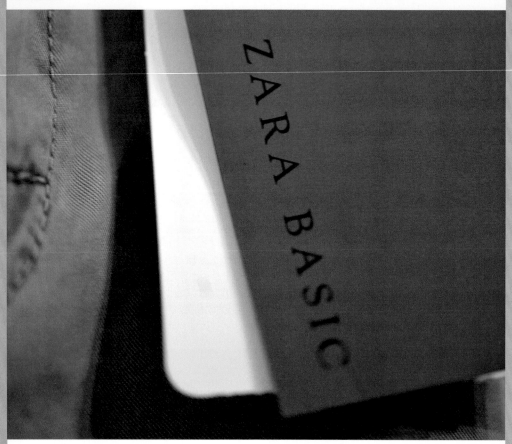

The Zara boutique-clothing store on Calle Real in the northern Spanish city of La Coruña is buzzing. Customers have made the journey here on a rainy Saturday morning to see what new and exciting styles are available this week. The red tank tops and black blazers seem to be a hit, but customers are pining for beige ones and bright purple ones too. Faced with this problem, most fashion companies would normally have to spend months retooling and restocking their range. Not Zara, however. Each store manager is able to spot these changes in trends and type them into their Casio handheld computer on Saturday in the safe knowledge that the items will arrive early the next week.

There is a very strong link between the store managers and the central design team based at Zara's head office in La Coruña. Each store is electronically linked back to the head office so that the head office can view and assess sales on a real-time basis. This allows the company to make sure that it can adapt quickly to customers' wants and desires. One example

of this was a new khaki skirt that the company initially just stocked in Spain to see how it would sell. In the La Coruña store, it sold out after being on the shelves for only a couple of hours. After speaking to Barcelona, it was apparent that sales were brisk there too. It was decided that the skirt should be tested out elsewhere, so overnight Zara sent out 7,800 skirts to over 1,300 stores worldwide. The results were clear. The skirt was a hit, and within the next few days stores in Europe, Asia and North and South America were being stocked with the khaki skirt.

It is this mix of intelligence gathering, fashion instinct and technological savoir-faire that is allowing Zara to set in motion something unique in the clothing trade. The combination of being able to translate the latest trends into products in less than 15 days and delivering them to its stores twice a week means that it is able to catch fashion trends while they are hot, responding quickly to the fast-changing tastes of young urban consumers. Few competitors, if any, can get new designs to their stores as quickly, giving Zara the edge over rival brands. The company continuously analyses its value chain and seeks to achieve control over as many sections of it as possible. By focusing on reducing the time between design and sale, it has developed a production cycle that is entirely different from fashion sector norms. The design team works throughout the season, studying everything from what clothes are worn in hit television series to how clubbers dress. This means there is a continuous stream of new products that ensure customers keep coming back to see what's new. Zara's clothing has filled an untapped niche: providing clothes with a designer feel at moderate prices.

Customers seem to love the results of this high-velocity operation. They are often known to queue up in long lines at Zara's stores on designated delivery days, a phenomenon that the Spanish press has dubbed 'Zaramania'. And this popularity is generating tangible, bottom-line results as well as admiration from the fashion world. Over the last five years, the company grew its profitability at a 30 per cent average annual rate, which is 45 per cent faster than its four industry rivals during that period.

A GLOBAL SUCCESS
Founded in 1963 as a maker of ladies' lingerie, Zara opened its first store in 1975 as a retail clothing company with a single location in La Coruña. By 1989, the company had 98 retail shops and production facilities distributed around Spain, and in the same year the company started its international expansion by opening a shop in Lisbon, Portugal. This was only the beginning of what was to become a huge expansion plan across the world. It is now the largest and most profitable unit of Inditex SA, the Spanish clothes manufacturer and distributor, with over 1,300 stores distributed throughout Europe, the Middle East, the Asia Pacific region and the Americas.

This rapid expansion has meant that Zara now has three characteristics that distinguish it from its competitors. First, it is the fastest-growing retail business not only in Europe, but also across the world. Second, the company has been able to export its formula internationally exceedingly well at a time when many other clothing companies in the middle and lower-middle market have found things difficult. Next, for example, is a fantastic company, but it has always struggled to export its particular format. And third, Zara has created a simple, singular message for all its customers. The shopping experience is upmarket, with modern designs reflecting current fashion trends, and the number sold being few enough to give the purchaser a feeling of exclusivity. Also, although the product finish is not to the highest specification, the fabrics, colours, patterns and styles are all high specification while the price is very competitive, a mix that has been the key to Zara's global success. Price tags are big and colourful, emblazoned with the flags of a dozen countries, each accompanied by a local currency price that is the same for that item around the world, from Madrid to Riyadh to Tokyo.

CHALLENGING THE COMPETITION
In times when a combination of recession and some merchandising mistakes have forced GAP and comparable European stores such as Sweden's H&M to retrench, Zara continues to expand. Much of its success is due to its unusual structure. For

decades now, the majority of clothing retailers have outsourced their manufacturing to developing countries in the pursuit of lower costs and greater efficiencies. Zara, however, bucked this trend and took a different stance. It felt that it would be better off developing a business that was able to respond quickly to shifts in consumer tastes, and thus made the decision to set up a vertically integrated business model spanning design, just-in-time production, marketing and sales. As such, it now produces more than half of its own clothes at its ultramodern factory in northern Spain, rather than relying on a network of disparate and often slow-moving suppliers. H&M, for instance, has 900 suppliers and no factories, whereas Zara makes 40 per cent of its own fabric and produces 60 per cent of its merchandise in house. While many analysts have argued that vertical integration has gone out of fashion in the consumer economy, Zara could be seen as a spectacular exception to the rule.

The result is that Zara has more flexibility than its rivals to respond to fickle fashion trends. It can make a new line from start to finish in three weeks, against an industry average of nine months. It is able to introduce 10,000 new designs into its stores each year, none of which stays there for over a month. This constant refreshment of the store offering creates a sense of excitement that attracts new shoppers and ensures that old ones return. Zara is also radically changing the way in which people shop. If customers see a product that they like in the store, they know that it will only be there for four weeks, rather than four months, and that they will probably not be able to find it after that. This stimulates customers to buy immediately and creates a greater velocity of shopping. This is quite a different situation from that of the traditional clothing retailer, and more and more retailers are finding it difficult to compete. Examples include C&A, which chose to exit the UK market, and the Japanese basics retailer Uniqlo, which has closed all but five of its UK stores. However, it's not just the traditional high-street chains that have been affected. Even supermarket clothing retailer George at Asda has been inspired to react, by producing a collection called 'Fast Fashion'.

Questions

1 What underpins the success of Zara in its chosen markets?

2 Outline Zara's production and distribution systems.

3 How do Zara's production and distribution systems meet the needs of the market? What features of the company's supply chain contribute to its success?

Lecturers: visit www.palgrave.com/business/hillessential for additional resources

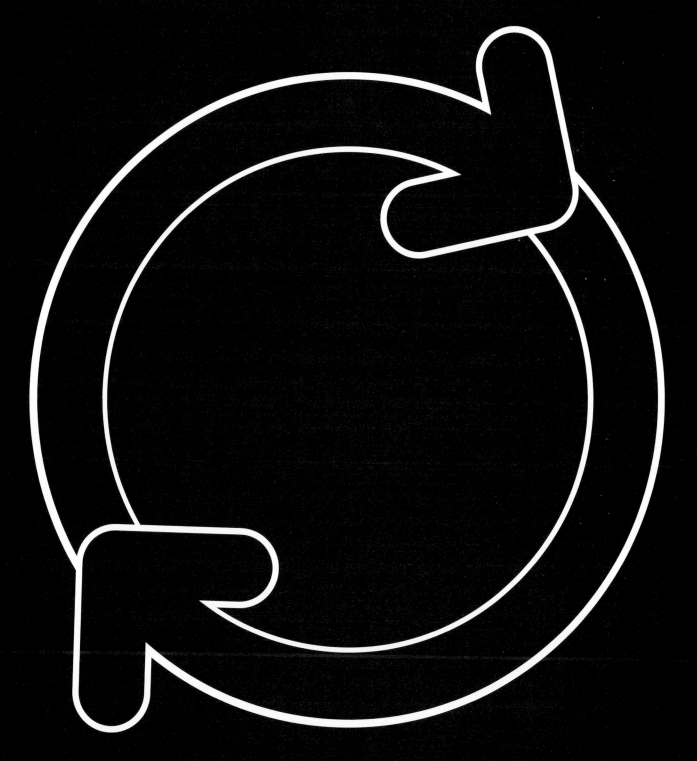

Improving Operations **12**

Learning objectives

After completing this chapter, you should be able to:

- Explain why companies need to improve their operations

- Understand how operations can be improved to release cash, improve market support and reduce costs

- Apply alternative improvement approaches, tools and techniques to identify improvement opportunities within a company

- Critically evaluate the differing improvement approaches used by organizations

- Understand the alternative approaches to making improvements

- Propose and substantiate improvements within a given operational context

Chapter outline

Introduction

Why improve operations?

- Releasing cash

- Improving market support

- Reducing costs

The process of improving operations

- Approaches to improving operations

- Improvement tools and techniques

- Making improvements

Critical reflections

Summary

Market support –
created by matching
the capability of an
operation with the
order-winners and
qualifiers required
by customers

Market support –
created by matching
the capability of an
operation with the
order-winners and
qualifiers required
by customers

Passive approach to
improvement – where
operations managers
respond to the need
for improvement
only after it has
become apparent

Proactive approach
to improvement –
involves anticipating
problems that may
occur and initiating
action ahead of time

Incremental
improvement (also
known as continous
improvement) –
involves making
a large number
of small, frequent
improvements that
often involve low
investment through
sources such as
'suggestion schemes'
or establishing an
'improvement culture'

Breakthrough
improvement –
improvements
result from major
changes to existing
practices and
normally involve large
investment either in
assets for 'process
and technology
investments' or the
time of the staff
working within
operations

Innovations – involve
changing something
established by
introducing a new
method, idea,
business model,
service or product

Stakeholders –
individuals or groups
who depend on an
organization to fulfil
their own goals, and
on whom, in turn, the
organization depends

Introduction

Organizations must continually look for ways to improve as markets are always changing and competition is constantly growing. There are several ways in which operations managers can help companies improve – by releasing cash to be invested elsewhere, by improving **market support** to grow sales revenue, and by reducing costs to increase profits. The process of making these improvements involves going through a never-ending cycle of four steps: *plan*, *do*, *check* and *review*. This can be done using either a **passive** or a **proactive** approach to make **incremental** or **breakthrough** improvements or **innovations**. As a result, a variety of tools and techniques are available to benchmark performance, map the customer journey, understand processes, identify the causes of problems, generate improvement ideas and re-engineer business processes, with the ultimate aim of either releasing cash, improving market support or reducing costs. Traditionally, companies have only used the people who worked for them to identify and make changes, but they are now starting to also use other **stakeholders**, such as suppliers and customers. This can lead to significant benefits, but it requires a radically different way of working.

Why improve operations?

As discussed in Chapter 2, improving operations allows the company to better meet a variety of different corporate objectives. However, the most common reasons for improving operations are, as mentioned above, to release cash, to improve market support and/or to reduce costs.

> **KEY IDEA**
> Operations can be improved to release cash, improve market support (and, with it, sales revenue) or reduce costs

Releasing cash

Once cash has been released by improving operations, it can be invested elsewhere, in either another aspect of operations or another function of the business. This can be done through a number of actions:

- *Reduce inventory* As explained in Chapter 9, companies need to conduct a causal analysis to understand why inventory is being held within operations. This is done by grouping inventory into one of the following categories: corporate, decoupling, cycle, pipeline, capacity-related and buffer (see Chapter 9). When the reason for holding the inventory has been identified, questions can then be asked, such as: Is it necessary? Why is it there? And what caused it? Once this is known, the systems, procedures and rules used can be challenged, reviewed and, if necessary, changed.

- *Change supplier payment terms* Another way to release cash is to delay paying suppliers. When doing this, however, companies must remember that although this will benefit them, it will also negatively affect their suppliers' cash flow. For small suppliers, this could have serious implications as they tend not to have much cash in their business. The company might even force one of its suppliers out of business.

- *Sell or lease equipment* Equipment that is not essential to the business can be sold off. Equally, equipment that is essential can be leased rather than bought. Although such a move would probably increase the overall cost of the equipment, leasing reduces the negative impact on cash flow by spreading it over a longer period of time.

- *Outsource* Processes requiring a high investment in equipment or inventory could be outsourced. However, as discussed in Chapter 11, companies need to review the strategic implications of making such decisions.

> **KEY IDEA**
> Releasing cash enables investments to be made elsewhere in the business

Improving market support

As described above, the second reason for improving operations is to increase the level of market support. This will, in turn, lead to greater sales revenue by improving the company's market share, establishing a new market or enabling a company to raise the price of its service or product. Case 12.1 gives examples of improvements made by Ritz-Carlton, Steinway & Sons and Massachusetts General Hospital. The process of making such improvements involves the following steps:

1 *Identify the order-winners and qualifiers* that operations must support from the market review, as discussed in Chapter 2.
2 *Translate these into strategic tasks* – for example, if price is a key order-winner, costs must be reduced throughout the business. Similarly, if quality conformance is a key qualifier, errors must be reduced and quality built into the process rather than being checked after the event.
3 *Review current performance* against each of these strategic tasks. Figure 12.1 shows examples of how to check current performance against order-winners or qualifiers.
4 *Identify and implement changes* to improve performance against each strategic task. Again, see Figure 12.1 for examples of how this can be done.

> **KEY IDEA**
> Improving market support leads to greater sales revenue by either increasing market share, establishing new markets or enabling prices to be raised

Having identified areas for performance review and typical improvements, let's now look at how they can be applied to some of the order-winners and qualifiers typically supported by operations.

Price

So that operations can understand whether price is being supported, it must check its current performance on a number of aspects. Analyses that help to highlight current or potential problems and typical areas for improvement are as follows:

- *Review the actual material, direct labour and overhead costs* Although all aspects of cost must be reviewed, materials and overheads are usually the main areas on which to focus as they tend to account for 70–90 per cent of total costs. Trends in costs for these should be reviewed so that operations personnel can understand historical and forecasted changes. In some instances, companies may wish to stabilize cost fluctuations by using supplier or employee agreements.

- *Map activities and identify areas of waste* As well as splitting costs by type, companies must also separate them into different activities. To do this, the entire business process from the customer placing the order through to the customer paying its bill needs to be mapped. Waste such as unnecessary process steps, movement, inventory, paperwork

Order-winner or qualifier	Reviewing current performance	Typical improvements
Price	• Review actual material, direct labour and overhead costs • Map current processes and identify areas of material and labour waste • Review the mix of operations volumes • Review annual operations volumes within a service/product range • Review production run lengths • Review the contribution per machine hour • Review product pricing	• Reduce large areas of costs –70–90 per cent of the total cost is usually accounted for by materials and overheads • Reduce material and labour waste • Reduce changeover and set-up times for the manufacturing process • Reallocate products across operations • Focus each operation on a particular market or resource
Quality conformance	• Review quality conformance levels for the following areas: services, products, orders, customers and market segments	• Reduce quality conformance errors • Build quality control into the system rather than checking conformance after the event
Delivery reliability	• Review the delivery performance for services/products, orders, customers and market segments • Analyse and compare the delivery lead-times that customers have requested against the actual delivery lead-times that operations supplies • Compare the actual processing with the overall operations lead-time	• Improve the scheduling of activities • Improve process reliability • Hold inventory at varying stages in the process
Delivery speed	• Analyse and compare the delivery lead-times that customers have requested against the actual delivery lead-times that operations supplies • Compare the actual processing with the overall operations lead-time • Map the actual operations process and identify any areas of material and labour waste	• Eliminate any waiting time between the steps in the process • Reduce the lead-time of steps in the process • Eliminate wasteful activities
Service or product range	• Review the capability of the process to meet the service or product range required now and in the future	• Develop the capability of the system to cope with the service or product range • Develop employee skill levels • Reduce changeover and set-up times
Demand fluctuations	• Assess the ability of the available capacity to respond to known or anticipated changes in demand	• Invest in capacity or inventory
Speed of new service or product development	• Map the new service/product development process and identify waste • Determine the length of activities and their dependency on other activities or key resources • Identify activities for which operations has responsibility	• Eliminate wasteful activities • Increase the capacity of any constraining resources • Reschedule activities so they are completed in parallel (rather than in sequence) with other parts of the process

Figure 12.1 **Examples of how to review performance and typical improvements to meet alternative order-winners and qualifiers**

CASE 12.1 IMPROVING PROCESSES: STEINWAY & SONS AND MASSACHUSETTS GENERAL HOSPITAL

STEINWAY & SONS

Steinway & Sons uses feedback from demanding concert pianists to help it design, manufacture and tune the pianos it makes. However, the company also promotes the fact that its pianos all have a different 'personality', as it believes that this indicates the richness of the materials and craftsmanship that goes into producing them, just as master winemakers know that their job is to make the most of the distinctive qualities of each year's harvest. **www.steinway.com**

MASSACHUSETTS GENERAL HOSPITAL

Massachusetts General Hospital continually looks for ways to reduce costs and improve quality by standardizing its patient care. With complex procedures like coronary bypasses, it standardizes most of the patient's preoperative and postoperative journey, but it then allows surgeons to maintain technical judgement over the detailed procedure. To appraise the patient's experience, the company then measures and evaluates 'standardized processes' against hard rules and metrics, but assesses 'artistic processes' through patient feedback. **www.mgh.harvard.edu**

Questions

1 Should processes always be standardized?

2 When should companies manage their processes more creatively?

or inspection can then be eliminated, and working practices for the remaining value-adding activities can be improved. Both sets of actions will help lower costs.

- *Review the mix of volumes in an operation* Cost-efficient operations typically focus on a narrow range of high-volume services or products. However, as markets mature, service/product ranges widen and volumes decrease. Businesses must therefore review the service/product and volume mix within their operations to help retain a focused approach.

- *Review service or product pricing* The range of profit margins typically generated from different services, products or customers is not always the result of varying operations costs. Instead, these profit margins often result from how the services or products are priced. The standard costing methods used often do not reflect the true costs of all the services or products. In addition, once a price is set, it is rarely reviewed and increased or decreased to reflect volume, material cost and other cost changes. Once services or products with low profit margins have been identified, improvements and developments can be made to reduce costs, negotiate higher prices with customers or delete the service or product from the range offered to customers.

Quality conformance
Quality conformance levels of services, products, orders and customers must be reviewed to assess how well markets are being supported. Specific reviews are best in that they can identify areas for improvement and lead to lasting change.

Reliability of delivery
Collecting and analysing delivery performance information is important in order to understand how reliability of delivery varies by service, product, order or customer. Comparing delivery on-time performance with aspects such as order size, customer lead-times, delivery lead-times and supplier lead-times helps to identify causes of above- or below-average reliability in terms of delivery performance, as well as highlighting areas and actions for improvement.

Speed of delivery
A number of analyses can be used to identify current areas and causes of poor performance, so that a start can be made in terms of identifying where improvements need to be achieved:

- *Analyse the total customer lead-time* from receipt of order to point of payment.
- *Map the actual operations process* to determine all the steps that make up the operations lead-time.
- *Analyse the actual delivery lead-time of operations* and break it down into the relevant elements of service or product delivery,
- *Analyse the lead-times that customers expect* and compare them with actual delivery lead-times.
- *Identify areas for improvement* by comparing the lead-time for each step of the process with the actual time it takes to process a service or product.

Other order-winners and qualifiers
Companies often have to support several other order-winners and qualifiers besides those discussed above. In all instances, current operations performance must then be reviewed against each of these to check whether they are supported and, where not, to identify areas for improvement. The following areas, for example, can be analysed:

- *Service or product range* Review the capability of operations to process the current range on offer and any future proposed changes. This needs to be completed for all the steps involved.

- *Demand fluctuations* Assess the ability of the current operations process capacity to respond to known or anticipated changes in demand.

- *Speed of new service or product development* Map the current new service or product development process and identify areas of **waste**. The length of each activity and its dependency on other activities or key resources can then be determined, and the activities for which operations has responsibility can be identified.

Waste or 'non-value-adding' activities – those which a customer is not willing to pay for, such as waiting for resources, transportation between operations or unnecessary paperwork and documentation

Reducing costs

Even when price is not an order-winner, costs often have to be reduced to increase profit margins. The reviews that need to be carried out here are similar to those identified in the section 'Price', above, and companies need to:

- Review where they can reduce actual material, direct labour and overhead costs
- Map activities to identify and eliminate areas of waste
- Review and reduce the mix of volumes within operations
- Review and, where appropriate, increase the price of services or products
- Review and, where appropriate, stop selling services or products.

> **KEY IDEA**
> Reducing costs leads to increased profits

The process of improving operations

As we mentioned earlier in the chapter, improving any aspect of operations involves going through four key steps – plan, do, check and review. These are shown in Figure 12.2 and discussed below:

Figure 12.2 **Improvement process**

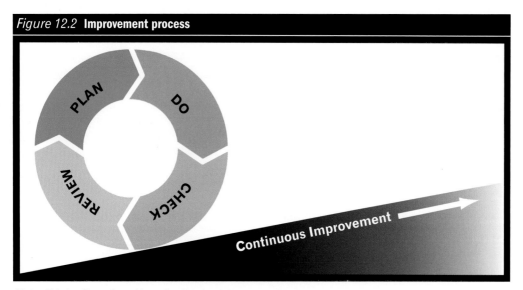

Note: This is often referred to as the Deming improvement cycle.

1 Plan

The first step is to identify a problem or aspect that needs to be improved. In other words, where do you want to release cash, improve market support and/or reduce costs? It usually helps to involve the managers and employees who work in the area being reviewed as they have a better idea of the issues being faced, the areas that need to be improved and how best to fix them. Initially, this can be a 'gut feel' analysis, but it must then be supported with data or evidence clearly showing the types of problem that exist and how frequently they occur. Based on this analysis, areas for improvement and development can be identified, and these then need to be prioritized before action is taken. Working out where to start can be helped by assessing each potential improvement using the following criteria:

- *The cost of implementing the improvement* – the cost of making the change, the amount of investment involved (the cash that will be tied up) and the reduction in day-to-day operating costs

- *The ease with which the improvement can be implemented* – the time and resources required for implementation will reflect the size of the change, the type and number of stakeholders involved and whether they agree on the course of action suggested

- *The impact of making the improvement* – how much cash will be released, the ongoing costs of operating differently and the benefits achieved, such as improved market support, additional sales and increased profits.

Again, this analysis can start as 'gut feel', with each aspect rated out of 5, where 5 represents low cost, high impact and easy implementation. The scores for each action can then be totalled, and improvement teams can be set up to look at each action in greater detail. Once a more in-depth analysis has been completed and the cost, ease and impact are better known, an organization can decide which improvements it is going to make. Two key aspects that help to create a focus when prioritizing actions and allocating resources to implementing them are:

- *The impact of doing nothing* – how much cash will be tied up, the ongoing 'unnecessary' cost of the current operation and the result of existing market support in terms of reduced sales and profits

- *Speeding up implementation* – how many resources are required and how these need to be used to implement the improvement actions in a shorter time.

2 Do
Once the improvement plan has been developed, it then needs to be implemented. Involving employees in the first step helps this to occur as they feel more empowered, more involved and more responsible for the improvement that is to be made. The next section explains how companies can choose to take a 'passive incremental', 'proactive incremental', 'passive breakthrough' and/or 'proactive breakthrough' approach to improving operations and creating a change.

3 Check
Once a change has been made, it is important to check whether the anticipated level of improvement has been achieved. In other words, the impact of the actions made in Step 2 must be measured against the improvement objectives identified in Step 1. The measures identified earlier in Figure 12.1 can also be used here to review the change in performance against different order-winners and qualifiers.

4 Review
Finally, the checks must be reviewed to determine whether the improvement objectives have been sustained. This will highlight gaps that will, in turn, identify further problems or aspects to be improved, and this will then lead back into Step 1.

> **KEY IDEA**
   Improving operations should be a continuous, ongoing process

'Organizations must **continually** look for ways to **improve** operations'

Approaches to improving operations

Once the necessary improvements have been identified, an organization needs to decide what approach it will take. Although improving any aspect of operations involves going through the same four key steps, these improvements can be either stepped or incremental and made on a passive or proactive basis, as shown in Figure 12.3 below. In practice, of course, companies will use a variety of approaches to improve their business as they all have a number of different features, as described in Figure 12.3.

Figure 12.3 **Typical features of alternative approaches to improvement**

Typical features			Incremental		Breakthrough	
			Passive	Proactive	Passive	Proactive
Level of investment in	Assets	Low	✓	✓		✓
		High			✓	
	Employee time	Low	✓			
		High		✓		✓
Improvement typically changes		Procedures	✓	✓		✓
		Process activities	✓	✓		✓
		Process technologies			✓	
		Layouts		✓		✓
		Roles and responsibilities		✓		✓
Time frame to develop and implement the improvements		Short-term	✓	✓		✓
		Medium-term	✓	✓		
		Long-term			✓	
Type of improvement		One-off			✓	✓
		Ongoing	✓	✓		
Number of people involved		Few			✓	✓
		Many	✓	✓		
Led by		Operations	✓	✓		✓
		Specialist function			✓	
When benefits occur from improvement		Occur during activity	✓	✓		✓
		Require further actions			✓	
Ease of sustaining improvement activity		Easy		✓		✓
		Difficult	✓		✓	

Companies must first decide whether they want to take a passive or a proactive approach to improvement:

- *Passive* – improvements are identified and implemented through activities such as 'suggestion schemes' and 'process and technology investments' made by support functions such as IT and engineering, with operations responding to suggestions from other areas.
- *Proactive* – conversely, operations takes control and drives change by developing an 'improvement culture' and using '**kaizen blitz events**' to make improvements.

> **KEY IDEA**

A proactive approach is better than a passive approach for driving improvement

The next step is then to decide whether to take an 'incremental' or 'breakthrough' approach to improvement:

Kaizen is Japanese for 'improvement' or 'change for the better'; occurs when everyone in the organization continuously looks for ways to improve how it operates

Kaizen blitz events – focused improvement activities used to address a particular issue within five days or less, such as changing the process, layout or procedures used

- *Incremental* Improvements come from a larger number of smaller, more frequent improvements that often involve low investment through sources such as 'suggestion schemes' or establishing an 'improvement culture'.
- *Breakthrough* Improvements instead result from major changes to existing practices and normally involve committing large resources either in assets for 'process and technology investments' or in the time of the people who work within operations for 'kaizen blitz events'.

> **KEY IDEA**

Organizations should improve their operations through a combination of incremental and breakthrough changes

Figure 12.4 compares the improvement in performance resulting from either breakthrough or incremental change. In reality, however, most companies use a combination of passive incremental, proactive incremental, passive breakthrough and proactive breakthrough approaches to suit their particular situation as these approaches vary in terms of:

- The level of investment required
- What they typically change
- The time taken to develop and implement the improvement
- The types of improvement that occur
- The number of people involved
- Who leads the improvement
- When the benefits of the improvement occur
- How easy the improvement activity is to sustain after it has been started.

Case 12.2 gives examples of the different types of breakthrough and incremental improvement that have been made by South African gold mines and Metro.

Looking at the advantages and disadvantages of the different basic improvement approaches in more detail will give an idea of when it is best to use each type of approach (Figure 12.5).

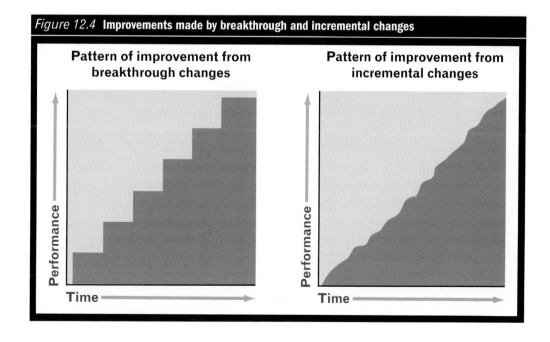

Figure 12.4 Improvements made by breakthrough and incremental changes

Pattern of improvement from breakthrough changes

Performance

Time

Pattern of improvement from incremental changes

Performance

Time

PROCESS AND TECHNOLOGY INVESTMENTS

BREAKTHROUGH

Specialist support functions identify and make investments in operations through new process and information technology investment

SUGGESTION SCHEMES

INCREMENTAL

Staff are asked to identify areas for improvement that are then reviewed by management who judge whether they should be implemented

KAIZEN BLITZ EVENTS

Operations resource is taken out of

day-to-day activities for a concentrated

period of time (normally up to five days)

to identify and make improvements

BREAKTHROUGH

IMPROVEMENT CULTURE

Staff are trained to use improvement tools

and techniques. Part of their working week is

then allocated for analysing existing working

methods and making improvements

INCREMENTAL

Proactive

CASE 12.2 BREAKTHROUGH VERSUS INCREMENTAL IMPROVEMENT: SOUTH AFRICAN GOLD MINES AND METRO

GOLD MINING

South African gold mines have dramatically increased their productivity by applying stone quarrying methods. Instead of using dynamite to blast the rock, they now use a steel cable studded with industrial diamonds to cut the rock into large chunks. Although the cable costs $290 per meter, it can operate 24 hours a day, requires less labour, minimizes the amount of rock wasted and eliminates the 900,000 blasts the company had previously made each day.

METRO

In 2003, the German retailer Metro launched its 'Future Store'. Customers have a computer on their shopping trolley that directs them to where the product is located in the store, scans it as it enters the trolley, shows the total cost of the items in the trolley and signals any special offers as the customer walks around the store. It also has a built-in camera for identifying and pricing fruit and vegetables. All of these initiatives have helped to reduce Metro's costs and have simplified their customers' shopping experience.

www.future-store.org

Question

Would you classify these approaches to improvement as breakthrough or incremental?

Passive incremental

A passive incremental approach to improvement involves activities such as suggestion schemes where employees are asked to identify improvements within their working area. These suggestions are then typically reviewed by managers or an improvement group to determine whether they should be implemented. The advantages of this improvement approach includes its low level of investment in assets and employee time. Disadvantages, however, include that its typical focus is on small changes in procedures or process activities, and the difficulty of sustaining employee engagement over a long period of time. Some organizations use financial rewards for employee improvement ideas, that are then implemented, but this often ends up preventing the flow of ideas from staff as they want to be paid for them. Futhermore, it can also build resentment between employees with the decision to give a higher reward for one idea than another.

Proactive incremental

If companies wish to start driving incremental change within their businesses, they need to establish an 'improvement culture' by training everyone in the use of improvement tools and techniques and then allocating time within their working week for employees to analyse parts of the business, identify improvements and implement changes. As discussed earlier in Case 10.6, 3M found that creating an improvement culture requires a significant change in attitude, behaviours and working practices throughout an organization. Most experts believe it takes 10–15 years to achieve this, but it tends to be easier to sustain improvement activity once it has become an established part of an organization's DNA. Compared with a passive incremental approach, a proactive incremental one requires more investment in employee time and will eventually lead to larger structural changes, such as improving layouts and modifying employees' roles and responsibilities.

> **KEY IDEA**

Establishing an 'improvement culture' helps to drive and maintain improvement

---

Case 12.3 shows how Porsche has established an improvement culture within its business using a proactive approach, while Case 12.4 describes how Volvo and Ricoh are constantly looking for ways to improve their businesses. These sorts of approach are guided by the following three key principles:

- *Process reviews* The process across the whole supply chain is reviewed, from the initial design of a service or product through to its delivery to a customer.
- *Success comes from people* Success relies on people's knowledge of and insights into the systems and procedures they use, as well as their ability to identify and make improvements. High levels of skill, employee participation and management support for these programmes are also essential to bring about these changes.
- *A constant need for change* The current processes within the business, however good they are, must never be considered adequate. Employees must constantly want to improve, look for aspects to change and implement results.

> **KEY IDEA**

Proactive improvement requires employee participation and involvement throughout the business

---

Passive breakthrough

The next approach that can be used is a 'passive breakthrough' one in which operations relies on support functions such as IT and engineering to identify and make improvements in processes and technologies. Unlike the incremental approaches to improvement change, these can lead to significant performance improvements, but they tend to take a longer time to develop and implement. The benefits of such improvements are

In 1993, the car manufacturer Porsche was on the verge of bankruptcy as sales had fallen dramatically from 53,254 cars in 1986 to fewer than 13,000 in 1993. Since then, however, it has used a mix of breakthrough and incremental change to turn the business around. For example, it has introduced new working methods that have helped it to reduce its workforce by 34 per cent, halve the time to produce a car from 120 to 60 hours and reduce its inventory by over 50 per cent. In addition, it has slashed the number of suppliers it uses from 900 to fewer than 300, and it also now uses parts across a number of its cars. For example, around 36 per cent of the parts used in its 911 cars are now identical to those used in its Boxsters. The impact of these improvements has been dramatic, with sales increasing to 98,652 cars in 2008. Equally, it now can produce 8.6 cars per employee compared with 2.4 in 1994.

www.porsche.com

Questions

1 How do the improvements at Porsche show the need to continuously drive change?

2 Check on the Porsche website **www. porsche.com** and identify current areas where improvements are being made.

Students: www.palgrave.com/business/hillessential provides learning resources for this case

VOLVO GROUP

Five employees competing for Volvo Group's Internal Environmental Award came up with a simple way to save energy. Instead of using heat to dry newly painted engine blocks before they were assembled into their vehicles, the company now uses dry air. As a result, parts of the same quality are now produced using 90 per cent less energy – 70 rather than 650 kW per hour.

www.volvogroup.com

RICOH

At Ricoh's copier plant in Shenzhen, China, the 3,500 staff are encouraged to come up with suggestions to cut costs. On average, 18 suggestions are made per day. For example, one worker recently suggested narrowing the distance between two work stations from 120 to 90 cm, the distance of one stride. This might not seem that significant, but implementing changes helps to motivate people and demonstrates the importance of their contributions. The cumulative impact of all of these changes is essential as the company's profit margin is less than 2 per cent.

www.ricoh.com

Question

Use these examples to illustrate the three points guiding continuous improvement that are listed in the chapter.

Lecturers: visit www.palgrave.com/business/hillessential for additional resources

often not realized until some time after the change has been made due to the further staff training and changes in working practices that are required. In fact, the suggested benefits on which an investment was initially justified are sometimes never fully achieved due to the poor selection or implementation of the new process technology.

Proactive breakthrough
The final approach involves making proactive breakthroughs through activities such as kaizen blitz events. In these blitz events, small groups of operations employees (usually five or six) are taken out of their day jobs for a small period (usually between two and five days) to analyse part of the business, identify changes and make improvements. Essentially, this is a more focused and concentrated version of the proactive incremental approach. By dedicating employee time in this way, significant changes can be made to procedures, paperwork, process activities, layout, roles, responsibilities and the like within a few days; in addition, it often leads to subsequent projects working with IT and engineering. The advantage of this approach is that changes are made quickly by people who work within the process and have an incentive for making it work better.

....
> KEY IDEA
Kaizen blitz events are just kaizen events completed in a compressed timescale by taking employees out of their day jobs and dedicating them to improvement activities for between two and five days
....

Lean improvement approach
As explained earlier in Chapter 8, the concept of 'lean' or 'lean operations' has developed to represent a philosophy of operations management that necessitates changes in emphasis, attitude and approach.

The application of these changes has been extended to all the major aspects of operations, and the title 'lean operations' is appropriately used to highlight the fundamental nature of the changes involved and the need for these to be applied across the whole of the operations function. It also gives additional weight to the importance of such changes in emphasis and the contribution that they make. The areas of operations activity include:

- Managing operations within a business (dealt with in this chapter).
- Scheduling operations (see Chapter 8)
- Managing the supply chain (see Chapter 11).

Improvement tools and techniques

Let's now discuss some of the various tools and techniques that can be used to analyse and improve operations. These can be used by organizations in several ways: to benchmark their performance against that of other businesses; to map their customers' journeys; to review within their business the processes used to deliver services and products; to identify problems; to generate improvement ideas; and to re-engineer their business.

Benchmarking
The first of these techniques, benchmarking, involves comparing business practice and performance between companies. It can be used to help start or maintain an improvement process by identifying, setting and measuring improvement targets against:

- Other parts of the same organization
- Direct competitors
- Companies within the same sector who are not direct competitors
- Latent competitors
- Companies outside the industry.

> **KEY IDEA**
> Benchmarking helps to start and maintain improvements

As an example, Case 12.5 shows how Ford improved its 'accounts payable' department by benchmarking itself against rival Mazda. Similarly, McDonald's reduced the lead-time for building a restaurant from 18 to 10 days after adopting best practice from the British Airports Authority.

Mapping the customer journey

Another useful tool to help an organization consider which services and products to deliver and how to deliver them is to map the **customer journey** through the following steps:

1 *Map the journey that customers take* – the steps customers go through from becoming aware of the need for a service or product through to its final delivery and the subsequent after-sales service
2 *Identify the points of interaction that customers have with the business* – where on their journey do customers interact with the business? Where are they **picked up**, **dropped off** and passed between departments within the business?
3 *Determine where on the journey you wish to interact with customers* – should the customer be picked up earlier? Or should the customer be dropped off later? And why?
4 *Determine how best to manage these interactions* – should customers be passed between different departments, and, if so, how should these **hand-offs** be managed within the business? In addition, how should information about the customer be managed and communicated across the organization?

> **KEY IDEA**
> Mapping the customer journey helps to identify which services and products to deliver to a customer and how best to deliver them

Customer satisfaction tends to increase when customers are in contact with a business for a longer part of their journey and when the interactions meet their needs. For example, Figure 12.6 shows the typical journey of a business class air traveller. British Airways and Virgin Atlantic interact with customers at different points of their journey and have made different developments at each interaction. A key difference between them, however, is the limousine service used by Virgin Atlantic to collect customers at the start of their journeys and deliver them to their final destination. Interacting with customers for more of their journey and offering them more relaxation options within the lounge and on the flight have led to Virgin Atlantic recently surpassing British Airways to win the Business Traveller Award for 'Best Business Class' service.

Mapping processes

A process needs to be mapped to understand how it currently operates before determining how to improve it. In reality, a number of these tools will be used to understand a process before identifying areas for improvement:

• *Process charts* The principal activities within a process are operations (completing tasks), checks or inspections, transportation, delays and storage (as shown in Figure 12.7). A process chart is used to show the sequence of steps that occur and the time taken to complete each step. As with other analyses, it must be checked using actual information and evidence.

> **KEY IDEA**
> Mapping processes helps to understand how a business currently operates

• *Service maps* These are used to map the movement of customers, information and materials through a process using the symbols shown in Figure 12.8. As discussed in

CASE 12.5 FORD MOTOR COMPANY: BENCHMARKING ITS ACCOUNTS PAYABLE DEPARTMENT AGAINST MAZDA

After reviewing its accounts payable department, Ford felt it could reduce its staff from 500 to 400. It was very enthusiastic about this level of improvement until it realized that Mazda only employed five people in its accounts payable function. Further analysis showed that Ford's account payable department spent most of its time checking, querying and investigating 14 items of information on three different documents that it received from three different groups: purchasing staff, the goods inwards department and suppliers. The company therefore decided to use a paperless system with automatic checks. It also asked the goods inwards personnel simply to accept only goods in line with the information on the computer system, and told suppliers that it would pay on receipt of goods.

www.ford.com

Question

How did benchmarking help Ford to improve its business?

Chapter 4, a key feature of service delivery is determining the number of customer interfaces, and therefore the line of visibility that separates front-office from back-office activities.

- *Information and material flow charts* These trace the flow of information and/or materials through the process. It is important to show both physical and electronic documents as well as computer screen shots showing the level and type of information used within a process, system or procedure.

Figure 12.6 **Customer journey for business class air passengers and examples of service developments made by British Airways and Virgin Atlantic**

Customer journey	Examples of developments on certain long haul flights	
	British Airways	Virgin Atlantic
Select and purchase flight	· Book online or over the telephone · Frequent flier programmes record customer preferences and use these to tailor the service (such as meal and seat preferences)	
Checking in	· Check in online · At airport using self-service points or dedicated business class desks	
Travel to airport		· A limousine collects passengers from any destination within 75 miles of the airport
Check in baggage	· Checking in of baggage is at 'Fast bag drop' points or dedicated business class desks	· Not required – baggage is checked in when placed in the boot of the limousine
Travel through immigration and security	· Dedicated business class areas speed up the process up	
Wait for flight	· A dedicated lounge for business class customers with a number of areas in which they can work or relax	· A dedicated lounge for business class customers with more relaxation options, including: · A delicatessen, brasserie, bar or roof garden · Games or a cinema · A beauty and hair salon, spa pool, sauna, steam rooms and showers
Board flight	· A dedicated business class area to speed up the process	
Fly to destination	· A number of features to help customers work or relax including: · Flat beds · Flexible eating times	· A wider variety of options to help customers relax, including: · Bar and dining areas · Massages · Flat beds
Collect baggage	· Baggage belonging to business class and first-class customers is unloaded first	
Travel through immigration and security	· A dedicated business class area to speed up the process	
Freshen up	· A dedicated lounge for business class customers with: · Showers · Clothes pressing service · Hot/cold breakfast	
Travel to destination		· A limousine takes passengers to any destination they wish within 75 miles of the airport

Figure 12.7 Process chart symbols

Symbol	Activity	Used to represent	
		Material or information	**Person doing the task**
 ○	Operation	Materials, products or information are modified or acted upon during the operation	Person completes an operation or task. This may include preparation for the next activity
▢	Inspection	Materials, products or information are checked and quality, quantity or accuracy is verified	Person checks and verifies for quality, quantity or accuracy at this stage in the process or procedure
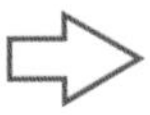 ⇨	Transport	Materials, products or information are moved to another location without being part of an operation or inspection	Person moves from one position to another as part of the process or procedure without being part of an operation or inspection
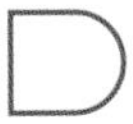 D	Delay	Temporary storage or filing of an item. Not recorded as 'in store' or filed and not requiring authorization for its withdrawal	Person unable to complete the next part of the task
 ▽	Storage	Controlled storage, governed by authorized receipt and issue; document filed and retained for future reference	Not used
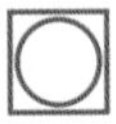 ◎	Combined activities	To show activities performed at the same time or a person competing two tasks at the same time	

Figure 12.8 Symbols used in service maps

Symbol	Explanation
 ••••• •••••••••	*Line of visibility* – used to divide the part of the operations visible to the customer (including telephone and written communication) from the rest of the service delivery system
 △	*Fail points* – points in the process where there is a high level of service failure
 ➡ ⇨	*Service paths* – the optimal and 'when things go wrong' service paths are shown as follows: • Optimal service path • Path where things go wrong
 ⬠ P	*Problem* – indicates where problems occur in a process
 ⬡ D	*Dialogue* – indicates where customer interface with the delivery system takes place – the line of interaction

- *Person flow charts* These map the movements of staff as they carry out a task. As with information or material flow process charts, these flow charts show all the operations and inspections that take place, together with any movements and delays.

- *Videoing* As well as charting a process, it is useful to video it to see what happens. Videoing has a number of advantages over the other charting methods as it:
  - *Is more accurate* – it provides a complete record of the activities that take place
  - *Helps process analysis* – it is often easier to assess the process as it can be reviewed many times and allows any number of people to review what happens

- *Increases acceptability that problems exist* – those involved in the process more readily accept the record of events (as the camera shows things as they really are) as well as their role within it.

Identifying causes of problems

Once a process has been mapped, the root cause of the problems can be identified using a number of tools and techniques:

- *Cause and effect diagrams* These help solve problems by identifying the causes and effects involved (as discussed in Chapter 10). Figure 12.9 gives an example of a cause and effect analysis of a company that is unable to supply products on time and in line with the agreed design specification. This detailed and systematic analysis enabled the company to identify where improvements needed to be made.

- *Why–why reviews* This approach starts with the problem and then asks why it occurred. The process is then repeated by asking why each problem occurred. The logic is that continually asking 'why?' (usually seven or more times) will get to the root cause of the problem.

> **KEY IDEA**

Cause and effect diagrams and why–why reviews help in understanding what has caused the problems identified

---

Generating improvement ideas

Once the root cause of the problems has been identified, ideas for improvement can be generated. Most people, because of their training and background, are good at analytical thinking, but few are good at divergent or creative thinking. Some barriers that often prevent the generation of ideas are:

- Self-imposed limits on possible solutions
- An inherent belief that there is one right answer
- A fear of being wrong
- Conformity to behavioural norms
- An unwillingness to challenge the obvious.

Analytical approaches restrict imagination as they often prevent the development of ideas outside apparent norms or perceived boundaries. Creative thinking, on the other hand, encourages ideas that were previously unrelated by consciously suspending judgement and evaluating ideas at a later stage. This allows the mind to think laterally by going through five different steps:

1 *Preparation* – collecting the known facts, defining the problem in different ways and restating or clarifying the problem
2 *Generation* – concerning the need to generate ideas, both in themselves and as a stimulus to creating other perspectives
3 *Incubation* – leaving the problem in the subconscious state as a way of creating new thought and the process of association
4 *Insights* – linking ideas to possible solutions
5 *Evaluation* – analysing all the facts on which evaluations of possible solutions could be based.

Whereas Stages 1 and 5 are based on analytical approaches, Stages 2, 3 and 4 are based on creative thinking. Deliberately separating these two phases is key, with the creative stages (2, 3 and 4) best carried out in groups, and with the aim of creating quantity rather than quality of ideas. By creating a large number of ideas, new directions and thoughts can be sparked off. To help achieve this, it is important to:

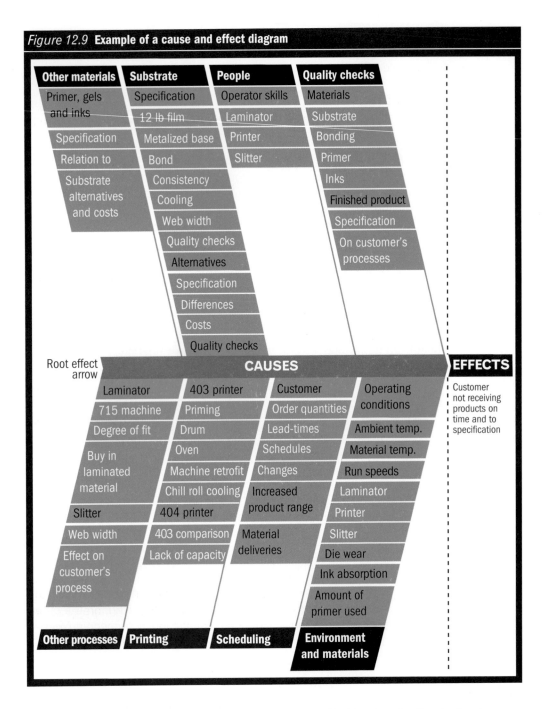

Figure 12.9 **Example of a cause and effect diagram**

- *Suspend judgement* Criticism of ideas is not permitted, and evaluation instead comes after the creative stage. Bringing these two phases together will lead to implied criticism and may make groups members reluctant to contribute. The key to success is discouraging self-evaluation from entering the process.
- *Freewheel* Wild ideas are deliberately fostered as they lead to better results.
- *Cross-fertilize* At set stages, participants are given the task of combining and improving on the ideas of others.

In addition, the generation of ideas can be helped by using a number of contributory techniques, including:

- *Brainstorming* – between six and 20 people take problems and, working with the above rules, seek solutions to them. All the ideas are written down so that they remain visible throughout the process. Typically, Stages 1–5 earlier form the basis for using this technique

- *Reverse brainstorming* – which asks, related to the idea being considered, 'In how many ways can this idea fail?'
- *Listing attributes* – lists the main attributes of the idea or object and examines how it can be changed
- *Forging relationships* – which lists the ways in which ideas or objects can be combined. These approaches generate what is referred to as 'effective surprise'. The eventual improvements are typically not of an 'off-the-map' nature but, in fact, have the quality of obviousness. The element of surprise is that, in retrospect, the solutions or improvements were obvious – indeed, 'How else would it have been solved?' The role of creative thinking is to push down the self-imposed barriers to alternatives so that we can access these alternatives.

> **KEY IDEA**

Improvement ideas can be generated by brainstorming, reverse brainstorming, listing attributes and/or forging relationships

----

An example of how to do this is described in Case 12.6 for IDEO, the US design consultancy.

Re-engineering business processes

Once improvement ideas have been generated, processes can be re-engineered. Essentially, this involves developing processes that provide the highest value for customers by eliminating waste, and then reconstructing management structures and functions around these. This process involves going through a number of steps, as shown in Figure 12.10:

Value-adding steps – those services, products or features for which a customer is willing to pay

1 *Map the process* – to establish facts rather than perceptions of how the business currently operates.
2 *Identify* value-adding *activities* – for which activities would a customer be prepared to pay? For example, customers are not really interested in the internal procedures and controls within the business as long as the service or product delivered meets their expectations.
3 *Eliminate waste* – remove the unnecessary procedures and processes within a business.
4 *Make the value-adding steps flow* – once you are left with the essential, value-adding steps for which a customer is prepared to pay, these must be made to flow by re-engineering the interfaces between successive steps, operating them in parallel rather than sequentially and removing any delays between each step
5 *Repeat the cycle* – once this point has been reached, the new process needs to be mapped, and the re-engineering process started again.

> **KEY IDEA**

Business processes can be re-engineered by mapping them, identifying value-added activities, eliminating waste and making the value-added steps flow

----

Case 12.7 shows how Mutual Benefit Life and JetBlue Airways have re-engineered their processes and describes the benefits they have achieved.

Making improvements

After deciding on the appropriate improvement tools and techniques to use, businesses then need to determine who is to use them and the areas that need improving. A good starting point for doing this is to identify the different stakeholders for the business and map them onto the power and interest matrix shown in Figure 12.11, in which:

- *Power* is the ability of individuals or groups to persuade, induce or coerce others into following a certain course of action.

CASE 12.6 IDEO: RULES FOR BRAINSTORMING IMPROVEMENT IDEAS

Founded in 1991, IDEO is considered to be the most successful design consultancy in the world. By 2009, it had won over 300 design awards, held over 1,000 patents and developed solutions for over 4,000 clients from a variety of industries including health care, fast-moving consumer goods, hospitality, financial services, automobiles and charities. Unlike other design firms who keep their design processes and methodologies secret, IDEO believes in open-source innovation and discloses its secrets to encourage clients to think creatively and foster innovation within their own organizations. It also runs educative workshops for its clients and encourages brainstorming using the rules below.

www.ideo.com

Questions

1 How is IDEO's approach different from that of other design consultancies?

2 Why are the rules it suggests so important when brainstorming new ideas?

Lecturers: visit www.palgrave.com/business/hillessential for additional resources

Rule	Practice
Defer judgement	• Don't dismiss any ideas • Any idea is good, no matter how crazy • Nothing can kill the spirit of a brainstorm quicker than judging ideas before they have a chance to gain legs
Encourage wild ideas	• Embrace the most out-of-the-box notions because they can be the key to solutions • The whole point of brainstorming is coming up with new and creative ideas
Build on the ideas of others	• No 'buts', only 'ands' • Sometimes people say crazy and bizzare things, like 'make it on Mars', but there is some element of truth in it. When you build on the ideas of others, you might bring those crazy ideas back down to earth and make them real innovations
Stay focused on the topic	• Always keep the discussion on target. Otherwise you can go beyond the scope of what you are trying to achieve
One conversation at a time	• No interrupting, no dismissing, no disrespect, no rudeness • Let people have their say
Be visual	• Use yellow, red and blue markers to write on big 30-inch by 25-inch 'Post-it' notes that are put on a wall • Nothing gets an idea across faster than drawing it. It doesn't matter how terrible a sketcher you are
Go for quantity	• Aim for as many new ideas as possible. In a good session, up to 100 ideas are generated in 60 minutes • Crank the ideas out quickly

MUTUAL BENEFIT LIFE

The Mutual Benefit Life Insurance Company used to handle customer applications through a series of departments: credit checks, quotations, rating, underwriting and document preparation. It typically took 5–25 days to process an application due to the delays, checks and rechecks within the process. So Mutual Benefit Life decided to re-engineer the process, creating case managers who were responsible for processing a whole application from start to finish. By removing all the hand-offs, delays and backtracking, it was then able to process an application in two to five days using 100 fewer staff, each handling twice as many applications as before.

JETBLUE AIRWAYS

JetBlue's pilots now use sleek laptops to advise how much engine thrust they should apply for take-off based on information such as outside temperature, fuel load, number of passengers, baggage weight, number of bags in each bin and length of the allocated runway. Moving away from a paper-based system with manual calculations and estimates has reduced the amount of fuel the company uses, lightened engine wear and cut down noise. As a result, operating and maintenance costs have reduced by 5 per cent, which accumulates to millions of dollars over the life of an aircraft.
www.jetblueairways.com

Questions

1 Identify the changes made and the benefits achieved by these two companies.

2 Are these examples of 'breakthrough' or 'incremental' improvements?

Lecturers: visit www.palgrave.com/business/hillessential for additional resources

© Alex Hill and Terry Hill 2011

Figure 12.10 **Re-engineering business processes**

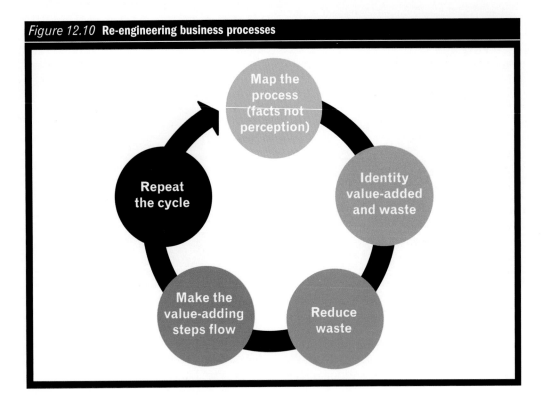

- *Interest* reflects how concerned each group is with impressing its expectations on an organization's purpose and the choices it makes.

Once stakeholders have been mapped, individuals or groups who have a high interest in the activities of the organization can then be used to help identify and make improvements. Typically, this involves using employees, suppliers or customers by giving them more power than they have as part of their normal role. Organizations such as Apple take a very closed approach to making improvements, in which innovations are guarded secrets and employees are the predominant source of improvement ideas within the organization. Google, however, uses a more 'open' approach by involving customers and suppliers in developing new services and ways of working. Both approaches, described in Case 12.8, have been highly successful, but they involve completely different ways of developing and improving services, products and processes. The key issues to consider when involving employees, customers and suppliers in this way will now be discussed in more detail.

> **KEY IDEA**

Improvements can be made by anyone who is interested in the business, as long as they are given the power to do this

Figure 12.11 **Mapping stakeholder power and interest**

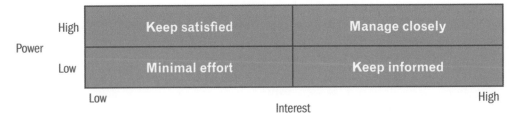

Involving employees

Involving employees is essential if companies want to establish an improvement culture within their business and to start driving incremental change, as discussed earlier and

CASE 12.8 CLOSED VERSUS OPEN INNOVATION: APPLE VERSUS GOOGLE

Computer firm Apple Inc. and Internet search engine Google, both headquartered in California, USA, have been voted in a survey of 2,700 executives by *BusinessWeek* as the world's most innovative companies. However, they have very different approaches to developing and improving their services, products and processes.

APPLE

Apple's hardware innovation and research is a closely guarded secret. For each potential new product or product feature, it creates 10 different designs, encouraging its employees to explore all different possibilities. After a few months, these are whittled down to three, and then after a few more months the company finally ends up with one strong decision. Throughout this process, teams of designers and engineers meet twice a week to discuss the product and explore alternative options, even towards the end of its development.

Apple's strategy is to put all its resources into developing a few products and make them exceedingly well. Steve Jobs, Apple's CEO and co-founder, comments, 'One of the keys to Apple is that we build products that really turn us on.' Innovation of products tends to be undertaken by a small group of individuals, who identify a gap in the market. There are no hierarchies in the design team, and they work without a formal structure.

www.apple.com

GOOGLE

Unlike Apple, Google uses an open approach to innovation in which it acts as a fertile ground for ideas offered by its employees, customers and suppliers. It has achieved this by developing an informal company culture that encourages employees to exchange ideas and continually make incremental improvements and added enhancements to their products. Employees are also encouraged to spend at least 20 per cent of their time working on their own ideas, even if they do not immediately relate to Google's current services or products. This approach has led to a number of developments such as the Google Directory, which provides the ability to search different topics and is offered in more than 10 different languages so customers can search in their own language.

As well as tapping into its employees' ideas, Google has also developed a number of partnerships with key customers to help develop new products and enter new markets. For example, its alliances with Universo Online in Latin America and China Mobile Limited in Asia. It has also partnered with major libraries such as the University of California and University of Wisconsin to digitize their holdings and make them easier to search.

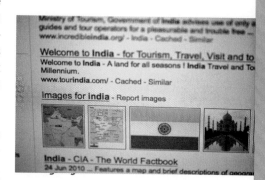

Sources: Morris, B. (March 3, 2008) What makes Apple golden *Fortune Magazine*. Available from: http://fortune.asia/2008/02/29/news/companies/amac_apple.fortune/index.htm (retrieved August 5, 2010).

Questions

1 Compare the approaches to innovation used by Apple and Google.

2 What are the advantages and disadvantages of these approaches?

Lecturers: visit www.palgrave.com/business/hillessential for additional resources

illustrated in Figure 12.3. Case 12.9 shows how Unipart uses its employees to identify and drive improvement within its business. For this to be effective, employees must be involved throughout, from agreeing the aims of the programme to identifying and making improvements. This ensures that everyone within the business is committed, involved and empowered to make a difference. A key challenge within this is creating a working environment that helps employees to develop their full potential, want to do a good job and contribute fully to improving all aspects of the organization. Essential factors to making this happen include:

Self-managed teams – self-organized, semi-autonomous small groups who determine, plan and manage their day-to-day activities with little or no supervision

- *Creating* self-managed teams This involves creating teams that are responsible not only for completing certain operations activities, but also for making decisions, implementing their ideas and being held accountable for the results they achieve. Figure 12.12 shows the four stages through which teams develop, from initial 'involvement and collaboration' to 'shared responsibility' and then 'empowered ownership', before finally becoming 'self-managed teams'. Achieving this transition requires a very different organizational structure and management approach.

- *Sharing information* Everyone in the organization needs to be aware of how it is currently performing against its competitors and against other parts of the business, as well as the types of improvement that it is making. This helps employees to set the objectives for their own team, and encourages them to keep looking for better ways to work.

- *Creating time for improvement* As well as being expected to manage themselves and complete the operations activities for which they are responsible, teams must also be allocated time within their working week to identify and make improvements. For example, employees at Google are encouraged to spend at least 20 per cent of their time working on new ideas, even if they are not immediately related to Google's current services or products (see Case 12.8).

Figure 12.12 The four stages of involving employees in improvement activities

STAGE 4	**Self-managed teams**	· Teams are responsible for all aspects of the process and site · Self-directed teams with integrated support from specialist groups · Site-based group for medium- to long-term decisions · An organization without rank
STAGE 3	**Empowered ownership**	· Traditional structure with overall control retained by management · Self-directed teams with some integrated support and overviewed by an operations manager · Teams are responsible for all aspects of the process
STAGE 2	**Shared responsibility**	· Traditional structure with overall control retained by management · Team-based – with appointed leader · Teams are responsible for the output of the process and participate in problem resolution and improvement activities
STAGE 1	**Involvement and collaboration**	· Traditional structure · Teams with supervisory control · Participate in problem resolution and improvement activities · Supervisor is responsible for output and behaviour · External specialist support

CASE 12.9 UNIPART GROUP

Unipart, the UK manufacturing and logistics company, has a training centre in each of its plants and warehouses where small groups meet to share their ideas on and experiences of how to improve the way they work. The training centres are also linked to each other through the company's intranet to help them collectively identify and solve the problems it faces across the business. In addition, over 400 internal facilitators are used to train and coach staff, and help pass on solutions and ideas between different groups.

www.unipart.com

Questions

1 What aspects of Unipart's approach illustrate the concept of continuous improvement?

2 How is employee involvement central to this initiative?

Students: www.palgrave.com/business/hillessential provides learning resources for this case

> **KEY IDEA**

Using employees to make improvements requires giving them more power than they usually have

Involving suppliers

As well as looking inside the organization, businesses can also identify other stakeholders, such as suppliers, and involve them in making improvements. As with involving employees, this requires a very different approach to managing and working with suppliers, as described earlier in Figure 11.15, and ultimately moving to a situation where customers and suppliers are mutually dependent on each other.

> **KEY IDEA**

Using suppliers to make improvements requires giving them more power than they usually have

For example, Philips, the Dutch electronics company, turned its research and development facility in The Netherlands into an open campus for more than 7,000 researchers from its Tier 1 and Tier 2 suppliers. Suddenly, the facility changed from being a cost centre to a profit centre as the researchers paid to rent space within the facility. It also found that the campus expanded its ecosystem and encouraged knowledge-sharing among its suppliers.

This is just one example of how suppliers can be used to improve a company's business. Case 12.10 shows how Apple has worked with both courier FedEx and the Chinese manufacturers of its iPods to produce and deliver a tailor-made iPod to a customer anywhere in the world in less than 90 hours. Case 12.11 describes how TED (Technology, Entertainment, Design) and Apple have used suppliers to develop new services and products that they then distribute to their customers through the **www.ted.com** website and Apple's iTunes 'App Store'. Involving suppliers in this way has radically changed how these businesses work, and has led to improvements that they would never have made on their own.

Involving customers

Just as businesses can get customers to serve themselves (see Chapter 4), they can also use them to improve their services, products and processes. Case 12.12 describes how Wikipedia and Threadless use customers to improve their businesses. As with companies such as Facebook and eBay, this collaborative way of working essentially involves giving customers the tools to develop and improve the services and products that the company sells, as well as helping decide how these are then delivered to its customers. Although customers have always been interested in the activities and actions undertaken within organizations, these sorts of initiative give them more power than they have traditionally had. And, as with involving employees and suppliers, this makes companies and customers more mutually dependent on each other than before. The advantage of this sort of approach is that customer loyalty increases, research and development costs are reduced, and there is almost instant demand for the services and products developed.

> **KEY IDEA**

Using customers to make improvements requires giving them more power than they usually have

A hundred and fifty years ago, it took a cargo-laden ship 90 days to travel from Shanghai to New York, but now Apple can take an online order for a tailor-made iPod, manufacture it in China and deliver it to a home address in Pittsburgh in less than 90 hours. This is achieved by its:

- Just-in-time manufacturing agreements with its Chinese suppliers, who only make an iPod after they receive an order from a customer anywhere in the world, and a
- Priority Direct Distribution agreement with FedEx to deliver the iPods to their destinations and allow customers to track their orders by scanning them up to 12 times during their journey.

As a result, Apple is able to offer customers iPods with their names engraved on the back in less than 90 hours with significantly less inventory.

www.apple.com

Questions

1 How did Apple manage to reduce the lead-time for supplying a tailor-made iPod?

2 How can other companies learn from these developments?

Lecturers: visit www.palgrave.com/business/ hillessential for additional resources

CASE 12.11 USING SUPPLIERS TO DEVELOP NEW PRODUCTS AND SERVICES: TED AND APPLE'S APP STORE

TED

TED (short for Technology, Entertainment, Design) is a US private, not-for-profit organization devoted to 'freely spreading ideas' through the Internet in the belief that these ideas can change attitudes, lives and, ultimately, the world. They see themselves as both a clearing house for free knowledge and inspiration from the world's most inspired thinkers, and also a community of curious souls engaging with these ideas and each other.

Initially TED started as a one-off event in 1984. It now holds annual global conferences in Oxford, UK and Long Beach/Palm Springs in the US. The lectures held at these events are 18 minutes in length and are then published on TED.com, where they can be watched for free by anyone. Although initially more technology focused, the talks now cover most aspects of science and culture, and have been given by a wide variety of people such as Bill Clinton, Al Gore, Gordon Brown, Richard Dawkins, Bill Gates, Bono, Jamie Oliver and various Nobel Prize winners.

By 2010, talks had been viewed over 300 million times and translated into more than 77 languages by more than 3500 translators. In 2005, it also introduced 'TED Prizes', where $100,000 was awarded to three winners wishing to 'change the world'. However, TED felt this was spreading its resources too thinly, and in 2010 it awarded a single $300,000 prize to one winner – Jamie Oliver – who has plans for a scheme to 'teach every child about food'. **www.ted.com**

APPLE'S APP STORE

Apple's 'App Store' is a service that allows its iPhone, iPod and iPad users to browse and download applications from its iTunes Store for free, or at a cost. These applications are developed by third-party programmers using a code that is developed and published by Apple. Developers produce software applications using the code and then submit them to Apple, which then decides whether or not to accept them into its store.

In December 2009, 58 million App Store users (34 million iPhone and 24 million iPod touch) downloaded 280 million Apps, generating $250 million sales; of this, 30 per cent goes to Apple, and the rest to the developers. As of April 8, 2010, there are at least 185,000 third-party applications officially available on the App Store, with over 4 billion total downloads since it first opened in July 2008. This success has led to the launch of similar services by its competitors. However, Apple have actually trademarked the term 'App Store'.

www.apple.com

Question

What do you think the advantages are of these approaches to developing new services and products?

Lecturers: visit www.palgrave.com/business/hillessential for additional resources

CASE 12.12 USING CUSTOMERS TO IMPROVE OPERATIONS: WIKIPEDIA AND THREADLESS

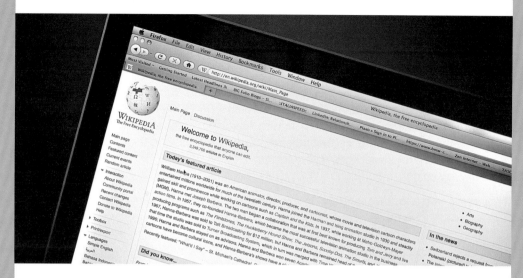

WIKIPEDIA

Wikipedia is a free, web-based, collaborative and multilingual encyclopaedia supported by the non-profit Wikimedia Foundation. Its 15 million articles have been collectively created by thousands of contributors from across the world and can be edited by anyone with access to its site. It is a move away from the previous style of in-house, 'expert-driven' encyclopaedia development and has also become a frequently updated news resource, with articles appearing soon after an event has occurred.

www.wikipedia.org

THREADLESS

Anyone can design a T-shirt, submit it in a weekly contest and then rate their favourite designs. Online clothing store Threadless then selects which designs to produce from those with the highest ratings, giving prizes and royalties to the winning designers. In this way, the company uses over 500,000 people to design and select the T-shirts it produces.

www.threadless.com

Questions

1 How do these two organizations develop their products?

2 What are the advantages of involving customers in this way?

Critical reflections

As we said at the beginning of the chapter, businesses need to constantly look for ways to improve how they operate in order to maintain their place in the market. If a company is not moving forwards, it is actually moving backwards as there is always someone else trying to take its customers. Improving operations can therefore help a business progress by doing one or more of the following:

- *Releasing cash* – which can then be invested elsewhere within the business, such as in new equipment or research and development
- *Improving market support* – which, in turn, leads to increased sales revenue by either increasing market share, developing new markets or enabling the business to charge a higher price for its services and products
- *Reducing costs* – resulting in higher profit margins.

To achieve this and drive their businesses forward, organizations need to take a proactive approach to improvement, one in which all stakeholders continually look for ways to do things better. Although the tools and techniques for improving operations are not revolutionary and have been around for many years, organizations are starting to use them in very different ways. Historically, businesses have used their own employees to identify and make improvements, but many are now rethinking the boundaries of their organizations and starting to give more power to suppliers, customers and other individuals who are interested in the organization.

In part, the Internet has helped facilitate this by improving communication between stakeholders and by starting to build communities that are more powerful when acting together rather than as individuals. But it has also come from a realization that significant benefits and advantages can be gained from tapping into a broader resource of knowledge and ideas. As a result, even organizations like Apple, which have traditionally taken a 'closed' approach to innovation, have used an open approach with its App Store. Not only is this service key to the future success of its iPhone, iPod and iPad products, but it is now generating over $75 million profit a month for Apple. Making these changes, however, requires a radically different approach and a willingness to move to a situation where customers and suppliers are mutually dependent on each other.

Summary

- Operations needs to be improved to meet a variety of different corporate objectives, the most common reasons being to release cash, improve market support (leading to increased sales) and/or reduce costs.

- Improving operations involves going through four key steps – plan (develop an improvement plan), do (implement the improvement plan), check (measure the impact of the actions made in Step 2 to see whether they have met the objectives set in Step 1) and review (review the checks made and identify further problems or aspects to improve, which leads back to Step 1).

- Companies need to decide whether they want to take a passive or a proactive approach to development, and also whether they want to attain incremental or breakthrough levels of improvement.

- A wide variety of tools and techniques is available to organizations wishing to improve their operations. The key ones include benchmarking, mapping the customer journey, mapping processes, identifying causes of problems, generating improvement ideas and re-engineering business processes.

- After deciding which improvement tools and techniques to use, businesses need to identify their 'high-interest' stakeholders and start using them to help identify and make improvements. Organizations can take either a closed approach to making improvements by only using their own employees and closely guarding their secrets, or a more open approach, involving customers and suppliers when developing new services and ways of working.

- Involving employees is essential if companies want to develop an improvement culture, which is necessary to drive and sustain change. To make this happen, they need to establish self-managed teams, share information and create time to work on improvement activities.

- Involving suppliers requires changing the relationship with suppliers and moving to a situation where customers and suppliers are mutually dependent on each other for developing new services or products and improving how they are delivered.

- Just as businesses can get customers to serve themselves, so they can also use them to improve their services, products and processes. This can increase customer loyalty, reduce research and development costs, and help tailor services and products to customers' needs.

Study activities

Discussion questions

1 A retail outlet offering a range of high-specification women's clothes wishes to develop relevant performance measures. Suggest those that you consider appropriate.

2 Explain the difference between stepped and incremental change programmes. What are the advantages and disadvantages of each?

3 Draw an outline process chart when arranging a holiday for which the hotels and flights are directly booked by you.

4 Why is the use of video gaining widespread application in the field of continuous improvement?

5 Why is there actual conflict between management and staff over productivity levels? What actions can operations managers take to resolve these differences?

Assignments

1 Develop a cause and effect diagram to explain lengthy service at a restaurant.

2 Use the Deming cycle approach to suggest and implement improvements to the library lending delivery system.

Exploring further

Journal articles

Chesbrough, H.W. and Garman, A.R. (2009) 'How open innovation can help you cope in lean times'. *Harvard Business Review*, **87**(12), pp. 68–76. This article proposes that 'open innovation' can play an important role in helping companies in the current challenging business environment. Open innovation allows intellectual property, ideas and people to flow freely both into and out of an organization and includes placing some of its assets and projects outside.

Swank, C.K. (2003) 'The lean service machine'. *Harvard Business Review*, **81**(10), pp. 123–9. To establish itself as the independent life-insurance advisers' preferred partner, Jefferson Pilot Financial successfully at reduced turnaround time on policy applications, simplified the submission process and reduced errors. The company's approach and the outcomes are examined in this article.

Thomke, S. (2001) 'Enlightened experimentation: the new imperative for innovation'. *Harvard Business Review*, **79**(2), pp. 67–75. Experimentation lies at the heart of every company's ability to innovate and at the heart of a company's ability to create and refine its services and products. To maximize the outcomes of innovation, this article puts forward a new way of looking at such approaches and explains the essentials of what it refers to as 'enlightened experimentation'.

Books

Hill, A. and Hill, T. (2009) *Manufacturing Operations Strategy: Text and Cases*, 3rd edn. Basingstoke: Palgrave Macmillan. The text provides a useful supplement to the current book by outlining an in-depth approach for developing and implementing operations strategy within manufacturing organizations.

Hill, T. (2005) *Operations Management: Text and Cases*. Basingstoke: Palgrave Macmillan. This provides a useful supplement to the current book by offering a more comprehensive explanation and further examples (including long case studies) showing how service and manufacturing companies have applied these concepts.

Hill, T. (1998) *The Strategy Quest: Releasing the Energy of Manufacturing Within a Market Driven Strategy: A Dynamic Business Story*. Available from AMD Publishing, 'Albedo', Dousland, Devon, PL20 6NE, UK; e-mail: amd@jm-abode.tiscali.co.uk; fax: +44 (0)1822 882863. This book (written as a novel) describes how an art business and a manufacturing organization restructure themselves to meet the changing demands of their customers.

Senge, P.M. (2006) *The Fifth Discipline: The Art and Practice of the Learning Organisation*. London: Random House. This book looks at how organizations expand their capacity to create results by nurturing an environment where people continually learn together.

Womack, J. and Jones, D. (2003) *Lean Thinking*. New York: Free Press. This book looks at how organizations should identify and eliminate waste within their businesses, citing examples from companies showing how their theories can be put into action.

Films

Best Shot. Director: David Anspaugh, 1986. Based a true story, this movie chronicles the story of a coach with a chequered past transforming a high school basketball team and leading them to the state championship final.

Big Chef Takes on Little Chef. TV documentary, 2009. This documentary describes how the Little Chef Restaurant management team bring in Michelin three-star award-winning chef Heston Blumenthal to help it try to recapture the commercial success it once had.

Dead Poet's Society. Director: Peter Weir, 1989. English professor John Keating inspires his students to sieze the day and challenge the status quo. Each, in their own way, does this, and they are changed for life.

HARLEY-DAVIDSON

Like all motorcycle manufacturers, Harley-Davidson has been hit hard by the current economic crisis with sales and profits declining rapidly in the last few years. In 2009, it announced a company-wide restructuring plan closing two factories and one distribution centre, and eliminating almost 25 per cent of its total workforce (around 3,500 employees), with plans to reduce annual operating costs by $260 million. Later that year, it ended the Buell product line, and in 2010 it sold the MV Agusta business bought only the previous year, announcing further plans to cut manufacturing costs by another $54 million.

THE STORY

Harley is no stranger to tough times. Established in 1903, William Harley and Walter, William, and Arthur Davidson built their first three motorcycles in a shed in Milwaukee. Six years later, they introduced their trademark two-cylinder, V-twin engine bike able to reach speeds of 60 mph, the fastest at that time. During the First World War, overseas demand grew, and by the

1920s Harley-Davidson was the largest manufacturer in the world and considered to be a leader in innovative engineering. The US motorcycle industry was booming, but then the Great Depression hit, which the company only managed to survive through its police, military and international sales.

Then came the Second World War and production soared to record levels as a result of supplying over 90,000 military cycles while earning the Army-Navy 'E' award for wartime production excellence. After the War, Harley-Davidson started developing recreational bikes, introducing the K-model in 1952, XL Sportster in 1957 and Duo-Glide in 1958. But again the industry was struggling, and soon it was the last remaining major US motorcycle manufacturer. It continued to do well and was sold to the American Machine and Foundry (AMF) company in 1969.

Then disaster struck as Japanese manufacturers flooded the US market with high quality, low-priced bikes. Harley-Davidson's market share fell from 78 per cent in 1973 to 23 per cent by 1981, and AMF put the company up for sale. In 1981, 13 of Harley's management team bought the company, hoping to reverse its fortunes and take on Honda, which now had 44 per cent of the market. But Harley's market share continued to fall, and it was left with a large number of unsold bikes. It decided to drastically cut production and reduced its 4,000 workforce by 45 per cent. In 1983, to help the floundering US motorcycle industry, President Ronald Reagan increased tariffs on large Japanese motorcycles from 4 to 49 per cent. While this increase was only effective for five years (declining each year), it did help to postpone the inevitable, but by 1985 Harley-Davidson was on the edge of bankruptcy.

TURNAROUND
In a last-minute bid to save the company, CEO Richard Teerlink convinced investors to fund a restructuring plan based on new management principles, marketing strategies and manufacturing techniques. He decided to reduce the high inventories and high operating costs that had made the company vulnerable to unpredictable market fluctuations. Instead of trying to make short-term improvements through quick fixes, such as throwing in computers and state-of-the-art machinery, Teerlink felt that the company needed to start listening to its employees and working with them to improve the business.

EMPLOYEE INVOLVEMENT
The first challenge was to earn the respect and trust of employees and get them to share in the vision built on the five values of 'tell the truth', 'be fair', 'keep your promises', 'respect the individual' and 'encourage intellectual curiosity'. Harley also decided to work with its unionized workforce rather than against them. Through its words and actions, the Harley management team showed that this was a new way of life, not just another 'programme'. They set up the Harley-Davidson Learning Center for employees to come with requests for specific job-training courses, and introduced a gain-sharing programme with cash incentives for maintaining and improving quality, profitability and delivery. Over the following year, everyone was trained in problem-solving and quality control techniques applicable to their area of expertise. The company also tried to insource as much work as possible, giving the union control over what was outsourced. When times are good, the company outsources, but it brings work back in-house in tough times to maintain jobs.

The unions even censure their own workers for shoddy performance and have helped to introduce cross-trained, 'self-managed' teams that set their own work schedules and have responsibility for production, quality and preventive maintenance.

INVENTORY REDUCTION
The first problem to address was inventory. At the time, inventory was high and only turned over four times a year, and the company needed to work out how to reduce it to free up cash to invest elsewhere in the business. At the time, Harley-Davidson used a complex material requirements planning computer system to schedule operations, which kept inventory high to ensure the assembly line was

not halted by any manufacturing problems. To solve the situation, the company moved to just-in-time (JIT) methods, making products only as they were required using visual systems to schedule production and manage stock. As inventory was reduced, problems were exposed and then solved. This resulted in a number of projects to improve material control and flow, reduce machine set-ups and improve machine reliability. The JIT system allowed quality to become the focus as inventory levels were smaller and more manageable. Once JIT was working well, the company then started working with suppliers to improve the way they worked. As a result, inventory levels reduced by 75 per cent and inventory turnovers increased steadily over the following 20 years (Figure 1).

PROCESS IMPROVEMENT

Rather than buying new machinery, the company focused on improving its use of existing equipment in order to increase the quality of its products. Harley-Davidson started an initiative called 'statistical operator control' that made operators responsible for the quality of the products they produced. Staff were given extensive training in tools such as control charts and histograms, and, as a result, the company saw a substantial improvement, with a 68 per cent reduction in scrap and rework and a 50 per cent increase in productivity (Figure 2). Operators could now monitor the manufacturing process to understand whether it was 'in control' (operating in a stable and predictable range) and 'capable' (consistently within specification). If a problem occurred, employees could immediately stop the process and fix it.

PRODUCTION CELLS

Harley-Davidson's factories comprised a huge, maze-like operation in which products were made in large batches on machines with high set-up times. There was no logical flow, and operators had to use forklifts to move materials around the facilities. The improvements made through involving employees reduced inventory, improved processes and enabled the company to move from a traditional batch production process to 'U-shaped' cells where one to four people worked together to produce a finished part. Each manufacturing department contained a number of cells that were easier to manage and required 25 per cent less space. Lead-times fell from over six weeks to a few hours, and inventory reduced as suppliers delivered raw materials and components directly to where they were required rather than to a central stock room.

Figure 1
Business performance (1985–2009)

$million	1985	1990	1995	2000	2002	2004	2006	2008	2009
Sales revenue	288	624	1,350	2,943	4,091	5,015	5,800	5,578	4,287
Profit	3	38	112	478	734	1,137	1,387	976	314
Inventory	79	60	84	191	218	227	287	379	323
Cash	28	13	31	420	192	275	239	569	1,630

Source: Harley Davidson Annual Reports (1985–2009)

Figure 2
Costs (1985–2009)

$million	1985	1990	1995	2000	2002	2004	2006	2008	2009
Direct	214	435	939	1,979	2,673	3,116	3,567	3,647	2,901
Overheads	71	151	299	486	684	762	846	943	851
Restructuring	–	–	–	–	–	–	–	12	221

Source: Harley Davidson Annual Reports (1985–2009)

TODAY

Sales and profits have grown significantly since the turnaround in the 1980s. Nevertheless, the company is constantly looking for ways to do things better. For example, when there was a capacity squeeze on its wheel production plant in Kansas City, layouts and processes were reconfigured to gain capacity. As a result, work-in-progress and handling were both reduced by 50 per cent. Equally, its Paint Group recently improved the sequencing and delivery of painted parts to assembly lines using visual management tools, while its new financial software has improved demand forecasting. Work has been undertaken to transform its York operation to make it much more flexible and efficient. The company is also looking at how it can grow international sales in order to move away from being too reliant on the US market, for example in India, where there is sufficient demand to overcome the high import duties.

THE FUTURE

Harley-Davidson's past growth and success has been built on loyal customers, some of whom tattoo its logo onto their bodies. But despite its rebellious image, its average customer is now a 47-year-old white male with a $84,300 annual salary! The huge bikes that drive most of its sales don't appeal to the younger generation (15 per cent of customers are under 35) or women (only 12 per cent are female); 52 per cent of its customers owned a Harley-Davidson earlier in their life, and the company needs to think about how to enter new markets. It has always been careful that production does not exceed demand and likes to keep its customers waiting 6–18 months for a new bike. In the past, this has helped maintain prices, so a year-old Harley usually costs 25–30 per cent more than a new one. Rather than cutting prices and offered financing like its competitors, Harley believes that cutting production is a better long-term strategy. Some analysts have debated whether this is the right decision for Harley, particularly given that its financing arm is still haemorrhaging cash. The questions that many critics have asked include: When will demand stop falling? Will it ever regain its market share? And can it successfully penetrate new markets?

Questions

1 List the improvements that Harley-Davidson made, and explain the benefits that resulted.

2 What are the issues that Harley-Davidson faces today?

3 How did it use 'continuous improvement' tools and techniques to turn the business around before? What are the lessons from that turnaround for its current situation?

Sources: Strumph, D. (August 27, 2009) 'Harley-Davidson to sell motorcycles in India'. Available from http://www.cbsnews.com/stories/2009/08/27/business/main5269000.shtml (retrieved January 7, 2011).

Lecturers: visit www.palgrave.com/business/hillessential for additional resources

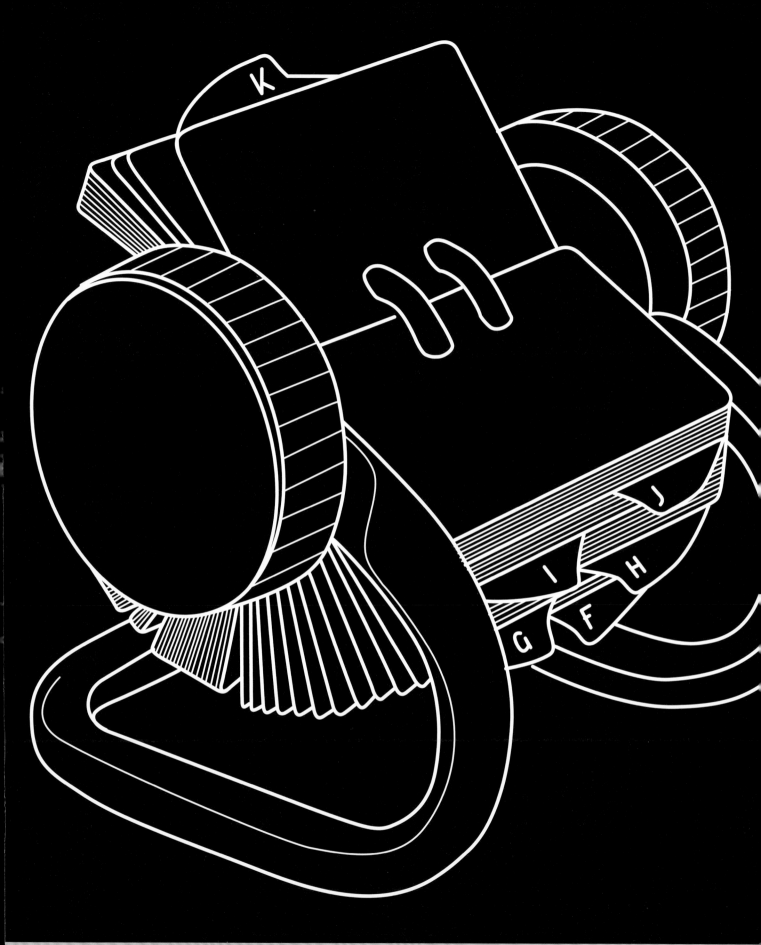

INDEX

Note: Page numbers in **bold** indicate where key term is defined.
Page numbers in ***bold italic*** indicate where term is featured in a case study.